How Ancient
Narratives Persuade

How Ancient Narratives Persuade

Acts in Its Literary Context

Eric Clouston

ROWMAN & LITTLEFIELD
Lanham • Boulder • New York • London

Published by Rowman & Littlefield
An imprint of The Rowman & Littlefield Publishing Group, Inc.
4501 Forbes Boulevard, Suite 200, Lanham, Maryland 20706
www.rowman.com

6 Tinworth Street, London SE11 5AL, United Kingdom

Copyright © 2020 by The Rowman & Littlefield Publishing Group, Inc.

All rights reserved. No part of this book may be reproduced in any form or by any electronic or mechanical means, including information storage and retrieval systems, without written permission from the publisher, except by a reviewer who may quote passages in a review.

British Library Cataloguing in Publication Information Available

Library of Congress Cataloging-in-Publication Data Available

ISBN 978-1-9787-0660-6 (cloth)
ISBN 978-1-9787-0662-0 (pbk.)
ISBN 978-1-9787-0661-3 (electronic)

Contents

Preface and Acknowledgments		vii
List of Figures and Tables		ix
List of Abbreviations		xi
1	Why Study the Persuasiveness of Narrative?	1
2	How to Identify the Persuasive Features of a Narrative	17
3	Narrative Persuasion in Philo's *Embassy to Gaius*	45
4	Narrative Persuasion in Josephus's *Jewish War*	65
5	Narrative Persuasion in *Joseph and Aseneth*	87
6	Narrative Persuasion in the *Letter of Aristeas*	107
7	Basic Literary Analysis of Acts	127
8	Narrative Persuasion in Acts	143
9	Case Study: The Cornelius Episode, Acts 10:1–11:18	177
10	Comparison Between the Five Texts	195
11	Revisiting the Purpose of Acts	209
12	Conclusions	221
Appendix A: List of Techniques of Persuasion		231
Appendix B: List of Accrediting and Discrediting Devices		233
Appendix C: Accrediting and Discrediting in Luke-Acts		235

Appendix D: Distribution of Accrediting and Discrediting in Luke-Acts	241
Appendix E: Overview of Accrediting and Discrediting	245
Bibliography	249
Index	261
About the Author	267

Preface and Acknowledgments

Acts is full of persuasion. But the reported speeches are, naturally, only summaries, compiled later, and sometimes translated, so our access to exactly how the apostles persuaded is not quite direct. On the other hand, the act of persuasion that we can most directly analyze is persuasion of the audience of Acts by the text of Acts. That is what the wording and storyline have been arranged to do. But what is the persuasive thrust of Acts? Who is being persuaded about what?

This book started as an attempt to analyze Acts as *persuasive narrative*; in particular, to investigate what can be learned from the way Acts has been constructed about the persuasive influence this narrative would have exerted on its early audiences. But there did not seem to be any credible method for doing this. So it was first necessary to define, and attempt to validate, a systematic method for analyzing persuasiveness in ancient narratives.

I am grateful for the consistent inspiration provided by Prof. Steve Walton, and for his meticulous comments. I would also like to acknowledge the careful and perceptive insights provided by Dr. Bridget Gilfillan Upton and Prof. Eckhard Schnabel, and the encouragement, example, and helpful advice of Dr. Cor Bennema, Rev. Dr. Dexter Maben, Rev. Adrian Watkins, and Rev. Dr. Glyn Ackerley. I am indebted to Dr. Roger Sewell for the mathematical analysis behind Chapter 5, note 49, which indicates that *Aseneth* is a Jewish, rather than a Christian, text.

Figures and Tables

Figure 8.1.	Distribution of Accrediting Through Luke	147
Figure 8.2.	Distribution of Accrediting Through Acts	147
Table B.1.	List of Accrediting Devices	233
Table B.2.	List of Discrediting Devices	234
Table C.1.	Accrediting in Luke and Acts	235
Table C.2.	Discrediting in Luke and Acts	236
Table C.3.	The Characters Accredited in Luke and Acts	236
Table D.1.	Distribution of Devices Through Luke	242
Table D.2.	Distribution of Devices Through Acts	243
Table E.1.	Overview of Accrediting and Discrediting	246
Table E.2.	Accrediting Devices in All the Texts	247
Table E.3.	Discrediting Devices in All the Texts	248

Abbreviations

A1 to A27	Devices for Accrediting (see Appendix B)
Aristeas	The *Letter of Aristeas*
Aseneth	*Joseph and Aseneth*
BAFCS	The Book of Acts in Its First Century Setting. 5 vols. Eerdmans, 1993–1996.
D1 to D24	Devices for Discrediting (see Appendix B).
Embassy	Philo of Alexandria, *Embassy to Gaius*
LCL	Loeb Classical Library
LSJ	Liddell, Henry G., and Robert Scott. *A Greek-English Lexicon.* 9th ed. Oxford: Clarendon, 1996.
LXX	Septuagint (edition used here: Alfred Rahlfs, ed. Stuttgart: Deutsche Bibelgesellschaft, 2006).
MT	Masoretic Text of the Hebrew Scriptures
NA^{28}	Eberhard Nestle, Barbara Aland, Kurt Aland, Johannes Karavidopoulos, Carlo N. Martini and Bruce M. Metzger, eds. *Novum Testamentum Graece*. 28th ed. Stuttgart: Deutsche Bibelgesellschaft, 2012.
NT	New Testament
OT	Old Testament
OTP	James H. Charlesworth, ed. *The Old Testament Pseudepigrapha*. 2 vols. New York: Doubleday, 1983–1985.
P1 to P5	Techniques of Persuasion (see Chapter 2 and Appendix A).
War	Josephus, *Jewish War*.

Chapter One

Why Study the Persuasiveness of Narrative?

Charles Dickens was fully convinced of the power of narrative to persuade. He had planned to write a pamphlet entitled, "An Appeal to the People of England on behalf of the Poor Man's Child." Within days he had another idea, writing to a friend, ". . . you will certainly feel that a sledge-hammer has come down with twenty times the force—twenty thousand times the force I could exert by following out my first idea."[1] The result was his influential novel *A Christmas Carol*.

Reading or hearing a story, some might not even notice that they are being influenced. But if you are trying to interpret the meaning of a persuasive narrative, you need some way of identifying and understanding the techniques of persuasion that are built into it. Stories may inform; stories may entertain; but, especially in the ancient world, stories would also influence and persuade. A story may challenge some assumptions and allegiances, while encouraging others. It may provide a good example to follow, or a cautionary tale. For a hearer familiar with Genesis 19, Jesus could evoke a powerful warning with the simple words, "Remember Lot's wife!" (Luke 17:32). For a later generation, familiar with Acts 5, one could evoke another powerful warning with the simple words, "Remember Ananias and Sapphira!"

In attempting to interpret a text, it is necessary to notice (among other things) the various ways in which it would have a persuasive impact. It is harder to answer, but also helpful to consider, the related question of why it was written—its *purpose*. Bible commentaries often include a section on the author's purpose in writing the book or letter. For this, it is helpful to glean as much information as possible about the author, audience, and context. Occasionally a purpose is mentioned in the text—for example, Paul's overt appeal to Philemon on behalf of the slave Onesimus (Philemon 10). But, generally, only limited information is available, and an author's purposes may be complex. Nathan's report to David about the poor man's ewe-lamb (2 Kingdoms 12:1–7 LXX; 2 Sam 12:1–7 MT)[2] shows that the real purpose of an account is not necessarily obvious straightaway. Any claim to have discerned the author's purpose should, somehow, allow for all available evidence. But how?

The discerning of purposes is a challenge, with any text. With *narrative*, it is especially challenging. Narrative is particularly likely to give little or no direct indication of purpose or of intended audience; narrative involves possibilities for the narrator to be rather different from the real author; and although narrative can have a deep impact on its audience, it is not normally overt in doing this. These difficulties help to explain why narrative criticism has usually focused on obvious literary features, such as structure and themes, rather than on persuasiveness or purpose.

Most ancient narrative seems to have included elements of persuasion. Texts can, of course, have a wide variety of purposes. If the aim is mainly to entertain or to inform, there may be no evident persuasive purpose; so a text might have no persuasive intent if it is a technical treatise, a plain chronicle of events, or perhaps even a legal or moral code.[3] On the other hand, the texts that are most overt in their persuasive intent are generally not narrative but speeches (e.g., Demosthenes, *Philippics*, denouncing Philip II of Macedon), dialogues (e.g., Plato, *Gorgias*, promoting philosophy rather than rhetoric), treatises (e.g., Josephus, *Against Apion*, defending Jews and Judaism), or, perhaps, even love poems.[4]

Nevertheless, throughout history, there have also been significant examples of persuasive narrative, whether presented as fact or fiction. Among the Greeks, Aristophanes not only entertained but also used both storyline and *parabases* (direct address to the audience) in his comedies *Acharnians* and *Lysistrata* to campaign against the Peloponnesian War, and Plutarch expects the audience of his biographies not merely to be informed, but to join him in being influenced, learning moral lessons.[5] Among Jewish authors, surviving passages from the historian Artapanus suggest an attempt to inspire respect for Jews by claiming that Egypt and Greece depended on Jewish patriarchs for key innovations.[6] Among Christians, *The Shepherd of Hermas* shows how visions may be reported with overt persuasive intent, urging wholehearted devotion. Within Scripture, brief stories are certainly used with persuasive purpose: Nathan's story of the ewe-lamb (2 Kdgms 12:1–7) contributed to David's repentance;[7] the story of Abimelech being killed by a woman dropping a millstone on him became a warning—a cautionary tale (2 Kgdms 11:21–22; cf. Judg 9:50–55); and parables were used, especially by Jesus, to provoke rethinking. The whole book of Jonah is a narrative conveying a message that includes persuasion against xenophobia. Indeed, of biblical narrative in general, it can be said that "the biblical authors deploy a narrative rhetoric which aims to convince without neglecting the pleasure of the narrative."[8]

Many of the tools of modern literary criticism were developed for the study of fiction, which is written to display the creative art of the author for the entertainment of the reader. So advertising, propaganda, and overtly didactic or apologetic texts have, at times, been deliberately excluded.[9] However, in the ancient world, it was rhetoric, and therefore persuasion, that lay at the heart of education. The surviving guidance tends to treat written composition as merely one among the various skills involved in rhetoric. So it is not surprising that the purposes scholars discern in ancient narrative often involve persuasion. With narrative, as with speeches, this does not only mean persuading an opponent to reconsider. Persuasion can equally involve convincing supporters that their support is well-founded and should continue; or introducing open-minded strangers to a situation that one wishes to portray in a particular light to influence their involvement. Persuasion is not confined to adversarial apologetics.

In the case of the Acts of the Apostles, the text should certainly be seen as a persuasive narrative—even though most scholars envisage a Christian audience[10] and so do not see it as evangelistic. Acts does not simply provide historical information; it suggests how events should be interpreted and that a response is necessary. The author seems to have exercised significant editorial freedom—for example, imposing his own style on the various speeches he reports[11]—so that one can hope to find consistent evidence, throughout the text, of the author's own persuasiveness. Acts may inform; it may also entertain; but it contains strong ideological elements, so Acts surely also has the effect of shaping the worldview of its hearers—it influences and persuades. In order to interpret the speeches within Acts, it is helpful to understand rhetoric; similarly, to interpret the book of Acts as a whole, it is helpful—and, this book argues, it is necessary—to understand how ancient narratives persuade.

Scholars who detect a persuasive purpose in an ancient text naturally point to particular supporting evidence within the text. But there has been rather limited discussion of method for this. One reason is that key literary-critical methods have, in the past, tended to exclude issues of persuasion. Another is that many historians have avoided overt attempts to persuade, which makes their persuasiveness hard to detect and analyze.[12] In contrast, persuasion is addressed by modern studies of advertising, propaganda, and campaigning, so that the present generation can learn both how to write persuasive stories and how to read them critically. But care would be needed in any attempt to apply these modern ideas to Acts, which is rooted in the very different cultural and literary conventions of its dual (Jewish and Greek) ancient context. "Socio-rhetorical" criticism has begun the process of considering persuasion within biblical narrative, including Acts.[13] But it is not clear that the techniques of persuasion used in speeches have yet been appropriately replaced by awareness of the rather different and less-well-documented techniques of persuasion relevant to narrative texts.

In this book, I argue that Acts is a persuasive narrative, and if the text is structured so as to have a persuasive impact, one cannot safely claim to have discerned that persuasion without the support, not only of particular pieces of textual evidence, but also of a systematic method for handling the evidence—a method for discerning techniques of persuasion within ancient narrative.

THE PURPOSE OF THIS BOOK

My aim in this book is to address the question: *What can be learned, from the way Acts has been constructed, about the persuasive influence the text would have exerted on its original audiences?*

Acts undeniably tells a story, so this question lies within the remit of biblical "narrative criticism." This focuses on the "final form" of a text, rather than sources or earlier stages of redaction, and considers engagement with the "original audience"—most simply understood as the audience(s) the author had in mind while finalizing the text. So it attempts to set aside twenty-first century perceptions and concentrate on what can be known about the attitudes, expectations and responses of ancient audiences. Those who wish to apply the text to the lives of modern readers will find that narrative criticism provides helpful, and probably necessary, groundwork, but such application is beyond the scope of this book.

The distinctive feature of this book is its focus on "narrative persuasion."[14] Rhetorical criticism has already focused on persuasion, but it uses methods more suitable for speeches than for narrative. Reader-response criticism has raised the question of how a first-time reader or hearer would respond but, again, has not yet provided a systematic method for addressing persuasion.

So, here, significant adaptation of narrative criticism is necessary. A further aim of this book is to develop *a systematic method for identifying techniques of persuasion within ancient narrative*. This method uses a taxonomy, which aims at completeness: a systematic list of "Techniques of Persuasion" that an author might build into narrative, supported by a systematic list of devices for "Accrediting" or "Discrediting" characters.

Persuasion within narrative is not generally overt, so there is no guarantee that it can be detected accurately, or at all—although, if there is no coherent persuasion, this method may be the best way to discover that. There are certainly challenges in identifying persuasiveness. So, in order to demonstrate how the method works and provide opportunities for comparison and for checking against previous scholarship, the method is applied to four nonbiblical texts as well as to Acts. Comparison with these texts allows Acts to be considered within its literary milieu. Since the Third Gospel is also a narrative text, the method could be applied to the whole of Luke-Acts. But that has not been attempted in this book; instead, the Third Gospel is referred to briefly, as providing necessary context for Acts.

Whether persuasiveness arises from some deliberate purpose of the author or, perhaps, emerges subconsciously, it remains relevant in interpreting a narrative. One cannot be certain of an ancient author's purpose, so this study focuses primarily on the expected persuasive impact of the text. It is often helpful in interpreting the text to form an opinion about purpose, as a working hypothesis; nevertheless, this study aims to minimize such assumptions and presuppositions. In that way, without creating a circular argument, the conclusions about persuasiveness may be used as *evidence for or against various suggestions about the author's purpose*.

So possible purposes of Acts, as suggested by others, will be listed in this first chapter, with some comments, but without prejudicing the following study. Only after gathering evidence about persuasion in Acts (Chapters 2 to 9 of this book) will the implications for these possible purposes of Acts will be discussed (Chapter 11).

THE TEXTS STUDIED

Before applying the method to Acts, it is demonstrated by applying it to four other texts: Philo's *Embassy to Gaius*; Josephus's *Jewish War*; *Joseph and Aseneth*; and the *Letter of Aristeas*. This approach allows the persuasiveness of Acts to be compared directly with persuasion detected in these other texts. Each claim to have identified a particular technique of persuasion within one of the texts is based on an analysis of that entire text. A technique of persuasion identified in Acts can be compared in some detail with examples of a similar technique being used in one or more of the other texts.

These texts have been selected on the basis of being similar to Acts in the following ways: being narratives; being written in Koine Greek; being approximately contemporary with Acts; and addressing Jewish issues. Classical Greek literature, earlier than Acts, had certainly influenced the Greek-speaking world and is of some interest here. But Acts has also been influenced by Jewish approaches to narrative,[15] at least through the Septuagint (LXX), whereas works written for Greek audiences, with Greek culture and using the Greek mother-tongue, lack that connection. Acts deals with Jewish characters and

Jewish Scriptures and, I will argue, has target audiences that include Greek-speaking Jews as well as Greek-speaking Gentiles.

Philo and Josephus were selected as authors whose wider corpus gives us insights into their context and style. Such insights are not necessary for this method, but they do at least reduce the uncertainties about the context and the relationship between narrator and audience. *Embassy* and *Flaccus* are the two works of Philo that, like Acts, narrate near-contemporary events, but *Flaccus* is significantly shorter than Acts, so the longer *Embassy* was chosen. *Embassy* has the unusual advantage of including, within the persuasive narrative, sections of overt rhetoric in the mouth of the narrator (addressed to the now-dead Gaius), thus providing a connection between conventional rhetoric and narrative persuasion. Josephus's *War* was selected because, unlike *Antiquities*, most of it narrates the recent past. The narrator of Acts is reticent so, in style of narration, *War* provides a closer comparison than *Life*, which is primarily autobiographical. However, compared with Acts, *Embassy* and *War* lack the prominence of the supernatural and the close connection to the Septuagint, so *Aseneth* and *Aristeas* were selected to provide balance, even though *Aseneth* deals with events of the more distant past. Analysis of more texts will be worthwhile, but these four provide a range of comparisons suitable for this introduction to the method.

CONTRIBUTION

The main contribution of this book is to identify the need for a systematic approach to analyzing the persuasiveness of ancient narratives and (with a particular interest in Acts) to attempt to provide that. Many scholars have analyzed some aspect of this, but only in a piecemeal way. Thanks to Aristotle, a systematic approach has, throughout history, been taken to understanding persuasiveness in speeches. The task of understanding persuasiveness of narratives may be more difficult, but our approach to it should surely be no less systematic. So this book provides a systematic approach to attempting to detect the persuasive aspects of a narrative. It also provides an approach to identifying the force of that persuasion—of what is the hearer being persuaded?—and therefore its significance. In the process, this book makes two further contributions relevant to persuasion: It identifies the significance of the accrediting and discrediting of characters, and it adds the key concept (previously neglected) of characterization with respect to the well-established concepts of empathy and sympathy. Respect allows a character to address the hearer with perceived authority. This method provides evidence for or against the various proposals for the purpose of Acts. It also provides insights by identifying the persuasive force of particular aspects of the narrative such as the use of repetition (retelling) and the significant changes in the characterization of Peter.

THE APPROPRIATENESS OF ANALYZING PERSUASION

Persuasion has always been susceptible to both appropriate and inappropriate use; indeed, Paul seems to indicate suspicion of rhetoric and to deny using it (1 Cor 2:4).[16] Scholars may, in the past, have been reluctant to consider narrative as deliberately persuasive not only because authorial intent is a notoriously complicated issue, but also because of negative connotations—the association of persuasion with aggressive proselytization, deception, political propaganda, or advertising. But persuasion should not automatically be perceived negatively. Paul does seek to persuade (2 Cor 5:11). Although Jesus comments that those who do not listen obediently to Scripture will not be "persuaded"[17] (πείθω, Luke 16:31), even by somebody rising from the dead, his purpose is arguably to persuade his hearers not to be like that. The frequent speeches in Acts indicate great interest in persuasion, and rhetorical criticism has indicated how helpful it can be to analyze techniques of persuasion.

A further criticism of the analysis of persuasion, especially within biblical narrative, might be that it depends on the assumption that the author invented at least parts of the narrative, to suit his (or her, although ancient authors were mainly men) persuasive purposes. Some scholars may indeed make that assumption, but it is not a necessary assumption. Rather, the method presented here can be applied to either fact or fiction. For persuasion to be detectible, it is only necessary that the author exercise the freedom to select, arrange, and present material. Without necessarily handling historical events and sources inappropriately (and the approval of the author's community would be the initial test of that), this may include selecting the material that best makes the author's point, arranging it to suggest particular causality and links, and providing introductions, asides, and comments to guide the audience. Even the most respected ancient historians did all of these things, and they also carefully arranged the conversations and speeches attributed to their characters. Even in a work claiming to represent facts, by the standards of Luke's[18] day, it would have been normal and generally acceptable to arrange and present his material according to his purposes. Persuasive analysis of biblical narrative is not incompatible with respect for its credibility as history or status as Scripture.

Attempts to discern the purpose(s) of Acts have led to a wide range of ideas, some of which are mutually incompatible. So one might dismiss such attempts as mere speculation. But discussion of purpose is a helpful aspect of interpretation, provided there is relevant evidence and provided there is (as this book attempts to provide) a credible method for handling that evidence.

POSSIBLE PURPOSES OF ACTS

There has been much discussion of the purpose of Acts, involving a wide range of theories rather than a clear consensus.[19] The text may, of course, have multiple, simultaneous purposes. This section will discuss possible purposes under broad headings, followed by brief comments on how relevant persuasion is to each of these suggestions.

1. *Further Scripture.* The scriptural (septuagintal) style of Acts and its frequent quotations from Scripture suggest the possibility of an intent to be (with the Third Gospel) a continuation of (OT) Scriptures, to provide further Scripture for the Jesus movement.[20] But Scripture includes a variety of genres with, inevitably, a variety of purposes. Even if this was the author's intent, more detailed consideration of purpose is still required.
2. *Church history.* Acts might have been written in order to provide later generations with a history of the early church.[21] Ancient history sometimes explicitly had later generations in mind.[22] Indeed, even if the main purpose were to influence initial hearers, the author might well also want to influence later generations.
3. *Christian teaching* (διδαχή). Even if not aspiring to be Scripture, Acts might nevertheless have been written as authoritative Christian instruction[23]—for example, clarifying the movement's relationship with Israel,[24] addressing concerns about the *Parousia*,[25] achieving "moral formation in the audience,"[26] or encouraging them, like the characters within the text, to persist in prayer.[27] Such Christian instruction may also "create identity in the reading/speaking community."[28]
4. *General publication.* Dibelius suggests that Acts was intended for general publication, to compete in the "book market" of the time.[29] This idea has not proved popular,[30] partly because scholars have doubted that the text is aimed at non-Christians; it is not clear that Acts would have the necessary popular appeal.
5. *Self-promotion.* It was not uncommon for books to have the purpose of raising the status of the author and/or patron.[31] The author of Acts is so reticent that his own status seems unlikely to be his main concern. But some part of the Jesus movement, especially those associated with Paul, might have acted as patrons for the preparation and publication of Acts, for the purpose of raising the status of the movement as a whole, or at least of their group.[32]

6. *Paul's legal defense.* The movement faced ubiquitous accusations (Acts 28:22), so some have seen Acts as defensive. Luke-Acts repeatedly declares Jesus and Paul innocent, so the idea that Acts contributes to Paul's legal defense has its advocates;[33] but it has generally been dismissed because so much material would be neither relevant nor acceptable to a Roman court.[34]
7. *Defense of Paul's memory.* Acts might respond to later attacks on Paul. These might be from Jewish Christians.[35] Or, by defending Paul against accusations (e.g., of revolt against Rome), Acts may help to defend later Christians facing similar accusations.[36]
8. *Defense of the Jesus movement.* Acts may be trying to persuade influential Romans to tolerate Christians, despite accusations, as acceptable and even legitimate (a *religio licita*).[37] This idea of political apologetic overcomes the problem of the text seeming unsuitable for the courtroom, but is not widely supported because it still fails to account for much, especially evangelistic, material.[38]
9. *Defense of Roman authorities.* The reverse is also possible—that Acts attempts to persuade believers that Romans are acceptable,[39] although few would regard this as the main aim.[40]
10. *Evangelistic proclamation.* Green asserts that, "Evangelism is the supreme concern of the writer,"[41] suggesting the purpose of proclaiming the gospel to nonbelievers, persuading them to join the Jesus movement. O'Neill speaks of Luke's "desire to win over the Roman Empire to the side of Christianity,"[42] so that the text is "primarily an attempt to persuade educated Romans to become Christians."[43] But many doubt whether pagans, who would be unfamiliar with the Jewish Scripture Acts refers to, can be the target audience.[44]
11. *Inspiration for evangelism.* Acts may be intended to inspire and train the next generation of evangelists,[45] providing "perspective and guidance" to inform the apologetic witness of Christian readers.[46] Defense speeches may provide a "model for the later church."[47] Indeed, Acts may offer the entire pattern of the "apostolic model" of mission as a model for the Church's continuing mission.[48]
12. *Promotion of one Christian faction.* If the early church included groups with various identities and beliefs, Acts may be a campaign document produced by one group in response to competing groups of believers.[49] For example, Tyson suggests a second-century date and anti-Marcionite purpose, defending the Twelve and the Jewish roots of Christianity against a movement that venerated Paul at their expense.[50]
13. *Legitimation of the Jesus movement.* A proposal that has wide current acceptance[51] is that of Esler, that the purpose of Acts is "legitimation" of

the Jesus movement—that is, the text reassures its members, some time after its founding, of its credentials and appropriateness.[52] Similarly, Maddox concludes that the aim is to confirm the gospel for believers.[53] Penner adds that Acts not only supports, but actively builds a new Christian cultural identity—an "emerging *politeia* under Christ."[54] Legitimation may be provided through answered prayer,[55] through appeal to Scripture,[56] or through depiction of the Church as a "Jewish philosophical school."[57] This is effectively apologetic addressed to insiders; indeed, even apologetic aimed at outsiders generally also involves legitimation aimed at insiders, because insiders are an inevitable part of the audience who actually hear such a text.[58]

In summary, among the proposed purposes of Acts, the most widely accepted is legitimation of the Jesus movement to its existing members—whether converts or second-generation members. There are also some who, whether or not combined with legitimation, assert an apologetic or even evangelistic purpose, but many reject this, generally on the basis that the implied audience is taken to be believers familiar with the Jewish Scriptures.

To what extent is persuasion a part of these purposes? Some of these evidently require persuasion because they are directly apologetic, i.e., the purposes involving evangelistic intent or providing a defense. The most significant proposed purpose, in terms of acceptance among scholars, is legitimation—which involves making "objectively available and subjectively plausible" the meaning of a social institution.[59] Plausibility features in this definition, which shows that an element of persuasion is intrinsic to legitimation. On the other hand, many see Acts as a history; but even a historian may intend to persuade—indeed, Acts has been described as "apologetic historiography."[60] By others, Acts might be seen as authoritative instruction, but that also involves an element of persuasion. Christians were certainly aware of persuasion in the OT (noting conditional promises, Eph 6:1–3; interpreting narrative as warning, Luke 17:32; 1 Cor 10:6–11; Heb 4:1, 11); and, in their own teaching, showing an interest in persuasion and conviction (e.g., 1 Thess 1:5); and tempering authoritative instruction with persuasive appeals (e.g., 1 Cor 10:15; 2 Cor 5:11). So even if Acts is primarily didactic, one may expect the author to write not only authoritatively but also persuasively.

Thus some of these purposes are primarily persuasive and others include some element of persuasion. But there is no widely accepted proposal for the purpose of Acts that does not involve persuasion, since even suggestions that it is a work of history or teaching have come to be combined with acceptance, at some level, of the relevance of persuasiveness.

This overview shows that analysis of Acts as persuasive narrative can be expected to make a useful contribution to the question of its purpose(s). But beyond that, I suggest that analysis of persuasion is worthwhile in its own right, as an approach to interpreting the text.

OVERVIEW OF THIS BOOK

Chapter 2 gives details of the method proposed and used here. After some discussion of how narratives persuade, it provides two systematic lists (which attempt to be complete, at least for the five texts studied in detail): a list of devices for Accrediting and Discrediting characters; and a list of the Techniques of Persuasion that may be employed—along with some indication of what persuasive impact each would have. These lists are summarized in Appendices A and B.

Chapters 3 to 6 provide analysis of four nonbiblical texts: Philo's *Embassy to Gaius*; Josephus's *Jewish War*; *Joseph and Aseneth*; and the *Letter of Aristeas*. These chapters allow conclusions reached by this method to be compared with conclusions reached by other scholars. Each chapter gives a brief demonstration of how the method can be used. The method brings out a few fresh insights. It gives conclusions that are generally in line with current scholarship, but it provides a firmer basis for accepting some conclusions and rejecting others.

Chapters 7 (preliminaries) and 8 (analysis of persuasion) provide a similar analysis of Acts, in the context set by the Third Gospel. Care is taken to do this without prejudging the purposes or persuasiveness of the text. Appendices C and D list all the instances of Accrediting and Discrediting in Luke and Acts. The analysis in Chapter 8 provides notable examples of persuasive techniques used. For example, it highlights the persuasive significance of the various retellings. It also identifies the Cornelius episode (Acts 10:1–11:18) as a particular focus of persuasion. Chapter 9 goes on to consider the Cornelius episode as a case study, working sequentially through that section of text in more detail. This demonstrates that the method is capable of being used at a much finer level of detail than has yet been attempted with any other section of text.

Chapter 10 compares these five texts, with Appendix E providing data on Accrediting and Discrediting. These comparisons and contrasts make it possible to reach conclusions about Acts, allowing for its literary milieu. The analysis demonstrates that the main approaches to persuasion used in Acts were in common use. In its style of Accrediting and Discrediting, Acts is shown to be more similar to *Aseneth* than to the other texts. Acts is shown to be distinctive in quoting Scripture frequently and in the intensity of its emphasis on the supernatural, including the Holy Spirit.

Chapter 11 returns to the question of the purpose(s) of Acts. Possible purposes are reassessed in the light of the identified techniques of persuasion. The suggestion that Acts is anti-Marcionite is undermined. The way Acts is constructed is suitable for winning over hearers who are unconvinced about the legitimacy of mission to Gentiles, hearers who are unconvinced about Paul (before his death), and also hearers who are unconvinced about the gospel.

Chapter 12 draws conclusions and discusses the possibility of wider application of this method, to the Gospels or to OT narrative.

This document is not a narrative but an academic book, written with the purpose of making a contribution to the discipline of biblical criticism, especially of the book of Acts, by persuading those who study and interpret Scripture that it is worthwhile and, indeed, necessary to attempt a systematic study of persuasiveness in biblical narrative. I hope that this introduction has persuaded you to read on.

NOTES

1. Letters dated 6/3/1843 and 10/3/1843: C. L. Lewes, *Dr. Southwood Smith: A Retrospect* (Edinburgh: Blackwood, 1898), 91–92.

2. Throughout, OT references are to the Septuagint, because the author of Acts used it. Hebrew (MT) references are added where necessary. The default LXX text is Alfred Rahlfs, *Septuaginta: Id Est Vetus Testamentum Graece Iuxta LXX Interpretes* (Stuttgart: Deutsche Bibelgesellschaft, 2006).

3. If enforcement or encouragement to conform is provided in other ways, external to the text.

4. Nicolas P. Gross, *Amatory Persuasion in Antiquity: Studies in Theory and Practice* (Newark, NJ: University of Delaware Press), 1985.

5. "[E]fficacious for moral improvement," Plutarch, *Life of Timoleon and Aemilius Paulus* 1:2, quoting from LCL, which is, where available, used by default throughout this book.

6. Gregory E. Sterling, *Historiography and Self-Definition: Josephos, Luke-Acts and Apologetic Historiography* (Leiden: Brill, 1992), 167–86.

7. A woman of Tekoa made similar use of a story: 2 Kgdms 14:5–11; cf. 3 Kgdms 21:35–43 (1 Kgs 20:35–43, MT).

8. Daniel Marguerat and Yvan Bourquin, *How to Read Bible Stories: An Introduction to Narrative Criticism* (London: SCM, 1999), 141.

9. Echoing Socrates's suspicion of rhetoric, e.g., Plato, *Gorgias* 459, questioning whether rhetoric even involves knowing right from wrong, or is simply the skill of persuading ignorant people. For example: "I am not primarily interested in didactic fiction, fiction used for propaganda or instruction." Wayne C. Booth, *The Rhetoric of*

Fiction, 2nd ed. (Chicago: University of Chicago Press, 1983), xiii. Among didactic works, he mentions Jonathan Swift's *Gulliver's Travels* (1726), John Bunyan's *Pilgrim's Progress* (ca. 1678), and George Orwell's *1984* (1949).

10. Philip F. Esler, *Community and Gospel in Luke-Acts: The Social and Political Motivations of Lucan Theology* (Cambridge: Cambridge University Press, 1987), 24–26; Beverly R. Gaventa, *The Acts of the Apostles* (Nashville: Abingdon, 2003), 52.

11. Marion L. Soards, *The Speeches in Acts: Their Content, Context and Concerns* (Louisville: Westminster/John Knox, 1994), 10–12.

12. Plain, unbiased presentation of facts, although an unrealistic expectation, was at times presented as an ideal: Lucian, *How to Write History*, 39; Polybius, *Histories* 1:14:4–5 (despite 16:14:6); Cicero, *On the Orator* 2:62.

13. Ben Witherington III, *The Acts of the Apostles: A Socio-Rhetorical Commentary* (Grand Rapids: Eerdmans, 1998), 39–46.

14. The phrase "narrative persuasion" is used, for convenience, to indicate the techniques and processes involved in persuading through a narrative text.

15. Todd Penner, *In Praise of Christian Origins: Stephen and the Hellenists in Lucan Apologetic Historiography* (London: T. & T. Clark, 2004), 329.

16. οὐκ ἐν πειθοῖς σοφίας [λόγοις], not with persuasive [words] of wisdom. Throughout, the NT Greek text is from NA.²⁸

17. LSJ s.v.

18. The author of Acts will, for convenience, be referred to as "Luke," without prejudging actual identity.

19. Mark L. Strauss, "The Purpose of Luke-Acts: Reaching a Consensus," in *New Testament Theology in Light of the Church's Mission,* ed. Jon Laansma et al. (Eugene, OR: Cascade, 2011), 135–50.

20. William S. Kurz, *Reading Luke-Acts: Dynamics of Biblical Narrative* (Louisville: Westminster, 1993), 6; C. K. Barrett, "The First New Testament," *Novum Testamentum* 38, no. 2 (April 1996), 102. Acts provides useful background for Paul's epistles, but it betrays no awareness of the epistles, so that is unlikely as its purpose.

21. Paul W. Walaskay, *Acts* (Louisville, KY: Westminster John Knox, 1998), 2, "the first chronicle of the church"; Craig S. Keener, *Acts: An Exegetical Commentary* (Grand Rapids: Baker Academic, 2012–15), 1:436, starts with "the communication of historical information."

22. Polybius, *Histories* 3:4:7–8; Lucian, *History*, 42.

23. To "edify," Ernst Haenchen, *The Acts of the Apostles: a Commentary* (Philadelphia: Westminster John Knox, 1971), 22–23; Richard I. Pervo, *Profit with Delight: The Literary Genre of the Acts of the Apostles* (Philadelphia: Fortress, 1987), 11, 137–38.

24. Robert Maddox, *The Purpose of Luke-Acts* (Edinburgh: Clark, 1982), 21, 31–65.

25. Maddox, *Purpose*, 21, 100–56.

26. Kathy R. Maxwell, *Hearing between the Lines: the Audience as Fellow-Worker in Luke-Acts and Its Literary Milieu* (London: T. & T. Clark, 2010), 175.

27. Geir O. Holmås, *Prayer and Vindication in Luke-Acts: The Theme of Prayer within the Context of the Legitmating and Edifying Objective of the Lukan Narrative* (London: T. & T. Clark, 2011), 265–66.

28. Todd Penner, "Civilizing Discourse: Acts, Declamation, and the Rhetoric of the *Polis*." In *Contextualizing Acts: Lukan Narrative and Greco-Roman Discourse*, ed. Todd Penner (Atlanta: SBL, 2003), 65–104, citing 101–2; Strauss, "Purpose," 141.

29. Martin Dibelius, *Studies in the Acts of the Apostles* (London: SCM, 1956), 135.

30. Loveday Alexander, *The Preface to Luke's Gospel: Literary Convention and Social Context in Luke 1:1–4 and Acts 1:1* (Cambridge: Cambridge University Press, 1993), 193–94, dismisses as misleading the very idea of a "book market."

31. Lucian, *History*, 7, 11.

32. Penner, "Civilizing Discourse," 102, sees Acts as asserting to any reader that only Christianity "can reasonably respond to the social, political and moral decay and disarray of the empire."

33. John W. Mauck, *Paul on Trial: The Book of Acts as a Defense of Christianity* (Nashville: Thomas Nelson, 2001), 221.

34. Strauss, "Purpose," 137.

35. Maddox, *Purpose*, 21.

36. Frederick F. Bruce, *The Book of the Acts*, rev. ed. (Grand Rapids, MI: Eerdmans, 1988), 10.

37. An idea reviewed by Esler, *Community*, 205–6; Haenchen, *Acts*, 23–24.

38. Strauss, "Purpose," 137.

39. Paul W. Walaskay, *And So We Came to Rome: The Political Perspective of St. Luke* (Cambridge: Cambridge University Press, 1983), 64–67.

40. Maddox, *Purpose*, 96–99; Keener, *Acts* 1:443–44.

41. Michael Green, *Evangelism in the Early Church* (Eastbourne: Kingsway, 2003), 349.

42. John C. O'Neill, *Theology of Acts in Its Historical Setting* (London: SPCK, 1961), 58.

43. O'Neill, *Theology*, 168.

44. Esler, *Community*, 25.

45. Babu Immanuel, *Repent and Turn to God: Recounting Acts* (South Perth, Australia: HIM International Ministries, 2004), 216, 219.

46. Richard J. Cassidy, *Society and Politics in the Acts of the Apostles* (Maryknoll, NY: Orbis, 1987), 159; Sterling, *Historiography*, 386.

47. Robert C. Tannehill, *The Narrative Unity of Luke-Acts: A Literary Interpretation*, 2 vols. (Minneapolis: Fortress, 1986–1990), 2:329.

48. Keener, *Acts* 1:440, 458.

49. Bart D. Ehrman, *Lost Christianities: The Battles for Scripture and the Faiths We Never Knew* (Oxford: Oxford University Press, 2003), 172–79, 184; an idea opposed by Maddox, *Purpose*, 185. A purpose of defense against Gnosticism lacks evidence: Strauss, "Purpose," 137–38.

50. Joseph B. Tyson, *Marcion and Luke-Acts: A Defining Struggle* (Columbia: University of South Carolina Press, 2006), 78.

51. Strauss, "Purpose," 140.

52. Esler, *Community*, "to explain and justify Christianity to the members of its community" (222), who "needed strong assurance that their decision to convert and adopt a different life-style had been the correct one" (16); Richard I. Pervo, *Acts: A Commentary* (Minneapolis: Fortress, 2009), 20–21.
53. Maddox, *Purpose*, 186–7.
54. Penner, "Civilizing Discourse," 101–2.
55. Holmås, *Prayer*, 261–63.
56. James A. Meek, *The Gentile Mission in Old Testament Citations in Acts: Text, Hermeneutic and Purpose* (London: T. & T. Clark International, 2008), 7; Penner, *Praise*, 328.
57. Charles H. Talbert, *Reading Acts: A Literary and Theological Commentary on the Acts of the Apostles*, rev. ed., (Macon, GA: Smyth and Helwys, 2005), xv.
58. Loveday Alexander, "The Acts of the Apostles as an Apologetic Text," in *Apologetics in the Roman Empire: Pagans, Jews and Christians*, eds. Mark Edwards, Martin Goodman, and Simon Price (Oxford: Oxford University Press, 1999), 22.
59. Esler, *Community*, 18.
60. Sterling, *Historiography*; Penner, *Praise*, 223–61.

Chapter Two

How to Identify the Persuasive Features of a Narrative

EXTENDING NARRATIVE CRITICISM TO ALLOW FOR PERSUASIVENESS

This book aims to contribute toward a better understanding of the book of Acts by developing and using a systematic method for discerning techniques of persuasion built into ancient narrative. This chapter defines that method. So how can one discern techniques of persuasion built into a narrative? In order to answer that question systematically, it is necessary to consider all of the various ways in which a narrative may be made persuasive.

Ideas could be taken from modern literary analysis and from other modern media for persuasion, but there would be a danger of taking modern ideas and imposing them anachronistically on an ancient text. So this method is based on ancient sources—modern ideas and examples may be mentioned at times for convenient illustration, but they are not definitive. The ideas arise from ancient narratives and ancient comments on them, including handbooks on style, supplemented by ideas that scholars have derived by analyzing ancient Greek and Hebrew texts.

The method starts with some conventional aspects of narrative analysis, particularly analysis of narrator and implied audience. Then the distinctive elements are two systematic lists, which I have not been able to find elsewhere: a list of devices for "Accrediting and Discrediting"; and a list of "Techniques of Persuasion" that are relevant to a narrative such as Acts. The audience will be referred to as "hearers" rather than "readers" on the basis that the vast majority could not read (let alone read fluently),[1] so most of the audience would have heard the text read aloud by a reader—a "lector"[2]—to a group. Ancient orators, authors, and readers were generally male, but women would have been included in at least some audiences.

From Aristotle onward, the ancients systematically analyzed persuasion through speeches, and the handbooks on rhetoric do explain how a "narrative" (*narratio*) may form part of a speech. Concerning persuasion through a work that is a narrative and not a speech, classical sources provide some comments,[3] but the ancients did not carry out any such systematic analysis. Penner argues that the function of a narrative text, as written by a historian, "is, for all intents and purposes, identical to the function of the *narratio* of speech."[4] Admittedly there is much overlap in the persuasive techniques used, but Penner is misleading in his suggestion that they are the same. Rather, the rhetorical situations are significantly different. An orator, on an occasion when he is including a section of narrative in his speech, is not the same as a storyteller, on an occasion when he is including a persuasive message in his narrative. What is appropriate for one is not the same as what is appropriate, effective, and acceptable to the audience, for the other.

With a speech, an orator directly addresses his or her immediate audience, face-to-face; but with a narrative text, an imagined (but not entirely known) range of future audiences is addressed by the author through the persona of the narrator and through the voice of the lector. With a speech, persuasion is acceptable and expected, whether overt or not, but with a narrative text, although there may be an expectation that it will inform, explain, and entertain, it is far from certain that overt attempts at persuasion are expected or acceptable.[5] A speech will be either deliberative (e.g., addressed to a senate), or forensic (e.g., to a jury), or epideictic (e.g., at a funeral), and cannot be a mixture of these (although declamation, for display, may involve showing off a mixture of these styles), but a narrative text does not address any of these specific rhetorical situations (except, perhaps, showing off the author's skill)[6]—its purposes and audiences are broader. The *narratio* within a speech builds on an existing, earlier-established relationship between orator and audience; but a narrative text has to establish the relationship between narrator and audience, and can choose to what extent the narrator is associated with the actual author. The *narratio* is only one step in a line of argument, and other parts will generally include explicit, intellectual discussion, argument, and perhaps an overt appeal, but a narrative text generally stands alone—the narrative itself must lead the audience's thoughts wherever the author wishes them to end up. The rhetorical handbooks are about speeches and are not, in general, even attempting to explain how narrative texts persuade. So here, in analyzing narrative texts, the concepts and terms from classical rhetoric can certainly, with caution, be used in helping to describing these narrative techniques, but they should not be treated as defining them.

On rhetoric, the ancient sources consulted include: Aristotle, *Rhetoric*; *Rhetoric to Alexander*; *Rhetoric to Herennius*; Cicero, *Orator* and *On the Or-*

ator; Quintilian; and the *Progymnasmata*, especially Aelius Theon's. Sources more relevant to narrative include: Aristotle, *Poetics*; Dionysius, *Critical Essays*; *On the Sublime*; Demetrius, *On Style*; Lucian, *On How to Write History*; and Theophrastus, *Characters*. References in this chapter give the key connections between the method and these ancient sources (with a few modern examples for convenient illustration). This method is based on approaches to persuasion that (whether or not described in the ancient handbooks) are actually used in ancient narratives—as detected by modern scholars.

THE GENERAL PROCESS OF PERSUASION THROUGH NARRATIVE

The rhetorical handbooks demonstrate awareness of how hearers should respond at various stages of a well-crafted speech. In contrast to a speech, a narrative generally appeals less to the intellect and more to the emotions, and it depends on flow of plot rather than flow of argument. Narrative follows a different trajectory from rhetoric, requiring a rather different structure. In general, a persuasive story needs to get six responses from the audience.

- *Attention.* A story, as much as a speech, must hold the attention throughout,[7] or everything else automatically fails.[8]
- *Consent.* The hearer must be persuaded, imaginatively, to "enter into" the story (as a story, requiring openness and, ideally, trust, but not necessarily belief—a story may openly be presented as fiction). This may be influenced by the hearer's relationship with the lector, author, and author's community, but the main concern here is how it is influenced by the narrator.[9] It is worth noting the opposite of consent—there is a danger of revolting a hearer;[10] or, if they are insulted, the likely outcome is antagonism, not persuasion.[11]
- *Engagement.* As the story gets going, the hearer is exposed to the narrator's perspectives, especially on each character introduced. Persuasion requires that, to some extent (even if only imaginatively, in the world of the story), the hearer should adopt these points of view—approving of heroes, despising villains.[12] This requires both coherence (that the story be internally consistent) and fidelity—fitting with the hearer's own experience.[13]
- *Participation.* As events unfold, the hearer is led through change and development—frustration, suspense, surprise, and final outcomes. In this way, engagement with the narrator's point of view can be deepened. Dramatic performances might involve vocal audience participation but, during a serious reading, the audience might well remain silent. Nevertheless,

this process of imaginative participation ("transportation")[14] provides the opportunity for moving the audience, beyond their preconceived values, in whatever direction the author sets.[15]

- *Response*. Rhetoric might aim not only at approval and applause, but, on occasions, at a specific vote or verdict. A persuasive narrative normally has less immediate and more general aims. But, by the end, the audience will have engaged with ideas in the world of the story that can influence their attitudes and behavior in the real world (whether consciously or subconsciously).[16]
- *Follow-up*. The way historians criticized the works of others suggests that, having heard a text, the audience would discuss it and would, in time, listen to other texts and continue the debate. Lucian's criticism of flattering historians (*History* 11) indicates that some authors performed their own works, concerned to influence their personal reputation and relationships. So, the persuasive process can extend far beyond the text itself. But such "follow-up" lies rather beyond the scope of the textual criticism here.

The main focus of this method is on identifying the use of particular Techniques of Persuasion within the text—where, for each technique, it is of interest to identify not only that it is being used, but also of what the hearer is, by this approach, being persuaded. In Chapters 3–8, in order to analyze the persuasiveness of the texts studied, every listed Technique of Persuasion has been searched for and the findings used to build up a picture of the overall persuasive thrusts of each text.

When a character speaks, the persuasive force depends on trust—in particular, on whether the hearer (of the text) has been encouraged to regard this character with sympathy, empathy (e.g., through "direct inside views" into their thinking), respect (through Accrediting), aversion, or even antipathy (through Discrediting). So, some Techniques of Persuasion depend on whether a character has been accredited or discredited, and before these techniques can be analyzed, it is necessary to notice all the processes of "Accrediting and Discrediting." It is not impossible for Accrediting or Discrediting to be, in itself, a persuasive thrust—if giving that character a good or bad reputation is an overall purpose of the text. But, in general, these devices simply contribute to the higher-level Techniques of Persuasion. Accrediting and Discrediting need to be analyzed in enough detail to clarify the level of trust established for each significant character. (See Appendix E.)

Many other literary devices may be relevant to persuasion, usually as building blocks that contribute either to Accrediting and Discrediting or to the Techniques of Persuasion. Identifying the use of one of these literary devices does not generally amount to identifying a persuasive thrust of the text, and it is not realistic to search for every such literary device. So I will mention only a few literary devices that have been noted as contributing to persuasion in the texts studied and will therefore be mentioned again in the later chapters.

PROPOSED METHOD FOR DISCERNING NARRATIVE PERSUASION

The method starts, as is conventional in narrative criticism, by analyzing the narrator and the implied audience. It then considers evidence of persuasion in the way the hearer is guided through the story and in how characters are presented—taking a particular interest in whether they are either accredited or discredited. Finally, the method identifies Techniques of Persuasion, using a systematic list of techniques that are relevant to narrative, with a brief statement of the specific persuasive effect of each one. I treat a "Technique of Persuasion" as an approach that may be used by the ancient author of a narrative text to give it a persuasive thrust, and where the use of the technique can be detected by a modern critic and the persuasive thrust identified.

The method used here is not strongly dependent on genre. Compared with nonnarrative texts (e.g., speeches, dialogue, or didactic treatises), persuasive techniques in narrative are less sensitive to whether the events described are regarded as historically true or invented[17]—narratives such as fables and parables can persuade even though clearly fictitious. The way a story is introduced may have some influence, but persuasive narrative operates in largely similar ways across genres.

More directly relevant to persuasion than the question of genre is a related issue—the extent of the author's (or editor's) freedom in composing and arranging their material. In composing fiction (such as fable or parable), the author may have great freedom. But in retelling an established story (e.g., Greek theater, drawing on earlier myths and epics),[18] the author had to be sensitive to the audience's expectations; there was some freedom, but some hearers would object if the events or characters seemed "wrong." The issue here is not primarily whether the earlier story was "true" (historical), but whether it was established—well-known and in some way respected. Finally, in presenting recent events or other verifiable information (e.g., geography), the author is particularly constrained, because some of their audience—whether initially or later—would know some details and would be able to check other details with independent sources.[19] So there are constraints on the author's freedom, depending on how well-known the information was and how strongly people might object.

In making a narrative persuasive, selection and arrangement of material can play a part—for example, suggesting similarities or contrasts. In interpreting whether the sequence of a narrative has been arranged with persuasive intent, care is needed to think through what level of freedom the author had. With fiction, they presumably chose the details, but with narrative presented as recent, verifiable fact, a detail might not have persuasive intent; it might simply have happened that way. Other details of how the author presents the narrative may still be persuasive, and the author can choose much about what to include and how, but care is needed to make a realistic assessment of the author's freedom. For example, when recounting recent, verifiable events, an author would have the freedom to decide whether and at what point in the narrative to include an episode—perhaps as an *analepsis* ("flashback" to the past) or *prolepsis* (used here to mean a "flash-forward")—and these decisions may well have persuasive significance, but he would have little choice in his presentation of the (actual) chronological sequence of events.

The texts studied here have been selected because of similarities to Acts, but they represent a range of genres. *Embassy*, which contains a persuasive letter and various speeches, can be summarized as a historical monograph of which parts are autobiographical. *War* is historiography[20]—a seven-volume history of the Jewish War—and also includes some autobiographical sections. *Aseneth* has much in common with the rather broad classical genre of "romance,"[21] but the tone is scriptural (echoing the Septuagint),[22] and the supernatural encounter with an angel provides an element of apocalyptic.[23] *Aristeas* begins and ends in the form of a personal letter, but the rest of its contents suggest that it would have been heard by its early audiences as an autobiographical historical treatise with didactic intent.

The proposed method does not require a clear genre to be identified—differences in persuasion between genres are not so significant and identifiable as to require them to be built into the method. A detailed study of how persuasion varies with genre would be a challenging task; nevertheless, the analyses in the following chapters will allow a few conclusions to be drawn from these particular texts.

Analysis of Narrator and Implied Audience

In rhetoric, a key factor in persuasion is the relationship or rapport between orator and audience. In a narrative text, the narrator's relationship with the hearer is less immediate or intense, but remains a key factor in persuasion.

When studying Scripture, some assume that the narrator can simply be treated as infallible;[24] and when studying fiction, it may often be appropriate for the narrator to be regarded as "omniscient." But in general, and especially when attempting to persuade, the narrator has to establish, not simply presume, the level of authority which it is appropriate for him to assert, given the target audience. So, first, the narrator can be analyzed in terms of his *ethos*—how he builds credibility. This can be established by building rapport through self-disclosure, or through claiming status as an eyewitness or as an expert—for example, claiming the virtues of a reliable historiographer. Secondly, the narrator can be analyzed in terms of his prominence (level of narration, especially the level of personal authority he assumes); and, thirdly, in terms of the content of his direct address or "asides"[25] (especially ideological or judgmental content, including judgment of characters). Whatever can be known, from the text, of the cultural context(s) of author and implied audience should be noted, and linked with what is generally known about this context from other sources. If the author is named, then the effect of this must be considered (e.g., does this confer authority? Is the author evidently attempting, by writing, to influence his personal reputation?). Details about the author from sources outside the text (e.g., that author's wider corpus) may be helpful, if that identification of the author can be made with confidence. But the purpose here is to investigate the interaction of the narrator with the implied audience, so such details are necessary only to the extent that they illuminate that interaction.

The implied audience should be analyzed from whatever clues can be found within the text, e.g., presupposed shared knowledge; or indications of the audience's ignorance, where the narrator has to explain[26]—combined, of course, with a wider awareness of the social context.[27] It has been common to define the "implied audience" as though this were inherently a monolithic entity;[28] but an orator was expected to be aware of different groups within his audience,[29] and this suggests that one must consider the range of possible groups which may be represented in the audience of a narrative text. The "implied audience" should therefore be seen as the range of groups of hearers who are implied by the details of the text. Consciously or subconsciously, the author must have had them in mind when writing. On the other hand, the "target audience" is not quite the same—it may be narrower. It is the specific audience at whom the persuasiveness of the text is targeted. Hearers who are already fully persuaded of the text's message are not likely to be the target audience, but may well be among the implied audience. On the other hand, hostile hearers who are not open to persuasion (e.g., the author's competitors) will not be the target audience but may, on occasions, form an inevitable part of the implied audience.

It would be tempting to use the text's persuasive thrust as evidence to help in deducing the implied audience, but since I am interested here in making deductions about persuasion from what is known about the audience, such an approach must be avoided, to prevent circularity of argument.[30]

Building Blocks of Persuasion

Not every literary device amounts to a Technique of Persuasion, but many literary devices can be used as building blocks. For example, if an event is described more than once, that is easy to detect and suggests that the author has a particular interest in that event. But the mere fact of this retelling does not, in itself, clarify the nature of the author's interest, and in order to discern whether the retelling is arranged in such a way as to have a persuasive impact, attention also needs to be paid to other details, e.g., who speaks and how they are characterized. So, before moving on to the Techniques of Persuasion, it is worth mentioning a few literary devices that make a contribution and will be encountered later in this book.

Vividness (ἔκφρασις, description) is an established feature of rhetoric—the process of vividly "bringing what is portrayed clearly before the sight,"[31] which is also a powerful and evident feature of persuasive narrative.[32] Vividness holds the attention and stirs the emotions. It may be prerequisite for effective persuasion. It influences how much the hearer is "caught up" in the narrative, e.g., David's indignation aroused by Nathan (2 Kgdms 12:1–6). The ancient concepts of vividness or spectacle (ὄψις, Aristotle, *Poetics* 1453b), arousal of emotions (*exsuscitatio*, *Rhet. Her.* 4:55), oracular demonstration (*demonstratio*, *Rhet. Her.* 4:68), engaging storyline (*Rhet. Her.* 8:13), and personal engagement (*On the Sublime* 26:3) are related to the modern term "transportation." Under that name, modern analysis provides an understanding of how this ancient technique works, which may be necessary here. In his reader-response approach to Thucydides, Connor suggests that vividness serves "to make the energy of our own response contribute to the power of the text"—which may be true—and that it serves "to awaken our critical and evaluative faculties."[33] Modern research shows that this is a misunderstanding of how narratives persuade. Whereas a hearer naturally responds to an argument with systematic, rational analysis, transportation by a vivid narrative leads to a less intellectual approach to persuasion—through "realism of experience," emotional responses and "reduced negative cognitive responding"—that is, *less* prominent use of the hearer's critical faculties.[34]

Comparison is a common literary device, indicating similarity between two things, e.g., two people or two actions. Typically, the audience has an established opinion of one, and the comparison is used to help to establish the audience's opinion of the other. *Contrast* is a related device, indicating difference between two things, e.g., one can seem taller by standing next to somebody short (*Rhet. Alex.* 3:8); the decisive women Deborah and Jael contrast with the men Barak and Sisera (Judg 4).[35] Juxtaposition or *patterns* and "echoes" within the text, perhaps connected by key words or *themes*,[36] can provide these comparisons and contrasts.[37] When an incident is told out of sequence (analepsis or prolepsis), that suggests a specific decision by the author—perhaps in order to achieve a desired juxtaposition.[38]

Emphasis (or *foregrounding*) can be achieved by repetition, arrangement[39] (e.g., who has the last word), or the use of forceful language (e.g., comparatives and superlatives). It helps to indicate which material is most significant.

Irony can also be used forcefully—where the text indicates a sense opposite to what others expect, subverting the meaning of a discourse or a situation,[40] e.g., Haman ending up hanged on gallows he himself set up for Mordecai (Esth 7:9–10). Related devices include sarcasm, hyperbole, and presentation by negation. *Sarcasm* is a cutting remark, especially where the intended meaning is the opposite of the natural meaning, e.g., καλῶς ἀθετεῖτε τὴν ἐντολὴν τοῦ θεοῦ, "You set aside the commandment of God *excellently*" (Mark 7:9—actually meaning *badly*).[41] *Hyperbole* involves obvious exaggeration for dramatic effect, e.g., seeing the speck (κάρφος) in another's eye without noticing the plank (δοκός) in one's own (Matt 7:3).[42] *Presentation by negation* involves stating what did *not* happen, reflecting or setting the hearer's expectations by providing a specific alternative to what did happen,[43] e.g., Philo provides a dramatic list of lethal weapons that were *not* found in Jewish possession (*Flaccus* 90), thus emphasizing how peaceable the Jews actually were.

Riddles and puzzles engage the attention and encourage the hearer to search for answers—to consider, discuss, or ask—but do not necessarily offer any overt or specific persuasive suggestion. Jesus's parables and allegories are puzzles—although not generally as obscure as riddles, such as Samson's (Judg 14:12–18).[44] In particular, when overt comment would be unsafe or unseemly, a text may have *subversive undertones*, making comments indirectly, through subtle "figured" speech (not necessarily detectable today),[45] e.g., thinly veiled references to Rome as "Babylon" ("seven hills" indicates Rome, Rev 17:9).

Retelling is a device evident in Acts. In general, telling something more than once provides emphasis (although, with care, it might even be possible to deemphasize, through revealing details in "gentle steps").[46] But retelling can have a wide variety of functions. It can: *remind*, e.g., David gives details of why Solomon should act against Shimei (3 Kgdms 2:8–9, summarizing 2 Kgdms 16:5–13; 19:16–23); *make connections*, e.g., Luke retells Jesus's prediction of Peter's denial, in the form of Peter's sudden recollection upon its fulfillment (Luke 22:61—even though the original account is recent, Luke 22:34); *reveal the point of view* of the character who retells already-familiar events, e.g., Josephus has Titus describe the (already-narrated) misfortunes of the Jews and proceed to assert that God is angry with them and helping the Romans (*J.W.* 6:40; cf. Eleazar's more extensive review and interpretation,

7:361–74); *indicate competing versions* of events, e.g., Josephus reports various such intrigues and disputes (*J.W.* 1:622–36; 2:26–36, 84–92); *indicate that a character is not truthful*, e.g., Gaius's rumors about Macro (*Embassy* 58; contradicting the narrative, 32, 35, 41); John of Gischala's claims about his retreat (*J.W.* 4:121–25; contradicting 106–11);[47] and perhaps Claudius Lysias's letter (Acts 23:26–30, which glosses over Paul's harsh treatment, 22:24–29); or *indicate that a character is truthful*, e.g., although, on their last meeting, Joseph refused to let her embrace him, Aseneth takes the risk of reporting her heavenly vision truthfully, including mention of their betrothal, without even checking whether Joseph's attitude has changed (*Jos. Asen.* 19:5–7, longer text). So retelling is a literary device that can contribute in a variety of ways. It does not normally amount to a Technique of Persuasion, but it may sometimes be used directly to persuade; in particular, when it is used to *persuade the hearer to trust an account*, polyphonically (P5c, below)—by retelling in different, mutually affirming voices.

Acts is exceptional in telling some events, not only twice, but more than twice—in the texts studied, the only comparable example is Josephus's prophecy of Vespasian's accession (*J.W.* 3:351–53, 399–402; 4:622–29). Chapters 7 and 8 make the case that these retellings in Acts amount to a "gentle steps" (P5e, below) approach to persuading the hearer.

Many other literary devices exist. The hearer may be impressed by elegant use of style (or variety of styles),[48] wide vocabulary or reference to a wide range of history, literature, and learning. If the purpose is to impress the hearer and build the author's reputation, then this may in itself be persuasive.[49] But for persuasion concerning anything else, such literary features are hardly relevant, except perhaps in building the narrator's credibility.

Accrediting and Discrediting

Some of the Techniques of Persuasion depend on the hearer trusting or, sometimes, distrusting a character. So, before moving on to those techniques, it is necessary to consider the Accrediting and Discrediting[50] devices that provide a foundation for persuasion by indicating which characters are trustworthy and which are untrustworthy. Whether consciously or subconsciously, a hearer will develop trust or distrust in particular characters as the narrative unfolds (and a character rarely develops or changes).[51] Accrediting devices within the text establish trust in that character, and that allows their words and actions to communicate to the audience with authority. In contrast, Discrediting prevents a character from being heard as authoritative, although their knowledge and opinions may still be worth hearing. In this way characters or groups (or even ideas and causes)[52] may be presented positively (i.e., accredited) or negatively (i.e., discredited). This positive or negative characterization might, in itself, amount to a technique of persuasion in the particular situation where that characterization is a significant persuasive thrust of the text. But Accrediting and Discrediting are listed separately because, in the texts studied, they play a significant role—and, in many cases, this is their main role—by providing the necessary characterization to support the other Techniques of Persuasion.

The simplest and most common accrediting device is a positive *epithet*—a word or phrase used to provide *positive characterization*. This is usually a description that would universally be recognized as positive (e.g., "virtuous," "wise"). But care is needed with epithets whose implication depends on culture or context, e.g., "uncircumcised" might be neutral elsewhere, but it means "foreign" to Jews, often with negative connotations (e.g., Acts 7:51). So an epithet might be "contextually" positive—that is, perceived as positive by the particular target audience. Or it might be contextually positive, as established by the way earlier parts of the text have set the scene.[53] In a similar way, negative epithets have the effect of discrediting. Accrediting may, at times, involve the supernatural (e.g., heavenly voices, omens, miracles, fulfillment of prophecy).[54] Portrayal as supernatural (e.g., heavenly messengers), or even as divine, is a particularly forceful form of accrediting, but this will fail if the hearer rejects the narrator's authority to make such an assertion. So, rather than the narrator personally attempting to wield that kind of authority, an alternative is to present evidence and allow the hearer to reach their own conclusions, e.g., an omen, a prophecy, or a miracle may be reported without comment, perhaps with the focus on the immediate response of the bystanders. So Accrediting and Discrediting are possible not only through loaded (positive or negative) epithets, but also through actions and events—such as a portent accompanying a character's birth; the performance of a miracle; or the amazed response of a crowd.

Analysis of trust, through Accrediting and Discrediting, underlies the analysis of persuasion reported in the next five chapters. Appendix B lists these devices—a list that aims to be complete (at least, concerning the texts studied)—and Chapter 8 provides some more detailed discussion. Accrediting devices A1–6 and discrediting devices D1–3 could, in general, be described as conventional, but the remainder (A7–27, D8–24) are particularly characteristic of a text that focuses on the supernatural (e.g., in Luke-Acts, even "reported evidence" largely points to the supernatural). Appendices C–E summarize the results of the analysis. The aim is to include all instances that would have an impact on the hearer's trust in a character (whether consciously or subconsciously). The instances can be categorized according to the device used, the character who is accredited/discredited, and the character (if any) who is involved in doing the accrediting/discrediting. Where more than one type of device is present in the same sentence, all are listed. Where one device is used repeatedly, in the same way, within the same sentence or adjacent sentences, that is only counted once, on the basis that a second instance, straightaway, would have limited extra impact.[55]

This analysis shows which characters are trustworthy and which untrustworthy; it also reveals which characters are most forcefully presented.

Techniques of Persuasion

This section provides a list (summarized in Appendix A) of the Techniques of Persuasion that may be detectable in ancient narrative. Each technique is described, with comments about what specific persuasive influence it is expected to have.

- P1) *Overt instruction*. The audience is being persuaded to follow the instruction or adopt the understanding presented.[56] This involves rational persuasion (*logos*), but the credibility (*ethos*) of the narrator or speaker is also significant.
- P1a) *By the narrator*, direct to the implied audience (e.g., in "asides").[57] A familiar example would be, "The moral of the story is . . ." The narrator may be prominent—for example, addressing the audience directly at the start of the text (e.g., *J.W.* 1:1–30; *Let. Aris.* 1–8; Luke 1:1–4; Acts 1:1–2). But comments to the audience may be provided at any stage throughout the narrative, and such asides are not necessarily prominent.
- P1b) *By a trusted character*.[58] The character's comments (especially generalizations that can be applied to everyone) are heard as authoritative if that character has been portrayed with respect (accredited) or if his/her point of view has been shown to coincide with the (trustworthy) narrator's. This arises when a narrative reports as authoritative a speech with ideological or hortatory elements.
- P1c) *By an "other" character* who has not been accredited. This becomes persuasive if there is some other form of accreditation, e.g., an untrustworthy enemy ends up forced by events to accept, perhaps reluctantly, a known tenet of the trusted character(s);[59] or if an untrustworthy character's instruction is so evidently inappropriate that the intended response is for the hearer to reject it (e.g., Gaius's desire to be considered divine, *Embassy* 265).

It is also possible to provide instruction by including, within a narrative, a *report of a dialogue*. By the end of a dialogue, two (or more) contrasting points of view have been heard; or, as a simpler version of this, narratives may simply include an opposing pair of speeches. Overall, this becomes persuasive, rather than merely thought-provoking, if the hearer is guided by the narrative toward one point of view, e.g., if one side is presented as "winning" the argument. Logically, strength of argument should be the decisive factor, and the approaches employed in philosophical dialogues (and in rhetoric) might be added here, as techniques of persuasion. But that is beyond the scope of this book, on the basis that narrative texts do not primarily influence the hearer through strength of argument, but through narrative techniques, such as characterization (who seems trustworthy?), arrangement (e.g. who has the last word? Luke 20:26, 39–40), and outcome (e.g., if a decision was made and followed through). Thus the opposing pair of speeches by Jesus, the respected chief priest (*J.W.* 4:238–69), and Simon, a leader of the denigrated (4:231) Idumaeans (4:272–82) permit both points of view to be heard, but the characterization leaves the hearer in no doubt about whose opinion to respect. Even Polybius, who expresses a concern for truth without prejudice (*Histories* 2:56:7), often makes it clear where his sympathies lie, and not always overtly: Concerning whether Rome was right to sack Carthage, he reports the views of four different groups, but emphasizes one by his arrangement—both by placing it last and by explaining it in rather more detail.[60] So, even though a narrative may report dialogue and logical arguments, it is still these techniques of narrative persuasion that (certainly in the texts studied) determine the persuasive impact on the hearer.

- P2) *Worldview.*[61] The audience is being persuaded to adapt their worldview for consistency with the worldview presented by the text.[62]
- P2a) *Worldview of the text* is revealed by a narrative event or narrator's description, e.g., when Aseneth receives supernatural protection from ambush (*Jos. Asen.* 27:11), this event communicates that God protects those who put their faith in him.
- P2b) *Trusted character's worldview* is revealed—perhaps by their words (a trusted character gives a speech promoting a particular point of view),[63] perhaps by their actions.
- P2c) *Untrustworthy character's worldview* is revealed—in order to be rejected.[64]
- P3) *Characterization* (usually of an individual, but sometimes of a homogeneous group) involving some degree of identification:
- P3a) *Positive characterization and empathy.*[65] Empathy involves identification, whether realistic or aspirational—so, from the hearer's point of view, the character must not be too exotic and must be acceptable, not despicable. Empathy is often built with a character who is at the center of events (a protagonist), especially if the narrative adopts their point of

view. It can be strongly built by a *direct inside view* into that character's thinking (whether expressed in their own words or mentioned by the narrator) or emotions.[66] The audience is being persuaded to accept whatever that character represents (e.g., them personally, especially if still living; or their character traits, and thus other people who share those traits;[67] or their community or successors in the real world). This might well involve a realistic, good example to follow.[68]

- P3b) *Positive characterization and respect.* Respect arises from stronger positive characterization, but less identification, than empathy. With empathy, one can imagine *being* that character; with respect, one can imagine *following* their lead. Respect is not normally considered in narrative criticism, but it is important when considering persuasion, because it builds trust in that character. By respecting this character, the audience is being persuaded to respect whatever they represent (e.g., them personally; or their words; or their actions; or their character traits, and thus other people who share those traits; or their community or successors in the real world). Such a character might act as a trusted adviser (P1b, P2b), or as an ideal to admire, e.g., Phinehas (Num 25:7–13; Ps 105:30–31, LXX; Ps 106:30–31, MT).

  Respect may, on occasions, be presumed rather than generated within the text. For example, among Greeks and Romans, respect could generally be presumed for Homer (for his epics), Aesop (fables), Socrates (philosophy), or Thucydides (history). Among Jews, God-fearers, and Christians, respect could be presumed for the OT and for the characters it portrays with respect (e.g., Moses or David).

- P3c) *Positive characterization and sympathy.* Sympathy involves pity for a character's plight, generally with some degree of identification. By developing sympathy for this character, the audience tends to become sympathetic toward whatever they represent (e.g., them personally; or their character traits, and thus other people who share those traits; or their community or successors in the real world, i.e., those in the same plight). For example, Euripides's *Trojan Women* employs this technique, which could be described as a "sob story."[69]

- P3d) *Aversion.* This involves the initial possibility of identification, but the hearer is then encouraged to avoid the sort of situation or behavior portrayed. The hearer is ultimately encouraged to distance themselves from this character and thus from whatever they represent (perhaps them personally; generally, their behavior or character traits, and thus other people in the real world who share those). Any identification is ambivalent: The hearer is encouraged to respond: "Although I could be like that, I do not want to be!" This might well involve a realistic, bad example to avoid, e.g., Simon the Pharisee (Luke 7:36–50).[70]

- P4) *Antipathy*: The text provokes hostility without identification.[71] Whereas direct inside views into an acceptable character's thinking can evoke empathy (P3a) by affirming their acceptability, any *direct inside views* into a repulsive character's thinking tend to serve, rather, to strengthen antipathy by exposing what makes them repulsive.[72]
- P4a) *Repulsive character (through traits)*. Through negative personal character traits, the audience is encouraged to reject the character's attitudes and behavior, and people who exhibit those attitudes or that behavior. Such a character is generally portrayed as a villain, e.g., the disrespectful fool, Nabal (1 Kgdms 25:2–42).[73]
- P4b) *Repulsive character (through identity)*. Here, the focus is not (primarily) on personal character, but on group identity, e.g., Idumaeans (*J.W.* 4:231, 310); perhaps the Sidonian Baal-worshiper Jezebel (3 Kgdms 16:31; cf. Rev 2:20). The audience is intended to develop hostility toward the group represented by this character (e.g., their community or successors in the real world). A xenophobic caricature epitomizes this category.

  In theory, it is also possible to persuade through the use of a *repulsive narrator*, whereby the audience is intended to reject the narrator's views and people who hold such views, e.g., Lucian's satirical and sarcastic *A Professor of Public Speaking*, presented as a treatise (not a narrative) by an incompetent, unethical rhetorician. This approach is very rare, and not found in the texts studied.[74]
- P5) *Plot* and arrangement: The plot is relevant to any good example to follow or bad example to avoid. Three persuasive approaches are significant here. First, the narrative may indicate whether an action is good or bad by direct comment (generally in the mouth of the narrator, P1a, or of a trusted character, P1b). Secondly, it may indicate the appropriateness of an action through positive or negative characterization of the person or group who performs the action (P3 and P4). Indeed, where it is not immediately obvious whether the action is good or bad, it is generally characterization that is the key to guiding the hearer and making the narrative persuasive. This is not entirely logical (a bad person may be capable of a good action), and would not on its own be adequate in a philosophical dialogue or a speech, where anything less than a rigorous proof could be picked apart by one's opponent, but it is the way ancient narratives generally "work."[75] Thirdly, the outcome may also be used to indicate the appropriateness or inappropriateness of the action which led up to it (P5a and P5b below). Modern analysts may expect a text to provide rigorous evidence of the link between cause and effect, between action and (final) outcome, and some ancient texts may aim or claim to provide this (e.g., Polybius, *Histories* 12:25b1–3),[76] but with an absorbing and carefully arranged narrative, cau-

sality does not actually need to be demonstrated (or even claimed) for the hearer to infer it.⁷⁷ In addition, there may be more subtle ways in which a narrative could indicate the appropriateness or inappropriateness of an action (e.g., omens; or associating an action with some earlier precedent that has already been shown to be good or bad), but in the findings of this study, any such subtle approaches have not made a significant contribution compared with these three approaches of direct comment, characterization, and outcome.

- P5a) *Positive change or outcome*. This encourages the audience to accept such an outcome as a possibility, and to value what led up to it.⁷⁸ Identification (especially empathy) will reinforce this, but it is not necessary. Examples include comedy, e.g., Dikaiopolis achieving the peace he desired in Aristophanes's *Acharnians*.
- P5b) *Negative change or outcome*. This gives a warning—aversion to this outcome leads to aversion to what led up to it. Identification (especially empathy) may reinforce this, but it is not necessary. This acts as a cautionary tale, e.g., against going too close to defenders, like Abimelech, who came to a "sticky end" (Judg 9:50–55).⁷⁹
- P5c) *Polyphonic affirmation*. This involves the hearer receiving the same persuasive idea from multiple voices—probably trusted characters (P1b or P2b) and perhaps also the narrator (P1a or P2a). To present the idea once could be persuasive, but this technique provides an extra dimension to the persuasion, not merely by repetition, but by giving the impression of independent affirmation by multiple people, e.g., in *Embassy*, multiple voices emphasize Jewish horror at the idea of a statue in their Temple (Jewish ambassadors, 192; Jewish elders, 229–30; Agrippa, 308).
- P5d) *Journey of discovery*. The audience identifies with a character, who learns a lesson (whether gradually or suddenly) as the story unfolds.⁸⁰ The audience is thus encouraged to learn the same lesson. Empathy is probably necessary.⁸¹ Examples include Aseneth,⁸² and as I argue in Chapter 8, Peter (in Acts 10:9–11:18).⁸³
- P5e) *Gentle steps*. The hearer is led, ideally unaware, through a cumulative series of minor developments in their attitude or thinking. This can be more persuasive than a direct challenge, which risks provoking immediate rejection. Philo describes this technique (without actually using it) when he mentions that Gaius publicized his desire to be considered a god gradually, "as if on stepping-stones" (ἀναβαθμός, step, *Embassy* 77). Helicon, knowing that Gaius was annoyed with Jews and open to humorous accusations (*Embassy* 168–69), successfully drip-fed him with slander (*Embassy* 171, 205). I argue in Chapter 8 that the retellings of Saul/Paul's conversion

involve a "gentle steps" approach to persuading the hearer of the validity of his call.

Shock of recognition is also a possible persuasive technique. The hearer is led, unawares, to a position where they can be ambushed by a persuasive surprise, e.g., Nathan's story to David (2 Kgdms 12:1–7).[84] Peter's temple speech may include this, when he claims that Jesus, whom "you killed" (while releasing a murderer, Acts 3:14–15), was actually the Christ (3:20).[85] Although characters within narratives receive such shocks (common in tragedy, Aristotle, *Poetics* 1455a), the audience is normally already aware; this study has not identified examples of ancient authors using such surprises to shock their audience.

It is also worth noting that material is *not* likely to be persuasive if presented in the mouth of somebody the hearer distrusts (e.g., somebody they hate, despise, or who offends them), or if it is unacceptable (i.e., a huge leap away from their existing ideas) or boring.

The persuasion in any one narrative work is likely to employ several—perhaps most—of these techniques, although it is assumed that they all derive from and contribute toward the same purpose (or, more realistically, set of purposes). An entire narrative is made up of various episodes and many characters. There may well be episodes and characters that are not, in themselves, persuasive, but simply make a contribution to the main plot. So an attempt to discern the presence of these techniques should start with the overall text, before proceeding with a more detailed search of a particular section. Even a minor character or episode may have an identifiable persuasive effect, but one should not leap to a conclusion without checking that this is coherent with persuasion in the overall narrative.

This list of Techniques of Persuasion aims at completeness, but it has omitted techniques that are particularly indirect or covert and therefore hard for a modern reader to identify—techniques that are not explained in the text, such as symbolism, allusion, covert allegory,[86] figured speech, subtle irony or humor, or hints at esoteric knowledge. These can certainly have persuasive effect, but cannot properly be understood without further information. So, although some scholars may wish to provide speculative interpretations, these aspects of persuasion are beyond the scope of this book. Similarly, the author's selection of material may play a significant part in their approach to persuasion, but unless the text has left an overt gap (e.g., explaining what has been omitted, Josephus, *J.W.* 2:250–51), or the events are widely known from other sources, we do not generally have enough information to assess the significance of what has been omitted.

These techniques have been listed because they are relevant to ancient narrative—although many may also remain in use in modern narrative. Characterization with respect is important here, because this study suggests that it is the predominant ancient approach to establishing a persuasive character. Given the hierarchical nature of ancient societies, respect is based not only on fame or achievement (as in modern celebrity or expert endorsement), but on status, nobility (by birth), virtue, reputation, and divine accreditation (which might not receive the same respect from modern hearers). On the other hand, whereas modern hearers tend to value the opinion of a peer (one "like me," e.g., *vox pop.*), it does not generally seem to have been assumed that an ancient audience would do so.[87] In the texts studied here, "trusted characters" are generally those characterized with respect rather than empathy.

WHAT IS THIS METHOD USEFUL FOR?

This method is designed to allow the modern critic to discern techniques of persuasion within an ancient narrative text and thus to assess the particular persuasive impact it would be expected to have on its early hearers.

The method is designed for narrative, with a primary interest in narrative presented as fact, although it is not unsuitable for fiction. Narrative may fit within such diverse genres as history, myth, comedy, tragedy, or biography.[88] It would normally involve prose, although narrative can sometimes be in poetic form, such as Greek drama and epic. A narrative work may, and normally will, include spoken elements such as speeches, songs, and dialogue—indeed, plays generally consist entirely of these, but they may still be narrative, in that they tell a story. This method has been developed with prose but could probably be used with any of these types of narrative. However, it is not suitable for a text that, overall, is not a narrative, e.g., a speech (where rhetorical criticism is needed), a technical treatise, or a philosophical dialogue.

The method is designed for persuasive narrative.[89] Persuasiveness may arise because the author had a deliberate persuasive purpose, but not necessarily. An author might have an intuitive sense that a story should be told in a particular way, without realizing that this "way" is persuasive. Narrative techniques may be used instinctively by authors who have never studied literary criticism, so the usefulness of narrative criticism does not depend on authorial training or intent.[90] It is possible that the author of Acts employed persuasive techniques simply because he felt most comfortable with that style of storytelling. Detection of persuasive techniques within a text does not amount to proof of the author's intent, although it is generally the best evidence available. Even when there is a stated purpose within a text, that is not necessarily an accurate or complete reflection of the author's true purpose(s). Despite these complications, study of persuasion within the text is possible even if the author had no training in persuasive composition and made no conscious formulation of a persuasive purpose. This method demonstrates the persuasive influence that the text would be expected to have on its original audiences—a particular, limited, but nevertheless valuable insight into the meaning of the text.

The method assumes unity (at least, unity of purpose) within the text. It is worth noting that multiple volumes, even by the same author, do not necessarily share the same purpose.[91] The use of various sources is not a problem, provided that the final editor exercised enough freedom to impose one particular set of purposes throughout the "final" (extant) form of the text.

With ancient texts, although there may be a variety of evidence, it is not possible to know the exact composition of and character of the "original audience(s)" of the work. Some texts may be overtly addressed to a particular audience, the "stated audience," but this does not necessarily represent the real audience (e.g., Philocrates seems to be a fictitious recipient of the *Letter of Aristeas,* see Chapter 6). The "intended audience," which the author had in mind at the time of composition, is of interest but cannot be identified with certainty. So literary critics generally work with the "implied audience," deduced by piecing together the relevant evidence from the text (which requires some wider awareness of the general linguistic and cultural context). Unless there happen to be other sources of information beyond the text, what is actually available for scholars to work with is this "implied audience."

Similar issues apply to the author. Even where an author is named, care is needed to assess whether the claim is credible (e.g., Aristeas, the "stated author," seems to be a pseudonym). If they were already well-known, their reputation would play a part in the impact of the text. It is, further, necessary to distinguish narrator from author. Although there is uncertainty concerning information about the author, it is the text itself that defines the narrator. It may be the (real) author/editor who addresses the intended audience, but in working with the text, a scholar is most directly considering how the implied audience interacts with the narrative as presented by the narrator.[92]

Narrative criticism in general has been accused of being subjective,[93] rhetorical methods have not always proved convincing, and the process of discerning purpose (especially in narrative) has been noted as a difficult task.[94] Narrative criticism has evident limitations, in that other forms of criticism are necessary if one is to address issues of historicity, sources, redaction, or subsequent reception of a text. Nevertheless, scholars in various disciplines, including biblical studies, remain willing to discuss the purposes of texts. That is an indication of the need for this book.

This method makes some use of accepted approaches to narrative and rhetorical criticism, but it is a significant development of them. It has the advantage of addressing directly, based on relevant ancient sources, the question of what persuasive techniques may be used, and are worth searching for, in ancient narrative.

SOME CONNECTIONS WITH CLASSICAL SCHOLARSHIP

How does this method compare with methods already used by classical scholars? Certainly, in studying Greek historiography, scholars have become increasingly interested, not only in historical events, but also in persuasiveness. Each scholar has a particular approach to this.

Overt persuasion in the mouth of the narrator is the easiest technique of persuasion to detect. Thomas focuses on this in her analysis of Herodotus, noting that he "delights in using the language of proof and open argumentation"[95] with, at times, an "egocentric"[96] and "flamboyant" rhetorical style suitable for speeches and display performances.[97] Noting the persuasive style of his contemporaries, especially in medical treatises, she associates Herodotus with the oral performance lectures of his day. In sections where his persuasion is overt, Herodotus was persuading his audiences, not only about the topic at hand, but also to take him seriously as an authority on a wide range of knowledge and deductions. So even overt persuasion in the mouth of the narrator can be more complex—in this case, the persuasive force also includes the less overt message that Herodotus himself is authoritative and should be listened to with respect.

But this is rather a limited approach. In general, overt persuasion is not the only, and not necessarily the most powerful, form of persuasion through narrative. Thucydides gives the impression of abstaining from value judgments yet, by applying reader response criticism, Connor detects implicit judgment in his "selection, shaping and shading" of material. It is not surprising that, as a scholar, Connor's approach is analytical. But he also seems to assume that Thucydides's narrative evokes an intellectual, analytical response from anybody in his audience—even for instance, in the *pathos* of accounts of suffering. Connor is keen to shield Thucydides from any accusation that these might be "the manipulations of a ideologue,"[98] but in doing so, he neglects the inevitable, and not necessarily inappropriate, emotional and relational aspects of the hearer's response whenever the text evokes sympathy (or, indeed, empathy or respect).

Those studying narratives of other genres (e.g., epic, drama) have yet other approaches. Some approaches will be more credible and more fruitful than others, depending on the text being studied. My purpose is not to discuss the relative merits of specific approaches, but to suggest that, in interpreting any of these texts, a better (and, until now, neglected) starting point is to attempt a systematic understanding of *all* the techniques by which such narratives may persuade.

SOME CONNECTIONS WITH BIBLICAL SCHOLARSHIP

Biblical scholars have adopted and adapted various ideas from the wider discipline of literary criticism, including narrative criticism, rhetorical criticism, and some aspects of reader-response criticism.[99] All this provides a helpful starting point. For example, Sternberg uses narrative criticism to analyze how Hebrew stories engage with their audiences,[100] but with the severe constraint that he only considers persuasion about how the audience is to regard events and characters *within* the narrative, not in their own world beyond it. Narrative criticism has also been applied to the NT,[101] including Acts.[102] For example, Finnern tabulates various kinds of persuasive and dissuasive effect (strengthening or weakening particular attitudes, beliefs, or behavior), influenced by whether characters are portrayed positively or negatively, with empathy, sympathy, or antipathy[103]—but he does not adequately address issues of respect and trust.

Rhetorical criticism (based on classical rhetoric, especially Aristotle)[104] has been most directly and appropriately applied to speeches—and Acts contains many[105]—considering how each speech would have influenced its narrative audience (the hearers, as presented within the world of the narrative). But this, while valuable, is not the same as considering—as this book does—the persuasive impact this report of a speech would have, probably decades later, on hearers of Acts. Setting Acts in its rhetorical context, Satterthwaite moves in this direction, by considering not only speeches but the entire narrative, concluding that "such a study helps us to understand Luke's purposes in writing Acts, and to form a clearer picture about how Acts might have been received by an audience aware of rhetorical conventions."[106] His essay has influenced later work, including "socio-rhetorical" criticism, and is a significant precursor to this book. For example, he begins to identify the significance of respect when he notes the narrative's positive characterization of believers "gives implicit support" to the gospel message presented in the speeches.[107] Socio-rhetorical criticism continues this development, deliberately considering both social context and rhetorical conventions,[108] but not adequately addressing narrative conventions.

Analysis of audience is important. Interest in the specific audiences and "communities" associated with each Gospel has not arrived at consensus and may have become over-speculative; rather, it is quite possible that these texts (along with Acts) were intended for wide circulation.[109] It has been common to treat the "implied audience" as though it were a single, monolithic entity. But, especially when considering what would be persuasive, it is necessary to consider the various relevant groups of different cultures and opinions. For example, in considering persuasive phenomena associated with evangelism in Acts, Liggins appropriately differentiates between what would be persuasive for Jews and what would be persuasive for Gentiles among its various audiences.[110]

All of this biblical criticism is relevant, but it does not amount to a systematic method for identifying techniques of persuasion in NT narrative.

OVERVIEW OF THE METHOD

Having selected a text to study, preliminary investigation involves gathering key details from it and about it. Thus in Chapters 3–7, the following will be presented: details about the text; a summary of the story; narrator and author; audience (stated audience, if any, and implied audience); date and context; any overt indications of purpose; and possible purposes, as suggested in the secondary literature. Next, evidence of persuasiveness is gathered from the text. Various literary devices may be noteworthy but not, in themselves, conclusive about persuasion; limited space prevents their presentation in detail here. The devices for Accrediting and Discrediting (A1–27, D1–24) must be systematically noted (as summarized in Appendices C–E), to establish which characters are trusted and which are untrustworthy. It is then possible to identify the Techniques of Persuasion (P1–5). By considering who is being persuaded of what, conclusions can then be drawn about narrative persuasion.

This analysis should consider the whole text, lest important information be missed. But the method can be used in much greater detail than presented in Chapters 3–8. To demonstrate this, a case study on Acts 10:1–11:18 is presented in Chapter 9.

Four extra-biblical narratives, approximately contemporary with Acts, have been selected for analysis on the basis of being similar to Acts. This shows how the method can be used with texts comparable to Acts. (A wider range of texts would also be of interest, but is beyond the scope of this book.) Comparison with these texts provides some indication of what is conventional and what is distinctive about Acts.

NOTES

1. Chris Keith, *Jesus' Literacy: Scribal Culture and the Teacher from Galilee* (London: T. & T. Clark, 2011), 71–123.
2. William D. Shiell, *Reading Acts: The Lector and the Early Christian Audience* (Boston: Brill, 2004); Walaskay, *Acts*, 19. Indeed, *Let. Aris.* 127 indicates a positive preference for such hearing rather than reading.
3. Penner, *Praise*, 180–222, emphasizing completeness, plausibility, vividness, use of speeches, and arrangement, to reveal character, motivation, and causes of events.
4. Penner, *Praise*, 189.
5. Lucian, *History*, 39.
6. Polybius, *Histories* 36:1:6–7, denounces historians who do this.
7. Or, for long texts, at least throughout the section read/performed at one sitting.
8. Aristotle, *Rhet.* 3:12:7, 9; suspense and surprise can help, Quintilian *Inst.* 4:2:107; but Strabo (*Geographica* 11:6:3) and Thucydides (*War* 1:22:4) accuse others of trying too hard to entertain.
9. Polybius, *Histories* 1:5:4–5; Lucian, *History*, 53, asserts that the historian should not seek goodwill, merely request to be heard with an open mind.
10. Aristotle, *Poetics*, 1452b; Polybius, *Histories* 15:36.
11. An orator should not appear as a "sage among fools," with the hearers feeling that they are treated as foolish, Cicero, *On the Orator* 1:221.
12. Aristotle, *Rhet.* 1:10:4; 2:8:13; Polybius notes the possibility of failing to achieve this engagement, *Histories* 1:5:4–5; Josephus engages Gentiles through allusions to classical literature, Gottfried Mader, *Josephus and the Politics of Historiography: Apologetic and Impression Management in the* Bellum Judaicum (Leiden: Brill, 2000), 156.
13. Penner, *Praise*, 196.
14. E.g., filling "gaps": Roman Ingarden, *The Cognition of the Literary Work of Art*, trans. Ruth A. Crowley and Kenneth R. Olsen (Evanston, IL: Northwestern University Press, 1973), esp. 50–63; Meir Sternberg, *The Poetics of Biblical Narrative: Ideological Literature and the Drama of Reading* (Bloomington: Indiana University Press, 1985), 189; Maxwell, *Hearing*. Modern studies describe the degree to which the hearer is absorbed into the story (a significant factor in persuasion) as "transportation": Melanie C. Green and Timothy C. Brock, "The Role of Transportation in the Persuasiveness of Public Narratives," *Journal of Personality and Social Psychology* 79, no. 5 (November 2000): 701.
15. E.g., evoking the desire to emulate a good example, Aristotle, *Rhet.* 2:11:1; Cicero considers not only persuasion to adopt a new point of view, but also to relinquish an old one, *Orator*, 97.
16. Demetrius, *On Style*, 292, considers subtle, rather than overt, persuasion; Polybius, *Histories* 1.1.2, considers direct instruction; nevertheless, persuasion involves not only the intellect (*logos*) but also the emotions (*pathos*); Steve Walton, "Rhetorical Criticism: An Introduction," *Themelios* 21, no. 2 (January 1996): 4–9, citing 4.

17. Concerning Acts, see Loveday Alexander, "Fact, Fiction and the Genre of Acts," *New Testament Studies* 44, no. 3 (July 1998): 380–99.

18. Aristotle, *Poetics*, 1453b.

19. Polybius, *Histories* 31:22:8, claims credibility on the basis that he cannot distort facts about Romans, because some of them will inevitably be in his audience.

20. Arguably "apologetic historiography," Sterling, *Historiography*, 392–93.

21. Randall D. Chesnutt, *From Death to Life: Conversion in Joseph and Aseneth* (Sheffield: Sheffield Academic, 1995), 254; Barclay, *Diaspora*, 204–5; Christoph Burchard, *Gesammelte Studien zu Joseph und Aseneth* (Leiden: Brill, 1996), 305.

22. Edith M. Humphrey, *Joseph and Aseneth* (Sheffield: Sheffield Academic, 2000), 31.

23. Gideon Bohak, Joseph and Aseneth *and the Jewish Temple in Heliopolis* (Atlanta: Scholars, 1996), 88, 101.

24. Sternberg, *Poetics*, 476.

25. Steven M. Sheeley, *Narrative Asides in Luke-Acts* (Sheffield: Sheffield Academic, 1992), 14–25.

26. For implied audience of Acts, see Joseph B. Tyson, *Images of Judaism in Luke-Acts* (Columbia: University of South Carolina Press, 1992), 19–41; John A. Darr, *On Character Building: The Reader and the Rhetoric of Characterization in Luke-Acts* (Louisville: Westminster/John Knox, 1992), 26–29.

27. I.e., aspects of the general sociocultural and linguistic context—the "extratext"; Darr, *Character*, 22–23.

28. E.g., Tyson, *Images*, 19–41. Love stories demonstrate the inadequacy—if both hero and heroine are portrayed to the audience as sexually attractive, the monolithic implied audience would be bisexual.

29. E.g., *Rhet. Alex.* 29:10; Lucian notes, of flattering accounts, that "everybody apart from the one flattered is disgusted" (Lucian, *History*, 11); Polybius addresses both young and old (*Histories* 31:30:1), contemporaries and posterity (3:4:7–8), cf. 1 Cor 7; 1 John 2:12–14.

30. Step 1: The persuasive thrust of the text suggests this kind of audience. Step 2: Since this is the audience the persuasive thrust must be this. Such a circular argument might be internally consistent, but it cannot provide evidence against other internally consistent hypotheses.

31. Aelius Theon, *Progymnasmata* 118 (trans. Kennedy, *Progymnasmata*, 45); *Ad Herennium* 4:68 (§LV), treats *demonstratio* as putting "before the eye" (*ante oculos*).

32. Penner, *Praise*, 190–96.

33. W. Robert Connor, *Thucydides* (Princeton: Princeton University Press, 1984), 16–17.

34. Green, "Transportation," 701–02.

35. Sternberg, *Poetics*, 479.

36. E.g., It is through themes that Tacitus guides his (Roman) readers' judgment; Olivier Devillers, "The Concentration of Power and Writing History: Forms of Historical Persuasion in the *Histories* (1.1–49)," in *A Companion to Tacitus* (eds. Victoria E. Pagán; Chichester: Wiley-Blackwell, 2012), 162–86, citing 165.

37. "Because [these techniques] involve the reader in the interpretative process, they can be particularly persuasive, more persuasive, perhaps, than an explicit interpretation or evaluation on the part of the writer": Philip E. Satterthwaite, "Acts against the Background of Classical Rhetoric," in *The Book of Acts in its Ancient Literary Setting*, eds. Bruce W. Winter and Andrew D. Clarke (Grand Rapids: Eerdmans, 1993), 367.

38. Tim Rood, *Thucydides: Narrative and Explanation* (Oxford Classical Monographs. Oxford: Clarendon, 1998), 21–22, 109–32.

39. Or "compensation" (involving emphasis or deemphasis), Devillers, "Concentration," 171.

40. Marguerat, *How to Read*, 175; Cicero, *On the Orator* 2:262, 269; *Rhetoric to Alexander* 21:1; Quintilian, *Inst.* 6:2:15; 8:5:54 (Latin *illusio*).

41. Cf. 1 Cor 4:8. Socrates was famous for this in dialogue, as mentioned by Cicero, who employed it in speeches, *On the Orator* 2:270–72, cf. 2:262; cf. Quintilian, *Inst.* 6:3:34 (Latin *male etiam dicitur*), e.g., praising while intending to ridicule one's opponent.

42. Cf. Matt 23:24; *Rhet. Her.* 4:67; Demetrius, *On Style*, 124; *On the Sublime* 38:3; Quintilian, *Inst.* 8:5:67 (hyperbole lies, but without intending to deceive).

43. Simon Hornblower, "Narratology and Narrative Techniques in Thucydides," in *Greek Historiography* (ed. Simon Hornblower; Oxford: Clarendon, 1994), 131–66.

44. Demetrius, *On Style*, 243; Quintilian, *Inst.* 8:6:53.

45. Demetrius, *On Style*, 289; Quintilian, *Inst.* 9:2:65–66.

46. It has been suggested that iterative presentation can deemphasize facts: Hornblower, *Historiography*, 131–66. No example was detected in the texts studied here.

47. The narrators identify these as false (*Embassy* 59; *J.W.* 4:125).

48. Dionysius of Halicarnassus, *On Literary Composition*; Stanley F. Bonner, *The Literary Treatises of Dionysius of Halicarnassus: A Study in the Development of Critical Method* (Cambridge: Cambridge University Press, 1939), 59–80.

49. Cicero, *Orator*, 28. For historians, Thucydides, *War* 1:22:2–4; Polybius, *Histories* 36:1:6–7; and Lucian, *History*, 42, decry this. Quintilian, *Inst.* 10:1:31, focuses on the author's future, not present, glory.

50. "Accrediting" and "discrediting" are, here, used as nouns. ("Accreditation" and "discreditation" seem cumbersome.)

51. Heinrich Lausberg, *Handbook of Literary Rhetoric: a Foundation for Literary Study*, trans. Matthew T. Bliss, Annemiek Jansen, and David E. Orton (Leiden: Brill, 1998), 544. Polybius is unusual in directly addressing issues of how character may develop; rather than providing his own judgment of them straightaway, his comments draw out moral lessons from each incident, Frank W. Walbank, *Polybius* (Berkeley: University of California Press, 1972), 92–96.

52. E.g., The Jewish Law and its Greek translation are accredited, *Let. Aris.* 31, 177, 310–11, 317.

53. Sternberg, *Poetics*, 476.

54. Maarten J. J. Menken, "Fulfilment of Scripture as a Propaganda Tool in Early Christianity," in *Persuasion and Dissuasion in Early Christianity, Ancient Judaism and Hellenism* (ed. Pieter van der Horst et al.; Leuven: Peeters, 2003), 179–98.

55. Plot might influence characterization, but is more forcefully used as a Technique of Persuasion.

56. "Instruction" may occasionally be a command to obey; more often, information or interpretation (whether or not presented as teaching) to assimilate; or a generalization, presented as universal, Aristotle, *Poetics* 1451.

57. E.g., John 20:31; 4 Macc 18:1–2. Sheeley, *Asides*, 32–39; "Narrative asides may be defined as parenthetical remarks addressed directly to the reader which interrupt the logical progression of the story" (36). Ancient fables often included a "moral" (at the beginning, *promythium*, or end, *epimythium*), a statement of the "meaning" (Theon, *Progymnasmata*, 72). This category might include allegory, if the key to its explanation is provided, e.g., Isa 5:1–7, the allegory of the vineyard—once the key is given (v. 7), it arguably becomes instruction.

58. 4 Macc 9:18. Satterthwaite, "Background," 365–66, notes that narration and dialogue can complement each other; e.g., in Acts, the viewpoints of narrator and key speakers coincide.

59. Haman's associates, Esther 6:13; Nebuchadnezzar, Dan 4:1–37; Antiochus Epiphanes, 1 Macc 6:10–13; Eleazar, Josephus *J.W.* 7:323–36, 341–88; the final soliloquies of the villain, Flaccus, in Philo, *Flaccus*, esp. 170.

60. Polybius, *Histories* 36:9; Walbank, *Polybius*, 175–6.

61. "Worldview" involves the ideological aspects of the narrative "point of view": Mark A. Powell, *What Is Narrative Criticism?* (London: SPCK, 1993), 169–96; i.e., "evaluative point of view" (23–25, 53–54).

62. "Defamiliarization," i.e., "decontextualization" and then "recontextualization" (Marguerat, *How to Read*, 145); or, if affirming a worldview, "legitimation" (Esler, *Community*).

63. Elijah, 3 Kgdms 18:37 (1 Kgs 18:37, MT).

64. E.g., Gaius's thoughts on his own status, Philo, *Embassy* 53–56, 58, cf. 255–58.

65. Joseph, Gen 42:23–24. On empathy and sympathy, see Powell, *Narrative Criticism*, 56–57; Marguerat, *How to Read*, 70.

66. For empathy, the character is generally positively portrayed (not necessarily in modern literature, e.g., Dickens's meanhearted Scrooge).

67. Cf. a *topos* makes a general point about character traits, whereas *encomium* (or invective) considers a specific person: Theon, *Progymnasmata* 106.

68. Jas 5:10–11; Polybius, *Histories* 15:36:7.

69. cf. perhaps Mephibosheth, 2 Kgdms 4:4; 9:1–13; 19:24–30; 21:7.

70. E.g., also, the protagonist of a typical tragedy (Aristotle, *Poetics* 1453a, 1454a); perhaps Cain (Gen 4:1–16; 1 John 3:12).

71. Marguerat, *How to Read*, 70; Powell, *Narrative Criticism*, 57.

72. Sternberg, *Poetics*, 477.

73. Although a villain may simply be a foil for the hero(es) rather than directly persuasive.

74. For a modern example: Clive S. Lewis, *The Screwtape Letters*, presented as letters between two devils (who are thus, effectively, the narrators).

75. The doomed Hasdrubal is portrayed negatively (*Histories* 38:7:1, 20), because (even) Polybius "is inclined to identify success with moral worth": Walbank, *Polybius*, 178.

76. Penner, *Praise*, 180–83.

77. Evident causation is most powerful (Powell, *Narrative Criticism*, 33); but causation need not be rigorously demonstrated to be inferred, if that "helps the narrative to make sense" (42).

78. Elijah, 3 Kgdms (1 Kgs, MT) 18:38, 45; 4 Kgdms 2:1–12 cf. Jas 5:16b–18.

79. E.g., also Sodom, Gen 18:16–19:29; Jude 7; Korah's rebellion, Num 16:1–40; 1 Cor 10:11; Heb 3:7–4:11; Polybius, *Histories* 1:31:1; 2:4:3–4.

80. A narrative might lead the hearer on their own "journey" (*On the Sublime* 26:2) in various ways. But, as used here, the "journey" belongs primarily to the character.

81. It might be possible to learn from a villain's journey of discovery. This might reinforce an existing opinion of the audience's (e.g., Flaccus's discovery that God favors Jews, addressed to a Jewish audience, Philo, *Flaccus* 170), but it is questionable whether it would be effective in changing an opinion. I have not noticed evidence that ancient literature took this approach.

82. Persuasion through a "journey of discovery" does not seem to be discussed in the ancient literature. But it is employed (consciously or not): *Aseneth* (see Chapter 5); *1 En.* 17–36.

83. Modern examples include Bunyan's Pilgrim and Dickens's Scrooge.

84. Cf. "unexpected turns," Quintilian, *Inst.* 4:2:107. Aristotle addresses recognition by a character as a theatrical device, *Poetics* 1452a; but there is most persuasive impact when it is the audience, not only the character, who is shocked.

85. Witherington, *Acts*, 181.

86. Demetrius, *On Style*, 100–01.

87. Aristophanes is unusual in including some characters from lower levels of society, but care is needed: Two "slaves" in *Knights* are actually thinly disguised representations of Athenian leaders.

88. Or vision-report, e.g., *Shepherd of Hermas*.

89. Although if a text lacks any element of persuasion, the method will reveal that.

90. Powell, *Narrative Criticism*, 93.

91. For example, there is a distinct change in Polybius's purpose in the later volumes of his *Histories* (see 3:4:4–6), Walbank, *Polybius*, 27, 182–83.

92. Powell, *Narrative Criticism*, 27, suggests: Real author addresses real reader; implied author addresses implied reader; narrator addresses narratee. But "real" audiences will not be discussed here because, hearing the work after completion, they did not directly influence it. Any preliminary audiences, hearing earlier works, drafts or excerpts, will be treated as influencing the intended or "target" audience.

93. Powell, *Narrative Criticism*, 91–97.

94. Dale Patrick and Allen Scult, "Rhetoric and Ideology: A Debate within Biblical Scholarship over the Import of Persuasion," in *The Rhetorical Interpretation of Scripture: Essays from the 1996 Malibu Conference*, ed. Stanley E. Porter and Dennis L. Stamps (Sheffield: JSOT, 1999), 64.

95. Rosalind Thomas, *Herodotus in Context: Ethnography, Science and the Art of Persuasion* (Cambridge: Cambridge University Press, 2000), 170.

96. Thomas, *Herodotus*, 242.

97. Thomas, *Herodotus*, 221.

98. Connor, *Thucydides*, 236.

99. Darr, *Character*, 29.

100. Sternberg, *Poetics*, even through gaps and ambiguity, 186–229.

101. Powell, *Narrative Criticism*; Marguerat, *How to Read*; Cornelis Bennema, *The Theory of Character in New Testament Narrative* (Minneapolis: Fortress, 2014).

102. Notably Tannehill, *Narrative Unity*; Charles H. Talbert, *Reading Luke: A Literary and Theological Commentary on the Third Gospel*, rev. ed. (Macon: Smyth & Helwys, 2002); and idem, *Acts*; Luke T. Johnson, *The Acts of the Apostles* (Collegeville: Liturgical, 1992); Kurz, *Reading*, 135–55; Paul C. Borgman, *The Way According to Luke: Hearing the Whole Story of Luke-Acts* (Grand Rapids: Eerdmans, 2006).

103. Sönke Finnern, *Narratologie und biblische Exegese: eine integrative Methode der Erzählanalyse und ihr Ertrag am Beispiel von Matthäus 28* (Tübingen: Mohr Siebeck, 2010), 238–45.

104. Stanley E. Porter, ed., *Handbook of Classical Rhetoric in the Hellenistic Period 330 B.C.–A.D. 400* (Boston: Brill, 2001); for significant later sources, see George A. Kennedy, *Progymnasmata: Greek Textbooks of Prose Composition and Rhetoric* (Atlanta: SBL, 2003); and Libanius, *Progymnasmata*; George A. Kennedy, *New Testament Interpretation through Rhetorical Criticism* (Chapel Hill: University of North Carolina Press, 1984); Walton, "Rhetorical Criticism"; Ben Witherington III, *New Testament Rhetoric: An Introductory Guide to the Art of Persuasion in and of the New Testament* (Eugene, OR: Cascade, 2009); Clare K. Rothschild, *Luke-Acts and the Rhetoric of History: An Investigation of Early Christian Historiography* (Tübingen: Mohr Siebeck, 2004); Edith M. Humphrey, *And I Turned to See the Voice: The Rhetoric of Vision in the New Testament* (Grand Rapids: Baker Academic, 2007).

105. Soards, *Speeches*, passim.

106. Satterthwaite, "Background," 337. Awareness and appreciation of rhetorical style might have been a factor in a hearer's response to a speech; but I would add that narrative persuasion could not have depended on audience awareness of the techniques involved, since even writers, let alone audiences, seem to have received little instruction in this. Indeed, undetected persuasion might be more effective than overt persuasion.

107. Satterthwaite, "Background," 376.

108. Most notably, Witherington, *Acts*.

109. Richard Bauckham, "For Whom Were the Gospels Written?" in *The Gospel for All Christians: Rethinking the Gospel Audiences,* ed. Richard Bauckham (Grand Rapids: Eerdmans, 1998), 9–48.

110. Stephen S. Liggins, *Many Convincing Proofs: Persuasive Phenomena Associated with Gospel Proclamation in Acts* (Berlin: De Gruyter, 2016), 236, 250, who notes the absence of coercion.

Chapter Three

Narrative Persuasion in Philo's *Embassy to Gaius*

AN OVERVIEW OF *EMBASSY*

This chapter identifies techniques of persuasion in Philo of Alexandria's *Embassy to Gaius*, a narrative that was probably written only a few decades earlier than Acts. Philo was a member of a prominent Jewish family in Alexandria and had clearly received a good (Greek) education. His main body of surviving works expresses his Jewish belief, in Greek, using the style of philosophical treatises. In contrast, *Embassy* consists largely of historical narrative, recounting events in which Philo himself played a part. It shows clear signs of being persuasive—it contains a persuasive letter (276–329) and various speeches, including rhetorical material in the mouth of the narrator (81–92, 208, 347–348). Surprisingly, the ending seems inconclusive and the introduction (1–7) makes no mention of the historical setting—rather, it uses the style of Greek philosophy to introduce the Israelites and their God.[1] Nevertheless, it is historical narrative that provides the overall framework. The text studied, and quoted, is the Loeb edition.[2] All references in this chapter are to *Embassy*, unless otherwise stated.

Summary of the Story

After an introduction (1–7), which has a strong didactic and philosophical tone, Philo reports the general optimism when Gaius become emperor in Rome (8–21) followed, however, by Gaius's removal of his cousin (22–31), his mentor Macro (32–61), and his father-in-law, Silanus (62–73). With Gaius then adopting divine attire (74–80), the narrator launches into a lengthy tirade, first addressed to Gaius (81–92), then recounting more about him (93–119). In Egypt, the Alexandrians take this as an opportunity to perse-

46   Chapter Three

cute the Jews living there (120–131), although, unlike Gaius, previous rulers had respected Jews (132–161). Egyptians, particularly the ex-slave Helicon, encourage Gaius in his belief in his divinity, and in his hatred of Jews (who deny his divinity, 162–177). So, the Alexandrian Jews send an embassy, including Philo, to Rome (178–183), where they hear with horror of Gaius's plan to erect a statue of himself in the Jerusalem Temple (184–206). Jewish elders plead with Petronius, governor of Syria (207–242). Petronius requests a delay, and Gaius is angered by this (243–260). Visiting Gaius, Agrippa[3] is horrified by his plan (261–275) and writes in an attempt to dissuade him (276–329). Gaius, embittered, permits delay while forming even worse plans (330–346). The narrator addresses Gaius again (347–348). Finally, the Jewish ambassadors get to meet Gaius, but he is sarcastic and dismissive and hardly lets them present their case (349–367). The ambassadors are frustrated by this theatrical travesty (368–372). The text ends with a puzzling mention of a "palinode" (373),[4] indicating that, whether or not the text is complete, this is certainly not the end of the overall story.

Narrator and Author

The narrator is prominent, regularly putting himself in the foreground[5] and providing his personal comment[6] or interpretation.[7] In the autobiographical sections,[8] the narrator becomes also a character within the narrative. He is explicitly a Jew (118) whose home is Alexandria (150). He mentions his advanced age (δί ἡλικίαν, 182; cf. γέρων, old, 1), which suggests that *Embassy* was written later than his philosophical works. He claims a good education (182). His familiarity with and commitment to Jews and Judaism are evident,[9] along with his commitment to the study of Jewish traditions and Scriptures.[10] His use of the concepts and vocabulary of Greek philosophy[11] and religion[12] indicate a Greek education[13] and that there is much about Greek culture with which he is comfortable. His frequent references to education suggest an ongoing concern, and perhaps involvement, with education. He speaks approvingly of Augustus's thorough study of philosophy (310 and 318, both through the pen of Agrippa),[14] scornfully of Helicon's limited education (166), and with horror at Gaius's hatred for his instructors (64).[15] Indeed, the narrator is not afraid to adopt a didactic tone with his implied audience (a tone set in 1–2).[16] The narrator is evidently conscious of rhetoric[17] and of its use and abuse.[18] Within the narrative, persuasion is a significant theme[19] (although the ambassadors' carefully prepared presentation is completely thwarted by Gaius's preoccupations: 364–366).[20] The narrator also demonstrates awareness of structuring his own arguments.[21] The narrator is occasionally explicit about sources, not only indicating when he was present[22] but also at times identifying hearsay as such.[23] This suggests concern for the credibility of the material presented.

There is no need to make a firm distinction between Philo the narrator and Philo the character within the narrative. They are hardly distinguishable from each other in their point of view; indeed, at 195, the narrator's voice, in the first person singular, shows through in a passage ostensibly in the mouth of the ambassadors as a group (including Philo himself).

The author is likely to have been known to many of his early hearers, since the narrator is prominent, personally making direct address to the audience (1), to Gaius (now dead, 91), and to opponents (141–142). Philo's authorship is not in doubt for most of his corpus, and especially not for *Embassy* (and *Flaccus*), because of the autobiographical content.

Audience

It cannot be presumed that all of Philo's works were written for the same reason or for the same audience. So this audience analysis should start from *Embassy* itself, only with caution supplementing that with input from the rest of his corpus or from elsewhere.

The implied audience is certainly Greek-speaking. There are also (without apology or explanation) Greek cultural allusions, e.g., ideas from Greek theater.[24] There may be parts of Philo's corpus where familiarity with philosophical ideas is helpful, but it is not clear that such familiarity is required of the audience of *Embassy*. It is assumed that the audience is receptive to the narrator's passion for Greek education. In contrast, when he discusses Jewish education, he makes his case more carefully, so he does not presuppose that his audience has a positive attitude towards Jewish training.[25] The élitist tone with which he mentions "the multitude" (οἱ πολλοί, 7)[26] suggests that the implied audience either see themselves as set apart from the crowd (by birth, rank or—most likely here—education) or at least aspire to that. "We old ones" (1) suggests that, although it is normally the young who receive education, this text is aimed more at seniors. The implied audience is urban, if they share the narrator's association of the city with progress and civilization, in contrast to the denigrated alternative of being nomadic and feral (θηριώδης, 20).[27]

The native Egyptians are not the target audience, and not intended to be part of the audience at all (although, in Alexandria, at least some of them would know Greek). The narrator's references to them, and to their religious practices (worship of animals), are negative to the point of being insulting.[28] Negative references to the general population of Alexandria refer to the Egyptians of the city.[29] There was a large population of Jews (*Flaccus* 43);

since its founding, Alexandria had contained Greeks[30] and, now that it was within the Roman Empire, at least some Romans.[31] Philo's negative portrayal of Alexandrians excludes native Egyptians from his implied audience, but not these Jews, Greeks, or Romans.

In Philo's references to the Roman Empire, he presents Jews, including himself, as loyal subjects,[32] suggesting that the implied audience is also within the Empire and assents to such loyalty. The Germans beyond the northern borders are grouped with other "more savage nations" (θηριωδέστερα ἔθνη, 10 cf. 147)—treated as outsiders, no part of the audience. Jews in the East are mentioned,[33] but the audience needs explanation of their offerings to Jerusalem, so they are not the main audience.

Jews in Palestine might know Greek and be interested in Philo's story, especially since he and the ambassadors found themselves unexpectedly representing them as well as Alexandrian Jews (194). But Philo is highly overt in appealing to Greek thought, even at one stage contrasting Gaius with "the true Paean" (Apollo, 110).[34] Such language, even when deployed so effectively for the purposes of rhetorical argument, would hardly be acceptable to any Jews who still shared the zeal of the Maccabees. This text could not be read to Palestinian Jews without offending at least some of them.[35]

There is no reason to exclude Alexandrian Jews, especially their leaders, from the implied audience. Philo represented them in Rome and would certainly have reported back. This text is surely influenced by and probably developed from whatever material (written or oral) Philo presented to Alexandrian Jewish leaders at that time. Although *Embassy* gives no indication of divisions among the Jews, other parts of Philo's corpus suggest that there were skeptical or apostate Jews, and those tempted in those directions.[36] There is no reason to exclude them from the implied audience of *Embassy*. Simply through their race, they were inevitably involved in the persecution which made the embassy necessary;[37] and, in *Embassy*'s presentation of Jewish faith and traditions, it is not the hearer's commitment to the God of the Jews that is presupposed but, rather, Greek assumptions about praise and blame. Although it would be harder to get the work to them, other Jews of the western Diaspora may be among the audience—those in Rome are mentioned (155–156);[38] those elsewhere are listed at length (in Agrippa's letter, 281–282).

The explanations of Jewish practices[39] suggest that Gentiles are also assumed to be present. Philo's presentation of Greek ideas does not give the impression that he is attempting to Hellenize traditional Jews. He does not question the adequacy of traditional Jewish customs and thought. In contrast, although some Greek values are presupposed, other Greek ideas are accepted only selectively and with reservations.[40]

Greeks, among whom Philo must have practiced his rhetorical skills, and perhaps Romans are included among the implied audience. The Jewish concept of "Gentile" is not used, but rather the contrast between "Greek" and "barbarian" (e.g., 83).[41] Philo expects his audience to accept "Greek" as a general description of what is positive within the Empire.[42] He intertwines Roman and Greek values when he denigrates the practice of obeisance (προσκύνησις, 116)[43] as both against Roman freedom and "barbaric." Greeks elsewhere, beyond Egypt, need not be excluded from the audience, although it is not clear how their attention would be engaged.[44]

Any Greek-speaking Roman in Alexandria might be included in the audience, if they could be persuaded to listen, but Romans in Rome are not the target audience.[45] If they were, Philo would surely present Rome as the center of the world, whereas he makes Greece-centered assumptions[46] and even once treats Alexandria as central.[47] The text is not tailored for Rome.[48]

Is it possible to discern whether Philo addresses his audience (and expects them to respond) as individuals or corporately? The Greek motto "know thyself" (69) is clearly individualistic. But the situation and response of the Jews, represented by their five envoys, is strongly corporate (369–370). There are times when Philo mentions people's situations simultaneously both as individuals and corporately (22, 48, 190). He mentions the conflict between personal concerns (as an Alexandrian Jew) and the corporate need (of all Jews, 193) and prioritizes the latter. As narrator, his address to Gaius switches between using "us" (86, 89) and "me" (91). These addresses to Gaius as an individual (81–92, 208, 347–348) are counterbalanced by direct address to an imaginary group of opponents (141–142). The situation is mixed, but may involve a call for Jews to prioritize the common (Jewish) good and for Greeks to use their independence of thought to come as individuals to a (countercultural) acceptance,[49] or at least tolerance, of Jewish beliefs.

Finally, is it possible to discern whether the text is designed for local and temporary use (e.g., for Philo himself to deliver in Alexandria) or for distribution and perhaps with future generations in mind? Philo's status and extensive corpus suggests that he already had a local audience whom he could reach by performing himself or distributing through those who had already performed his other works. The rhetorical device of addressing the (now dead) Gaius, on behalf of both "me" (the narrator/performer, 91) and "us" (with the audience, 86, 89), would be so forceful when well delivered that it might well have been written for Philo himself to perform.[50] The account of Gaius's chaotic second audience with the ambassadors (352–367) denies them the opportunity for a set speech, but provides the lector with the opportunity for a highly dramatic episode, in which Philo was personally involved and which he probably relished recounting—not many people would get to meet the emperor.

The repeated use of sarcasm may also indicate that Philo intended to deliver the material himself. Appropriate tone of voice is vital to indicate the actual meaning.[51] Any other performer would need careful preparation. He suggests that this work is worthy of attention (3), including by future audiences; but this might simply be intended to grasp the attention of initial audiences. The narrator makes a variety of observations that are presented as though eternal truths—suitable for future audiences, but equally the stuff of education in his own time. Agrippa reviews how earlier generations, especially the Imperial Family, had treated Judaism (291–320), but this serves an immediate purpose, not an interest in history *per se*. So it is not obvious that Philo had future generations primarily in mind.[52] In the aftermath of the events related, he surely hoped to influence his own generation,[53] especially in continuing his ambassadorial task of influencing the powerful, towards tolerance and protection for Jews in Alexandria.

In summary, although others might also be included in the implied audience, there are two key groups who should particularly be borne in mind when assessing persuasion within the text: first, Philo's fellow Alexandrian Jews; and, secondly, any Greeks who could be persuaded to listen—especially those with education and influence, and especially those in Alexandria, as they would be the most interested and accessible.

Date and Context

The events described in *Embassy* occurred in AD 38–40.[54] The work was composed before AD 70, since the Jerusalem Temple is treated as currently functioning (157). Most scholars assume that the work was written within a few years of Gaius's death in AD 41.[55] The text is directly concerned with Jews in Alexandria, Philo's home, and this is the most likely location for initial publication and performance.

Previously Proposed Purposes

Previous discussion of Philo's purposes as an author has, naturally, focused on the exegetical treatises that comprise most of his corpus, where he interprets the OT in terms of Greek philosophy.[56] He seems to be encouraging Jews to follow the Law[57] and providing them with "moral lessons from the Bible,"[58] but these texts might also be apologetic, to attract proselytes.[59]

Nevertheless, in *Embassy* (and *Flaccus*), Philo has taken a step away from being interpreter of Scripture toward becoming interpreter of political events. Here, his purpose may be different. Of *Embassy*, Colson comments, "it is a 'Philippic,' an invective . . . and nothing else."[60] Borgen identifies a more specific lesson: Although Flaccus and Gaius evidently proved to be enemies of the Jews, they were "in reality enemies of God himself" (by proud arrogance, *Flaccus* 124, 132; or claiming divine status, *Embassy* 75).[61] Williamson adds that Philo is concerned to show that, despite the suffering of the Jews, "God in the end punishes the perpetrators of evils," especially of evils against the Jews.[62]

LITERARY DEVICES, ACCREDITING AND DISCREDITING

In each text, the literary devices are far too numerous to list, so only a few examples can be mentioned—those most relevant to the text's persuasive impact. In *Embassy*, *sarcasm* is noteworthy, used against Helicon and Apelles by the messengers (203) and by the narrator (206)—evoking antipathy against Helicon and Apelles, while accrediting the messengers, because they speak with the narrator's style and point of view.[63] *Direct inside view* is used to build empathy with Philo, presented as a perceptive character (avoiding the ill-founded optimism of his colleagues, 182, 184),[64] and also to build antipathy toward the scheming Gaius (255–258).

See Appendix E for an overview of the Accrediting and Discrediting devices in all of the texts, including *Embassy*.

NOTABLE EXAMPLES OF PERSUASIVE TECHNIQUES

- P1a) *Overt instruction by the narrator*. *Embassy* starts with a rhetorical question about how long "we" (who are old, but naturally inviting the hearer of any age to identify with the narrator) will take to learn properly lessons upon which (it is implied) light is about to be shed. *Embassy* is presented as instruction for those willing to learn.

  What is the content of that instruction? The narrator approves of self-restraint (ἐγκράτεια) and condemns unrestraint (ἀκρασία) as leading to serious illness (14, applied to Gaius). The "divine form cannot be counterfeited as a coin can be"[65] (110, responding to the theme, introduced at 75, that Gaius wanted to be thought divine). The narrator describes the activities of the Alexandrian mob against Jews (120–122) as "terrible" (δεινός, 123). On the delay in availability of a statue for the Romans to erect in the Jerusalem Temple, he comments that this was "to my mind through the providence [πρόνοια] of God, who stretched out his hand, unseen, to protect the wronged" (220). On Petronius's decision to delay, he comments that God suggests "good decisions to good men," so that, "benefitting others, they receive benefits" (245). When Gaius decreed that people could set up statues of him, yet nobody actually did so in Jewish territory, this was "by the providence [πρόνοια] with justice [σὺν δίκῃ]" of God (336). When Gaius ended their final audience in a softer tone, the narrator explains that God "having compassion on us, turned [Gaius's] anger to mercy" (367).

Flaccus ends its account of some of the same events with an overt, didactic conclusion (P1a): "the nation of the Jews were not deprived of the help which is from God" (*Flaccus* 191). The narratorial comments in *Embassy* suggest that a similar conclusion would be appropriate, as an answer to those (4–5) who doubt God's concern for humans, particularly for Jews.

Other asides indicate the narrator's didactic tendencies (but are uncontroversial[66] or only briefly relevant).[67] Philo cannot resist lecturing: Indeed, his scientific aside on health, in the middle of an account of Jews suffering, distracts unhelpfully from the *pathos*.[68]

- P1b) *Instruction by trusted characters*. The Jewish ambassadors (including Philo) assert that "those who are noble are full of hope and the laws create good hope for those who take more than a sip of them" (i.e., by study; 195), and that, "Perhaps these things are to test the present generation, how they are in terms of virtue and whether they are schooled to bear misfortunes with resolution" (196). The (Palestinian) Jewish elders ask (rhetorically), "what more profitable gain is there for men, than holiness?" (242).

- P1c) *Instruction by untrustworthy characters*. There is little,[69] although even Gaius acknowledges (with surprise) the commitment of Jews to their customs (268).[70]

- P2a) *Worldview of the text*. Events are not left to speak for themselves—the narrator is more than willing to comment (P1a). His appeal, in support of his interpretation, is as much to reason as to the events. He cites no supernatural occurrences or divine visions as evidence for his interpretations. For Philo, it is with the Jewish law and traditions that authority lies, not with present signs and wonders. Rather, God's intervention is "unseen by us" (220). It is understood only by the "reason" (λογισμός) that can take a long-term view (2), abandoning ignorance (ἀμαθία) and blindness (21).

- P2b) *Worldview of trusted characters*. The ambassadors think out loud (190–196) in ways that seem to merge with the narrator's point of view. The Jewish messengers narrate events (198–205) in a style very similar to the narrator's, including sarcasm (203) and invective (205),[71] so that it is hard to be certain where their speech ends and the narrator resumes. Palestinian Jews speak to Petronius (224, 229–242) in a style similar to the narrator's.[72] Finally, King Agrippa is presented as a Jerusalem Jew,[73] and his letter to Gaius (276–329), while appropriately tailored to its author and (narrative) audience, is also united with the narrator in its point of view.[74]

Agrippa's overview of how Romans have treated Jews in the past (291–322) has similarities to the narrator's account of the dealings that Tiberius and Augustus had with them (141–161). The striking difference is that Agrippa's letter is careful to woo the favor of the living Gaius,[75] whereas the narrator, addressing the now dead Gaius, can freely vent invective.

The material presented in the mouths (and pen) of all these Jews, while adapted to some extent to the immediate narrative context, contains no sign of contradictions or conflicts between the Jews. Rather, they speak with one voice—just like the Palestinian Jews who are presented as spontaneously approaching Petronius in one body (225).

- P2c) *Worldview of untrustworthy characters*. Reports of Gaius's thoughts (53–56, 58, cf. 255–258) expose his inappropriately self-centered view of his role as emperor.
- P3a) *Positive characterization and empathy*. The character of Philo within the story is closely linked to the narrator. His unease at Gaius's apparent goodwill (182, 184) provides insight into his emotions, which builds empathy. After that, his group of five ambassadors behaves as a single character, whose emotions are also expressed (206, 357, 366, 369, 372), developing empathy with the whole group. Direct inside views of Agrippa (261–262) build empathy with him.

   Petronius, in charge of Syria, is caught uncomfortably in the middle of events (throughout 207 to 260). The narrator gives lengthy and detailed insight into his thinking (209–218, including thoughts presented as direct speech in 218, 223, 243–253). He is caught between his duty to and fear of Gaius (209) and his sensitivity to the concerns of the Jews (243), trying to avoid violence (217, although the Jews threaten only self-harm, 234). He is presented positively—informed about Judaism, a "good man" to whom God imparted a "good decision" (245) to allow delay and provide plausible reasons. Petronius's impossible situation highlights the inappropriateness of Gaius's demands. To a Jewish audience, his character provides reassurance that Roman officials are capable of acting with wisdom and compassion. A Greek or Roman, identifying with Petronius, would be impressed by and more benevolent toward Jews.
- P3b) *Positive characterization and respect*. Philo is presented as a man whose age and education (182) have brought wisdom.
- P3c) *Positive characterization and sympathy*. The Palestinian Jews act in complete unity, as a single character, presented with *pathos* (with dust and tears, 227–228; great emotion, 243). Petronius reacts with pity (περιπάθησις, intensity of passion), suggesting that the audience should also. Agrippa gains a sympathetic (συμπαθής, 273) response from onlookers (encouraging the same response from the hearers) when incapacitated

with horror (266–275) at Gaius's statue proposal. Indeed, each group of Jews responds to Gaius's proposal with horror, described at length. This complements the more intellectual discussions of Jewish belief and attachment to their traditions by providing graphic and emotional demonstration of them. For Jews among the audience, this encourages them to admire and share in this emotion, strengthening their commitment to Judaism. For Greeks (and any Romans) in the audience, this encourages them to admire this wholehearted commitment, to question the appropriateness of emperor worship, to avoid similarly offending Jewish beliefs, and perhaps also to be intrigued or attracted.

- P3d) *Aversion.* Macro is a Roman whose seniority, status, education, and role as mentor (for Gaius) suggest parallels with Philo himself. His lecture to Gaius (43–51) is very responsible. However, his earlier representations to Tiberius on Gaius's behalf (35–38) had been misguided and deceptive, an abuse of rhetoric (albeit successful, 37). Macro's death is partly due to the outspoken boldness of his advice (πεπαρρησιασμένα, 41).[76] Public opinion accuses him of arrogance (69), but the narrator indicates how sincerely he had helped Gaius (60). He would be a suitable protagonist for a tragedy, as proposed by Aristotle[77]—a man of status, with whom the audience can identify, whose character is noble but who makes an error—in this case, attempting to improve Gaius (whose response was the opposite, 52), with a tragic outcome. The audience is encouraged to avoid making that kind of error themselves.

  Macro is also a foil—his nobility, wisdom, and sincerity make Gaius's behavior all the more appalling. The portrayal of Macro (along with Silanus, 62–65) accentuates the negative portrait of Gaius (using Greco-Roman standards at this stage, when Jewish issues have merely been hinted at, in 4). Just as Queen Vashti sets the stage for Esther, by highlighting the volatility of King Ahasuerus (Xerxes; Esther 1:9–22) so that dramatic tension builds when Esther approaches him (Esther 4:11–5:2), so also Macro highlights the volatility of Gaius, so that the audience understands how risky the ambassadors' task is.

- P4a) *Repulsive character (through traits).* Various individuals are presented negatively: Gaius, Helicon, Apelles, Capito, and Isidorus—although Romans as a whole, their rule and institutions, are presented with respect and loyalty.[78]

  Isidorus is introduced, at the final audience with Gaius, as a "bitter sycophant" (355).[79] He is the only one named among the ambassadors' opponents, who otherwise act as a group character, influencing Gaius through slander and mockery, so that the narrative abandons the language of an orderly hearing (350) for that of theater (351, 359, 368). The audience is encouraged to be hostile to those who resort to theatrical techniques over serious issues.

Capito, the tax collector for Judea, is introduced by the Jewish messengers as becoming rich through corruption,[80] so any respectable member of the audience will view him negatively. He initiates a dispute over a non-Jewish altar, sending an exaggerated (μετεωρίζω, to elevate, 202) account to Gaius. Thus the audience, whether or not initially sympathetic to Judaism, is sucked into the narrator's disapproval of Capito's troublemaking.

Apelles is presented in ways that, while unattractive to Greeks, would be utterly repugnant to Jews—as one who had in the past sold his sexual services and, now old, had resorted to the stage, with implications of inappropriate verbal seduction (203–204) and direct accusation of his "venom" (205).[81] The audience is thus warned against such poisonous speech and encouraged to distance themselves from anti-Jewish comments and those who make them.

Helicon, the Egyptian slave who gains Gaius's ear, is described negatively throughout.[82] His soliloquy (168–170) exposes his scheming—abusing rhetoric by pandering to Gaius's openness to slander and sycophancy (τὸ βλασφημεῖν τῷ συκοφαντεῖν, 169). He is a striking contrast to the noble character of Macro, Gaius's former mentor—a slave rather than noble, poorly educated rather than well-educated, and devious rather than open. This portrayal, while discouraging sycophancy, also suggests that there was, among the sneering, actually no valid argument or accusation against the Jews.

The portrayal of Gaius starts with his position upon succession—his opportunities and responsibility, and the high hopes and expectations of his subjects (8–13). The office of emperor is presented positively, but Gaius himself negatively throughout. The mechanisms are numerous, including: *negative epithets*, such as his appetite for boys and women (14; with lack of restraint, ἀκρασία); his eagerness to be thought a god (75), a contextually negative epithet, in that Roman society had been used to this idea ever since Augustus,[83] but this text (from Jewish perspective) builds up multiple negative associations for such an aspiration. The narrator comments that he was "naturally untrustworthy" (339), acting with only the "appearance of friendship" (344). Messengers call Gaius quarrelsome and contentious (δύσερις ... καὶ φιλόνεικος, 198). Nonverbal judgment can be detected in his sickness (14) and death (107), although the narrator also comments. Negative *direct inside views* of Gaius are found in his resentful asides about Macro (53–56, 58), silent anger at Petronius (255–258), and egotistical emotions when acquiescing to Agrippa's request (331–332). Gaius is *foregrounded*, as the first individual introduced (8), the focus of attention of the whole Empire

(10–13). Echoes are prominent in the form of detailed contrasts between Gaius and his predecessors (Tiberius, 141–142; Augustus, 143–161; and others, 291–322). Relevant *themes* include the suggestion that, whereas Gaius should have been a restrained statesman, his preference was for the theatrical (despite Macro's advice, 42–51, especially 44; influenced by Helicon, 168–169, and Apelles, 203; culminating in the appalling farce of the ambassadors' audience, 368). *Vividness* depends on dramatic delivery of the work, e.g., the passionate speeches addressed to the dead Gaius and the tumultuous account of the final audience. Through this negative portrayal of Gaius, hearers are encouraged to avoid a lifestyle of excess and egotism in general (especially delusions of divinity) and, most forcefully, to avoid interfering with traditions held sacred by the Jews.

- P4b) *Repulsive character (through identity)*. Egyptians, as a group, are presented negatively, especially those in Alexandria, who took a leading role in the aggression against the Jews (120). Egyptians are condemned unequivocally as unstable (120), worshipers of animal deities (139, a contextually negative description), flatterers (162), involved in folly and impiety (163), and as being like crocodiles and asps (166). The audience is warned not to share in their character or religious ideas, as some "dimwits" (ὀλιγόφρων, 163) do. This language is hardly designed to win over Egyptian hearts. Rather, it would reaffirm Jewish hostility toward Egyptians, and encourage Greeks and Romans to maintain a distance from Egyptians and their ideas.[84] The audience is encouraged to distrust and perhaps even to hate Egyptians.
- P5a) *Plot: Positive change or outcome*. That Gaius's statue plan is delayed (245) and eventually interrupted by his death (107) implies a positive outcome for Jews—God is acting on behalf of his people (220).
- P5b) *Negative outcome*. Three villains come to a "sticky end." In *Flaccus*, this motif is a key part of the story; in *Embassy*, it is less prominent, arising in two brief prolepses (jumping ahead in time). Helicon and Apelles, who have been characterized (since their introduction in 166 and 203) as villains and enemies of the Jews, are the subjects of a prolepsis devoted to their executions (206), the result of their "impiety" (ἀσεβεία). For Gaius, there is a mere phrase of prolepsis: "had he not first been put to death by justice" (107),[85] containing within it the narrator's judgment. Although the characterization of these villains is complex, appealing to both Jewish and Greek values, ultimately the narrator and the events of the text are united in employing the well-established Greek concept of justice as inevitable fate, or divine retribution, and applying it to enemies of the Jews and of Jewish traditions. Although most of the narrative concerns difficulties for the Jews, the narratorial comments keep looking forward to their resolution. The subsequent death of Gaius was certainly known to the entire audience

beforehand and represents a significant factor in the audience's hearing of the story. Throughout, it is already known that his ambitions will be thwarted. Those who are like these various villains, however powerful they may seem, are ultimately doomed—following both the Greek concept of inevitable justice (107) and the Jewish belief in the God who acts on behalf of his people (220). Thus, the story answers the doubters mentioned at the outset (3–4).

- P5c) *Polyphonic affirmation.* There is a key theme of Jewish horror at the prospect of Gaius's statue, expressed emotionally by the messengers (186–188; ταραχώδης, troubled, 186), ambassadors (189–194; θρηνέω, wailing, 190), Jewish leaders (223–224; with tears, δάκρυ, 223), Jewish population (225–243; κλαυθμῶν καὶ στερνοτυπιῶν, weeping and smiting their breasts, 227) and Agrippa (266–275; τρόμος τε καὶ σεισμός, trembling and convulsing, 267). Thus, Philo emphasizes the inappropriateness of such a statue in their Temple.

- P5d) *Journey of discovery.* There are minor elements of this. Philo's embassy (349–373) reveals Gaius as adversary rather than judge (180, 349); and Petronius's encounter with the Jews (209–253) may affirm his opinions (209) more than changing them, but it does evoke his sympathy (243) and the hearer's.

- P5e) *Gentle steps.* Philo starts by emphasizing the inappropriateness of Gaius's general behavior, especially his claims to deity, using Greco-Roman ethical and religious criteria (22–114). Only then (115, nearly a third of the way through the work—with, before that, only a very brief mention at 4) does he introduce Jews, as opposing him on the basis of their own traditions (117). This introduces the Jews gently but positively to culturally Greek hearers who are not already favorable toward them.

NARRATIVE PERSUASION

This analysis has confirmed that, of the literary devices considered, almost all of them are used with reference to the character of Gaius, let alone in other ways within this text. Philo has certainly made extensive use of them in engaging with his audience. Nonverbal indications of judgment are hardly used, partly because the narrator is so willing to comment, and partly because the text is completely devoid of supernatural events (except in a very general sense of God's control over human affairs). Although Scripture may claim to speak for God, Philo does not.

Notable here is the use of sarcasm, which is not generally characteristic of Philo[86] nor of Scripture. For example, angry with the Jews, Gaius calls them

Agrippa's "excellent and good citizens" (καλοί σου καὶ ἀγαθοὶ πολῖται, 265). Gaius's sneering (σαρκάζων, 352) tone is initially mentioned as "mild and kind" (ἐπιεικῶς καὶ φιλανθρώπως, 352). Each instance involves the use of a good word—which ought ideally to apply—and then revealing the bad truth explicitly. This provides a striking contrast, and sharpens the criticism.

Of the persuasive techniques listed, most are used, and used extensively, suggesting that persuasion is indeed a key element throughout this text. The narrator repeatedly emphasizes the authority of and respect due to Jewish Scripture and tradition. However, Scripture is not quoted, and tradition is explained when necessary for the narrative (particularly concerning images and the Jerusalem Temple) rather than for its own sake. The narrator himself is prominent, so that much of the authority asserted by the text rests with him personally. The Jews are presented as completely united (at least on the issues faced here), providing further support for the Jewish worldview presented. The narrator also appeals, especially early in the text, to the values espoused by Greek education (especially philosophy)—treating them as values naturally shared with his audience. So the persuasion in this text is aimed primarily at Greeks.

Most of the persuasive techniques are evident in this text. The worldview of the text is communicated mainly through the comments and judgments of the narrator (P1a), not merely through events themselves (P2a). This is not surprising for a narrative by an author whose main corpus consists of didactic treatises—it fits what is known of Philo's character. It is certain that this text has extensive persuasive content, so it is very likely that Philo had persuasive intent. But what has this analysis revealed about the persuasive impact of this text?

CONCLUSIONS

The analysis here fully confirms Colson's assertion that *Embassy* includes invective against Gaius, but he goes too far in adding that it is "nothing else."[87] Even his description "Philippic" needs care: The original examples, both of Demosthenes and of Cicero, were speeches attempting to influence ongoing political situations by denouncing the living.[88] But *Embassy* denounces the dead. It would allow people to vent their anger against Gaius in language they could not have used while he was in power, but it would not have been able to influence the succession after Gaius.

Embassy is more than invective. Gaius was gone, but the concept of emperor worship[89] lived on, with the danger that this struggle might be repeated, so *Embassy* also provides a warning to those who might trouble Jews in future. This analysis also suggests an attempt to win the support of Greeks and a positive encouragement to Jews to stand firm in their traditions.

Philo has not, here, abandoned his habit of teaching. But, in *Embassy*, his teaching starts, not from Scripture, but from political events. He does not personally claim any divine revelation or prophetic insight. His implied authority comes from status and education, but the authority he promotes is that of Jewish tradition and Scripture. Nevertheless, his appeal to his audience is not based on any such asserted authority, but rather on the basis of commonly accepted Greek ideas.[90] He does not attempt to impose his view on the audience, but encourages them to use their reason—although he also uses persuasive narrative (surely intended to be combined with dramatic delivery) to engage their emotions.

The narrator's asides propose that, although the Jews seemed powerless, in reality God protected them, because of their faithfulness to their traditions and because of justice. Gaius deserved his early death. Here is not merely a negative message, that Gaius was bad, but more strongly a positive message, that faithfulness to Jewish traditions is good and should be encouraged, or at least permitted. The portrayal of the Jews is of complete unity and selfless dedication to their traditions—an aspiration for Jews to work toward, and a puzzle for Gentiles, which may serve to them as a warning or even as an invitation.

If the work were intended to persuade Roman authorities to tolerate Judaism, there would be a difficulty in the intellectual arguments that underlie it. The Jewish messengers make it clear that Jews did not and will not tolerate any pagan practice by aliens within their "Holy Land" (200–202), not even a single, makeshift altar. Yet Philo also seems to be requesting the authorities to tolerate the practice of Judaism by Jews who are effectively aliens in Alexandria and, presumably, elsewhere also. Unsurprisingly, there is in *Embassy* no direct attempt to explain why an apparently intolerant religion should be granted toleration—indeed, to express the situation in those terms would hardly be persuasive. The medium of narrative permits such questions to be marginalized, e.g., by the negative portrayal of the Gentile aliens in contrast to the positive portrayal of the Alexandrian Jews. Delivered appropriately, the narrative of *Embassy* might be more persuasive than an intellectual discussion of the relevant politics and policies.

It is not, however, likely that *Embassy* was written as a discussion document, attempting to influence the political decision-makers directly—the didactic features might not be adequately respectful to a powerful audience. It seems highly likely that it was aimed at influential Alexandrian Greeks, to build their sympathy for, tolerance of, and even support and protection for the Jews, and also to turn them against the idea of emperor worship. Given the difficulty of gaining the attention of Greeks, it is likely that Philo assumed that the many of the hearers would be fellow Jews, and the text certainly also provides encouragement for them.

NOTES

1. E.g., φύσις, nature, 1; ἀρετή, virtue, 5.
2. Francis H. Colson, *Philo* (Cambridge, MA: Harvard University Press, 1962), 10:1–187. For the minor variations between manuscripts, see E. Mary Smallwood, *Philonis Alexandrini Legatio ad Gaium. Edited with an Introduction, Translation, and Commentary,* 2nd ed. (Leiden: Brill, 1961), 36–37.
3. Herod Agrippa I, king of Judea.
4. λεκτέον δὲ καὶ τὴν παλινῳδίαν "the palinode must also be told" (παλινῳδία, recantation, LSJ s.v.; "'counter-story' or 'reversal'" Colson, *Philo*, 10.186 n. a). In context, Philo surely intends no retraction. Perhaps he intended to write more; perhaps this simply refers to the well-known outcome, Gaius's death.
5. Most prominently, at 6, 10, 91, 116, 133, 141, 152, 195 (seemingly within a speech by the ambassadors).
6. 4, 32, 39, 42, 91, 99, 110, 123, 210, 227, 338, 360.
7. 57, 196, 220, 245, 336, 366.
8. The narrator's presence as a character is explicit at: 178-190, 197, 206, 349–367.
9. 4, 118, 157, 159, 161, etc. Ronald Williamson, *Jews in the Hellenistic World: Philo* (Cambridge: Cambridge University Press, 1989), 1:3.
10. 115; (195–196, in the mouth of the ambassadors).
11. Evident in themes such as: virtue (ἀρετή: 5, 98, 312); reason (λογισμός: 2, 196); knowledge (ἐπιστήμη: 21, 69); and a Delphic quotation, γνῶθι σαυτόν—"know thyself."
12. Especially in the sustained comparison between Gaius and the various deities with which he associated himself (78–113).
13. Also *Spec. Laws* 3:1–4.
14. Cf. Petronius in 245.
15. Associated with lusts and murder, 65. Instruction and instructors are mentioned at 5, 26, 27, 31 (ironically, a first and final lesson on suicide), 41–51 (Macro as Gaius's instructor), 53–56 (Gaius's response), 196, 310, 318, 319, 320. Jewish instruction is emphasized in 115, 210.
16. Philo suggests that even "we" who are old lack reason (λογισμός: 2) and misunderstand fortune (τύχη; "Chance," perhaps as a goddess, Smallwood, *Legatio*, 152) and nature (φύσις: 1)—providing an incentive to listen to what he is about to teach.
17. Manuel Alexandre Jr., *Rhetorical Argumentation in Philo of Alexandria* (Atlanta: Scholars, 1999), 15, 18, 248.
18. Abuse of rhetoric is a repeated theme: 36–38 (Macro on Gaius's behalf), 57–58 (Gaius against Macro), 67–72, 165 and 202 (distorted written reports), 168–169, 176–177 (Helicon's jesting and malice).

19. E.g., Agrippa's letter to Gaius (276–329; 311 introduces two of many possible stories; 322, an imaginary speech from Gaius's ancestors).

20. 350 discusses due process; 360, flawed circumstances when silence becomes the best defense.

21. E.g., 114 indicating that enough has been demonstrated; 138 indicating what is about to be demonstrated; 141–142 rhetorical questions to imagined adversaries; 152 asking and answering rhetorical questions; 212 offering the strongest proof (τεκμήριον δὲ μέγιστον); 218 both sides of Petronius's personal deliberations, 373.

22. Esp. 349, recording what "we" saw and heard.

23. 24 public speculation; 30, 39, 61, 76, 172 hearsay; 39, 203 gossip about sexual behavior; 172 about bribery; 223 (cf. 306) appropriately reports a private meeting with the disclaimer "they say" (φασιν); 315 Agrippa overtly quotes Flaccus's letter.

24. 75, 79, 111, 166, 202, 204, 234, 351, 359, 368. Theater is culturally Greek, not Jewish. 111, 116, 202, 359, 368 carry negative connotations, although 204 is positive.

25. 115, Jewish customs are contrasted with others, and Philo elaborates on (rather than presupposing) their authority; 195–196 promotes study of Scripture in dialogue with an imagined questioner, so Philo's audience is not assumed to agree.

26. Crowds of Jews are presented positively (226, 300); but not general crowds (67); generally held opinion may be either accepted (89, 152) or refuted (70).

27. 107 also suggests an assumption that it is the people in every city who are significant.

28. 139, 163 calling their religion "godlessness" (ἀθεότης); 166 comparing them to crocodiles. Sarah J. K. Pearce, *The Land of the Body: Studies in Philo's Representation of Egypt* (Tübingen: Mohr Siebeck, 2007), 80. In general, for Philo, Egyptians were the "ultimate other," Maren R. Niehoff, *Philo on Jewish Identity and Culture* (Tübingen: Mohr Siebeck, 2001), 45–74.

29. 120–121 their "most brutal rage" (θηριωδεστάταις ὀργαῖς); 162 hypocrisy (ὑπόκρισις); 163 the impiety (ἀσέβεια) of having animal gods; 170.

30. Williamson, *Philo*, 6; Peder Borgen, "Philo of Alexandria," in *Jewish Writings of the Second Temple Period: Apocrypha, Pseudepigrapha, Qumran Sectarian Writings, Philo, Josephus,* ed. Michael E. Stone (Assen: Van Gorcum, 1984), 2:2:249.

31. Not least, Flaccus Avillius, whom Tiberius sent to govern Egypt, *Flaccus* 1–2.

32. 116, 119, all subjects as loyal; 161, 230, Jews as peaceable; 236, Jewish respect (εὐλαβείας) for the emperor; 309, Agrippa applauds Augustus's achievements.

33. 216–217; also Josephus, *Ant.* 11:133.

34. Similarly, Hermes's attire is appropriate for the "interpreter and prophet of the divine things" (τὸν ἑρμενέα καὶ προφήτην των θείων, 99). Dishonorable deeds deserve "farthest Tartarus" (ἐσχατιᾶς Ταρτάρου, 103); "they say" (φασιν, 103) is added, perhaps for Jewish hearers, to soften this Greek phrase. (LXX uses Tartarus only three times: Job 40:15; 41:23; and Prov 24:51 [30:16, MT]; whereas Hades is the usual translation for Sheol.)

35. Whereas Alexandrian Jews were "thoroughly hellenised," Williamson, *Philo*, 6. Philo is not fully syncretistic, e.g., treating the Gorgon as a mere "mythical fabrication" (μύθου . . . πλάσμα: 237, via the mouths of Jewish elders), but he does treat the Greek story as containing some truth.

36. *Names* 62; *Moses* 1:31; (possibly *Embassy* 3); Borgen, "Philo," 2:242, 244.

37. Whatever divisions there may have been between Jews, the persecution united them; it was a threat to them all: 157, 159, 184, 330, 370.

38. But not mentioned when the ambassadors were in Rome (178–206, 349–372; unless among those who seemed helpful but then fled, 372). Such silence makes them unlikely to be part of the target audience.

39. 156 (offerings); 158 (Sabbath restrictions); 210–212.

40. 112 distinguishes between the Ares of mythology (surely meaning traditional understanding of the Greek deity) and of reason (ἐν τῇ φύσει λόγου: a more philosophical concept); 237.

41. With a Greece-centered view of the Empire (102, 141, 145, 162, 292).

42. Approving of Augustus "hellenizing" (147), treating Rome as a new version of Greece.

43. Whereas προσπίπτω is used of Jewish elders before Petronius (230).

44. There is no evidence of Philo going on lecture tours—only on visits to Rome (*Embassy*) and Jerusalem (*Providence* 2:64).

45. Colson, *Philo*, 10:xxii n. a: "The story in Eus. ii. 18, that he [Philo] read the Περὶ ἀρετῶν or part of it to the whole senate in Rome does not sound very probable."

46. 102, 141, 145, 162, 292.

47. 173, Alexandria is accessible to the whole inhabited world (τῆς οἰκουμένης).

48. The idea of Rome hellenizing (147) might please Greeks, but not necessarily Romans.

49. Philo claims that Jews "welcome no less than their own countrymen" (οὐχ ἧττον τῶν ἰδίων ἀποδέχονται πολιτῶν) foreigners who pay homage to Jewish laws (211). Proselytes receive positive mention (*Rewards*, 152); Williamson, *Philo*, 23.

50. Personal address ("We old ones," 1; cf. 141–142) is also particularly suitable for Philo himself to deliver.

51. Sarcastic words: 60, 163, 203 (by Jewish messengers), 206, 265 (by Gaius), 352. Longer, sarcastic comments would be easier to perform: 91 (98 highlighting the contradiction, παράλογος), 101 (intensified by 99).

52. Alexandre, *Argumentation*, 250 (of Philo's whole corpus).

53. Work primarily for posterity would be more measured: Colson, *Philo*, 9:301 (on *Flaccus*).

54. Colson, *Philo*, 1:ix.

55. Gaius's death is alluded to in 107; Alexandre, *Argumentation*, 1 n. 1; Borgen, "Philo," 2:233.

56. Colson, *Philo*, 1:xvi; Alexandre, *Argumentation*, 7.

57. Borgen, "Philo," 2:233.

58. *On the Cherubim*, 35–39.

59. *Praem*, 152.

60. Colson, *Philo*, 10:xxii.

61. Borgen, "Philo," 2:251.

62. Williamson, *Philo*, 17.

63. The slave Helicon is called "aristocratic" (εὐπατρίδης); he and Apelles are "advisers . . . noblest and most wise" (συμβούλοις . . . τοῖς ἀρίστοις καὶ σοφωτάτοις,

203) cf. the narrator calls them "admirable advisers of admirable actions" (καλῶν πράξεων καλοὶ σύμβουλοι, 206).

64. Which also helps to accredit him as narrator.

65. παράκομμα here means counterfeit, echoing mimicry (μιμούμενος) in the previous sentence.

66. Probably too innocuous to represent an attempt to persuade, e.g., "for flattery always attends success" (32); "the gifted . . . can make plausible arguments" (57); "neither a god nor a wise man will become a bringer of bad news" (99); "for misfortunes themselves teach people what their situation is" (227).

67. These primarily move the plot along: e.g., the power of a wheedling wife (39); "a sleeping man is at risk" (42).

68. 125–126, cf. *Flaccus*, 186–187, an aside on why it is better to die on land than at sea distracts from Flaccus's death.

69. Although used forcefully in *Flaccus*, 170–175.

70. Echoing a theme of the narrator's, e.g., 225–243.

71. Helicon as a venomous scorpion (205), cf. the narrator introduced him as "abominable and infamous" (ἐπάρατον καὶ ἐξάγιστον, 166).

72. The theatrical metaphor of tragedy is mentioned by the leaders (234) and narrator (351). Indeed, "saying such words as these" (τοιαῦτα ἐπιλέγοντας, 224) reveals that Philo himself composed "their" speech.

73. 278 (despite acknowledgment, in *Flaccus*, 39, of his Syrian connections).

74. And with the rest of the Jews. Agrippa's comments on their willingness to die (308) echo the narrator (117; 208–209), ambassadors (192; 369), and Palestinian Jews (233–234).

75. 323–326 shows gratitude, like an *exordium*, as Agrippa pleads that his country's traditions not be disturbed (τοῦ μὴ κινηθῆναι τὰ πάτρια, 327).

76. Boldness (παρρησία, 63) is also characteristic of Silanus, Gaius's next victim. Boldness is, here, noble but tragically unwise—whereas in Acts, it is consistently positive; Daniel Marguerat, *Les Actes des Apôtres* (Geneva: Labor et Fides, 2007–2015), 1:156.

77. Aristotle, *Poetics* 1453a, 1454a.

78. E.g., the narrator observes that "subjects are slaves of the emperor" (δοῦλοι δὲ αὐτοκράτορος οἱ ὑπήκοοι, 119) without complaint about the principle, only about Gaius's behavior. Jewish elders claim "respectful fear" (εὐλαβεία) of the emperor (236).

79. See also *Flaccus* 20, 135–145.

80. νοσφίζεται (199), the same verb used in Acts 5:2 of Ananias and Sapphira.

81. In the mouth of Jewish messengers, a trusted source. Mention of the ancient Philistine city Ascalon would associate him in the mind of a Jewish hearer with a history of rivalry.

82. 166 abominable; 203 dealing with tidbits of gossip (σπερμαλόγος, cf. Acts 17:18); 205 scorpion.

83. Augustus had been declared *divus* immediately after his death: Mary Beard, John North, and Simon Price, eds., *Religions of Rome: Volume 1: A History* (Cambridge: Cambridge University Press, 1998), 208.

84. Egyptian religious ideas had already been imported, in modified forms, via Greece to Rome, particularly the cults of Isis and Sarapis; Beard, *Religions*, 160–61.

85. εἰ μὴ ἔφθασε προαναιρεθεὶς ὑπὸ τῆς δίκης.

86. Colson, *Philo*, 10:xiv; he suggests that the title itself, "on virtues" (περὶ ἀρετῶν) might be sarcastic (along with ironical phrases at 163, 203, 352). (The dramatic list of weapons that were *not* found in Jewish possession, *Flaccus*, 90, is "presentation by negation"—another form of irony, close to sarcasm.)

87. Colson, *Philo*, 10:xxxii.

88. Demosthenes influencing Athens against Philip of Macedon; Cicero influencing Rome against Mark Antony.

89. Beard, *Religions*, 140.

90. Niehoff, *Philo*, writes of Philo's multiethnic approach (13), with a "sense both of affinity with Greek culture and superiority over it" (158).

Chapter Four

Narrative Persuasion in Josephus's *Jewish War*

AN OVERVIEW OF *WAR*

This chapter investigates the techniques of persuasion built into Josephus's *Jewish War*. The works of Flavius Josephus have long been used to provide contextual information for the New Testament. Various analysis has already been reported, comparing Josephus's works with Luke-Acts.[1] This is worthwhile because these narratives were written at about the same time, and both describe events in a primarily Jewish context for the benefit of Greek-speaking audiences at a cultural and geographical distance. *War* goes further back in time than Acts,[2] but when Pilate is first mentioned (2:169), the events become contemporary with those in Acts. Josephus is of particular interest here because, in *Life* and *Against Apion*, he is overtly persuasive.[3] He writes as a highly overt narrator, providing many comments. With large amounts of autobiographical material,[4] much information is available about Josephus and his context (to be read with critical caution). So, much research has been carried out on him, on his context(s),[5] and on his interaction with his implied audience(s).[6]

War, consisting of seven books, is significantly longer than the other texts studied.[7] There is little doubt about the unity or authorship of the work, although Josephus may have written Book 7 later. The text studied is from the Loeb Classical Library.[8]

Summary of the Story

War describes how Jerusalem and its Temple came to be destroyed by the Romans. Book 1 traces the earlier history of the Jews, including Herod the Great. Book 2 covers Herod's successors, explaining how the Jews came to rebel against the Romans, with Josephus commanding forces in Galilee. In Book 3, Josephus, surviving the Roman siege of Jotapata, is captured and appears before the commander, Vespasian (*J.W.* 3:392–408). In Book 4, the Jews retreat to Jerusalem, including the villain John of Gischala (4:121) and bands of brigands, identified as Zealots (4:138, 161). Chief priest Ananus opposes these ruffians (4:162–207). The Zealots summon Idumaeans, who ignore chief priest Jesus (4:238–269), overrun Jerusalem (4:300–333), but leave in disgust at the Zealots' excesses (4:353). John assumes power, but is opposed by another villain, Simon son of Gioras (4:503–584). After Nero's death, Vespasian's troops proclaim him emperor (4:592–604). Book 5 describes how the Romans, under Titus, besiege Jerusalem, using Josephus as negotiator, and eventually, in Book 6, take the city. Book 7 describes the aftermath—a triumph in Rome and the suicide of Jewish Sicarii at Masada.

Narrator

The narrator is highly overt. Josephus also appears as a character within the narrative and, for this, he uses the third person singular. But where the narrator addresses the audience directly (e.g., 1:1–30), he uses the first person[9]—introducing himself by name (1:3). The narrator is presented as identical with the author—Josephus himself—which contributes to the credibility of the work, and also suggests concern for his own reputation; the highly personal tone adopted at times[10] may be a strategy for evoking sympathy. This style may derive from the author's experience of personally delivering his story (probably including draft sections of *War*) and would be particularly appropriate if Josephus was writing with the intention of delivering the material himself, at least to its initial audience(s).[11]

Josephus claims to provide (unlike others, 1:6–7) a careful and thus reliable account (1:9; even claiming to have hidden nothing and added nothing, 1:26).[12] He emphasizes his own direct involvement (1:3, 18; as an eyewitness, 1:22) and criticizes those who rewrite earlier histories rather than contributing new material of their own (1:15). He identifies himself as Jewish (1:3; a "foreigner," ἀλλόφυλος, to his audience, 1:16), and openly admits that his sympathy and grief for his nation might be considered inappropriate for a historian (1:9, 11–12; 5:20 cf. 5:566; 6.111). The audience of *War* is thus encouraged to expect an account that can be trusted (more than others), but that will nevertheless be Jewish in its sympathies and interpretation of events.

Josephus claims various credentials: priestly descent (1:3, universally respectable); previous publication of an account in Aramaic (1:3)[13] which has already been influential in the East (1:6); and, rather than being motivated by profit like Greeks, he has invested in this work (1:16). Although he claims to be presenting truth rather than pleasing his audience (1:30 cf. 7:455), his prologue seems designed to attract the interest of a Greco-Roman audience, glossing over much of the work but providing a rapid-fire summary of the key military and political events to be covered, with the promise of details about Judaism (including the previously inaccessible Holy of Holies, 1:26), portents, sufferings, destruction, triumph, and treasures (1:28).[14]

The character Josephus is presented as prophetic, because his prediction came true, of Vespasian becoming emperor,[15] and also echoing the Jewish prophets, especially Jeremiah.[16] Nevertheless, although the narrator makes some direct assertions, his interpretations are at times carefully nuanced, e.g., it seems (ὡς ἔοικεν, 1:593); perhaps (τάχα, 1:607); I suppose (οἶμαι, 2:539; 4:323, 652; 5:566);[17] for I say (φημὶ γάρ, 5:257); so it seems to me (ἔμοιγε δοκεῖν, 6:4).[18] Josephus admits that there was suspicion of his prophetic claims.[19] These nuanced asides indicate to the audience that the narrator is assuming the role of a cautious historian rather than an inspired prophet.[20]

Author

Much more information about Josephus is provided elsewhere in his corpus. It is necessary here only to mention the points most relevant to his relationship with his audience(s). Our concern here is not primarily with the accuracy of his claims, but with the relationship with his audience that is assumed or established by mention of such details.

Born in AD 37 (*Life* 5), Josephus claims priestly and aristocratic descent (*Life* 2–6) and a good education (*Life* 9–12). His point of view matches this background.[21] Aged twenty-six, he led a successful delegation to Rome (*Life* 13–16) and was thereafter able to warn his countrymen about Rome's military power (*Life* 17). In *War*, Josephus leads Jewish forces in Galilee in a brief campaign.[22] Having surrendered to Vespasian, Josephus is then brought forward to reason with the defenders of Jerusalem, encouraging them to surrender.[23] After the destruction of Jerusalem, he claims he was housed in Vespasian's former home in Rome, with a pension and Roman citizenship (*Life* 423). He seems to have remained in Rome and done his writing there. He claims that, after Vespasian's death, both Titus and Domitian continued to favor him (*Life* 428–429); but he also continued to receive criticism,[24] particularly from Jews.[25]

Audience

There is a "stated audience" within *War*: The prologue commends Josephus's work to the subjects of the Roman Empire (1:3), both Greeks and Romans (1:16). Elsewhere, we learn that copies went to Vespasian, Titus, other

Romans who had been in the war, Agrippa II and various of his relatives (*Life* 361–362; *Ag. Ap.* 1:50–51), probably when they were in Rome—initial presentations of the work were probably to a local audience, since 1:22 addresses people who already know Josephus.[26]

The implied audience needs almost everything Jewish explained to them, whereas minimal explanation is provided of Roman affairs.[27] This shows that the primary audience is Greek-speaking members of Roman society,[28] and not Jewish. But multiple audiences need to be considered. First, the main "implied audience" consists of Greek-speaking members of Roman society. Secondly, the emperor (whichever was in power at the time of publication—probably Titus, for the final form of Books 1–6[29]—along with his loyal retinue), plays a key role as an audience who must not be antagonized, and will hopefully be pleased with whatever parts he might hear (with the possibility of any part being scrutinized and brought to the emperor's attention).[30] Thirdly, just as Josephus was responding to others with whom he disagreed (1:1–2, 6), so his own audience would certainly include personal opponents (implied in 1:30) who could in time gain access to the work—an "inevitable audience." Their response might include deliberate misinterpretations or distortions, aiming to discredit him. So Josephus had to write with care. Fourthly, another inevitable audience would be those hostile to Jews in general. Fifthly, although the main implied audience is Gentile,[31] Jews in Rome would certainly be interested in this history, whatever their opinion of Josephus.[32] Sixthly, since Josephus approves of writing for the benefit of posterity (1:15), he presumably has future generations in mind.[33] On the other hand, although Josephus's earlier Aramaic work had been aimed at Jews in the East (1:3, 6, with their neighbors), there is no indication that they remain part of the audience for this Greek work.

Diversity of audience, certainly in their openness to Josephus's allocation of praise (to Romans) and blame (to Jewish gangsters), is suggested by his comment that everyone may follow his/her own opinion about this (5:257).[34] Persuasion in *War* would naturally be aimed primarily at the main implied audience, but these other five audiences inevitably also have an impact on the way Josephus could write.

Date and Context

Books 1–6 seem to have been finished under Titus (AD 79–81, although much had already been drafted under Vespasian), and Book 7 under Domitian (AD 81–96).

In writing *War*, Josephus had help with his Greek (*Ag. Ap.* 1.50), as the consistently good quality of his Greek in Books 1–6 confirms, although in

Book 7 and the rest of his works, the less polished Greek suggests that this help ceased.[35] He may have started writing soon after the fall of Jerusalem, but *War* took years to complete. The "books" were presented to Vespasian (*Life* 361; *Ag. Ap.* 1:50), so some had been written before Vespasian's death in AD 79. Book 7 is generally dated to the reign of Domitian (AD 81–96) because, after only brief mention in Books 1–6 (4:646, 649, 654), Book 7 contains more flattering references to Domitian (7:37, 85–88, 120, 152). Nevertheless, Book 7 seems to be part of the original plan (1:29–30), providing material promised earlier.[36] The process of writing took time, including distribution book by book, which is how Agrippa II received it, apparently responding with sixty-two letters (*Life* 364–366).

It has been noted that Titus is treated more honorifically than Vespasian, suggesting material completed under Titus, after Vespasian's death.[37] I would add that "Caesar" is not used of Vespasian at all in Books 1–6 (although it is from 7:40 onward). The title becomes prominent in Books 5–6, where it means Titus, suggesting that at least those books (and similarly 1:1–30) were written during Titus's reign (AD 79–81)—by which time the dead Vespasian would more naturally be mentioned without a title, and "Caesar" could be applied with less ambiguity to the reigning Titus.[38]

Indications of Purpose

Within *War*, the narrator gives some indications of purpose, and *Antiquities* 1:1–4 (written later, referring to *War*) provides further evidence. There had already been malicious accounts of recent events (1:2, 7), so *War* aims to defend the Jews as a nation.[39] Jews had been dismissed as insignificant (1:8), whereas Josephus promotes their significance both throughout history (1:17; *Ant.* and *Ag. Ap.*) and as fighters in this noteworthy war (1:1, 8). Despite accusations of rebelliousness (a theme that starts at 1:10), Josephus blames a minority of ambitious and aggressive "bandits" and "tyrants,"[40] presenting traditional Jewish leaders (e.g., high priest Ananus, 3:151, 160–207, 325) and the general population (e.g., 2:304–306; 3:326–328; 4:86) as more reasonable.

Josephus's first, Aramaic account had been for Jews of the eastern Diaspora (1:3, 6), persuading them of the futility of military opposition to Rome. He indicates that this Greek version (*War*) is a translation, so one might expect it to retain that earlier purpose—of being written to Jews (1:3)[41] on behalf of Rome. But the Greek is not evidently translated from Aramaic,[42] and audience analysis suggests that the work has been rewritten for a Gentile audience. Nevertheless, the former purpose is reiterated: In describing Roman military organization, Josephus denies eulogizing but indicates his intention to console the defeated and to deter the rebellious (3:108).

The extreme character and behavior of Nero are indicated briefly, with a narratorial comment that dismisses such details as unnecessary here, and returns to Jewish history (2:250–251 cf. 4:493, 496), so *War* aims, not merely to retell engaging or entertaining stories,[43] but to focus on the history of the Jews. Josephus's imperial sponsorship (*Life* 423–429)[44] suggests that he was expected to show the Flavian emperors (Vespasian, Titus, and Domitian) in a good light[45] and probably also to instill fear in any who might oppose them.[46]

Josephus includes lengthy digressions detailing geographical and historical background[47] and explaining Jewish sects and practices.[48] He considers his digression on Roman military organization (3:70–107) to be useful for those who are not aware of these things and are interested (3:109), indicating didactic intent. Although historians sometimes wrote to show off their rhetorical skills, Josephus's limited Greek meant that he was hardly qualified for that;[49] but he might have intended his work for general educational use. The audience is offered, not only facts, but also thought-provoking lessons,[50] for example, on the sad fate of Jesus the prophet: "Thinking through [ἐννοῶν] these things, one will find that God sends warnings" (6:310).

In summary, the narrator is overt in wanting to refute slander against the Jews, before a Greek and Roman audience. He had previously written to persuade against conflict with Rome and that, along with consoling the defeated, remains one of his aims (3:108).

Previously Proposed Purposes

Given the wide range of indications of purpose, it is not surprising that scholars have drawn a wide range of conclusions. There is a popular view that *War* "apologises to the Romans for the Jews,"[51] easing postwar hostility toward Jews by refuting slander,[52] displacing blame to a (now dead) minority,[53] and arousing sympathy for the Jews as a whole.[54] Cohen suggests that "Josephus is especially eager to exculpate the members of his own class, the priestly aristocracy and rich nobility."[55] Josephus defends, not Jewish zealotry, but a kind of "enlightened, cosmopolitan, pro-Roman Judaism,"[56] seeking to persuade Gentiles that Judaism is respectable[57] and significant, through the challenging (to Gentiles) idea of Romans serving as instruments in "the Jewish god's plan for his people."[58]

More controversially, Rhoads suggests that Josephus goes beyond instruction and attempts to "convert" his readers, calling upon them to appeal to God (5:416).[59] This is overstated, since the appeal is in the mouth of Josephus the character (not the narrator) and is addressed to defenders in Jerusalem (not directly to the hearer); nevertheless, some support is lent to Rhoads's case by similar comments from the narrator, directed to Jerusalem (5:19) and to the audience (6:310). Further, the narrator's repeated asides, indicating that events were primarily under God's control, imply that the Roman Empire itself, and the reader's own life, are also actually in the hands of the God of the Jews. The brief mentions of proselytes and other Gentiles who engaged with Jewish religion are mainly positive.[60] Indeed, Mason suggests that Josephus here wished to address Gentiles who took a serious interest in Judaism,[61] as he later would again in *Antiquities*.[62] But this is speculative; the text of *War* itself does not indicate any overt intention to proselytize.

A traditional view, that Josephus attempts to shield Titus from blame, has been disputed by Mason who suggests instead that Josephus subtly attempts to "deny him the credit" for his victory.[63] Mason also suggests that Josephus presents himself as "a man to be reckoned with, a paragon of virtue and authority."[64] Similarly, Thackeray suggests that, in *Life*, Josephus "indulges his vanity to the full"[65]—and this suggestion would be hard to deny for parts of *War* also.[66] Some had made accusations against Josephus (e.g., of plotting against Rome, 7:448), so *War* clearly defends Josephus's reputation as honorable and no threat to Rome. The preface makes no mention of this, but the subsequent content suggests that it was a significant concern.[67] Mention of Jews regarding Josephus with suspicion, as a coward and traitor (3:439),[68] suggests a further aim of defending himself to Jews as capable and loyal to Judaism.[69]

Cohen suggests that Josephus aims to "blacken"[70] John of Gischala (introduced in 2.585–594). There is good evidence for that within the text, but Josephus's purposes were certainly broader. Downing notes that both Josephus and Acts assume some common ground with "the best anti-mythological pagans" and concludes that their intent is to "entertain high-minded pagans."[71] But this idea conflicts with Josephus's own claims (1:15, 30). It has also been suggested that Josephus seeks to persuade Jews that the destruction of the Temple was God's will, and thus inevitable,[72] and that they should accept the benefits of *pax Romana*.[73]

So, the following intentions have been suggested: to displace blame from and evoke sympathy for Jews; to present Judaism as respectable and even attractive; to present himself and the Flavian emperors positively and John of Gischala negatively; and to persuade Jews to accept Roman rule.

NOTABLE EXAMPLES OF PERSUASIVE TECHNIQUES

- P1a) *Overt instruction by the narrator*. The narrator does not give commands to be obeyed by the audience, but he does give explanations to be assimilated. Most striking is the report of a Jewish (messianic) prophecy, with the narrator's interpretation that its true fulfillment lay, not in a Jew, but in "the sovereignty of Vespasian, who was proclaimed Emperor on Jewish soil" (6:313), with the implication that the audience should submit to the Flavian emperors.

When Cestius failed to achieve an early Roman victory, the narrator's explanation is not that God supported the Jews, but (surprisingly) that God had "already turned away even from the sanctuary because of the evildoers."[74] The implication is that God had ordained instead the later, more devastating defeat for the Jews, with the insurgents[75] to blame. Similarly, when the villain John of Gischala escaped to Jerusalem, this was "an act of God, saving John," not through favor, but only for "the destruction of the Jerusalemites."[76] Thus not only the Jews' failures (e.g., 3:293) and internal struggles (e.g., 4:297), but even their apparent successes, are attributed to God's plan for their impending defeat. The language of God and of fate (e.g., 4:297; 5:355) is used interchangeably so, although the narrator consistently maintains a Jewish monotheistic worldview, he expresses this in language that is accessible to a Gentile audience.

The narrator places the blame on sedition (e.g., 5:257) and pollution of the Temple (4:150, 323, 388) by tyrants (2:276) and brigands (4:138), including the Zealots (4:388).[77] Absolution from blame,[78] although implied at various points within the narrative, is not expressed directly in the mouth of the narrator—except at 5:257, where its force is reduced because he allows for divided opinions by inviting the audience to draw their own conclusions.

Thus, the narrator's asides build up an interpretation of events. Despite biting accounts of corrupt Roman governance (2:272–283), the narrator's subsequent aside plays this down.[79] The narrator does not directly criticize the Romans.[80] He does, repeatedly, place blame on the Jewish brigand-chiefs (e.g., 4:135) and their groups of followers. God's plan, certainly after the death of the priest Ananus (4:318), was to allow Jerusalem and the Temple to be destroyed, because of the behavior of these brigands. So it was by the provision of God that the Romans had supremacy (5:367), just as it was in fulfillment of a Jewish prophecy that, on Jewish soil, Vespasian was declared emperor (6:313). This interpretation, far from pandering to the assumptions and expectations of leading Romans, subtly contradicts them. Rather than attributing Roman victory to the prowess of the Romans themselves, or to the power of their gods, the narrator subverts Roman triumphalism with the alternative suggestion that their victory was given to them by the God of the Jews, who was punishing his own people.[81]

- P1b) *Overt instruction by a trusted character*. Trusted characters express persuasive views rather more forcefully than the narrator does. Agrippa is presented as a trusted character, whose antiwar speech in Jerusalem

(2:345–401, 403–404) includes the assertion, capable of wider application, that the time for pursuing liberty is past, since "the man who once having accepted the yoke then tries to cast it off is a self-willed slave, not a lover of liberty" (2:356). In themes and tone, this speech is closely aligned to the narrator's point of view.[82] Nevertheless, the sentiments were presumably acceptable to Agrippa, since Josephus claims to have given him the opportunity to read and comment on the text (*Life* 362–367).

Ananus also echoes the narrator's viewpoint. While suggesting that bad fortune might justify obedience to the Romans, he criticizes Jerusalemites as inferior (ἀγενής, 4:179) if they were to give in to Jewish villains (πονηρός, 4:179; echoing the narrator's word, e.g., 2:539, 4:328). He goes on to suggest that, ironically, the Romans may be upholding the laws (Jewish laws, since associated here with the Temple), while it is murderous Jews (those within, ἔνδον, 4:184) who break them (4:183–184; cf. narrator at 5:443–445).

Vespasian, addressing his generals, interprets Jewish internecine strife as a sign of God handing victory to the Romans (χαρίζομαι, to give freely, 4:370; echoing the narrator's word, 3:293) with the Jews suffering worse from each other than they would if defeated by the Romans (4:375; cf. narrator at 5:19, 256).

- P1c) *Overt instruction by an untrustworthy character*. A penitent Zealot exposes the excesses of his group and urges the Idumaeans to distance themselves (346–352). The Sicarii are also presented as villains (7:253–258 cf. 4:400–409), and before their suicide at Masada (7:323–336, 341–388), their leader Eleazar speaks at length, stating that they ought to have "appreciated God's purpose, that the Jewish race, once loved by Him" (7:327) had been doomed, not because of Roman might (7:360) but because of the "many wrongs which, beside ourselves, we dared [to inflict] on our fellow countrymen" (7:332). The account of the mass suicide is followed by mention of survivors (two old women and five children), which explains how the events could be known, but surely does not amount to a claim that Eleazar's very words have been preserved; any alert hearer might detect aspects of Josephus's own voice here. This villain is presented as having learned a lesson; thus, the audience is warned against the subversive violence represented by the Sicarii.

- P2a) *Worldview of the text*. The narrator is not in the habit of leaving events to speak for themselves. In one rare example, the brutality of Herod the Great is emphasized by a "narrative event": He planned to have a leader from every village executed upon his death, to ensure universal mourning;[83] but straight after his death, Salome, his own sister, takes steps to release them (1:666).

Overall, an aristocratic Jewish worldview is evident, with respect for the Jerusalem Temple, along with the associated Jewish religious customs. Horror is expressed at the Zealots' bypassing of traditional high-priestly families, electing a high priest by lot from a wider group (low-born, ἀγενής, 4:148; a gross impiety, τὸ τηλικοῦτον ἀσέβημα, 157). Also characteristically Jewish is horror at unburied bodies (4:317, 324, 331–333, 360, 381–384 cf. Tob 1:17–19) and at men acting effeminately (4:561 cf. Deut 22:5).[84] Nevertheless, the narrator appeals to values more widely recognized within the Greco-Roman world. Ananus is praised for favoring democracy (4:320), which would impress those with Greek education.[85] In contrast, John is denigrated for unjustified pursuit of tyrannical power (4:208, 390) and those with a stake in the establishment would share the narrator's suspicion of such insurgents (στασιαστής, 4:410).

- P2b) *Trusted character's worldview.* Agrippa's antiwar speech (P1b above) includes various insights into his worldview; for example, "so great an empire [Roman] could not have been built without God's help" (2:390); and he speaks of the risk to all Jews if war were started "through the folly of a few men" (2:399). The audience is encouraged to adopt Agrippa's respectful and conciliatory approach to Roman power. The speeches of Ananus (4:163–192) and Jesus (4:238–269) express a similar worldview, which is also hard to distinguish from that of the narrator.
- P3) *Characterization.* Characterization is rarely ambiguous—significant characters are generally portrayed either very positively or very negatively, and these characters do not develop or change. Although many of the actions would speak for themselves, the narrator frequently also comments.
- P3a) *Positive characterization and empathy.* Josephus presents himself as a character with whom the audience can identify, through his introduction as a trusted narrator (1:1–30), his various speeches as a character,[86] and frequent *direct inside views* into his personal thoughts.[87] This characterization is suitable for evoking empathy toward Josephus as a character,[88] and therefore also toward Josephus the author (still living, of course, for his initial audiences). Insights are also given into the private thinking of Agrippa (2:319–325), evoking empathy with him in his attempts to calm an inflamed political situation.
- P3b) *Positive characterization and respect.* The portrait of chief priest Ananus is unambiguously positive, especially the narrator's encomium (4:319–325, on Ananus and his colleague Jesus).[89] The narrator asserts that, given the opportunity to lead, Ananus could have saved the Jews (4:151, 318, 321). This encourages the audience to respect such noble leaders, and the values of the traditional aristocracy.[90] The Flavian emperors, Vespasian, Titus, and Domitian, are also characterized extremely

positively (e.g., 4:594–600), encouraging respect for them—albeit with the danger of being seen as mere flattery.⁹¹ The portraits are nuanced, though. Vespasian is presented as wise in instructing his generals to wait while the Jews weaken each other, but his speech ends with a complete anticlimax—the idea that Roman victory might be attributed to the Jews' sedition (4:376) and infighting—which is hardly credible as Vespasian's last word at that moment, but surely betrays the narrator's agenda.

- P3c) *Positive characterization and sympathy*. The Jews, as a whole (especially the nobility, 4:327–329, 357), are presented as victims of the ruthless and deceitful brigand-chiefs. In Jerusalem, the followers of Ananus are presented as representative of the common people, rightly opposed to the excesses of the Zealots (4:193). Horrific details are given of their fate at the hands of the Idumaeans (4:306–313; more piteous, οἰκτρότερον, 4:312). Sympathy for such Jews is evoked.⁹² Blame is attached to a vicious minority, with the effect of shifting blame away from the Jews as a whole (while glossing over any religious roots of revolt).⁹³

- P3d) *Aversion*. The youth of Jerusalem, seduced into following John of Gischala, are contrasted with those who were older and wiser (4:128). The youth provide an example not to follow. Should Gentile subjects of the Empire identify with such Jews, the message is less against anti-Roman rebellion than against internal brigandry and sedition.

- P4a) *Repulsive character (through traits)*. Throughout *War*, those who promote war against Rome and strife among Jews are presented negatively, as bandits, with the Zealots and Sicarii being key groups. Attention is given to various leaders (reviewed in a digression, 7:259–274) and (along with Simon son of Gioras), John of Gischala is particularly prominent. John is introduced as self-seeking and unscrupulous,⁹⁴ and his leadership is shown to be violent and sacrilegious (e.g., 4:562–563). The audience should distance themselves from such people and such behavior.

- P4b) *Repulsive character (through identity)*. The Idumaeans are characterized extremely negatively, in words that reflect on their entire community—"a turbulent and idle people" (θορυβῶδες καὶ ἄτακτον ἔθνος, 4:231) and "naturally most savage in murdering" (φύσει τε ὠμότατοι φονεύειν, 4:310). These descriptions would evoke hostility not only toward these particular Idumaeans, but towards all Idumaeans.⁹⁵

- P5a) *Positive change or outcome*. It is the Romans, particularly the Flavian emperors, who have positive outcomes in *War*, as emphasized by the account of their triumphal procession (7:123–157). This is not encouraging the audience to want to be an emperor (which would be treason), but to be among the loyal subjects who benefit from their stable rule (7:157).⁹⁶

- P5b) *Negative change or outcome.* The story of the suicide of the Sicarii at Masada (7:320–401) is given emphasis through the inclusion of Eleazar's long speeches.[97] The Sicarii are always presented negatively (2:254–257, 425; 4:400–409; 7:253–258), and this tragic end provides a further indication that the audience should shun their violently subversive ways. The fate of Catullus (7:451–453) is also presented as deserved (although the deaths of Ananus and Jesus, 4:325, were not).
- P5c) *Polyphonic affirmation.* The narrator's opposition to lawless Jewish insurgents is a theme expounded early on, in Agrippa's warnings (2:345–404, e.g., 399), and raised again by Ananus (4:163–192, e.g., 185) and Jesus (4:238–269, e.g., 242). These speeches by trusted characters reinforce the narrator's characterization (P4a).
- P5d) *Journey of discovery.* Josephus leads his audience through the process that led up to his surrender to the Romans (3:341–392), including insights into his developing thinking (3:351–353; 3:362–382—"gentle steps," P5e). This suggests an attempt to persuade the reader of the appropriateness of his decision.

NARRATIVE PERSUASION

This work clearly has a variety of persuasive purposes and it employs a variety of persuasive techniques to achieve them. Overt persuasive techniques are evident, with more subtle techniques (such as letting events speak for themselves) hardly noticeable. The text engages differently with each part of its audience.

Greek-speaking Roman Subjects (the main implied audience). Overtly, the audience is encouraged to respect the emperors and Roman rule in general and not to blame the Romans for the destruction of Jerusalem. The audience would recognize this as required, of a Flavian-sponsored account, and would listen for subtle subversive messages, such as Josephus's possibly sarcastic denial of flattering Titus (5:97). Nevertheless, even reported Roman corruption and maladministration are not presented as the main problem, more as a fact of life. It is particular leaders and factions among the Jews—tyrants and brigands—who are blamed. The emphasis is not on rebellion against Rome, but on sedition against established local leadership, oppression of their own people, and impiety against their own God and traditions. Mention of Roman military prowess (3:70–109) is subverted by treating Roman victory not primarily as their own achievement nor as the gift of their own gods, but as the one God punishing these Jewish offenders. Josephus provides a barrage from a universally recognizable arsenal of positive concepts (e.g., virtue, piety, nobility, friendship) and negative concepts (e.g., villainy, impiety, baseness, betrayal) to evoke assent from his audience, as he draws them from these generalizations toward his own particular interpretation of events.

While overtly encouraging respect for Romans, Josephus directs fear away from them and toward God, fortune, and fate (consistently linked to the God of the Jews). By blaming a minority, Josephus encourages sympathy for Jews in general. In attaching blame to the ambitious, unscrupulous, and ruthless, he discourages association with such people. In praising Ananus and Jesus (and himself), he encourages his audience to respect and follow leaders of noble birth, noble character, courage, and ability. The audience is encouraged to take sides, not with Romans against Jews, but with established local leaders against power-hungry newcomers, not so much to join the Roman celebrations (although the triumph is dutifully described), as to join Josephus in mourning (or at least sympathy) for ordinary Jews. The text also encourages respect for Jewish heritage, for Josephus, and for the one God of the Jews.

Flavian Emperors (and their retinue). The Flavian emperors would probably find the text suitably flattering, and suitably loyal to Roman supremacy. Josephus's prophecy (3:401) that Vespasian and Titus would become emperors is presented as divine accreditation for them (as both of them accept, 4:625–626), with Josephus himself presented as divinely inspired. A cautionary tale against rebellion may be expected, and there are some elements of that. Despite maladministration by particular Roman governors,[98] the narrator makes no direct criticism; rather, Roman rule is supported, especially through Agrippa's antiwar speech (2:345–401). Titus and the Romans are exonerated from any impiety in destroying the Temple. The characterization of Jews as victims rather than rebels suggests that remaining Jews (including the Diaspora) are not a threat and should be tolerated, viewed with sympathy,[99] and perhaps even respected for their heritage (1:17).

Those hostile to Josephus personally. Gentiles inclined to dismiss or hate Josephus might not accept his self-portrayal, but would at least hear his claims to have been a capable leader, a prophet, and a wise (if unsuccessful) negotiator, caught in impossible situations but with honorable intentions. Jews among the audience (presumably in Rome), suspecting Josephus of treachery, are assured of his loyalty to traditional Judaism and of his concern for the Jewish people (apart from the brigands). Josephus admits no fault, placing blame on others and minimizing any grounds for accusations against him. Although he was undeniably a military leader, he treats others, but never himself, as warmongers—defusing any accusation that he instigated rebellion. He claims to have foreseen the Jews' defeat, but courageously continued rather than betray his country (3:136–137). On his final surrender, he provides a lengthy justification for not committing suicide (3:362–382), claiming to be God's servant, not a traitor (3:354). While admitting that Vespasian was initially skeptical (3:403), the text presents him as becoming fully persuaded (4:622–629, cf. 3:407). Thus, to question Josephus's divine inspiration would be to question Vespasian's judgment, and perhaps to question Vespasian's divine appointment—something no Roman subject would be wise to do. In negotiations with the defenders of Jerusalem (5:362–419; 6:96–111), in contrast to their folly (6:310), Josephus is portrayed as reasonable, echoing the respected Agrippa, and vindicated by the ultimate fall of Jerusalem (whereas John was proved wrong, 6:98). Enemies are not easily won over; but the text both denies them ammunition and encourages empathy and even respect. Hostile hearers might reject Josephus's supernatural attestation (3:400, cf. 386), but the way this is linked to Vespasian and Titus would make it hard to question publicly.

Those hostile to Jews. Although unlikely to listen to the whole work, those hostile to Jews would find little ammunition here. Using language accessible to Gentiles, and avoiding portraying Jews as insisting on special treatment,[100] Josephus defends Jews in general against accusations of rebelliousness by shifting the blame onto a particular minority, with the majority presented as victims. Those inclined to dismiss the Jews as insignificant (1:7–8) are answered with details of a lengthy war in which the Jews are generally courageous and committed. From both sides, notable acts of individual heroism are reported. The Jerusalem Temple is presented as internationally revered (e.g., 4:262, 275) and magnificent (5:184–237). *War* admits some fault, for example the (undeniable) treacherous massacre of the Roman garrison in Jerusalem (2:450–456), but blame is placed firmly on bandits (2:409). In contrast, "the people" want an end to revolt (4:449–450), appalled by this crime (4:454–455)—they are victims rather than perpetrators, with blame placed on tyrannical leaders and their violent associates, the Zealots and Sicarii. The horrors may evoke anger, but the text directs such anger against brigand-chiefs, leaving the common people to be objects of sympathy. Josephus uses categories universally recognizable to Greeks and Romans, such as friendship (e.g., 1:390; 3:349), tyranny (1:10; 2:276; 4:208), deceit (2:285; 4:208), and democracy (4:320) with little emphasis on issues of importance exclusively to Jews (e.g., food laws; circumcision, mentioned only at 2:454). Thus Gentile hearers, even if hostile, are invited to focus their antipathy on the miscreants (now dead) and to adopt a more sympathetic attitude toward Jews, including those in the real world of their own day.

Jews (especially in Rome). The generally positive portrayal of Romans and extensive discussion of the case against rebellion would encourage Jews not to resent or hate Romans. But dissuading Jews from further rebellion is not the main purpose, both because Gentiles are the main implied audience and because the reasons given for Jerusalem's destruction are not suitable: The emphasis is not on rebellion, but on impiety and brutality. Although rebellion against Rome is portrayed negatively in a few places (2:356, 455; 5:365), it is not the reason for defeat. Rather, God's wrath was kindled by bad behavior, especially toward fellow Jews (e.g., 4:150; 5:19; 6:3) and toward the Temple (e.g., 4:150, 171, 201, 323; 6:110). Sedition, although condemned, is primarily against local (Jewish) authority. The text might persuade a Jewish audience to be obedient to Rome, but it does more to encourage respect for appropriate Jewish leadership, behavior, and piety (necessarily reinterpreted, after the Temple's destruction).

Some aspects of *War* might alienate Jewish hearers. The way Josephus speaks of fate, fortune, and God interchangeably would be easy for Gentiles to relate to, but Jews might be offended that he does not overtly reject Gentile understandings. The text admits that Herod erected statues and temples at Caesarea, but it does not indicate disapproval (2:266, cf. 1:414, 650). The narrator expresses no opinion on the fervor of the young Jews who attempted to remove Herod's golden eagle from the Temple gate (1:653). Nevertheless, Diaspora Jews would generally understand the constraints of addressing a Gentile audience while under imperial sponsorship and might forgive this.

Jews might be horrified at Josephus's suggestion of God favoring the Romans,[101] but in mentioning the Babylonian destruction, he draws parallels with Jeremiah (5:391–394), providing scriptural precedent for such an idea. On the other hand, the suggestion that Vespasian fulfilled Jewish messianic prophecy (6:313) would be hard to accept, and no attempt is made to justify it to a Jewish audience.[102] Jews would be likely to dismiss this as a politically expedient idea, attractive for Vespasian and convenient for Josephus.

Nevertheless, Josephus goes to some lengths to address the accusation of having betrayed his people; it was from Jews themselves that such an accusation would be most pointed. Josephus portrays himself as loyal to his people and to God, even in surrender, and as wise in advising others to come to terms. His speech against suicide (3:362–382), while employing general arguments, includes Jewish aspects, especially that life is a gift from our creator to whom we are answerable (3:372, 379). He presents the tyrants as oppressing Jews, and his own behavior as reasonable and honorable by comparison. Overall, although Jews are not the main audience, Josephus does seem concerned to present himself positively, not only to Gentiles, but also to his fellow Jews.

Posterity. The narrator does not present himself as a prophet whose words should be preserved and venerated,[103] nor as a philosopher supplying enlightened ideas or memorable quotations.[104] Since Josephus is dismissive of historians who rewrite the work of others (1:13–15), it is unlikely that he wanted others to use his material as a source for their own histories. At times, the narrator assumes the role of a teacher, especially in the digressions (especially 3:70–109), addressing students (3:109), presumably in any generation. Appropriately for a historian, he explicitly mentions posterity as the audience of the accounts of heroic deaths (3:204, 229), both Jewish[105] and Roman.[106] One might expect Josephus to commemorate Jewish heroes especially, but Roman heroes are given slightly more prominence—he is not portraying Jews as more heroic than Romans.[107] Josephus's positive representation of himself may well be aimed, not only at the initial audience, but also at posterity, wanting future (as well as contemporary) audiences to regard the Jewish War, and Josephus himself, as significant.

CONCLUSIONS

The target audience seems to be aristocratic leaders within the Empire, with a Greek education. There is evidence of Josephus trying to win respect for himself, sympathy for Jews, and probably also respect for Jews—for their customs and established leadership. It would not be hard for contemporary Gentile hearers to relate to the tensions described, between conservative leadership and opportunistic adventurers. It is in general (not particularly Jewish) terms that Ananus is presented as a hero, and the aspects of John that make him a villain are also universally recognizable. The text provides instruction on good and stable governance, but asides also address the role of God and destiny in ordering events. Most Gentiles would naturally presume that a defeated people's deity was either defeated or won over by the Romans;[108] but counterculturally, the narrator suggests that the God of the defeated Jews was in control throughout.

War is not merely pro-Roman propaganda, since it subtly subverts Roman triumphalism. Nor is it a statement of Jewish consensus since, although generally orthodox and respectful toward Judaism, it is exceptional in its assertion of God going over to the Romans.[109] Josephus took some risks—of alienating Jews by his pro-Roman stance, and of alienating Romans by subtly denying them, and their gods, ultimate credit for victory. But overall, the text presents a favorable impression of Josephus, of Jews, and of Judaism, by offering a distinctively Jewish interpretation of events to the main target audience of Gentiles.

Josephus's persuasiveness has significantly influenced scholarly suggestions about his purposes. The analysis here provides a more explicit and comprehensive approach to this. It has identified examples of most of the listed techniques of persuasion and shown that such analysis can be used not only to check the credibility of the narrator's stated purposes, but also to indicate other (unstated) purposes.

Josephus's stated (or indicated) objectives are largely but not entirely confirmed: Jews are defended against slander, through positive portrayal of Jewish heritage (especially the Temple) and shifting of blame, leaving the general population portrayed as victims.[110] Jews might be deterred from rebellion,[111] but they are not the main, target audience. Any rebellion is deterred,[112] but sedition against local leadership is denigrated more than sedition against Rome. The text might console other defeated nations, but provides meager consolation to Jews. The claim not to flatter Romans or emperors is contradicted, although Roman triumphalism is subtly undermined. The claim not merely to entertain is confirmed, although the more dramatic episodes do grip the audience's attention, and those interested to learn are informed, especially in the digressions, with both Romans and Jews presented as noteworthy.

Concerning less overt purposes, this analysis has suggested the following: Josephus both defends himself against accusations and actively presents himself as worthy of respect (e.g., as an authoritative historian) and empathy (as a character). The negative portrayal of John of Gischala is not an end in itself,[113] but it deflects blame from Josephus (heroic, in contrast to this villain) and other Jews (as victims of this tyrant). But although the text presents the destruction as God's will, it is not clear that it aims to persuade Jews of this,[114] both because the main implied audience is Gentile, and because argumentation that would be persuasive for Jews is very limited (Jeremiah is alluded to, 5:391–93, but Scripture is never quoted).

Despite working hard to establish Josephus's authority as a historian and narrator, and even as a prophet, *War* does not then assume high levels of narratorial authority. The implied audience does not simply accept the narrator's authority but, rather, has to be drawn into the narrative if they are to be won over.

This analysis has largely affirmed the conclusions of recent scholarship. Mason has given persuasiveness some consideration[115] and this work can be summarized as affirming his conclusions. This chapter has not produced any surprises for Josephus scholarship, but it has demonstrated the use of the proposed method and its compatibility with relevant current scholarship.

NOTES

1. E.g., Sterling, *Historiography*; F. Gerald Downing, "Common Ground with Paganism in Luke and Josephus," *New Testament Studies* 28, no. 4 (October 1982): 546–59; Steve Mason, *Josephus and the New Testament*, 2nd ed. (Peabody: Hendrickson, 2003), 251–95, suggesting that Luke-Acts is dependent on Josephus.

2. *War* starts with Antiochus IV Epiphanes, second century BC.

3. Mason suggests that Josephus "wrote every word and phrase (as long as he was on the ball) according to the prescriptions of rhetoric," Steve Mason, *A History of the Jewish War, A.D. 66–74* (New York: Cambridge University Press, 2016), 80.

4. E.g., *J.W.* 2:568–3:442; *Life*.

5. Palestine and subsequently Rome, e.g., Shaye J. D. Cohen, *Josephus in Galilee and Rome: His Vita and Development as a Historian* (Boston: Brill, 2002); John Curran, "Flavius Josephus in Rome," in Jack Pastor, Pnina Stern, and Menahem Mor (eds.) *Flavius Josephus: Interpretation and History* (Leiden: Brill, 2011), 65–86.

6. Steve Mason, "'Should any wish to enquire further' (*Ant*. 1.25): The Aim and Audience of Josephus' *Judean Antiquities/Life*," in *Understanding Josephus: Seven Perspectives*, ed. Steve Mason (Sheffield: Sheffield Academic, 1998), 64–103.

7. Studied in full—except in Tables E1–3, where a shorter section allows more direct comparison.

8. Josephus, *The Jewish War*, in *Josephus*, trans. Henry St. J. Thackeray, vols. 2–4, (Cambridge: Harvard University Press, 1997). Although there are variations between manuscripts, one group is "decidedly superior," 2:xxix–xxx.

9. First person singular, with occasional first person plural, e.g., 5:140, 232; 6:400.

10. Especially 1:9, 11–12; 5:20; 6:111.

11. In Rome, according to Mason "Enquire," 67, 72–79; idem, *New Testament*, 95–99.

12. Josephus claims to write μετ' ἀκριβείας (1:9 cf. 7:454; truth, 7:455; cf. Luke's claim to have researched ἀκριβῶς, Luke 1:3). He even dares to make a favorable comparison with the respected Thucydides (*Ag. Ap.* 1:18, 27).

13. Now lost.

14. Mason, *New Testament*, 97–98.

15. 3:351 (visions of the fate of Jews and emperors), 399–402 (of Vespasian, and Titus, becoming emperor), 405–407 (that the siege of Jotapata would last forty-seven days), showing Josephus as prophetic (3:352, 405, 407; 4:623–629); Cohen, *Galilee*, 97–98.

16. 5:391–393. The destruction in Jeremiah's day: 5:391, 411; 6:104, 268, 437, 439; Mason, *New Testament*, 21, 92–93.

17. And, in the mouth of Josephus the character, 5:412.

18. Hearers are to decide for themselves: explicit at 5:257; 6:310, 399; implied at 7:453.

19. 3:403; perhaps "When he needed an excuse for surrender, he invented divine authorization." Cohen, *Galilee*, 100.

20. *Contra* Sterling, *Historiography*, 392.

21. E.g., *J.W.* 4:153–154; 326–333 (in Jerusalem); 4:447 (in Rome); 5:439–441; David M. Rhoads, *Israel in Revolution: 6–74 C.E.: A Political History Based on the Writings of Josephus* (Philadelphia: Fortress, 1976), 164; Mason, *New Testament*, 37–39.

22. 3:59–63, 127–140; Rhoads, *Revolution*, 7.

23. Especially *J.W.* 5:361–420; but also 5:114, 261, 325–36, 541–547; 6:94–118, 129, 365.

24. 7:448; *Life* 336–367.

25. *Life* 424, 429. Curran, "Josephus," 72. John M.G. Barclay, *Jews in the Mediterranean Diaspora from Alexander to Trajan (323 BCE–117 CE)* (Edinburgh: T. & T. Clark, 1996), 350, suggests, "Josephus makes no reference to the Jewish community in Rome, and his silence may betray his failure to gain its confidence." His point is reasonable, if exaggerated (Josephus mentions them briefly, 2:80, 105).

26. Mason, *New Testament*, 94.

27. Mason, *New Testament*, 96–99; e.g., 5:184–217 gives detail of the Temple in Jerusalem, but no explanation is given of figures of Roman history, e.g., Agrippa (1:118); Crassus (1:179); Cassius (1:180); Pallas (2:246).

28. Not primarily Roman by race: Romans are mentioned in the third person (e.g., 3:70–109).

29. Although Cohen, *Galilee*, 89, suggests several editions.

30. Josephus knew appropriate techniques (*Life* 367); John M. G. Barclay, "The Empire Writes Back: Josephan Rhetoric in Flavian Rome," in *Flavius Josephus and Flavian Rome*, eds. Jonathan Edmondson, Steve Mason, and James Rives (Oxford: Oxford University Press, 2005), 320.

31. Narrator is a foreigner (ἀλλόφυλος, 1:16) to his audience.

32. Curran, "Josephus," 84.

33. 6:200 (narrator; also *Ant.* 1:3); 3:204 (Josephus the character; in contrast to Titus, 6:46–53).

34. Agrippa seems to have approved (*Life* 362–367).

35. Cohen, *Galilee*, 87.

36. 7:420–436, on Onias's temple, fulfills 1:31–33; Mason, *New Testament*, 67.

37. Cohen, *Galilee*, 85–86; Titus approved publication (*Life* 363); the negative portrayal of Caecina (4:634–644) should be dated after his execution in AD 79.

38. Titus and Domitian had received the title "Caesar" at the time of Vespasian's accession; Cassius Dio, *Roman Histories* 65:1.

39. Cf. *Ant.* 1:4; Mason, "Enquire," 73; ibid., *New Testament*, 64.

40. Tyrants (τύραννος) appear at 1:24, 27; bandits/plunderers (λῃστής) at 2:228, 235; 2:275 brings both together. Blame: e.g., 1:10; 6:94–95, 124–128, 250; Barclay, "Empire," 325; Rhoads, *Revolution*, 12, 159–64.

41. Rhoads, *Revolution*, 159.

42. Mason, *New Testament*, 65; Thackeray, *Josephus*, 2:xv.

43. 1:15, 30; *contra* Downing, "Common Ground," 558.

44. Although Mason downplays patronage, "Enquire," 77.

45. His claim not to flatter Titus (5:97; cf. 1:2, *Ant.* 1:2) rings hollow (esp. 5:82, 89). In contrast, Polybius had (more than two centuries earlier) felt able to make "cynical comments on Roman policy" despite writing as an exile, held in Rome, Walbank, *Polybius*, 168.

46. Thackeray, *Josephus*, 1:xi.

47. 2:188–191; 3:35–58, 158–160, 506–521; 4:5–8, 54–56, 452–485, 530–533, 607–615; 5:136–247; 7:164–189, 280–303.

48. 2:119–166 on Jewish sects, or "philosophies"; 5:184–237 on the Temple.

49. Mason, "Enquire," 69–70; Josephus criticizes this approach, *Ant* 1:2.

50. Mason, *New Testament*, 65–66. Instruction was a common purpose, e.g., Polybius, *Histories* 1:1; Plutarch, *Alexander* 1:1; Aristophanes, *Frogs* 1009–1036.

51. Cohen, *Galilee*, 97; in contrast, Mason associates Josephus with the Flavians' desire to present "Judaeans" to Romans as "a foreign scapegoat"—Mason, *History*, 14.

52. Mason, "Enquire," 71.

53. Barclay, *Diaspora*, 352.

54. Barclay, *Diaspora*, 355.

55. Cohen, *Galilee*, 97.

56. Rhoads, *Revolution*, 13.

57. Bartlett, *Hellenistic World*, 75.

58. Curran, "Josephus," 76; cf. Barclay, "Empire," 321.

59. Rhoads, *Revolution*, 12–13.

60. *J.W.* 2:561; 5:15, 17, 187, 199, 402; 7:45, 357; but with the exception of 2:454, 463, and the restriction of 5:194.

61. Mason believes the intended audience to be the same: "Enquire," 68.

62. Mason, "Enquire," 96, cf. 80.

63. Mason, *New Testament*, 83.

64. Mason, *History*, 95.

65. Thackeray, *Josephus*, 1:xiv.

66. E.g., 3:142–144, 193–194, 200, 340, 436; Cohen, *Galilee*, 91–97.

67. But Mason, *New Testament*, 53: "a claim to have many accusers was itself a rhetorical commonplace . . . to generate sympathy . . . (e.g., Martial, *Ep.* 3.9; 4.27; 7.72)."

68. 5:375, 541; 6:129; *Life*, 424, 429; Mason, *New Testament*, 52.

69. John R. Bartlett, *Jews in the Hellenistic World: Josephus, Aristeas, The Sybilline Oracles, Eupolemus* (Cambridge: Cambridge University Press, 1985), 73–74.

70. Cohen, *Galilee*, 90; and "to dissociate Josephus from John" (93).

71. Downing, "Common Ground," 558.

72. Curran, "Josephus," 79.

73. Bartlett, *Jews*, 75; Mader, *Politics*, 147; Mason, *New Testament*, 69; Rhoads, *Revolution*, 12.

74. διά τοὺς πονηροὺς ἀπεστραμμένος ὁ θεὸς ἤδη καὶ τὰ ἅγια (2:539).

75. στασιαστής is used at 2:529.

76. θεοῦ δ' ἦν ἔργον ἄρα του σῴζοντος τὸν Ἰωάννην ἐπὶ τὸν Ἱεροσολυμιτῶν ὄλεθρον (4:104).

77. Rhoads, *Revolution*, 159–64 analyzes the interlinked use of: "brigand" (λῃστής), "insurgent" (στασιαστής), "tyrant" (τύραννος), "conspirator" (ἐπιβουλός), and "wicked one" (πονηρός).

78. For Titus (6:241, 254, 262, 284); for Romans (5:257, 6:123); Barclay, "Empire," 331.

79. Not an adequate reason/excuse (οὐκ ἀξίαν ἔσχεν πρόφασιν, 2:285), i.e., for war.

80. Praising them (3:70–71) despite denials (3:108); Barclay, "Empire," 320.

81. Cohen, *Galilee*, 76; Mason, *New Testament*, 55–64.

82. Tessa Rajak, *The Jewish Dialogue with Greece and Rome: Studies in Cultural and Social Interaction* (Boston: Brill, 2002), 148–49.

83. Herod is initially presented positively, but the narrator explicitly condemns this as lawless (ἄθεμις, 1:659).

84. Although Jewish practices that were hard for Gentiles to relate to, especially circumcision, are not emphasized.

85. Greeks pioneered and respected democracy (but not unquestioningly, Plato, *Republic* 8:544).

86. Direct speech: 2:605–607; 3:204, 260–261, 354, 362–382, 388–389, 400–402; 5:376–419; 6:99–110. Indirect speech: 2:580–582, 609, 638; 3:139–140 (a letter), 197–200; 5:363–374, 546–547; 6:97–98.

87. 2:570, 573, 577, 620, 642; 3:130, 136–37, 151, 171, 183, 193, 203, 258, 263, 346, 353–54, 361, 387, 391; 5:326.

88. Also, as ideal general (2:568–3:408, cf. *Life*); Bartlett, *Jews*, 73; Cohen, *Galilee*, 91–100.

89. Ananus's tragic death can be seen as the "narrative fulcrum" of the whole work, Steve Mason and Honora Chapman, *Judean War 2: Translation and Commentary*, vol. 1B (Leiden: Brill, 2008), 418 n. 3819.

90. Rhoads, *Revolution*, 164, 178.

91. Subversive undertones are possible, e.g., 5:367.

92. Also, for aristocrats (e.g., 4:327–330); and Jesus (6:300–309).

93. Mader, *Politics*, 52.

94. 2:585–589; 4:85, 208; Cohen, *Galilee*, 90.

95. Despite earlier portrayal as hostile Gentiles (Ps 82:6, LXX, although not Ps 83:6, MT), Josephus treats Idumaeans as Jews (4:272–274 cf. 4:136; *Ant.* 13:257–258 explains).

96. And not to end up like the executed villain, Simon, 7:154 (P5b).

97. The speeches are more than 75 percent of the account.

98. And the Flavians' predecessors (especially Vitellius, 4:647, 651–655) are negatively portrayed.

99. Sympathy is ascribed to Titus (1:10), which would help to promote such sympathy.

100. Except when John uses the Sabbath as a false pretext (4:9–103), but Josephus distances Jews in general from him.

101. From Agrippa, 2:361, 373, 390; Josephus, 3:354, 367; 5:412; narrator, 6:399.

102. Vespasian failed to fulfill Davidic descent (2 Kgdms 7:12–16), rule from Zion (i.e., Jerusalem, e.g., Ps 2:6, not merely appointment when nearby) and loyalty to one God.

103. Josephus the character is presented as prophetic, but not the narrator (who only provides interpretations, 4:387–388; 6:313), *contra* Sterling, *Historiography*, 392.

104. Josephus and/or his assistants occasionally use allusions or quotations, especially in speeches (Thackeray, *Josephus*, notes 3:496; 4:40; 5:501); but do not seem to compose quotable maxims.

105. Niger, 3:25–26; Eleazar et al., 3:229–233; others, 6:91–92; Jonathan, negatively portrayed, 6:169–176; Eleazar, 7:196–209.

106. Aebutius, 4:36; Gallus, 4:37–38; Longinus, 5:312–313; Sabinus, 6:54–67; Julianus, 6:81–90; Pedanius, 6:161–163; Longus, 6:186–187; Rufus, 7:199.

107. Daring charges are characteristic of Jews (6:17), but contrasted with Roman discipline (e.g., 3:13–21, 24, 153, 475; 4:45), not with cowardice.

108. Romans made vows (*evocatio*) to enemy deities to win them over; Beard, *Religions*, 34.

109. Only Vespasian and, to some extent, Ananus agree with the narrator on this.

110. Rhoads, *Revolution*, 13.

111. Bartlett, *Jews*, 75; Rhoads, *Revolution*, 12.

112. Thackeray, *Josephus*, 1:xi.

113. Cohen, *Galilee*, 90.

114. Curran, "Josephus," 79.

115. Mason, *New Testament*, 68–99.

Chapter Five

Narrative Persuasion in *Joseph and Aseneth*

AN OVERVIEW OF *ASENETH*

This chapter investigates the techniques of persuasion built into *Joseph and Aseneth*, another narrative, in Koine Greek, which is broadly contemporary with Acts. Like Acts, it deals with the interface between Jews and Gentiles—it tells how a Jewish patriarch, Joseph, came to marry a Gentile, Aseneth, the daughter of an Egyptian priest. Aseneth is portrayed as becoming the "City of Refuge" (*Jos. Asen.* 15:7; 17:6; 19:5, 8 cf. 16:16) for all subsequent proselytes. So this is not simply an entertaining romance, but a story with a prominent religious message and some obvious elements of persuasion.[1]

In looking for techniques of persuasion in ancient narratives, for comparison with Acts, it is helpful to consider a range of texts, and *Aseneth* helpfully extends that range. *Embassy* and *War* have provided relevant examples of historiography. But they are different from Acts in their prominent, named authors, emphasizing eyewitness accounts, and in their limited reference to Scripture and to supernatural events. *Aseneth* admittedly has the disadvantage of evidently being composed long after the period in which the narrative is set. But, in contrast to *Embassy* and *War*, it has the advantages of being, like Acts, an anonymous work, being closely linked to Scripture (based around some key relevant details from Genesis), and including supernatural visions and events, which are vital to the story.

Aseneth gives the impression of being a romance, but its style is septuagintal. Apart from narrative and dialogue, the text includes some lengthy soliloquies. Between the two sections of the story, the longer text includes a prayer by Aseneth (21:10–21), which takes the form of a penitential psalm, with (in some manuscripts) the refrain, "I have sinned, Lord, I have sinned," an arrangement that may be designed for congregational singing.[2] More integrated with the story are her penitential soliloquies (6:2–8; 12:1–13:15),[3] which work as part of the narrative. There are also prayers, in direct speech, from Joseph (8:9) and from Aseneth (27:10), both of which are answered within the narrative. So the text may be effective as an entertaining romance,[4] but the religious aspects betray a further agenda, with some didactic elements and some mystical elements.

There are significant complications with this text. First, large variations between the manuscripts show that there must have been extensive redaction, probably for all of the extant copies.[5] Secondly, scholars have not reached a consensus about whether the author was a Jew or a Christian (or perhaps a proselyte, a Jewish-Christian, or even a Samaritan).[6] Technically, for a story set in Joseph's day, his people are best described as Hebrews; nevertheless, by the time this text was written,[7] author and audience would have thought of these people as "Jews," so it is not anachronistic to use that word here, reflecting the way the audience would have thought of God's people in the story. This text uses various titles for God, always implying the God of Joseph and of the Jews. Here, it will be convenient to speak simply of "God," meaning the God assumed by the text, whatever faith community the author and audience may have belonged to.

There is general agreement that the original language of *Aseneth* was Greek.[8] Because of the significant variations (fifteen Greek manuscripts and eight translated versions survive),[9] attempts to reconstruct the Greek text have led to two published reconstructions: Philonenko's text,[10] based on the "shorter" group of texts, which he suggests are the earliest; and Burchard's text,[11] based on the "longer" group of texts, since he disagrees and assumes that the longer texts are actually earlier. Scholars continue to refer to both of these reconstructed texts.[12] For references, I have used Burchard's chapter and verse divisions (which are necessary for referring to the longer text).[13]

There is slight uncertainty about the unity of the text. The story divides into two separate episodes: 1:1–21:21 (concluded by a psalm, 21:11–21) and 22:1–29:9. The second episode presupposes the first, but otherwise they could be separate stories. Some question the unity of authorship,[14] and there are, admittedly, changes in theme, but the similarity of style and thought suggests common authorship.[15] Within the reconstructed texts, minor inconsistencies remain; for example, after Aseneth's destruction of her idols, the ongoing narrative gives no indication of any negative reaction from her family. But, in contrast, her soliloquies repeatedly dwell on her isolation and rejection by them and others.[16] Such inconsistencies may simply be the result of uneven redaction.[17] Perhaps the redactors wanted proselytes/converts experiencing persecution from their families to be able to empathize with

Aseneth's soliloquies,[18] but were reluctant to allow the narrative to portray pagans as persecutors, for fear of raising hostility from either side.

Summary of the Story

Aseneth is mentioned very briefly in Genesis. When Pharaoh gave Joseph power in Egypt, he also gave him as his wife "Aseneth, daughter of Petephres [Πετεφρῆς], priest of Heliopolis" (Gen 41:45),[19] who then bore his sons Manasseh and Ephraim (Gen 41:50). *Aseneth* is crafted to fit in with the characters and context set by Genesis, with the minor change that Petephres's name (LXX, cf. Potiphera in MT) comes out as Pentephres (Πεντεφρῆς) throughout *Aseneth*.

Aseneth begins by mentioning the seven years of plenty (*Jos. Asen.* 1:1, echoing Gen 41:47) and Joseph collecting grain "like the sand of the sea" (1:2, cf. Gen 41:49). As Joseph approaches Heliopolis, the audience is introduced to Pentephres (positively portrayed as noble and prudent) and his virgin daughter Aseneth, famed for her beauty (1:6), but so dismissive of suitors as to be arrogant (2:1). Hearing of Joseph's approach, Pentephres suggests Aseneth should marry him, but she is quick to refuse (4:9–12). Joseph's appearance is so dazzling that Aseneth is moved to repentance. Joseph refuses to let her embrace him, because he worships God but she worships idols. Seeing her distress, he prays for her. After his departure, she expresses her repentance by getting rid of her idols, fasting, and praying for a week. A heavenly man appears to her (14:3), announces her acceptance in heaven (15:4) and betrothal to Joseph (15:6), enacting her transformation through a supernatural honeycomb (16:1–17:4), and informing her that she will be known as "City of Refuge" (πόλις καταφυγῆς, 15:7 cf. Num 35:27) for all proselytes. Joseph then arrives and, having also heard from the heavenly man, now accepts Aseneth as his bride. Joseph approaches Pharaoh, who formalizes the marriage. The longer text recaps at this point with a penitential psalm by Aseneth (21:11–21).

The story moves on to a new scene, eight years later,[20] during the seven years of famine (22:1). Aseneth meets and is accepted by the elderly but beautiful Jacob. Pharaoh's firstborn, who had wanted to marry her (1:7–9), becomes jealous. He asks Simeon and Levi to help him assassinate Pharaoh and Joseph, so that he can take the throne and Aseneth (23). They firmly reject this. He then manages to persuade Dan and Gad, along with Naphtali and Asher (24). As they ambush Aseneth, Levi (positively presented as wise and prophetic) brings other brothers to the rescue (26). Heroic Benjamin stuns Pharaoh's son and kills his fifty soldiers (27:1–5). Attacked by the four scheming brothers, Aseneth prays and their swords disintegrate. Aseneth persuades Simeon to show mercy. Levi takes Pharaoh's son home, but he dies. Pharaoh dies of grief, and Joseph rules Egypt for forty-eight years, before handing over to a younger heir of Pharaoh's (29:9).

Narrator and Author

The author and redactors of *Aseneth* are entirely anonymous. The author was clearly familiar with Greek and with the Septuagint (not only Genesis), but not necessarily with Hebrew or Aramaic.[21] The text seems deliberately to sound like scriptural narrative, as it echoes and builds on details from Genesis. The narrator's style is in keeping with that—reticent, not directly addressing the audience, yet providing asides that speak with authority. For example, the narrator provides the positive assessment of Joseph, that he is "meek and merciful and fearing God" (8:8) and clarifies that "Pharaoh's son lied" to Dan, Gad, Naphtali, and Asher (24:7). But, to provide the direct religious teaching and effectively to speak for God, the narrator leaves it to the authoritative characters: primarily the heavenly figure (14:3–17:9), but also Joseph (8:5–7) and Levi (23:10–11; 29:3–4).

The process of redaction means that the narrators of the longer and shorter texts cannot be treated as entirely identical. For example, two similes may betray a male perspective in the longer text: Joseph sees Aseneth's fingers as like those of a fast-writing (male) scribe (20:5; whereas various women's skills would require dexterity and could have been mentioned); and Aseneth embraces Jacob like a man returning from fighting embracing his father (22:9).[22] The shorter text lacks these.[23] Similarly, the narrator twice describes Aseneth's breasts—when Joseph rejects her approach (8:5) and when she receives supernatural beauty (18:9)—with neither present in the shorter text.[24] So care has been taken here to work with material that is common to both reconstructed texts or, where they differ, to note that.[25]

The narrative takes a Jewish perspective—the underlying assumptions about God (or "heaven") are those of Jewish monotheism, not Gentile polytheism. Joseph ascribes to God the giving of life to all things (8:9, leaving no room for other life-giving deities); Aseneth amplifies this (12:1) and describes idols as "dead and dumb" (12:5); surprisingly, it is in the name of "the God of Joseph" that Pharaoh blesses Aseneth (21:4, 6). So, when the narrator speaks of God, it is these Jewish assumptions that set the context.[26] Aseneth is "nothing like the virgins of the Egyptians but in every way like the daughters of the Hebrews . . . tall as Sarah, good-looking as Rebecca and beautiful as Rachel" (1:5). This is not merely personal preference by the narrator, but part of a systematic idealization of Jews, as those who worship God (θεοσεβής e.g., 8:5; 23:10). Whereas Genesis indicates that Hebrews, as shepherds, were an "abomination" to the Egyptians (βδέλυγμα, Gen 46:34), *Aseneth* inverts this by explaining that Joseph ate separately, because to eat with Egyptians was an abomination to him (βδέλυγμα, 7:1).[27] That the heavenly figure is described as "in every way similar to Joseph" (14:9) may also "betray the Jewish bias of the narrator."[28] On the other hand, while hostility to polytheism is implicit in the narrative, it is in the mouth of the authoritative characters that it becomes explicit, e.g., Joseph describes idols as "dead and dumb" (8:5), which Aseneth echoes (12:5; also, in the longer text, 11:8 and 13:11). Any overtly didactic or polemical content is in the mouth of such characters. So, although the narrator consistently takes a Jewish perspective, he avoids drawing attention to this.

Audience

The hearers are assumed to have some familiarity with Genesis,[29] needing no explanation of "the seven years of plenty" (1:1; 3:1) or "the seven years of famine" (22:1); and Aseneth's accusation that Joseph slept with his master's wife (4:10) is never explicitly refuted (although his innocence is explicit to the audience of Genesis, Gen 39:12; and *Jos. Asen.* 7:3–5 builds on this).[30]

The hearers are either Jewish or others who are willing (at least within the context of the story) to accept the uniqueness and appropriateness of Judaism—for that is not only an idea reinforced by the narrative, but actually a presupposition. A hearer unwilling to accept that there is anything special about Jews would from the outset be alienated, e.g., by the association of Hebrew girls with beauty and desirability, in contrast to Egyptian girls (1:5); this makes it almost certain that Egyptians were no part of the intended audience—they would be offended by such a comment. On the other hand, awareness of Jewish beliefs and customs is only required at a very basic level. Monotheistic assumptions lie behind the introduction (by the pagan, Pentephres) of Joseph as "the mighty man of God" (3:4) and "(the) spirit of God is upon him" (4:8); and those familiar with Sabbath observance might understand that as the background of Joseph's explanation that he will come back on the eighth day (9:5)—but such awareness is not necessary to follow the plot.

There is some esoteric symbolism,[31] especially in Aseneth's encounter with the heavenly man (chs. 14–17), which involves a supernatural honeycomb and various bees. (Although scholars have explored symbolic meanings, that is not the focus in the analysis here.) It is possible that the hearer is expected, from other sources, to be aware of the significance of some of this symbolism. On the other hand, some of it remains obscure despite scholarly attempts relate it to other ancient texts, and it is quite possible that the purpose of such symbolism was deliberately to leave the hearer puzzled and eager to ask for an explanation from some teacher or group of those initiated into such mysteries. The text itself mentions mysteries: Asked his name, the heavenly man replies that names written in God's book are "unspoken" (ἄρρητος, 15:12x, absent from shorter text). When Aseneth is perceptive, the heavenly man comments that God's mysteries have been revealed to her (16:14).[32] Levi knows God's "unspoken" things (ἄρρητος, 22:13) and reveals them to Aseneth in secret.[33] These references suggest that some of the symbolism might only make sense if the hearer were already fully initiated, or else inquired further. The audience would therefore consist of those already involved in the author's (or redactor's) community and those interested in becoming involved, through seeking answers about these mysteries.

Date and Context

Estimates of the date of writing are interlinked with theories about the author's community and context. Earliest estimates are in the second century BC, after the Septuagint had become available. Latest estimates extend to the fifth century AD, if the text is Christian. But if it is Jewish (as the analysis below will indicate), it would not be later than AD 135, making the text approximately contemporary with Acts.

Most scholars treat *Aseneth* as a Jewish text from a period when proselytism was a realistic possibility, therefore before the Jewish revolt under Hadrian (AD 132–135),[34] because he proceeded to ban proselytism, and probably before the revolt under Trajan (ca. AD 115).[35] Philonenko suggests rural Egyptian provenance,[36] with the text wooing Egyptians to convert.[37] In contrast, Bohak makes the very specific suggestion that the esoteric symbolism refers to Onias's temple at Heliopolis, suggesting that the text was written by and for the Jewish community there (against the Jerusalem Temple) between 160 and 145 BC.[38] He sees mention of Ioakim as king of Moab (3:7) as anachronistic insertion into the story of Iakimos, Onias's rival in Jerusalem.[39] His interpretation depends on very specific, allegorical interpretation, with different groups of bees representing different groups of priests, honeycombs symbolizing temples, and Aseneth (as "City of Refuge") taking over symbolism from the Jerusalem Temple.

Some have suggested that *Aseneth* might be a Christian text. The absence of overtly Christian content would be appropriate, to avoid anachronism.[40] The heavenly man does make a cross-shaped, blood-colored mark (16:17), which might indicate Christian editing,[41] or possibly authorship. Comparison with Syrian Christian texts has led to the suggestion that *Aseneth* is Christian, from Syria and from the third to the fifth centuries AD. There may be parallels in the "adjuration of powerful divine beings"[42] (but such adjuration was pervasive). The absence of Torah commandments has been noted,[43] and bread, wine, and oil (e.g., 8:5–7) have been associated with the Christian eucharist. The text's focus on virginity has been associated with the Syrian Christian promotion of lifelong sexual abstinence for converts;[44] but this is hardly tenable, since the text mentions Aseneth bearing two sons (21:9; cf. Gen 41:50).[45] Overall, these arguments are far from convincing.[46]

Jewish authorship is the more credible explanation for a text with such emphasis on Judaism, and it is supported by the absence from the texts of any demonstrably Christian reference or any clear allusion to the New Testament. The case for Christian authorship depends on links in symbolism that seem rather tenuous, and on the absence of key Jewish practices, which can be accounted for by the story's pre-Torah setting and its atmosphere, emphasizing cordial relations with the Gentile hierarchy.[47] I would add a powerful (85 percent confidence) argument in favor of Jewish, not Christian, provenance: *Aseneth* treats Simeon and Levi as God's agents in slaughtering the Shechemites (23:14, cf. Gen 34), in accordance with early Jewish interpretation[48] whereas, in contrast, early Christian reception history consistently condemns the brothers.[49]

The provenance of *Aseneth* could be almost any Greek-speaking region.[50] Although set in Egypt, the text does not necessarily originate there—the information about Egypt could all have been gleaned from the Septuagint.[51] Some versions mention thick Ethiopian hair (22:7),[52] but Ethiopians had traveled widely.[53] A honeycomb being "white as snow" (16:8) is not a natural simile in the heat of Egypt; and a potentially offensive comment about Egyptian girls (1:5) might be unsuitable to publish in Egypt, where Egyptians might overhear.[54]

Whether the text is Jewish or Christian, the following groups can helpfully be considered: "pagans" (with some interested outsiders among them); "believers" (with some earlier converts among them); and "converts" (in the process or recently converted). Within the story, pagans are Egyptians; believers are Hebrews; and the convert is Aseneth.[55] There are hints at (perhaps priestly) hierarchy among the believers, in the prophetic role assigned to Levi. If the audience were Jewish, any earlier convert would forever be regarded as a proselyte (given Jewish interest in genealogies and tribal identity). In contrast, if Christian, a larger proportion of the believers might be "earlier converts"; but such converts might, in time, be fully assimilated into the community, as "believers."[56]

Previously Proposed Purposes

A wide range of possible purposes has been discussed, and naturally, scholars' proposals depend strongly on their understanding of the author and their community. Many accept the possibility of multiple purposes, aimed at multiple audiences.[57] It is generally agreed that the story arises out of a desire, within a community resistant to mixed marriages for fear of assimilation and loss of identity, to account for the surprising marriage of a Jewish patriarch to a Gentile.[58] Recent scholarship has included literary analysis and has taken some account of how narratives persuade.[59] Aseneth's conversion has prompted the idea that this text has missionary intent: Philonenko suggests that, as well as addressing Jews, it also addresses Gentiles (Egyptians) as a polemic against idolatry[60] and calls for them to take refuge in the Most High God.[61] Nir suggests that the text was composed among Syrian Christians, to persuade polytheists to become Christians, be baptized, and take a lifelong vow of sexual abstinence.[62]

The text would be most accessible to an audience familiar with the Septuagint and sympathetic toward Jews. This has prompted the idea that the text primarily addresses Jews. Philonenko suggests that, to them, it acts as an apology for mixed marriage (on the basis that the pagan partner converts to Judaism).[63] Barclay adds the idea that the text provides assurance of God's protection, to build the "religious confidence" needed to sustain a minority community.[64] Bohak suggests that the text specifically addresses the Jews of Heliopolis, providing justification for Onias's actions in establishing a Jewish temple and building their community there.[65] Burchard provides a nuanced view of the "Jewish" audience, noting that the text may also address converts to Judaism and perhaps interested God-fearers. Hence, for him, the text primarily reminds believers of the privileges they had either inherited or gained;[66] secondarily, it emphasizes ethics, such as not repaying evil for evil and avoiding non-Jewish women.[67] It may also compete with pagan romances, providing Jewish readers with an alternative.[68]

Scholars have reached their views based on their understanding of the audience and, whether explicitly or not, on their understanding of the message and persuasion built into the text. These various proposed purposes will, therefore, not be presupposed in the analysis that follows. The narrator gives no direct indication of purpose, so discussion of purpose can be delayed until the persuasive elements of the text have been considered.

NOTABLE EXAMPLES OF PERSUASIVE TECHNIQUES

Although many scholars have seen allegorical interpretation as key to understanding this text, they have not reached consensus in their conclusions. This study will limit itself to techniques of persuasion that are discernible in spite of such uncertainties over symbolism.

- P1a) *Overt instruction by narrator.* There is little. When Joseph kisses Aseneth three times, the narrator explains that this imparts to her the spirits of life, wisdom, and truth (19:11, absent from shorter text)—the narrator ascribes a significance that could not otherwise be known by the audience. But this is not directly applicable to them, and the narrator does not provide direct, generalized instruction.
- P1b) *Overt instruction by trusted character.* There is much. An obvious example is Joseph's assertion that, "It is not appropriate for a man who worships God to sleep with his woman/wife before the wedding" (21:1). A more significant example is Joseph's speech to Aseneth in 8:5–7, explaining his refusal to let her (an idol-worshiper) kiss him, including the same words, "It is not appropriate for a man who worships God . . ." (8:5).[69] This provides the inspiration for her repentance.[70] Joseph's similar warning to women who worship God (8:7) is not relevant to the narrative (which involves no Jewish women), but is surely directed at the audience, providing a clear indication that this narrative is intended to communicate a broader, more general message. The heavenly man also has much to say, primarily concerning Aseneth's acceptance and her ongoing role as "City of Refuge" for other Gentiles who convert[71]—suggesting the acceptability of such proselytes in the audience's own context.
- P1c) *Overt instruction by untrustworthy character.* Dan, Gad, Naphtali, and Asher, acting as villains up to this point, rightly affirm, "The Lord fights against us for Aseneth" (28:1) and the Lord "repaid [ἀνταποδίδωμι] us" for our actions (28:3). This plays a part in making God's judgment clear, affirming the ethical lessons indicated by chapters 22–29.
- P2a) *Worldview of the text.* Most of the worldview is expressed by the characters (next paragraph), but the supernatural also contributes. When Aseneth prays for deliverance, Dan, Gad, Naphtali, and Asher's swords fall and disintegrate (27:11).[72] This nonverbal indication of judgment supports the broader theme that God protects those who worship him and who, unlike those conspirators, behave appropriately.
- P2b) *Worldview of trusted characters.* Joseph's worldview is indicated both in his direct statements preventing Aseneth from kissing him (8:5–7) and in the theology of his subsequent prayer for her (8:9). These indications are significant because (at least in the narrative sections) it is these that provide Aseneth with the guidance she needs for meaningful repentance.

The heavenly man's worldview is particularly significant, since it is presented as a revelation from heaven. Although some elements are hard to interpret, it is very clear that Aseneth, because of her appropriate repentance, is accepted and that others—indeed, "many nations"—will similarly follow after her, sheltered under her wings (15:7). Of the honeycomb, the heavenly man affirms that "everyone who eats of it" will, forever, not die (16:14). Such a generalization can be applied to the audience's context, although the esoteric symbolism leaves questions about exactly how.

- P3a) *Positive characterization and empathy*. Aseneth is the central character, with whom empathy is developed. Her initial characterization emphasizes wealth, status, beauty, and virginity: She is highly desirable to men, and women might aspire to be like her. Her flaw of being over-dismissive of men (2:1; 4:9–12)[73] serves, not to make her repulsive, but to introduce a tension that the story must resolve. Her only other "flaw" is that of being an idolater (2:3; 3:6; contextually negative, from Jewish perspective), a further dimension to that tension. Her extensive soliloquies provide a *direct inside view*. Her encounter with the heavenly man provides a particularly striking inside view, involving all the senses: the sight of him (causing her to fall, 14:1–2), sound (as he calls her name, 14:4–8), touch (as she touches his knees, 15:14, and he her head, 16:13), smell (of the honey, 16:9), and taste (to be imagined, as she eats honey, 16:15). The audience is surely intended to identify with her throughout her experiences, and thus to approve both of her and of the course she has taken.
- P3b) *Positive characterization and respect*. Joseph is introduced with titles linking him to God (e.g., "the Powerful One of God," 3:4; "Son of God," 6:3), characterized by virtue and virginity (4:7), and comparable with the sun itself (with rays on his crown, 5:4–6). He is treated as almost superhuman, with no flaws mentioned.[74] The audience is given no direct inside view of his thinking and is thus hardly encouraged to identify with him, responding with respect rather than empathy. Similarly, the heavenly man (naturally, for a heavenly being, 14:1–9) evokes respect rather than empathy. The audience is encouraged to listen with respect to words from these trusted characters.
- P3c) *Positive characterization and sympathy*. Unusually, if there is sympathy evoked here, it is where the characterization has been negative. Dan, Gad, Naphtali, and Asher behave as villains, except that Naphtali and Asher are quick to show remorse (25:5–6). After God thwarts their ambush, they plead for mercy before Aseneth (28:2–6), and Aseneth pleads for them before Simeon. This scene primarily emphasizes how Aseneth and Levi handle the situation mercifully, pacifying the other brothers. But it may also evoke sympathy for the conspirators, which would encourage believers to act with compassion toward fellow believers who have behaved badly.
- P3d) *Aversion*. The conspirators Dan, Gad, Naphtali, and Asher are possible to identify with, as brothers of Joseph and thus tribes of Israel. But their envy and hostility (22:11; 24:2; along with their supernatural defeat,

27:11) suggests to the audience that they must distance themselves from such characters and such behavior.
- P4a) *Repulsive character (through traits)*. Pharaoh's firstborn is portrayed so negatively as to be repulsive. He is jealous of Joseph over Aseneth (23:1), treacherous in conspiring against his father (23:2–6; 24:14), and deceitful (24:7). Given also the negative outcome for him (P5b), the audience is encouraged to hate (or at least avoid) people with such traits.
- P4b) *Repulsive character (through identity)*. By contrast with Aseneth, the text implies that other Egyptian women are short and ugly (1:5). Ironically, her seven virgin attendants are the other Egyptian women described, and they are exceptional (1:6), like her. Nevertheless, anti-Egyptian prejudice, although not emphasized, is evident.
- P5a) *Plot: Positive outcome*. Aseneth receives (from God) at least three obvious positive outcomes: her marriage (21:1–8), salvation from kidnap (27:2–5), and salvation from murder (27:11).[75] The audience will naturally desire such positive outcomes and note that, in Aseneth's case, they arise from her new relationship with God.[76] Hearers who are already believers are thus encouraged to value and put confidence in their relationship with God. If there are hearers who are not believers, they are encouraged to follow Aseneth's example and convert.
- P5b) *Negative outcome*. Pharaoh's firstborn acts as a villain in plotting against his father and against Joseph and Aseneth. He is felled by Benjamin's stone (27:3) and subsequently dies (29:7). This acts as a warning against plotting murder, treason, or kidnap.[77]
- P5c) *Polyphonic affirmation*. The idea that Joseph is a powerful man of God ("firstborn," even, 21:4; and 23:10 in longer text) comes from Pentephres (3:4), Aseneth (6:2–6), a messenger (18:1), Pharaoh (21:4), and Levi (23:10). The idea that Aseneth is now acceptable comes from the heavenly man (15:4), Joseph (19:8), Pharaoh (21:4), and Jacob (22:8).
- P5d) *Journey of discovery*. The hearer is encouraged to identify with Aseneth and thus accompanies her on her journey of discovery. Initially, her idols (2:3; 3:6) represent an obstacle. Pentephres initiates her journey by praising Joseph to her (4:7–8), but her unfounded rejection (4:10) introduces a further obstacle. Her journey continues through experiencing Joseph's glory (which overcomes her objections, 6:1–8),[78] his refusal to let her kiss him (8:5–7), his prayer for her (8:9), her week of penitence and rejecting idols (chs. 10–13), and her encounter with the heavenly man (chs. 14–17). This journey culminates in her wedding, which becomes possible because she has thoroughly converted to Judaism. The romantic aspects of the story are set up so that the audience naturally wants to see the obstacles overcome and a wedding ensue. This leads the audience, imaginatively, to

participate in her journey from despising Joseph and all Jews[79] to respecting them, and from being steeped in idol worship to completely rejecting idols and turning to God. Well-established believers might not fully identify with Aseneth's initial obstacles, but they can identify with the other aspects of her character and enjoy seeing the obstacles removed to their satisfaction. This journey has the effect of reminding them of the privilege involved in being a believer and of persuading them that any proselyte who has wholeheartedly converted should be accepted. Any interested outsider hearing the story would be encouraged to join Aseneth on her journey of conversion.

Is it clear which of these audiences the journey has been tailored for? It is interested outsiders who could most directly identify with Aseneth. But the wider audience analysis (above) might suggest an audience of believers (who would appreciate the Genesis background to the story). Further, some parts of Aseneth's journey are more implied than narrated: She merely deduces Joseph's innocence of sexual misconduct (6:2–3), and she bemoans her rejection by family and others (11:3–6; 12:5, 7, 9–13; and, shorter text, 12:7, 8, 11, Philonenko's referencing), whereas the narrative indicates the opposite (20:6–7). She mentions aspects of God's character that she has heard from "many" (11:10, absent from shorter text), implying that people had told her about God separately from the events described here. Such minor omissions would not matter at all to believers, who would hardly notice them. The gaps are not so serious as to prevent interested outsiders from following Aseneth's journey. But, on the other hand, the text is not carefully prepared for outsiders who are suspicious or even hostile, because such gaps would weaken its case. Further, Aseneth's first experience of Joseph might need "gentle steps," if a suspicious hearer is to be drawn into respecting him. Pentephres's praise (3:4; 4:7–8) may help, but the text provides such a forceful description of the encounter (5:4–6:1) that is better regarded as a "shock of recognition." That would be suitable for a compliant hearer, but would be likely to alienate an initially-suspicious hearer. So this journey of discovery is particularly suitable for interested outsiders, reasonably suitable for believers, but unsuitable for outsiders who are suspicious or hostile.

- P5e) *Gentle steps*. A hearer who shares Joseph's commitment to Jewish men staying separate from foreign women (7:5; 8:5) is led through the gentle steps of Joseph's process of accepting Aseneth—first, as safe, like a sister (7:8); then as needing prayer (8:9); then as accepted by heaven (15:9; 19:5–7, longer text only); and only then finally accepted by Joseph (19:8; 19:2, shorter text).

NARRATIVE PERSUASION

The text is not aimed at pagans who are hostile to believers, since there is no evident attempt to persuade such a hearer to join Aseneth's journey of discovery—rather the gloriously regal description of Joseph would risk provoking scornful dismissal. On the other hand, interested outsiders are encouraged to respond to Aseneth with empathy, accompany her on her journey of discovery, and affirm the behavior that is presented as appropriate for believers. The persuasion built into the text seems appropriate for such a proselytizing purpose.[80] It provides an idealized example for converts to follow.

Recent converts would also naturally show empathy for Aseneth, and they might claim her as their own "city of refuge." Nevertheless, they might find the story problematic because her conversion is described in such idealized terms that any hearer's own conversion experience would (given the messy reality of many conversions)[81] seem pedestrian and halfhearted by comparison. It is also questionable whether their acceptance into the community of believers would have been as wholehearted as Aseneth's. Such a hearer, although surely reassured by Aseneth's acceptance, might also be worried that they themselves do not live up to her example. This ambiguity suggests that recent converts are not the target audience.

Believers already open to the idea of converts joining their community would easily be able to relate to the story, since it supports the possibility of conversion. However, the text has a challenge for them, because it is far from lax about the separation of believers from pagans; rather, it affirms the need for separation (7:7; 8:5), with the only exception being a wholehearted convert who has fully renounced idolatry and taken refuge in God (12:3–6; 15:2–8; 16:14). It is likely that believers would know of relationships and even marriages formed across the boundary without such clear conversion. The idealized form of this story suggests that this group would be challenged by this restriction—since complete rejection of idols is portrayed as prerequisite to conversion and acceptance into the community. The text does not address the practicalities of less-than-complete conversion or less-than-complete acceptance so, although this group is probably an inevitable part of the audience (their perspective is close to that of the narrative, so it is they who would be most likely to take an interest in the text), they are probably not the target audience.

Believers opposed to converts joining the community would, naturally, start by being suspicious of Aseneth. However, the fully respectful characterization of Joseph would help the narrator to win their approval. Aseneth's wholehearted repentance uses poetic language and orthodox theology that would further help to win them over. So the text does take appropriate steps to help such suspicious hearers to develop empathy for Aseneth. There may be relationships and even marriages across the boundary, of which they still disapprove,[82] but this story presents such an idealized conversion, along with accreditation from the heavenly man and from the community of believers, that even the most suspicious hearer is pressed to admit that Aseneth deserves acceptance. The persuasion built into the text is entirely appropriate for persuading suspicious believers that they should accept appropriate converts. However, there is little indication that Aseneth undergoes any rite of initiation performed by the community of believers—her wedding is hardly that, and the honeycomb is administered to her by the heavenly man independently of the community. Nir suggests that her washing (14:15, cf. 18:8–10) indicates baptism,[83] but, again, nobody else is involved in this action. Believers initially opposed to converts would, if persuaded that converts are acceptable in some cases,[84] surely be very interested in the conditions for that acceptance and this would naturally involve a formal process, involving the community or at least its leaders. If these believers opposed to conversion were the only target audience, one would expect the text to be more specific about the necessary conditions[85] and processes for conversion. It is likely that they are a significant part of the audience, but not its entirety.

If the text were created and used by a sect within the community of believers, those already initiated would presumably have been instructed in some esoteric meanings. For them, the text would provide accreditation for those teachings, by explaining how Aseneth had received mysteries from heaven itself and that Levi received ongoing revelation—perhaps pointing to an ongoing prophetic priesthood. For interested outsiders, the text might, through empathy with Aseneth, encourage them to become initiates into the sect. However, such a sect would surely attract initiates primarily from within the wider community of believers, and only secondarily from among pagans. It is not clear that the story of Aseneth, a pagan convert, is the most appropriate story for them. The text would only make sense as a sectarian text if the sect's converts were primarily from paganism, but that did not apply to any of the Jewish sects about which details are available[86] (although it might more plausibly apply to a Christian sect). The persuasion within the text points to the significant boundary being between believers and pagans, and not between initiates into an esoteric sect and other believers. It is not clear that the text arises from such a sect.

CONCLUSIONS

Much has been written about the mysterious symbolism in this text, which is certainly intriguing, but beyond the scope of this study. Analysis of the persuasive techniques discernible within the text provides a less speculative approach to interpretation.

Although it is conceivable that the work is Christian, evidence for that is not convincing—even if some wording could be shown to be Christian, it might have arisen from later editing. The text seems to presuppose (and address) suspicion, among some "believers," of "converts"—a suspicion that is natural among Jews, but not necessarily among Christians (where some communities might consist largely of "converts"). The evidence points more toward a Jewish provenance—although this analysis of persuasion has not depended on that assumption.

The text was evidently written and redacted by those sympathetic to converts joining their believing community. Young believers were surely discouraged by their community from getting romantically involved with outsiders, and the text does still emphasize that boundary. This analysis of persuasion suggests that the text is suitable for persuading other believers, suspicious of conversion, to accept converts (whether or not for the purpose of marriage)—albeit with important constraints, especially that the convert should abandon paganism. However, a story intended only for such an audience would surely be less vague about the processes involved in acceptance by the community. The text is also suitable for persuading interested outsiders to deepen their interest and to follow Aseneth's example, by wholeheartedly converting. Lack of familiarity with Genesis need not be a problem, if a little explanation were provided; rather, it is the symbolism, such as the honeycomb, that would present more of a puzzle. This seems designed to raise questions, so that any uninitiated hearer would have to inquire further.

Thus the most coherent explanation for the persuasive aspects of the text is that it was written in the hope of attracting converts (which is conceivable even if there were only a few interested outsiders), but with the constraint that the text also had to be acceptable to those within the community of believers who were opposed to relationships with pagans and inclined to oppose conversion. The romantic aspects of the story are enough to account for its preservation, for entertainment within a community of believers, whether or not conversion was an ongoing process.

Consideration of this text has extended this study, from works in the style of classical historiography (*Embassy* and *War*) to a work which adopts biblical style, linked especially to the Septuagint version of Genesis. Whereas Philo and Josephus, as eyewitnesses, are prominent narrators, the narrator of *Aseneth* is less prominent, with the main persuasive content put in the mouths of the characters. Concerning persuasion, this study of *Aseneth* has shown how the taxonomy can be applied to a text of rather different style. It has helpfully revealed prominent use of three approaches that were not noted in those examples of historiography: First, supernatural visions and events are vital to the narrative, with the heavenly man providing the most forceful authenticating device for the message, as well as providing much of its content. Secondly, *Aseneth* provides an example of a prominent "journey of discovery" as a way of encouraging the hearer to share in the experiences and responses of the main character. Thirdly, it employs puzzling imagery, which suggests that the text is designed to encourage the hearer to inquire further. This is a literary device, rather than a technique of persuasion—an indication that this text played a part in a wider process.

NOTES

1. Humphrey, *Aseneth*, 80–81, speaks of its "primary characteristic as a persuasive story" (80).
2. Cf. Ps 135 (136), which repeats, "His mercy endures for ever."
3. Also, in the longer text only, 11:3–14, 16–18.
4. Christoph Burchard, "Joseph and Aseneth," in OTP 2:161–212, citing 186.
5. The shorter versions of the text (Group d) are about a third shorter than the longest (Group a): Burchard, "Aseneth," 180.
6. Ross S. Kraemer, *When Aseneth Met Joseph: A Late Antique Tale of the Biblical Patriarch and His Egyptian Wife, Reconsidered* (New York: Oxford University Press, 1998), 247–74.
7. After LXX had become available, so no earlier than second century BC, Burchard, "Aseneth," 187.
8. Burchard, "Aseneth," 181.
9. Burchard, "Aseneth," 178–79; Uta Barbara Fink, *Joseph und Aseneth: Revision des griechischen Textes und Edition der zweiten lateinischen Übersetzung* (Berlin: De Gruyter, 2008), 14–197.
10. Marc Philonenko, *Joseph et Aséneth: Introduction, Texte Critique et Notes* (Leiden: Brill, 1968), 128–221; Greek, with French translation.
11. Christoph Burchard, "Ein Vorläufiger Griechischer Text von *Joseph und Aseneth*," in idem, *Gesammelte Studien zu Joseph und Aseneth* (Leiden: Brill, 1996), 161–212; Burchard, "Aseneth," 202–47, provides an English translation.
12. E.g., Kraemer, *Reconsidered*, prefers the shorter text but also refers to the longer text.
13. Burchard, "Aseneth," 200; conveniently, Burchard also shows Philonenko's divisions.
14. Rivka Nir, *Joseph and Aseneth: A Christian Book* (Sheffield: Sheffield Phoenix, 2012), 177 asserts; Kraemer, *Reconsidered*, 40, "not inconceivable."
15. E.g., similar links to Genesis at 1:1 and 22:1–2; Burchard, "Aseneth," 182.
16. 11:3–6; 12:5, 7, 9–13. (The shorter text omits most of chapter 11, including these references, but has similar references at 12:7, 8, 11, using Philonenko's referencing.)

17. Aseneth's receiving of bread-cup-ointment is also inconsistent: The narrative reports honeycomb from the heavenly man; he proclaims that she has received bread-cup-ointment (16:16, cf. promises at 8:5; 15:5), as does she (19:5), yet her prayer indicates provision by Joseph (21:21, absent from shorter text).

18. Barclay, *Diaspora*, 204–16, esp. 213.

19. τὴν Ἀσενὲθ θυγατέρα Πετεφρῆ ἱερέως Ἡλιουπόλεως (LXX).

20. Shorter text omits the year.

21. Burchard, *Studien*, 305–06, who lists scriptural allusions.

22. Both absent from the Greek, but reconstructed from Syriac and Armenian versions; Burchard, *Studien,* 193 n. 31; 199 n. 63.

23. The male child remains (12:7, Philonenko's numbering), but with added mention of his mother.

24. Humphrey, *Aseneth*, 73; cf. Song 4:5; 7:3, 8; 8:10; but comparison with apples (8:5) has Greek rather than Hebrew provenance (Burchard, "Aseneth," 211 n. h, citing Aristophanes and Theocritus). At 8:1–5, Pentephres encourages Joseph and Aseneth, as committed virgins, to embrace as brother and sister. But the narrator's comments on Aseneth's breasts (and sibling language used of sexual intimacy in Song 4:10; 8:1–2) suggests that the audience would hear the situation as sexually charged. Especially in the longer text, virginity is part of, and not a substitute for, the theme of erotic love.

25. Humphrey, *Aseneth*, 67–74.

26. The longer text has stronger monotheistic emphasis (11:7–8; 18:11; 20:7; 21:13; 27:10, all absent from the shorter text).

27. Barclay, *Diaspora*, 208.

28. Chesnutt, *Conversion*, 103. Philonenko, *Aséneth*, 106, speculates that the author was an Egyptian convert or one born of a mixed marriage.

29. Possibly also "city of refuge" from Num 35:6–28; Deut 4:41–43; 19:1–14; Josh 20:1–9.

30. Pentephres's affirmation that Joseph is a virgin (8:1) does not refute the accusation of attempted rape (Gen 39:14).

31. Kee, "Socio-Cultural Setting," 410; i.e., the meaning was known only within a particular group.

32. τὰ ἀπόρρητα μυστήρια τοῦ ὑψίστου.

33. τὰ ἄρρητα θεοῦ τοῦ ὑψίστου . . . κρυφῇ.

34. Burchard, *Studien*, 307.

35. Burchard, "Aseneth," 187; idem, *Studien*, 302.

36. Philonenko, *Aséneth*, 106–09.

37. Philonenko, *Aséneth*, 106.

38. Bohak, *Heliopolis*, 85.

39. Bohak, *Heliopolis*, 86.

40. Kraemer, *Reconsidered*, 251.

41. Burchard, "Aseneth," 187, "perhaps some Christian interpolations."

42. Kraemer, *Reconsidered*, 10, 250; using the shorter text.

43. Nir, *Christian Book*, vii. But there are hints at Joseph's observance of the Sabbath (9:5) and Jewish eating habits (7:1).

44. Nir, *Christian Book*, 179, with bees representing the souls of virgins, 90–115.

45. Nir, *Christian Book*, 176; *contra* Chesnutt, *Conversion*, 257.

46. Chesnutt, *Conversion*, 74.

47. Mention of distinctively Jewish practices would emphasize separation rather than cordiality. That Aseneth is a woman is enough to explain the absence of any reference to circumcision.

48. Judith 9:2–5; *Jub.* 30:17, 23; *Testament of Levi* 2:1–4; 5:3; 6:8; Philo, *On the Migration of Abraham* 224. There are four ancient Jewish authors who comment on Simeon and Levi's action, all positively. (Also Theodotus, quoted by Eusebius, *Preparation for the Gospel* 9:22, but he may well be Samaritan, not Jewish, since he calls Shechem a holy city. Josephus, *Antiquities* 1:337–342, mentions the incident, but without any decisive comment.)

49. Tertullian, *Against the Jews* 10:8–9; Ambrose, *Jacob and the Happy Life* 9:38; Chrysostom, *Homily on Genesis* 59:12; Gregory the Great, *Letter to Domitian*, Book 3, Letter 67 (*NPNF*2 12:142–43); Cyril of Alexandria, *Glapyhra on Genesis* 5:174B–C. There are five ancient Christian authors who comment, all negatively. (Saint Ephrem the Syrian, *Commentary on Genesis*, 31, mentions the incident, but without any decisive comment.) Bayesian analysis, based on these surviving known-Jewish and known-Christian views, indicates 85 percent probability that *Aseneth* (being positive about this incident) is a Jewish text.

50. Kraemer, *Reconsidered*, 291, although she expresses a preference for Syria.

51. Kraemer, *Reconsidered*, 286.

52. Some longer texts, but absent from the Greek manuscripts and shorter texts; in Syriac, "Ethiopian" is replaced by "Indian," Burchard, "Aseneth," 238 n.h.

53. E.g., Isa 18:1–2; Acts 8:27.

54. Barclay, *Diaspora*, 214: "'Egyptian' is a term of abuse throughout."

55. Aseneth's seven virgin handmaids are a further group character (with one separated from the rest momentarily in 10:4); a flat character, acting as an accompaniment to Aseneth.

56. Although divisions between Jewish and Gentile Christians did persist: Rom 3:30; Gal 3:28.

57. Kee, "Socio-Cultural Setting," 409; similarly Randall D. Chesnutt, "The Social Setting and Purpose of Joseph and Aseneth," *Journal for the Study of the Pseudepigrapha* 1, no. 2 (April 1988): 21–48, especially 40–41.

58. Eckart Reinmuth, ed., *Joseph und Aseneth* (Tübingen: Mohr Siebeck, 2009), 26–28; Kraemer, *Reconsidered*, 294. For Jewish prohibition on mixed marriages, even stricter than scriptural requirements and with no provision for conversion, see *Jub.* 30:7–17.

59. Humphrey, *Aseneth*; Chesnutt, *Conversion*, 97–117.

60. Philonenko, *Aséneth*, 106. Barclay, *Diaspora*, 204, 207.

61. Philonenko, *Aséneth*, 106. The case against a Gentile audience is made by Burchard, "Aseneth," 194–95, and Chesnutt, *Conversion*, 257–62, based on lack of accessibility and persuasiveness.

62. Nir, *Christian Book*, 178.

63. Philonenko, *Aséneth*, 106; Chesnutt, *Conversion*, 260.

64. Barclay, *Diaspora*, 216.

65. Bohak, *Heliopolis*, 101–2, by seeming to foretell these things.
66. Burchard, "Aseneth," 195; Chesnutt, *Conversion*, 262.
67. Burchard, "Aseneth," 195; Chesnutt, *Conversion*, 262; Humphrey, *Aseneth*, 100, 111.
68. Burchard, *Studien*, 305.
69. οὐκ ἔστι προσῆκον ἀνδρὶ θεοσεβεῖ. Similar phrases are used to introduce sayings against returning evil for evil (23:9; 29:3) or injuring (23:12, absent from longer text).
70. As indicated by Aseneth's echoing of Joseph's words, e.g., mention of idols in 12:5 (and 13:11, absent from shorter text) echoes 8:5.
71. 15:7; 17:6, then echoed (in the longer text only) by Aseneth (19:5) and Joseph (19:8).
72. The terrified response to Simeon and Levi's swords flashing "like fire" (23:15, longer text only) might also suggest the supernatural.
73. Her confessions echo this: 6:3, 5, 7.
74. Those aware of Gen 39:12 know that Aseneth's accusation that he slept with his mistress (4:10) is untrue. The characterization of Joseph here (with respect) is different from that in Genesis, which encourages empathy with direct inside views, Gen 42:7–9, 24; 43:30; 45:1.
75. Pharaoh also survives attempted assassination (25:1–4), but he is a flat character; he is not the focus, but his survival moves the plot along, and he soon dies, brokenhearted (29:8).
76. 15:2–6; 27:10–11. Benjamin and Leah's sons also played a heroic part (27:5–6).
77. His villainy is vital for the plot, in chs. 23–29; he provides a foil, allowing Simeon and Levi's virtue to show through when they refuse to join him (23:2–17).
78. She instantly designates Joseph as a "son of God" (6:3), apparently dismissing the rumors about him.
79. Any Jew could be dismissed as a "shepherd's son from the land of Canaan" (4:10).
80. Even those unfamiliar with LXX would have little disadvantage in trying to follow the story, although brief explanations from Genesis might be needed.
81. The existence of "God-fearers" who had not become full proselytes (e.g., Acts 13:26) indicates complexity within the concept of conversion to Judaism. Simon Magus (Acts 8:9–24) provides an example of an ambiguous conversion to Christianity; Arthur D. Nock, *Conversion: The Old and the New in Religion from Alexander the Great to Augustine of Hippo* (London: Oxford University Press, 1965), 68, notes limitations on wives' religious freedom; Pliny reports converts who claimed to have abandoned Christianity (156–163).
82. Timothy's Jewish mother and Greek father did not circumcise him (Acts 16:1–3).
83. Nir, *Christian Book*, 56–63.
84. An ongoing issue—other converts will follow Aseneth (15:7; and, longer text only, 16:14–16).
85. The text presents an idealized convert, but does not address the question of whether and how far a convert may fall short of the ideal and still be accepted.
86. Chesnutt, *Conversion*, 254.

Chapter Six

Narrative Persuasion in the *Letter of Aristeas*

Overview of *Aristeas*

This chapter investigates the techniques of persuasion built into the *Letter of Aristeas*. This text presents Jewish ideas in Greek through a narrative set in the culturally Greek context of Alexandria. An account of an embassy is provided, ostensibly for the benefit of a Gentile reader who values learning, but the pro-Jewish worldview and emphatic reverence for the Jewish Law and its Greek translation suggest an intent to influence, not merely to inform.

Aristeas may have been known to the author of Luke-Acts;[1] it was certainly used as a source by Josephus[2] and perhaps by Philo.[3] Christians preserved it, probably not for its literary merit,[4] but as the earliest surviving account of the origin of the Septuagint.[5] Although scholars were in the past primarily concerned with historical reliability,[6] the author's use of a variety of styles indicates the need for literary analysis, which has recently come to the fore in interpreting *Aristeas*.[7]

The contents of *Aristeas* suggest that it would have been heard by its early audiences as an autobiographical historical treatise with didactic intent. It describes itself as a narrative[8] for the "the soul's edification,"[9] for a lover of learning. It emphasizes historical reliability,[10] claiming eyewitness accounts,[11] copies of official documents[12] and access to official records (297–300). So it is presented as an historical narrative or treatise. It has the form of a personal letter,[13] but is evidently intended for general circulation.[14] Its literary style suggests composition with oral delivery in mind. Although the author has put effort into unifying the work, with narratorial asides linking the sections,[15] the text employs a striking variety of styles, characteristic of exercises in rhetorical education, *progymnasmata*.[16] The use of various sources might be a factor in this, but the author is surely demonstrating his Greek education.[17] The

Symposium is the longest section (187–294; with an apology for this, 295) with a tightly controlled structure (seventy-two questions and answers). It is reminiscent of Greek philosophical symposia[18] and, in kingship, addresses a well-attested theme of Greek literature.[19] The description of the king's gifts (51b–82) is an example of ἔκφρασις (vivid description).[20] Eleazar's exposition of the Law (130–169) is like an apologetic philosophical treatise.[21] The description of Jerusalem and its territory (83–120), with elements of ἔκφρασις,[22] also has elements of a Greek travelogue (despite omitting details of the journey, promised at 83). Idealized details[23] suggest this might be "utopian geography," but it is not clear that the hearer is expected to discern this—it is presented as a reliable account of an impressive journey.[24]

Greek quotations are from Thackeray's text.[25] Textual variations are relatively minor and have no significant bearing on this analysis of persuasion. The narrator ("Aristeas") has to be distinguished from the author (who will not be referred to as "Aristeas").

Summary of the Story

The narrator, who is also a key character, is Aristeas,[26] a courtier of King Ptolemy II (later known as Philadelphus)[27] in Alexandria.[28] Aristeas addresses the text to his brother Philocrates (*Let. Aris.* 1–8),[29] recently arrived (5, so events are portrayed as recent).

Demetrius of Phalerum suggests that the "laws of the Jews"[30] should be translated for the royal Library; the king agrees (9–11). Aristeas pleads for the release of Jewish slaves, which the king generously implements (12–27). Aristeas is sent to Jerusalem with the king's letter to the high priest, Eleazar (35–40; requesting six elders from each tribe, to translate),[31] and lavish gifts for the Temple (51b–82). Eleazar sends back a letter (41–46) and seventy-two elders (47–51). Aristeas provides glowing descriptions of Jerusalem (83–107, especially the Temple), of its surroundings (107–120), and of the elders (121–127). Questioned, Eleazar provides an exposition of the Law (130–69), which Aristeas applauds (170–171, cf. 133).

The king pays exaggerated respect to the scrolls and then to the elders, whom he invites to a banquet (173–186), provided according to Jewish customs (181–183). Seven banquets ensue (187–294, conveniently referred to as "the Symposium").[32] The king questions each elder on the general theme of kingship. Each answer would be recognizable to Greeks as a wise saying, but with a reference also to God's involvement (distinctive of Jewish wisdom, 200–201). The king is delighted (293–294).

The elders carry out the translation, reaching agreement and finishing, as if providentially, in seventy-two days (307). Demetrius assembles the Jews to hear it; their leaders approve (310), and anybody modifying it is cursed (311). It is read to the king, who is impressed (312); Greeks who had previously quoted these texts had been smitten (Theopompus and Theodectus, 313–316). The translation is preserved in the Library (317). The king provides lavish gifts and bids farewell to the elders (318–321). A brief epilogue (322) promises Philocrates a further document.

Narrator and Author

Aristeas, the narrator, is actively involved as a character almost throughout.[33] There is little to distinguish the narrator (prominent in prologue, narratorial asides, and epilogue) from Aristeas the character (involved in the events)—their literary functions are different, but their points of view coincide.

Aristeas is a trusted courtier of King Ptolemy (40). He is consistently portrayed as a Gentile—a Greek[34] who values education (1–2) and piety (2)[35] and wants to understand the things of God (3). He asserts that Jews and Greeks worship the same God by different names, and prays on behalf of Jews to the creator and lord "of all" (17–18)—pious by both Greek and Jewish standards. Aristeas is positively disposed toward Jews (humane and pious, 18), asking for explanations (129, 306) and showing respect (for Eleazar, 170, and the elders, 306). Aristeas has written previously to Philocrates concerning Jews (6), and he promises a further document (322); so this text is presented as the middle of three works—perhaps a literary device to indicate that much more is worth knowing.[36] The reference to an earlier work might indicate pseudepigraphy—there was a history of the Jews by an Aristeas,[37] but he was probably not prestigious enough to for his name to be worth adopting.[38]

The author of *Aristeas,* unlike the narrator, is evidently not a Gentile but a Jew (or, possibly, a well-informed proselyte). The tone is pro-Jewish,[39] the narrator's point of view seems Jewish,[40] and only a Jew would be aware of and concerned about some of the details, e.g., original arrangement of the twelve tribes (97);[41] detailed dietary regulations (mice, 144; cloven hoofs, 150); and ceremonial washing (306).[42] Aristeas's questions (129, 306) provide an opportunity for the answers Jewish respondents wish to provide; he acts as a foil. The author is aware of the Septuagint, with no evident awareness of the Hebrew.[43] He seems aware of the geographical details of Alexandria (301) and of court titles, language, and processes (maybe more appropriate to later generations of the Ptolemaic court,[44] and generally correct, so he might have had access to court).[45] Alexandria is his most likely location, given his Greek education, general awareness of philosophical ideas,[46] and respect for the Library there, with its literary scholarship.[47] Inconsistent tenses are far from conclusive, but might suggest a later author failing to be consistent in his attempts to present the text as near-contemporary with events[48]—present tenses suggest that Philadelphus (21)[49] and Eleazar (96–98)[50] remain alive; however, imperfect tenses are also used of royal activities, which would allow the possibility that the king is now dead.[51]

Aristeas is unusual, in that it seems to be written under an invented, but not famous, name. The Jewish author presumably expected to achieve more credibility by presenting the work as that of an educated and influential Greek courtier. The narrator accredits Eleazar and the Jewish elders, affirming, through "Greek" eyes, the appropriateness of the (Diaspora) Jewish worldview this text associates with them.[52]

Audience

The stated audience is Aristeas's brother, Philocrates, who has an interest in holiness (5) and learning (7). All who love learning will also be interested (7), and future audiences are mentioned—those who will have the work passed on to them (296).[53]

The implied audience is in Egypt, since they are expected to realize that "the city" (4) means Alexandria. Initial audiences are likely to have been in Alexandria, which is central to the narrative. But native Egyptians are not among the intended audience; they are described as foolish because of their worship of animals (138),[54] and an Egyptian hearer would feel insulted. Nor are women the target audience, since women's reasoning is derided.[55]

The text assumes an audience aware of standard virtues from Greek philosophy—it is liberally scattered with them,[56] e.g., "justice and piety" (24);[57] "most philosophical and flawless" (31);[58] "the mean" (122).[59] The hearer is assumed to approve of Greek education and to be familiar with basic philosophical terms—which would apply to most Greeks, and many Jews of Alexandria (maybe not of Palestine); but anyone hostile to Greek culture[60] would be alienated—they are not the intended audience. The idealized description of Palestine (83–120)[61] suggests that the audience must be either unfamiliar with it or already well-disposed toward idealized presentations of it.

No more than a rudimentary awareness of Judaism is required, to follow the basic meaning. Hacham argues that knowledge of the book of Exodus is necessary, so that the (Jewish) audience interprets *Aristeas* as a new Exodus, a foundation story (justifying residence in Egypt).[62] Such connections may perhaps add a layer of meaning, but without them the text is certainly neither meaningless nor incoherent. Rather, I suggest that the audience is treated to an account of Judaism without any evident assumption of prior knowledge; explanations are given—about the language of the Law (11) and why Greeks had not previously heard excerpts (313–316). A hearer ignorant of Judaism would be neither confused nor embarrassed.[63]

The text does not address Greeks actively hostile to Jews—the narrator does not even acknowledge contentious issues,[64] let alone address them, leaving such an audience struggling to identify with either the characters or the plot. Rather, Aristeas would be dismissed as a stooge. Scholars have recently tended to exclude Gentiles from the audience altogether. Honigman assumes an exclusively Jewish audience, but this seems to be based on a circular argument linked to her proposed purpose of the text, a "charter myth" aimed at Jews. Her case for this is that the comparison between Jerusalem (an average city, συμμετρέω, 105) and Alexandria (of great size, "surpassing," ὑπερβάλλω, 109) is "clearly aimed at Jews" because it is derogatory about Alexandria—since Aristotle prescribes average size for the ideal city.[65] This is an obscure and unconvincing argument. Rather, Alexandria is said to surpass all other cities not only in size but also in εὐδαιμονία (prosperity, good fortune, 109), surely a positive epithet, and was so attractive that immigration had once caused problems for agriculture elsewhere. Gentiles should not be excluded from the audience on such a tenuous basis.

Some suggest that Greeks would be amused or offended[66] by the account of Philadelphus bowing before the Law. Admittedly, there would have been Jews who would be horrified at the idea of bowing before any symbol of a pagan deity.[67] But Greeks (and, later, Romans)[68] were generally willing to show respect and even worship foreign deities. Alexander the Great himself had traveled to Siwa, in the Libyan desert, to present gifts and consult the oracle of the Egyptian god Ammon.[69] A Greek hearer would not necessarily scoff at such respect for these scrolls, portrayed as the very oracles of God (177). Greeks should not be excluded from the audience on this basis.

There are aspects of the text that do suggest Greeks among the audience. An educated Greek would find in *Aristeas* affirmation rather than anything offensive.[70] The explanations would help any Greek hearer willing to listen. Apologetic is evident when Eleazar denies that Moses was preoccupied with mice and weasels (144), refuting an (albeit minor) allegation. Although there would have been those among the Jewish audience who would be delighted if Aristeas expressed respect for circumcision, Sabbath, and the avoidance of pork (as he does of other aspects of Judaism), these are not mentioned. The text surely glosses over such divisive issues for the sake of Greek hearers, to maintain a harmonious impression of Greek-Jewish relations.

A note of caution: Since Aristeas and Philocrates seem to be invented personas, there is a possibility that the implied audience may also be invented—distorted to add verisimilitude to the account. The text would not provide enough evidence for that to be identified, let alone resolved.

In summary, *Aristeas* is aimed at Greek speakers, probably in Alexandria (at least initially), who are familiar with and favorable toward Greek culture and who are not hostile toward Jews. Egyptians are excluded, but it is not clear that either Greeks or Jews can be excluded.[71] The effort put into presenting Judaism from a Greek perspective (and avoiding divisive topics) suggests Greeks within the implied audience, while other details seem to be of particular interest to Jews.

Date and Context

The date of composition is probably between 247 and 116 BC. It is not clear that one can be more specific, unless one proposes a specific purpose for the text, related to a specific historical situation. Composition in Alexandria seems likely. The events are presented as occurring during the reign of King Ptolemy II (Philadelphus, 285–247 BC) and Arsinoe.[72] There is scholarly consensus that *Aristeas* was actually written in Alexandria, but in a later generation, because various errors and anachronisms have been noted. Most significantly, *Aristeas* presents Demetrius of Phalerum as respected head of King Philadelphus's library; but Diogenes Laertius suggests that Demetrius supported Philadelphus's rivals and, upon Soter's death, was detained by Philadelphus and died mysteriously.[73]

Aristeas was certainly known to Josephus by about AD 100 and it seems to predate Roman power (30 BC).[74] Mention of some Jews holding offices of state (37) might suggest a date after ca. 180 BC, and Shutt suggests that *Aristeas* emphasizes toleration as a reaction against hostilities in Jerusalem around 170 BC. Murray considers a date as late as 100 BC, when Jews played a partisan military role under Cleopatra III (who reigned from 116 BC).[75] But this text gives no indication of a military role for Jews; evidence for such a late date is weak.

There is also significant work that has placed *Aristeas* earlier within the Ptolemaic period, although after Philadelphus's death in 246. Thackeray suggests that the political situation in Palestine indicates a date before the Seleucid conquest of 198 BC.[76] Hadas suggests that similarities to a known decree of Philadelphus point to an early date, and that the Zenon papyri of 259 BC reflect the same political situation between Palestine and Egypt.[77]

Previously Proposed Purposes

There has been a shift in the suggested audience from Greek (e.g., Meecham, 1935) to predominantly Jewish (e.g., Hadas, 1951) to exclusively Jewish (Tcherikover, 1958, and most scholars since). Proposed purposes reflect this evolution.

If addressed to Greeks, *Aristeas* may be apologetic, defending Jews and Judaism.[78] It may even aim to attract Greeks to the Septuagint.[79] If addressed to Jews, a wider range of possible purposes emerges. It may encourage Jewish confidence in their own community and doctrines,[80] perhaps aiming to "bring up a generation of educated Jews, who would be able to live on equal terms with the Greek citizens of Alexandria."[81] It may encourage positive engagement with their Greek neighbors.[82] It may aim to provide a charter myth for the Jewish community in Egypt, retelling Exodus to justify their residence there (despite the Torah's reservation about return to Egypt, Deut 17:16).[83] In contrast, Carbonaro associates *Aristeas* with Onias and Heliopolis, as "a political pamphlet urging the fall of the Hasmonaean dynasty."[84] But his allegorical interpretation is speculative and particularly hard to verify.

On the other hand, many scholars see the focus as being on some Greek translation of Scripture, presumably some form of the Septuagint. Kahle suggests that *Aristeas* supported the introduction of a new, authorized Greek version.[85] But he sees *Aristeas* as a story pretending to relate how Scripture had been translated many years before, and it is not clear how that would support a new translation. More credibly, *Aristeas* might support an old version against a new rival.[86] Such specific suggestions are speculative, but wider acceptance has greeted the more cautious suggestion that *Aristeas* provides a "charter myth"[87] or "foundation myth"[88] about the Septuagint's origins, demonstrating its quality and advocating its status as a sacred text. So, although various other suggestions persist, the general thrust of recent scholarly opinion interprets *Aristeas* as a text for Egyptian Jews, authenticating the Septuagint.

NOTABLE EXAMPLES OF PERSUASIVE TECHNIQUES

The text displays the literary abilities of the author, through its variety of literary styles, but such a display is unlikely to be the main aim. Since there seems to be a gap of a generation or more between Aristeas and the actual author, there would have been no opportunity for the author to take any credit.

- P1a) *Overt instruction by narrator.* The prologue indicates from the outset that the narrator adopts a didactic role, with early asides extolling learning and piety (2).[89] When Aristeas the character prays, the narrator explains that people are God's creation (17)[90] and that, when they think of a righteous act, God guides them (18).[91] The narrator's position fits within the overlap between an educated Greek and a Diaspora Jew. But the narrator's asides focus less on teaching under his own authority than on establishing the authority of the trusted characters, e.g., Eleazar is mentioned as having explained "accurately" (133).[92] At the end of Eleazar's speech, Aristeas (as narrator and character) commends him: "To me he seemed to make a defense in every respect excellent" (170, cf. 112);[93] of the seventy-two elders, he comments that they surpassed the philosophers "in their conduct and discourse" (235).[94]

- P1b) *Overt instruction by trusted character.* Eleazar, who is portrayed entirely positively, is permitted a long speech (130–169), a letter (41–46), and a noteworthy saying: A good life "consists in observing the laws; and this is achieved by listening much more than by reading" (127). This emphasizes the importance of the Law and that, rather than being a library book for a scholar to read (as Greeks might expect), a group or community should gather and hear it, presumably with the implication of discussing and intending to obey it.[95] Eleazar's speech (130–169) defends the Law as being, not arbitrary tradition, but suffused (through allegorical interpretation) with ethical meaning, e.g., eating domesticated but not carnivorous birds indicates that one must be "just and achieve nothing by force" (148); indeed, "All . . . supports justice" (169). The hearer is thus encouraged to accept that the Jewish Law makes good sense by the standards of Greek thought.
- P1c) *Overt instruction by untrustworthy character.* None of the significant characters is untrustworthy.
- P2a) *Worldview of the text.* This text mixes two cultural worldviews—Diaspora Jewish and Alexandrian Greek (with an emphasis on education and philosophy—although also on a singular God,[96] rather than on myths[97] or polytheism).[98] The narrator treats the Law with great respect (in writing "of gold," 176, a universally positive epithet). There is no hint of Greek hostility toward Jews, and little evidence of Jewish hostility toward Greeks.[99] The worldview presented consists of the overlap between these two cultures.[100] The hearer is encouraged to believe that Greeks can, without any abandonment of their ethical and intellectual ideals, not merely tolerate, but respect and even revere Judaism, and that Jews can, without any abandonment of their commitment and obedience to the Law, engage in friendly and constructive ways with educated Greeks.

The text finds limited place for the supernatural or miraculous. Having explained his belief that God answers pious prayers (18), the narrator interprets the freeing of Jewish slaves as simultaneously Philadelphus's generosity and God's answer to prayer (20). When the seventy-two translators finish in exactly seventy-two days, he cautiously comments that this is as though "by some deliberate design" (307).[101] The hearer is invited to see this as providential—a gentle claim of divine authentication, both of Judaism and of this translation, in wording acceptable both to those Greeks who might expect skepticism from a serious historian and to those Jews who might expect explicit faith in God as prerequisite for an authoritative writer.

- P2b) *Worldview of trusted characters*. Demetrius (a famous Greek writer) is portrayed here as a scholarly and conscientious librarian convinced of the importance of the Jewish Law, not merely as another book to collect, but because it is "most philosophical and flawless, since it is divine" (31).[102] The audience is invited to share his assessment. King Philadelphus is portrayed as scholarly (294) and generous (21, 26, 51–82). He hears advice and takes decisive action, but he has a less prominent role in teaching. Noteworthy are his benign attitude toward Jews (37–38) and extreme reverence for the Jewish Law (176–179) as "oracles" of God (177).[103] But, in persuasiveness, the most prominent trusted character is Eleazar. His worldview is communicated primarily through his teaching (see P1b), but also through the respectful and friendly terms in which he addresses Philadelphus (41–46) and his respect and concern for the elders (123–126).

- P3a) *Positive characterization and empathy*. The narrator indicates his own ideals, especially in the prologue and epilogue, and provides *direct inside views* of Aristeas, the character (12, 17–18), thus establishing his piety (3, 18) and building the audience's empathy with him—to the extent that they are led with him on a journey of discovery (P5d). The audience is thus drawn into Aristeas's respect for Jews and their Law.

- P3b) *Positive characterization and respect*. King Philadelphus is characterized entirely positively,[104] and with respect (e.g., his lavish gifts reflect his majesty, 79, and imply generous piety), although, when he is first introduced, this seems more assumed than emphasized. Since he was famous,[105] the audience would already be aware of his power and reputation as a patron of learning. So, *Aristeas*, rather than establishing his reputation, presumes it and uses it to show that such an important figure was favorable toward and impressed by Jews and their Law.

Eleazar receives respect, not only as high priest, but also for his achievements ("usefulness," 3) and character ("good character and renown," 3; "virtue," 122; "loved," 123).[106] So the hearer is to listen with respect to Eleazar's teaching and worldview. The seventy-two elders are selected for their expertise in the Law and in Greek, but they are further represented as exemplary (32, 39, 46), of esteemed (ἔνδοξος) parents (121), without conceit (122), and as giving outstanding answers (122, 235, 293–294). The audience will thus be attentive to their educational teaching on kingship, but their main task is to be translators, so respect for them also builds respect for the translation—for, although the Law and the translation are not

exactly characters, they are also presented entirely positively and as worthy of respect (31, 177, 310–11, 317).
- P3c) *Positive characterization and sympathy*. There are indications that Aristeas feels sympathy toward the Jewish slaves, whose "wretchedness"[107] he mentions to the king (15). The audience is aware of that, but the narrative does no more to develop sympathy. The king focuses on justice (23–24), not compassion.
- P3d) *Aversion*. There is none.
- P4a) *Repulsive character (by traits)*. "Informers" (ἐμφανιστής) are briefly mentioned, in an exchange between Eleazar and Aristeas (166–167). Eleazar characterizes them negatively, as people who speak with malicious intent, hoping to see others destroyed. Aristeas affirms that the king deals most severely with them. This might call to mind the sycophant (συκοφάντης) as stock villain of Greek comedy,[108] or the ninth commandment against false testimony (ψευδομαρτυρέω, Exod 20:16, cf. καταμαρτυρέω, used of Naboth's accusers, 3 Kgdms 20:8–14). Any hearer is expected to assent to this generalization, and regard informers with hostility.
- P4b) *Repulsive character (by identity)*. Eleazar comments that Egyptians (among others) are infatuated with theriolatry. For Jewish hearers, this affirms Jewish hostility toward idolaters (and idolatry, e.g., Exod 20:2–6). Educated Greeks were less hostile, but perhaps scornful of Egyptian religion.[109] Eleazar's comment is too brief to arouse hostility in a hearer who is not already hostile. Rather, this would be suitable to persuade a hearer already scornful of Egyptian religion to harden that attitude and to see Judaism as different and superior.
- P5a) *Plot: Positive outcome*. Having achieved their task, the seventy-two elders return home with valuable gifts and an open invitation to return (318–321),[110] further encouraging respect for them. The king is presented as gladly paying to liberate Jewish slaves and sending precious gifts (justice and piety being his aim, 24, cf. 42). In return, he receives profitable teaching (294) from "cultured" men (321; literally "educated," παιδεύω); scrolls worthy of inclusion in the Library (10) and of being "preserved reverently" (317);[111] and, by implication, his desired outcomes of benefiting all Jews (38) and achieving "renown" (39, cf. 79; perhaps an allusion to *Aristeas* itself). The king's pious interest in Judaism is rewarded, which would encourage Greek hearers also to take such an interest. But that is not a major purpose, since the text develops little empathy with the king and does not emphasize these positive outcomes for him. The text does more to encourage the hearer to identify with Aristeas (P3a), but in his case there is even less emphasis on a positive outcome;[112] the process is better described as a "journey of discovery" (P5d).

- P5b) *Negative outcome*. The brief stories about Theopompus (314–315) and Theodectus (316) are classic examples of cautionary tales. These men considered including material from the Jewish Law, but were physically afflicted; attributing this to God, they abandoned the idea and recovered. This explains why earlier Greek writers did not mention the Law (312). Contrast with the (unscathed) elders provides divine authentication of the seventy-two. The stories provide a warning not to quote, interpret, or translate these divine words (31, 177, 313) lightly,[113] and, perhaps, not to attempt to translate the Law into Greek again—the approved text should now be quoted (cf. 310–311).
- P5c) *Polyphonic affirmation*. There is polyphonic respect for the new translation, on which Demetrius and the seventy-two agree (302–303), and which is then wholeheartedly approved by the Alexandrian Jews (310–311) and by the king (312, 317).
- P5d) *Journey of discovery*. Aristeas was already positive toward Judaism (12, 15), so his experiences can hardly be said to change his attitude. But they do deepen his knowledge and respect. His confidence that God answers pious prayers (18) is affirmed by the king's release of Jews (20). The lavish gifts he takes to Jerusalem impress upon him the worth of both king and high priest (81). In Judea, he observes how exceptional the Temple is (84), the extent of the water supply (91), the skill of the priests (92), the glory of Eleazar (96), the strong defenses (100–102, cf. 118), fertile country (112), well-qualified (εὔθετος, 122) elders, and finally the admirable (καλός, 170) defense of the Law made by Eleazar (170). In Alexandria, he observes the remarkable respect shown by the king (175–177) and is presumably present to see how impressed the philosophers (200–201, 235) and the king (293–294) are by the wisdom of the seventy-two elders. Aristeas is impressed by their piety (305–306) and is presumably present to see the translation completed and approved (310–311, 317). The hearer naturally joins Aristeas in finding all these aspects of Judaism impressive and praiseworthy.
- P5e) *Gentle steps*. There is early mention of the history of Jewish slaves in Egypt (12–14), followed by their prompt and generous release by the king (15–27). A hearer aware that there has not actually been complete harmony in Alexandria between Greeks and Jews is thus introduced in gentle steps to the (remarkable) harmony presented in the rest of the text.

NARRATIVE PERSUASION

This text is not aimed at those actively hostile to Jews, nor at any Jews who might be hostile to Greek culture—it hardly engages with the issues that would be important to them and shows little sign of attempting to win their consent to engage with the narrative. Rather, the text claims to introduce Philocrates, and other interested, cultured Greeks (7), to Judaism, portrayed positively by a Greek courtier. But analysis of the text affirms the scholarly consensus that the real author is Jewish (or a well-informed proselyte), probably writing in Alexandria a generation or more later than the events described.

Alexandrian Jews are a significant part of the intended audience. As the author's peers, they would be an inevitable audience and, for them, the text is engaging from the outset, since they would be interested in the story of how their own forebears were brought to Egypt and were later granted freedom and respect. There are three main thrusts to the persuasion for them. First, they should respect and faithfully preserve (310–311, cf. 317) this Greek translation (Torah but probably, by association, the entire Septuagint, as available in their day), which has full Jewish authentication (via a respected high priest, the best Hebrew originals, qualified translators, and Alexandrian Jewish approval),[114] plus approval from Philadelphus and his Greek librarian. Secondly, Jewish hearers are invited to have confidence in Judaism as worthy of respect by the standards of educated Greeks and even (through Eleazar's speech, 130–169) to interpret the significance of the Law through that lens. *Aristeas* is written in Greek about the Greek translation of the Law, for Jews who, although fluent in Greek, were not necessarily fluent in Hebrew. It legitimates Jewish teaching and interpretation using not only Greek language but also the ideas provided by Greek philosophical education. Jews might not accept Aristeas's idea that Zeus and God are equivalent (18),[115] but this idea is put in the mouth of a Gentile, not a Jew,[116] which would make its expression easier to tolerate. Thirdly, Jews are invited to regard Alexandrian Greeks (but not Egyptians) with respect. Greeks (especially Aristeas and the king) are presented as people who, if enlightened and appropriately informed, will respect Jews.

Although the device of using a Greek narrator accounts for some Greek aspects of the text, other aspects suggests Greeks among the audience. If the text were intended exclusively for Jews, one would expect it to show some awareness of Jewish objections to Greek culture. Instead, educated Greeks are presented as already distanced from myths and theriolatry —effectively, as being in agreement with Jews.[117] The absence of any criticism, indeed the positive portrayal, of Greek customs,[118] suggests that the text is designed to encourage Greek hearers to listen and to join Aristeas on his journey of discovery. Judaism is associated with piety and wisdom, harmless and worthy of respect, with Jews portrayed as similar to a Greek city-state (with its own customs, 182, and made up of equally represented tribes) and their Law as similar to ancient Greek law-codes. *Aristeas* calls for interest in and respect for Jews and Judaism. But by associating Zeus with the Jewish God, it avoids direct proselytizing[119] and does not seem to expect Greeks to abandon their own culture. It would encourage Alexandrian Greeks to follow Aristeas's example of respect for Judaism and, therefore, for Jews. However easy or hard it might be to persuade a Greek audience to read or hear *Aristeas*, the persuasion within the text is suitable for building this interest and respect.

Philo mentions that, in the first century AD, Alexandrian Jews still held an annual festival on the island of Pharos, celebrating the translation of the Septuagint by feasting there, with family and friends, including "a great number" of people from other nations.[120] According to *Aristeas*, Philadelphus ordered an annual commemoration, throughout his life, of the arrival of the translators (180). It is quite possible that this is mentioned because a Jewish festival, such as that described by Philo, was already celebrated at the time *Aristeas* was written.[121] *Aristeas* could then provide a "charter myth" for the festival, attributing royal origins to it.[122] The king's reference to "throughout our life" (180) would explain why Alexandrian Greeks were not now required to be involved. Such a festival would have been an ideal opportunity for *Aristeas* to be read aloud, in whole or in part. Indeed, it is quite possible that the text was composed for exactly such an occasion—with Jews certain to be present, and with the aspiration that well-disposed Greeks would also attend.

CONCLUSIONS

The text would encourage Jews in Alexandria to have confidence both in their community and in their Greek Scriptures. Honigman's assertion that *Aristeas* acts as a "charter myth" for the Septuagint explains much of the persuasion within the text and receives some support here, but if the Septuagint were the focus, then most of the text would be mere "digressions,"[123] which raises doubts about this interpretation.[124] In contrast, Hacham regards the text as a foundation myth for the Egyptian Jewish community. Persuasion within the text points simultaneously to both of these as relevant and intimately interlinked. Jews are certainly a part of the audience, so *Aristeas* is not simply an apologetic tract aimed at Greeks. On the other hand, attempts to exclude Greeks from the audience have not proved convincing. Rather, the absence of tension between Greek and Jew (despite earlier enslavement of Jews) suggests their inclusion. The text is also suitable for encouraging Greeks toward interest in and respect for Jews and Judaism.

Analysis of persuasion excludes some possibilities:[125] *Aristeas* is not designed to engage with Greeks hostile to Jews, nor with Jews hostile to Greeks. In general, alongside their consideration of social, historical, and intertextual issues, scholars have been able to find evidence within the text to support for their various theories concerning its occasion, audience, and purpose. But the cases they have made against alternative audiences and purposes have generally been weak. This analysis has, rather, pointed toward the feasibility of two intended audiences—both Alexandrian Jews and well-disposed Greeks. This suggests a dual purpose for the text and leads to the speculative suggestion that the *Aristeas* might have been read out at, and might even have been composed for, an annual Jewish festival in Alexandria.

NOTES

1. Henry G. Meecham, *The Oldest Version of the Bible: "Aristeas" on Its Traditional Origin* (London: Holborn, 1932), 331–33; "possible reflections" in the NT.

2. Josephus, *Ant.* 12:12–118 is a paraphrase; Meecham, *Version*, 333–39; Moses Hadas, *Aristeas to Philocrates (Letter of Aristeas)*, trans. Henry St. J. Thackeray (New York: Harper, 1951), 18–19.

3. Hadas, *Aristeas*, 21–26; Philo, *Moses* 2:25–44 describes the same events.

4. Josephus rewrote extensively; Meecham, *Version*, 333–9; Hadas, *Aristeas*, 18–19.

5. *Aristeas* mentions Greek translation of only the Law (i.e., Pentateuch), but demonstrates awareness of other parts of the LXX; Meecham, *Version*, 102, 335 (cf. 97); Erich S. Gruen, *Heritage and Hellenism: The Reinvention of Jewish Tradition* (Berkeley: University of California Press, 1998), 211. The account is simplified; the hearer is probably not intended to distinguish between the translation described and whatever version of LXX they knew.

6. Meecham, *Version*, 133–72.

7. Sylvie Honigman, *The Septuagint and Homeric Scholarship in Alexandria: A Study in the Narrative of the Letter of Aristeas* (London: Routledge, 2003).

8. διήγησις (1, 8, 322).

9. πρός ἐπισκευὴν ψυχῆς, 5, where ψυχή (breath, life or spirit) need not carry any religious connotation (cf. διάνοια, mind, understanding, 322).

10. The narrator distances himself from writers of myths (μυθολόγος, 322).

11. 10, 91, 96, 100.

12. Royal decree (22–25); librarian's report (29–32); royal letter (35–40); Eleazar's reply (41–46).

13. An epistle, Meecham, *Version*, 204; Honigman, *Septuagint*, 1, denies this.

14. For "all who are like-minded" (πᾶσι τοῖς ὁμοίοις, 7), loving learning (φιλομαθῶς, 7), and others it will be passed on to (296).

15. 21, 28, 34, 51, 83, 120, 128, 171, 295–300, as well as prologue (1–8) and epilogue (322); Honigman, *Septuagint*, 25–27; but some suggest composite authorship, e.g., Solomon Zeitlin, suggesting that the account of the Temple (at least 83–97) was inserted after AD 70, Hadas, *Aristeas*, 138–39, n. 97.

16. Kennedy, *Progymnasmata*.

17. Honigman, *Septuagint*, 14–17 treats this as "*poikilia*—thematic and stylistic variation" (14) but admits that the only relevant example is poetry (Callimachus) not prose (as here).

18. Honigman, *Septuagint*, 18 notes similarities in particular to the *Deipnosophistae* of Athenaeus of Naucratis.

19. Oswyn Murray, "Aristeas and Ptolemaic Kingship," *Journal of Thelogical Studies*, n.s. 18, no. 2 (October 1967): 337–71, especially 344–53.

20. The glowing descriptions mention viewers (67); amazed reactions (78); leaf-motifs seeming to move in the breeze (70).

21. Hadas, *Aristeas*, 50, "homily" (χρεία); Honigman, *Septuagint*, 18, ἐργασία (elaboration) of a χρεία.

22. Billowing Temple curtain, a spectacle "hard to tear oneself from" (δυσαπάλλακτος, 86, cf. 99; Shutt translates "unforgettable"); R. J. H. Shutt, "Letter of Aristeas: A New Translation and Introduction," in OTP 2:7–34, citing 18.

23. Details, especially geographical, are an idealization (echoing Scripture); Hadas, *Aristeas*, 48–50; Honigman, *Septuagint*, 18; e.g., that there were still twelve tribes (32, 39, 46, cf. Ezek 48).

24. *Contra* Hadas, *Aristeas*, 50. *Aristeas* lacks the supernatural element (paradoxography, such as monsters and amazing customs) of the less credible travelogues: Honigman, *Septuagint*, 68–69.

25. Hadas, *Aristeas*.

26. Aristeas's name becomes explicit at 43 (whether or not it was in the original title).

27. Here named simply "Ptolemy"; his father was son of Lagos (12–13); his consort is Arsinoe (41, i.e., his second wife of that name, who was also his sister); Meecham, *Version*, 325–26; Hadas, *Aristeas*, 5.

28. 173—initially called simply "the city" (4; perhaps 22).

29. 1, 120, 295, 322, whose love of learning is emphasized, 7, 322.

30. τῶν Ἰουδαίων νόμιμα (10).

31. ἑρμηνεύω here indicates "translate," but can mean "expound"—a normal role for such Jewish elders.

32. Victor Tcherikover, "The Ideology of the Letter of Aristeas," *Harvard Theological Review* 51, no. 2 (April 1958): 64.

33. Explicitly present: 10–20, 83–173, 306; never explicitly absent; 296 is ambiguous, but may imply the narrator's presence throughout 174–294 and even 301–305, 307–321.

34. Aristeas is an outsider to Jews (6, 128–129, 306, 311); Hadas, *Aristeas*, 4; *contra* Shutt, "Aristeas," 7, who treats him as Jewish, leading to inappropriate translation at 16 and 170–171.

35. εὐσέβεια (piety), e.g., 2, 24, 42 (of the king), 229, 255; cf. σεμνότης (holiness, 5) and ὁσιότης (piety), 18, 306 (of the seventy-two elders); Honigman, *Septuagint*, 61.

36. The narrator comments on the brevity of one account (βραχέων τῶν ὑποδειχθέντων, 128).

37. Eusebius, *Preparation for the Gospel*, 9:25, preserves a fragment; Meecham, *Version*, 91.

38. Murray, "Kingship," 342, ascribes both *Aristeas* and that history to one, later, pseudonymous author.

39. Hadas, *Aristeas*, 5–6.

40. E.g., 170, 306, although the concept that Jews and Greeks worship the same God (16) would be controversial within Judaism.

41. κατὰ τὴν ἐξ ἀρχῆς διάταξιν (97); of interest to Jews (who would be aware of the questionable current reality of twelve tribes, presumed in 47–51); also, release of Jewish mothers and children (27) might be glossed over by a Gentile, but would be of sharper concern to Jews.

42. Further, no Gentile could come close enough to see details of the officiating high priest's vestments (96–99); Hadas, *Aristeas*, 137, nn. 96–99.

43. Following LXX rather than MT where they diverge concerning the gold of the table (57, cf. Exod 25:23–24); Hadas, *Aristeas*, 121; Noah Hacham, "The Letter of Aristeas: A New Exodus Story?" *Journal for the Study of Judaism* 36, no. 1 (2005): 12.

44. Thackeray, "Aristeas," 502; Hadas, *Aristeas*, 29–32.

45. Barclay, *Diaspora*, 139–40.

46. Meecham, *Version*, 142.

47. Honigman, *Septuagint*, 119–20.

48. Hadas, *Aristeas*, 6–7.

49. ἔσται . . . τοῦ θεοῦ κατισχύοντος αὐτόν (21); best translated "as God will give him strength"; present participle generally describes events concurrent with the main verb (ἔσται, future).

50. These might be understood as historic present, but such use is nowhere evident in *Aristeas*.

51. διῳκεῖτο, "used to be set in quick motion" (28; although a few MSS have present tense, Hadas, *Aristeas*, 109, n. 28; Meecham, *Version*, 139, n. 4).

52. E.g., a Diaspora viewpoint is indicated by mention that Eleazar was useful for Jews both with him and "in other places" (3, cf. 38); cf. Tcherikover, "Ideology," 83.

53. πᾶσι τοῖς παραληψομένοις τὴν ἀναγραφήν (cf. future generations, 38, renown 39).

54. πολυμάταιος, occupied with something worthless; blameworthy (14, 23–24), although their priests get some respect (6, echoing Herodotus, Hadas, *Aristeas*, 95, n. 6). M. A. L. Beavis, "Anti-Egyptian Polemic in the Letter of Aristeas 130–65 (The High Priest's Discourse)," *Journal for the Study of Judaism* 18, no. 2 (1987): 147, identifies "worthless persons" (142) as Egyptians.

55. 250, by an elder; this was a Greek commonplace, Hadas, *Aristeas*, 198, n. 250.

56. Meecham, *Version*, 239–42, 286–91.

57. τὸ δίκαιον . . . εὐσέβεια.

58. φιλοσοφωτέραν . . . καὶ ἀκέραιον.

59. "The mean . . . the best [course]": τὸ μέσον . . . κάλλιστον; an Aristotelian ideal; Hadas, *Aristeas*, 149, n. 122.

60. E.g., 1 Macc 1:11–15.

61. E.g., the Jordan flows only south, but is described as flowing around (περιρρέω, 116) the territory; Hadas, *Aristeas*, 50. Mention of what is "called Samaria" (107)

suggests that the hearer (although Philocrates might be in mind) is not familiar with it, Hadas, *Aristeas*, 143 n. 107.

62. Hacham, *New Exodus*, 1, 19.

63. *Contra* Honigman, *Septuagint*, 27.

64. Circumcision (1 Macc 1:15, 60–61; 2 Macc 6:10; 4 Macc 4:25), Sabbath observance (1 Macc 1:43; 2 Macc 6:6), and abstinence from pork (1 Macc 1:47; 2 Macc 6:18–20; 7:1; 3 Macc 3:7; 4 Macc 5:2; 6:15–16) were emblematic; Meecham, *Version*, 313; Hadas, *Aristeas*, 65–66.

65. Aristotle, *Politics* 7:4:4 (1326a5–b25).

66. Hadas, *Aristeas*, 65–66; Tcherikover, "Ideology," 177–78.

67. Dan 3:18, *Bel* 5, 24–25; cf. Philo, *Embassy*, 117–118.

68. Even importing foreign deities, through *evocatio*; Beard, *Religions*, 34.

69. As recorded by Callisthenes: Strabo, *Geographica* 17:1:43 (C814); Plutarch, *Alexander* 26:10–27:11 (cf. Arrian of Nicomedia, *Anabasis* 3:3–4), involving gifts and showing respect to Ammon (albeit associated with Zeus, Plutarch, *Alexander* 27:7, 10).

70. Even dismissal of myths (137, 168, 322) fits with Greek philosophy, e.g., Plato, *Phaedrus*, 229.

71. Ekaterin Matusova, *The Meaning of the Letter of Aristeas: In Light of Biblical Interpretation and Grammatical Tradition, and with Reference to its Historical Context* (Göttingen: Vandenhoeck & Ruprecht, 2015), 141, includes both.

72. 41; Arsinoe II, became queen between 277 and 273 BC; Meecham, *Version*, 325, 329; Hadas, *Aristeas*, 1, 5.

73. Diogenes Laertius, *Lives of Eminent Philosophers* 5:78; Hadas, *Aristeas*, 7.

74. Hadas, *Aristeas*, 9.

75. The Jews Ananias and Chelkias were Cleopatra's generals; Murray, "Kingship," 362, 368–369; cf. André Pelletier, *Lettre d'Aristée à Philocrate* (Paris: Editions du Cerf, 1962), 58, suggests early second century BC.

76. Henry St. J. Thackeray, *The Letter of Aristeas: Translated into English with an Introduction and Notes* (London: Macmillan, 1904), 3.

77. Hadas, *Aristeas*, 26, 32, 37–38, 46–47.

78. Meecham, *Version*, 7, 92; Hadas, *Aristeas*, 20, "perhaps."

79. Meecham, *Version*, 111.

80. Hadas, *Aristeas*, 20; Tcherikover, "Ideology," 82.

81. Tcherikover, "Ideology," 83.

82. Hadas, *Aristeas*, 21; Tcherikover, "Ideology," 68.

83. Hacham, *New Exodus*, 14, 19. Hadas, *Aristeas*, 71, n. 99, mentions yet further suggestions. Gruen, *Heritage*, 221, concludes that *Aristeas* "proclaims that Jews in the homeland and those abroad share a stake in their common tradition."

84. Paul Carbonaro, *La* Lettre D'Aristée *et le Mythe des Âges du Monde* (Pende: J. Gabalda, 2012), 178 (translation his).

85. Paul E. Kahle, *The Cairo Geniza*, 2nd ed. (Oxford: Blackwell, 1959), 209.

86. Mention of earlier, careless versions, 30–31, might refer to poorly copied Hebrew Scriptures recently used for a new Greek translation: A. F. J. Klijn, "The Letter of Aristeas and the Greek Translation of the Pentateuch in Egypt," *New Testament*

Studies 11, no. 2 (January 1965): 154, 157; or a new rival version might have come from Leontopolis, after Onias IV established a Jewish community and temple (ca. 154 BC): Sidney Jellicoe, "The Occasion and Purpose of the Letter of Aristeas: A Re-examination," *New Testament Studies* 12, no. 2 (January 1966): 148–50.

87. Honigman, *Septuagint*, 8–11.

88. Benjamin G. Wright III, *Praise Israel for Wisdom and Instruction: Essays on Ben Sira and Wisdom, the Letter of Aristeas and the Septuagint* (Leiden: Brill, 2008), 294–95.

89. προσμανθάνω, εὐσέβεια.

90. κτίσμα. Aristeas also suggests that the God of the Jews is Zeus by another name (16)—not a new concept for the Greeks, e.g., Plutarch, *Alexander* 27:10.

91. κατευθύνω (see 216 also).

92. ἐργαζόμενος ἀκριβῶς. Hadas's translation, "elaborated," neglects the implication of accuracy.

93. Ἐμοὶ μὲν οὖν καλῶς ἐνόμιζε περὶ ἑκάστων ἀπολογεῖσθαι. Eleazar's speech is an apology (ἀπολογία) for, i.e., defense of, the Law.

94. ταῖς ἀγωγαῖς καὶ τῷ λόγῳ.

95. ἀκρόασις (127) certainly means hearing, but can also imply obeying ("heeding", Hadas).

96. The narrator chooses to mention God in the singular at 17, 18, 20, 21; Aristeas the character does so at 15, 16; Sosibius at 19; the king at 177 (cf. 179); Demetrius at 313–316.

97. τὰ τῶν μυθολόγων βιβλία (322; cf. 137, 168); Greek myths (e.g., Homer) were polytheistic.

98. Eleazar attacks polytheism (134–138); the narrator approves of his speech (170).

99. In contrast to 3 Macc. (Eleazar does criticize theriolaters, 138, and Gentile immorality, 152.)

100. E.g., the translators' qualifications, by Greek (philosophical education, 121–122), Jewish (experts in the Law, 32, 121–122), and universal standards ("exemplary lives" καλῶς βεβιωκότας, 32, 39; "noble and good men," ἄνδρες καλοὶ καὶ ἀγαθοί, 46).

101. κατὰ πρόθεσίν τινα.

102. φιλοσοφωτέραν . . . καὶ ἀκέραιον . . . ὡς ἂν οὖσαν θείαν.

103. λόγιον.

104. Hadas, *Aristeas*, 160, n. 152, wrongly sees Eleazar's condemnation of mixed-up (ἐπιμισγόμενος) unions, defiling "mothers and daughters" (152), as criticism of the Ptolemies' brother-sister relationships (Arsenoe was the king's sister, 45). Rather than incest, this refers to the Jewish prohibition on a man having sex with both a mother and her daughter (Lev 18:17; 20:14).

105. Philo, *Moses* 2:29–30. Hadas, *Aristeas*, 122, n. 56.

106. ὠφέλεια (3); καλοκἀγαθία . . . δόξα (3); ἀρετή (122).

107. ταλαιπωρία.

108. Making malicious, false (or at least exaggerated) reports, e.g., Aristophanes, *Ach.* 559, 818.

109. Beavis, "Polemic," 149; though, despite suspicion, Isis and Sarapis gained a following, Beard, *Religions*, 160–61.

110. Despite Eleazar's fears (124; which serve further to emphasize their exceptional abilities).

111. συντηρεῖν ἁγνῶς.

112. Aristeas learned about "religious matters" (τὰ θεῖα, 3), but this is hardly emphasized as an outcome.

113. Hadas, *Aristeas*, 223, n. 313.

114. Divine accreditation is gently implied by providential completion in seventy-two days (307)—far short of Philo's claim of miraculous verbatim agreement between the translators (*Moses* 2:37–40).

115. E.g., Eleazar mentions the king's piety for "our" God (i.e., of the Jews, 42); cf. 2 Macc 6:2 indicates horror at such an idea.

116. To persuade Jews of Aristeas's idea, it would be vital for Eleazar to support it. He does not.

117. Eleazar emphasizes that Jews abstain from homosexual practice (152), but this he associates with "most of the rest of mankind," thus avoiding overt criticism of Greeks. Mention of defiling "mothers and daughters" (of no great concern to Greeks) also dilutes any criticism.

118. E.g., one of the seventy-two encourages the king to attend the theater (284, albeit for plays with περιστολή, "propriety," trans. Hadas), in contrast to later rabbis; Hadas, *Aristeas*, 211, n. 284.

119. *Aristeas* may encourage the hearer to find, not merely scrolls to read, but Jews to ask (127).

120. Philo, *Moses* 2:41–42.

121. This idea is speculative, but is given some support by 2 Macc 1:18, which indicates an interest (albeit in Jerusalem) in festival observance in Egypt.

122. The first reading would then have been presented as the discovery of an old document.

123. Hadas, *Aristeas*, 60.

124. Carbonaro, *Mythe*, 178.

125. E.g., Meecham's (subsidiary) suggestion that *Aristeas* attracts Greeks to the LXX (*Version,* 111) is undermined by *Aristeas*'s focus on the Jewish community, not only the translation.

Chapter Seven

Basic Literary Analysis of Acts

The Acts of the Apostles is the main focus of this study, so the same method is applied in more detail for Acts. This chapter provides the preliminary literary analysis, in preparation for a study of the techniques of persuasion in Chapter 8.

AN OVERVIEW OF ACTS

The question of how narratives persuade is particularly relevant to interpreting Acts, because Acts is a narrative and there is abundant evidence of persuasiveness within it. Some have treated Acts as a sequence of speeches,[1] and about half of the verses contain some direct speech.[2] Nevertheless, the main speeches[3] amount to less than a quarter of the text (226 out of 1,002 verses), and there are significant sections of narrative, especially Paul's journey to Rome (27:1–28:16), that do not set the scene for a speech. Thus, Acts is generally and rightly regarded as narrative—within which speeches, dialogue, and letters play a part—and narrative critical methods have increasingly been applied to it.

Acts includes *prima facie* indications that analysis of persuasion is required. First, the prologue associates Acts with the stated persuasive aim of the Third Gospel; in addressing Theophilus and mentioning an earlier text, Acts 1:1–2 surely refers back to the persuasive aim that Theophilus should know the ἀσφάλεια (assurance, certainty)—i.e., be convinced—of the things about which he has been informed (Luke 1:4).[4] Secondly, the speeches in Acts indicate interest in the persuasion of the various narrative audiences: A decision is encouraged (deliberative rhetoric, 2:38; 3:26; 26:29); audience responses are reported (positive, 2:41; 8:12; 10:44; negative 7:54;

divided, 13:42–45; 14:4; 17:32–34; 28:25); and there are indications of further debate (e.g., 6:9–10; 18:4, 28; 19:8–9). Acts uses the language of forensic rhetoric: witness (μάρτυς, notably at 1:8; 10:41), reported accusations (6:13–14; 16:20–21; 17:6; 21:38; 24:5–6; 25:7), evidence or proof (e.g., τεκμήριον, 1:3), attestation, especially supernatural (e.g., revealed by God, ἀποδεδειγμένον ἀπὸ τοῦ θεοῦ, 2:22; signs and wonders, σημεῖα καὶ τέρατα, 5:12; 14:3) and the verifiability implied by public events (26:26, cf. 4:16).[5] The author betrays at least some basic familiarity with rhetoric,[6] and these themes indicate his interest in persuasion. So it is worthwhile to investigate the persuasive impact of Acts itself upon its own hearers.[7]

Various genres have been suggested for the Third Gospel and for Acts. The two works need not necessarily have the same genre; a case can be made for the Third Gospel to be a *bios* (biography) of Jesus,[8] but Acts follows various characters and hardly fits that genre—except, perhaps, as a *bios* of a people.[9] Pervo suggests that Acts contains so much direct speech that it matches works of fiction better than works of history.[10] Nevertheless, the genre of "historiography" has been most frequently proposed, on the basis of the style of the pair of prologues, the links to world history, and evidence of concern for historical reliability.[11] The pair of Luke-Acts prologues suggests a concern with credibility, as is characteristic of historians[12]—mentioning eyewitnesses (αὐτόπτης, Luke 1:2), careful investigation (ἀκριβῶς, exactly, accurately, Luke 1:3), and certainty (ἀσφάλεια, Luke 1:4).

Acts seems to have been composed in Greek, so linguistic nuances are relevant and not mere artifacts of translation. This study uses the Nestle-Aland main text. This largely follows the Alexandrian text group, but there are significant differences between that and the "Western" group (particularly Codex Bezae), which is significantly longer (by 8.5 percent, more than 800 words)[13] with more honorific titles for Jesus and more references to the Holy Spirit. Ideally, a separate analysis would be conducted, of persuasion in the Western text, but that is beyond the scope of this book.

Relationship to the Third Gospel

The analysis below assumes that the implied audience of Acts is familiar with the Third Gospel (as indicated by 1:1). But the prologue of Acts shows that it is a separate text, so even if written by the same author, it may not have been written at the same time and would not necessarily have the same genre, intended audiences, or purposes.[14] So it is appropriate here to analyze Acts as the text, with the Third Gospel setting the context but not predetermining one's view of persuasiveness or purpose. Narrative persuasion in the Third Gospel is also worthy of study, but is beyond the scope of this book.

Acts has been selected, rather than the Third Gospel, for the following reasons. First, there is reasonable scholarly consensus that Acts, including the speeches within it, reflects the style of a single author who, whatever his sources, exercised enough editorial freedom to impose his own style[15]—which increases the likelihood of consistent, detectable persuasion. In the Third Gospel, although such editorial freedom seems to have been exercised in the ordering and introducing of episodes, it was not exercised to the same extent throughout, particularly not in words ascribed to Jesus.[16] Secondly, although the Third Gospel had "many" predecessors (Luke 1:1), there is no surviving evidence of any earlier account of the early church. This suggests that less care would be needed to ensure that Acts fitted with the style and content of other sources (oral or written) that hearers might already know and respect—a further indicator of editorial freedom.[17] Thirdly, the events described in Acts happen almost a generation later than the events in the Third Gospel. The growth of the church implies an accelerating rate at which relevant events occurred.[18] So the more recent the events, the more material was likely to be available and thus the more opportunity to shape it, through selection. Finally, Acts displays more evidence than the Third Gospel of being crafted into a closely interconnected narrative. This reduces the risk of it being an assembly of episodes faithfully preserved from separate sources, which thus might not display coherent persuasion. In Acts, causality or explicit geographical sequence links most episodes, leaving few episode transitions without such a link.[19] Several characters provide links by being introduced briefly, and then adopting a significant role later, e.g., Barnabas, 4:36–37; Stephen and Philip, 6:5; and Saul/Paul, 7:58. In the Third Gospel, although the birth and passion narratives are closely linked sequences, the ministry in between includes episodes where the connections are less clear.[20]

Some have argued that Acts was already envisaged when the Third Gospel was written, e.g., Witherington cites details of Stephen's death that echo Mark's, but not Luke's, passion narrative;[21] and this idea may be supported by links between the end of the Third Gospel and the start of Acts. The idea is plausible; but the analysis below does not depend on it—only on the assumption that both author and audience of Acts are familiar with the Third Gospel (in approximately the form available today).

Summary of the Story

The scene for the start of Acts is set by the Third Gospel, which tells the story of Jesus's earthly life and ministry, from his birth, accompanied by supernatural announcements, via his public ministry, involving teaching and miracles, to his arrest, execution, resurrection appearances, and ascension. As a story, it has an appropriate ending, since Jesus's earthly ministry is complete. But Jesus's final words point forward, to the apostles' proclamation to all nations (Luke 24:47–48) and to God's supply of "power" (δύναμις) from on high (Luke 24:49).

Acts retells the ascension in more detail: Jesus's promise of "power" is amplified (1:8), with mention of the Holy Spirit, and, effectively, a commissioning of the disciples to be "witnesses in Jerusalem and all Judea and Samaria and to the end of the earth" (1:8, echoing Luke 24:48). In Jerusalem, the dramatic arrival of the Holy Spirit upon the believers (2:2–4) leads to bold proclamation (especially by Peter, now characterized with respect) and performance of miracles (2:43). Thousands are baptized, but increasing opposition from Jewish leaders culminates in the stoning of the heroic Stephen (7:57–60). As disciples scatter, there is a positive response to Philip's preaching in Samaria. A vision transforms Saul, leading persecutor and thus villain, into Jesus's emissary to the Gentiles (9:15; thereafter characterized with respect). Visions lead Peter to preach to the household of Cornelius, a godly Roman centurion, and these Gentiles promptly receive the Holy Spirit (10:44). Saul/Paul and Barnabas preach to both Jews and Gentiles in Asia Minor, facing opposition but leaving behind groups of believers. The believers in Jerusalem are thus persuaded to accept Gentile believers without requiring them to become Jews (ch. 15). Paul's ministry reaches Greece, but while visiting Jerusalem, he is arrested by the Roman authorities due to false accusations by the Jews (21:28–29). After testifying at various hearings, Paul ends up transferred eventually to Rome, pending a hearing before the emperor. Acts ends rather inconclusively, with Paul still preaching, to all who come (28:30–31).

Narrator

The narrator is prominent only in the prologue, where he addresses Theophilus directly (1:1). His voice then transforms (1:4; ungrammatically, in midsentence) from reporting Jesus's words to becoming Jesus's voice in direct speech. Before reading to a group, the lector had to prepare, at least enough to recognize which words are said by which character, to ensure an appropriate tone of voice. Indeed, preparation is vital to navigate such vocal booby-traps as the narratorial aside (that there were about 120 believers, 1:15b) inserted unexpectedly between "Peter . . . said" (Πέτρος . . . εἶπεν) and the actual start of Peter's speech (1:16). Nevertheless, an ambiguous transition, such as 1:4, is rare in Acts.[22] It gives a subtle implication of a close link between the narrator and Jesus—they cannot, here, be entirely distinguished. This involves no direct claim to authority, which might be pondered with suspicion. In the Third Gospel, Jesus has been presented with great respect (e.g., attested by heavenly voices, 3:22; 9:35), whereas the narrator claims authority less overtly (having, nevertheless, authority to narrate events in heaven: "the angel Gabriel was sent by God," Luke 1:26). The transition at Acts 1:4 would be tricky but, however performed, blurs the distinction between lector speaking as narrator and lector as the voice of Jesus himself. This enhances the narrator's authority by subtle association with Jesus.

The "we" passages suggest the presence of the narrator during particular parts of Paul's journeys.[23] Scholars have discussed whether this might arise from literary convention in journey narratives, or from use by a later compiler of a travel diary by some companion of Paul's. There is no reason to suppose that the shift between "they" and "we" is a mere mistake, especially since this is repeated. In terms of persuasiveness, it acts as a claim by the narrator to have been a participant. The last "we" brings Paul and his companions to Rome (28:16), so, at the end, the hearer is left with the impression that the narrator was involved, alongside Paul. Use of "we" certainly contributes immediacy and dramatic impact (especially during the shipwreck, 27:18, 27, 29, 37; 28:1), but it is also a gentle narratorial claim to authority as eyewitness.[24]

The narrator of Acts claims significant authority, not merely as an "omniscient" narrator concerning earthly events, but also, at times, effectively claiming divine authority for his account.[25] The narrator of the infancy narratives (Luke 1–2) claims significant authority, declaring Zechariah and Elizabeth "righteous before God" (1:6) and explicitly identifying "an angel of the Lord" (1:11; 2:9).[26] Such comments speak for God, suggesting either that the author was citing sources already regarded as having authority equivalent to Scripture or even that the Third Gospel is itself presented as Scripture. In Luke 3–24, narratorial authority is claimed more gently (e.g., voices from heaven are reported, but not identified, 3:22; 9:35).[27]

In Acts, the narrator claims authority at a level similar to the narrator of Luke 3–24. He reports two men in white (1:10), without identifying them as angels (cf. Luke 24:4). When he mentions characters being "filled with the Holy Spirit" (e.g., Peter, 4:8; Stephen, 7:55; Barnabas, 11:24; Paul, 13:9), this is not merely on his own authority, but explicitly attested by public supernatural events such as the Spirit's dramatic arrival (2:2–4; 4:31; 8:17; 10:44; 19:6) and other signs and wonders (e.g., 6:8; 13:11). When the twelve are imprisoned, it is "an angel/messenger of the Lord" who frees them (5:19), but this claim depends more on the authority of the twelve (now portrayed with respect) than of the narrator, with their supernatural release providing evidence (cf. Peter's release, 12:7–9). Similarly, "an angel of the Lord" is credited with striking Herod (Agrippa I, 12:23), and his undeniable death attests to this. The narrator assumes the authority to describe various people as prophets

(Agabus, 11:27; 21:10; Judas and Silas, 15:32; Philip's daughters, 21:9) and Cornelius as devout, fearing God (10:2). The narrator identifies some actions of the Spirit: e.g., apparently transporting Philip (8:39) and speaking to Peter (10:19). On the other hand, some significant revelations are described simply as visions (to Cornelius, 10:3; to Peter, 10:10), and when Saul/Paul hears a voice, it is not the narrator but the voice who identifies this as Jesus (9:5).

Thus, the narrator of Acts describes many supernatural events and, at times, treats himself as having authority to authenticate them, but he is more inclined to allow events or characters within the story to act as the prime source of authority. In particular, claims of fulfillment of OT prophecy are included in speeches and not in the mouth of the narrator.[28] The narrator makes no attempt to appear incredulous or impartial; in this, his style is inappropriate for classical historiography, but is similar to much of the Septuagint. Thus the text of Acts comes at least close to claiming scriptural authority for itself;[29] it is certainly arguable that Luke 1–2 goes that far.

The narrator employs various asides to guide the hearer. For example, a brief prolepsis indicates that the famine prophesied by Agabus did eventually happen (11:28), indicating the narrator's desire to authenticate Christian prophecy (since this detail is not otherwise necessary). An intriguing comment, not presented as an aside, is that, when Stephen stands before the Sanhedrin, they "saw his face, like the face of an angel" (6:15). Technically, this reports their perception, but it is not entirely clear how the author would know this—although Saul may have been present (7:58), and other witnesses might also have become believers (cf. 6:7; 21:20)—and there would not have been agreement on exactly what an angel looked like (beyond the general expectation of shining, Ezek 40:3; Dan 10:6; cf. Exod 34:29–30; cf. an angel looking like "a god," Dan 3:25, is similarly vague). Whether or not based on reliable reports, the effect of this narratorial comment is to portray Stephen as having divine approval. The hearer (unless actively hostile) may not be conscious of this mechanism, but his/her perception of Stephen will certainly be influenced by it.

In summary, the narrator gives the impression of being reticent, and ascribing authority more to characters within the narrative than to himself;[30] nevertheless, the narrator is far from impartial, with no hint of doubt about the authority of the apostles or the truth of the supernatural events he recounts.

Author

The name "Luke" came to be attached to the Third Gospel, and no other ascription was attached to it or to Acts in the early centuries.[31] The author's identity was presumably known to some initial audiences,[32] but not necessarily to all the audiences he aspired to reach. Nevertheless, he is not named within either text, but is reticent—neither text treats the author's identity as their source of authority. The author of Acts is certainly competent in Greek, and he shows evidence of familiarity with the conventions of classical rhetoric[33] and historiography[34] and with the Septuagint, which is quoted extensively.[35] He was not necessarily familiar with Hebrew or with Palestine;[36] the text mentions Aramaic as "their" language (τῇ ἰδίᾳ διαλέκτῳ αὐτῶν, 1:19), so it is probably not the author's mother-tongue.[37] The subject matter suggests an interest in the urban, rather than rural, and elite and middle classes, rather than peasants and slaves.

Audience

The stated audience is Theophilus (1:1). The address "most excellent" (κράτιστος, Luke 1:3) might suggest the status of a Roman official (cf. 23:26; 24:3; 26:25 addressed to governors Felix and Festus).[38] Luke 1:4 indicates that Theophilus has heard something already. Although κατηχέω might indicate formal instruction (Rom 2:18 of Jewish instruction; Gal 6:6 of Christian instruction), that would not necessarily involve extensive instruction (1 Cor 14:19 suggests a mere five words!) nor exactness, nor baptism (Acts 18:25–26). The word can equally mean simply "inform" (Acts 21:21, 24, of a false rumor). Theophilus has heard about Jesus, but what he has heard is not specified. It is possible that Theophilus's name, indicating the love of God, points to an invented, idealized addressee. On the other hand, Witherington suggests that Luke-Acts be treated as addressed, personally, to one particular official in response to his inquiry,[39] with the further possibility that Theophilus acted as patron for publication.[40]

The implied audience of Luke-Acts has been analyzed in detail by Tyson,[41] considering especially what the text explains (implying audience's ignorance) or does not explain (implying audience's knowledge). He concludes that:

> Our reader is a generally well-educated person with a rudimentary knowledge of eastern Mediterranean geography . . . familiar with some public figures, especially Roman emperors. He has some knowledge about James and his position within the primitive Christian community[42] . . . represented in the text as a Godfearer, a centurion, an Ethiopian eunuch, and a Theophilus. . . .[43]

Tyson's approach makes careful use of the evidence within the text, but it has a severe limitation: It assumes one, literate reader. That is an unjustified assumption, since any hearer (whether literate or not) might be in the audience for a reading to a group.[44] It is also artificial in assuming a monolithic audience. Tyson notes that Acts explains both Jewish (Luke 20:27; Acts 23:8;

26:4) and pagan (the famous cult of Artemis at Ephesus, 19:21–40) religious practices so that "The implied reader has limited knowledge of both pagan and Jewish religions."[45] It is not clear who could have had such limited knowledge in both of these areas. More nuanced audience analysis is required, allowing for different groups within the implied audience—one group with limited knowledge of Judaism and another with limited knowledge of paganism. The use of Jewish festivals to indicate time of year (Passover, 20:6; Pentecost, 20:16; Day of Atonement, 27:9) is realistic in representing Paul's concerns, but also suggests the presence of Jews within the implied audience—otherwise the season could be given, or the Roman month.[46] The presence of Gentiles is strongly indicated by the explanation of Jewish factions (23:8). Although the text betrays an interest in the elite and middle classes, that does not require that the audience be rich and powerful; rather, within the implied audience, there are some who might react badly to a focus on the poor (whereas the poor generally have no difficulty with a story about the rich).

Tyson also concludes that, because some pagan practices are criticized in Acts, the implied reader must also, already, be critical of these practices.[47] But persuasive narrative would thus be discounted through the unjustified assumption that the text "preaches to the converted." Rather than artificially narrowing the implied audience in such ways, a more cautious approach is needed here.

It is certain that the implied audience can understand Greek fairly fluently, although not necessarily speak it fluently. It is not certain that Greek is their mother-tongue, since Greek was widely used as trade-language. It is far from certain that they are literate; literacy rates have been estimated at only 10 percent,[48] so it is more likely that they are not. The polished Greek of the Third Gospel's prologue should not be taken as indicating an audience with classical education, who could themselves have written it. Rather, to appreciate this style, it is only necessary that the hearer has, on some previous occasion, heard a reading or a speech that employed formal style.[49] That might exclude rural peasants, but it is not clear that others are excluded. Further, after the prologue, the text immediately reverts to septuagintal, Koine Greek, so if anybody should be excluded, it would be the highly educated—e.g., the antiquarian attached to classical Attic Greek, whose sensibilities would be offended.

The frequent quotations from Scripture require a hearer who is aware that Jews have sacred, well-respected Scriptures, and is respectful toward prophetic utterances, particularly those that come true. A pagan actively hostile to Jews would not engage with such respect, but any other pagan would be familiar with oracles, omens, and stories of their fulfillment, which were pervasive in Greek literature.[50] It is highly educated historians and philosophers who might be excluded, as the small minority who might be dismissive.[51]

Scholars have tended to assume that the implied audience has extensive knowledge of the Septuagint.[52] But, when somebody quotes Shakespeare (or, in India, Thiruvalluvar), they are not addressing only those few scholars who are familiar with the entire works. The implied hearer is, rather, aware of Shakespeare's reputation and not actively hostile (or the quotation fails to be persuasive). Undoubtedly, there are in Acts allusions to the Septuagint which can only be detected through detailed familiarity; but awareness of such allusions is not necessary for understanding and appreciating any part of the narrative of Acts. Undoubtedly, detailed knowledge allows the hearer to judge for themselves whether they agree with the interpretation presented in Acts, but it is far from clear that the quotations are included for the purpose of permitting such well-informed analysis.[53]

In Acts, quotations are clearly introduced as such, so that the uninformed reader is told that the following words are, for example, "written in the book of Psalms" (1:20) or "spoken through the prophet Joel" (2:16). Fifteen quotations are introduced thus, as scriptural (1:20; 2:16, 25, 31, 34; 4:25; 7:42, 48; 8:32; 13:33, 34, 35, 40; 15:15; 28:25). There are only two that are not so clearly introduced: Peter, addressing Jewish leaders, quotes Psalm 118:22 about the rejected stone, with no indication that this is a quotation (4:11), but the audience has previously heard this, quoted with clear introduction at Luke 20:17. Secondly, at Pisidian Antioch, Paul quotes Isaiah 49:6 with the ambiguous introduction "the Lord commanded us" (ἐντέταλται ἡμῖν ὁ κύριος, 13:47), but this is not entirely unclear, since it is the last of several quotations by Paul in that episode and the others are all clearly introduced. No detailed knowledge of the Septuagint is necessary to follow the significance of these quotations.[54] Indeed, detailed knowledge of the Septuagint might even be misleading; mention of τὸν παῖδα αὐτοῦ (his [God's] servant, 3:26) comes straight after mention of Abraham (3:25). The learned might wrongly assume that God's servant is Abraham, because God called him that (Gen 18:17, LXX but not MT).[55] But the key to understanding the speech lies, not in awareness of Septuagint background to this title, but in Peter's bold application of it to Jesus (3:13).

The implied audience is familiar with the Third Gospel: Pilate can be mentioned without explanation (3:13), because he is familiar from Luke 23:1–25; "that a murderer be released to you" (3:14) assumes awareness of Barabbas (Luke 23:13–25); and "the baptism of John" (1:22) is mentioned without explanation (although the apostle John was just mentioned, 1:13), requiring familiarity with John the Baptist (Luke 3:1–20).

A text may give indications of whether it is addressed: to an individual (e.g., reading the text privately); to a group, who are each expected to respond as individuals; or to a group expected to respond together, corporately. In the Septuagint, Proverbs is exceptional in that it may be designed for private study and individual response, given repeated address to "my child" in chapters 1–7 (although "children" also appears, at 4:1; 7:24). First and 2 Timothy and Titus are also addressed to individuals (although final greetings include others, suggesting that others are expected to "overhear"). Exodus 23:2 provides teaching addressed to an entire community,[56] but requiring individual response: "You [singular] shall not be [i.e., join in] with a multitude in wrongdoing." Similar use of the second person singular is found, notably, in the Decalogue (Exod 20:1–17). In contrast, most OT prophecy seems to demand a corporate response, e.g., "house of Israel, seek [plural] me and live" (Amos 5:4).[57] Some instructions, such as "talk about them" (Deut 6:7; cf. "encouraging one another," Heb 10:25) are only possible corporately.

Acts betrays a corporate focus.[58] There is no example in Acts of a plural audience within the narrative being addressed in the second person singular (although the Third Gospel has this, in Jesus's teaching: Luke 6:29, 41–42; 11:34–36; 17:3–4). There are speeches in which Paul addresses an individual—Felix (24:10–21) and Agrippa (26:2–29), but even these simultaneously consider plural audiences: "before . . . all people" (24:16); "all who are listening" (26:29; cf. Peter addressing all Israel, 2:36; 4:10). The only conversation presented as entirely personal is that between Philip and the Ethiopian (8:26–40, whose charioteer and attendants are implied, 8:38, but not mentioned), and it is not clear that the hearer is expected to identify with the exotic Ethiopian. Rather, the focus in Acts is strongly on groups of hearers, whether in the Temple (2:46; 3:11; 5:12, 25, 42), public spaces (2:6; 5:15; 14:11; 16:13, 16; 17:17; 18:28), synagogues (9:20; 13:14; 14:1; 17:1, 10, 17; 18:4, 19, 26; 19:8), households (2:46; 5:42; 10:24; 12:12; 16:34, 40; 18:7; 21:8–10), church assemblies (13:1–2; 15:30; 20:7–8), church councils (11:2; 15:6; 20:17–18; 21:18), or lecture hall (19:9). Personal discussions surely also happened, but Acts provides rather little indication of this.[59] Indeed, twice the personal authority of centurions is neglected, to the point of rudeness: Brought before Cornelius's family and friends, after an abrupt conversation with Cornelius outside, Peter addresses the whole group (twice using second person plural, 10:28, 29).[60] The narrative presents Cornelius, personally, as the one who sent for him (as Peter knows, 10:22), yet Peter now asks why "you [plural] sent for me" (10:29). Similarly, on ship, Paul neglects the authority of centurion Julius by addressing his soldiers along with him (27:31). If the text were aimed at one, particular Roman official, there are opportunities for the narrative to encourage that official to identify, personally with these centurions and to engage with the story from their point of view. Instead, the narrative focuses on the whole group, in a way that would be almost offensive to a responsible official or *pater familias*. The implied audience of Acts is not one official; it is plural.

That texts such as Acts would normally be read to a group rather than individually is supported, among Jews, by scriptural examples (Neh 8:2–8; Jer 36:10, 15, 21; cf. *Let. Aris.* 127); among Gentiles by such texts as *On the Sublime*;[61] and also among Christians (Col 4:16). The general focus within the narrative, which gives some indication of the author's mind-set, also points more to hearers than readers. First, the Ethiopian is the only solitary reader mentioned in Luke-Acts (8:30), in contrast to reading to groups in synagogues (13:15, 27; 15:21; Luke 4:16). Secondly, "hearing" is used (ἀκούω: 28:28; Luke 8:12; 11:28; 16:29), rather than reading, as the medium for the word.[62] Thirdly, a focus on hearing rather than reading may be implied by mention that God spoke "through the mouth" of David (1:16; 4:25; Luke 1:70) or of the prophets (3:18, 21, cf. the "voice" of the prophets, 13:27). This is not strong evidence, but it is directly from the text.

In summary, the implied audience of Acts: is aware of the Third Gospel; can understand spoken Greek; is aware of the general geography, history, and politics of the eastern Mediterranean; is aware that Jews have well-respected Scriptures and is not actively hostile to them nor to the idea of miracles and prophecies; is corporate rather than individual; and is more likely a group of hearers than a reader. Some among the implied audience are not entirely familiar with Judaism (needing the factions explained, 23:8, and Hebrew/Aramaic names translated),[63] and some are not entirely familiar with paganism (needing details of the cult of Artemis, 19:24–35).

Although many are more specific about the implied audience, the analysis here is cautious. In particular, it is neither necessary nor appropriate to presuppose that the audience already shares the worldview presented in the text.[64]

Date and Context

Acts must have been written after the last events described within it, which sets the earliest possible date around AD 62. The analysis in Chapter 8 suggests publication at about this time, but that will not be presupposed. Acts was surely written after the Third Gospel; many date that after AD 70, the fall of Jerusalem, but the evidence is far from conclusive.[65] Acts must have been written before the first clear references to it, around AD 160–180.[66] It demonstrates no evident awareness of Paul's letters, suggesting that Acts predates their collection and distribution, indicating a date before or around the end of the first century AD.[67]

Acts describes events around the eastern Mediterranean (from Jerusalem to Rome) and assumes general awareness of this region. It seems likely that both author and audience belong here. For each of the Gospels, scholars have attempted to identify their "communities"—as intended audiences, but also as influencing the way the traditions were preserved and told; similarly, for Acts, Pervo identifies the author's perspective with that of Ephesus.[68] But Bauckham questions these attempts to identify "communities," making a good case that the texts were intended to reach wide audiences.[69] Nevertheless, these texts were inevitably influenced by the communities with which the authors were most familiar—influencing the form in which material was preserved and the style in which the authors became used to presenting it. These communities may have provided an initial audience (perhaps also for early drafts) and may have helped with initial publication and dissemination.

Detailed research has been carried out on the cultural context of some of the churches, including those at Corinth, where rich and poor, slave and free valued the idea of being Roman,[70] and Rome, the metropolis where immigration from the entire Empire provided the context for diverse and "fractionated" groups of believers who were largely poor[71] and, judging by social conditions in Pompeii, likely to have consisted mainly of slaves, some sexually exploited, and craft workers, many near-destitute.[72] Such research provides some general indications of the social and cultural context(s) within which Acts originated and affirms that the majority of hearers were probably not particularly wealthy or educated.

Indications of Purpose

By referring back to the Third Gospel (1:1), Acts associates itself with the purpose indicated in Luke 1:1-4—to give the audience confidence (ἀσφάλεια) in what they have heard (about Jesus and his followers). Gospel proclamation in Acts indicates that this includes confidence particularly about the resurrection of Jesus (1:3; 2:24, 32; 4:2, 10; 10:40; 13:30, 34; 17:18, 31; 23:6; 24:15, 21; 26:8, 23), involving a call to repent and believe in his name (2:38; 3:19, 26; 5:31; 10:43; 13:38–39; 16:31; 17:30; 26:18, 20).[73] Purposes previously proposed by scholars have already been discussed in Chapter 1.

This chapter has used conventional literary critical methods to provide a preliminary analysis of Acts. The narrator is reticent, but he comments authoritatively on spiritual matters, which suggests that scriptural authority is being claimed for the text itself. The implied audience is not monolithic but broad, including both Jews and Gentiles; and it is plural, not an individual. Indeed, a Roman official (as some suggest Theophilus might have been) would more likely be offended than engaged by the way Peter and Paul neglect and even bypass the authority of centurions by addressing their people directly. Building on this literary analysis, the next chapter will consider persuasion in Acts.

NOTES

1. Borgman, *Way*, structures his analysis thus.
2. Richard I. Pervo. "Direct Speech in Acts and the Question of Genre," *Journal for the Study of the New Testament* 28, no. 3 (March 2006): 288, 304, claims 516 verses out of 1,002; but, omitting quoted letters, 500 verses contain direct speech.
3. Twelve speeches: Colin J. Hemer, *The Book of Acts in the Setting of Hellenistic History* (Tübingen: Mohr, 1989), 415–16.
4. Persuasive, whether to an "insider" or an "outsider"; Alexander, *Preface*, 192.
5. Soards, *Speeches*, 199.
6. Satterthwaite, "Background," 337–80; echoed by Witherington, *Acts*, 46.
7. Keener, *Acts*, 1:451–68.
8. Richard A. Burridge, *What Are the Gospels?: A Comparison with Graeco-Roman Biography*, 2nd ed. (Grand Rapids: Eerdmans, 2004).
9. Like Dikaiarchus, *Bios Hellados*: Talbert, *Acts*, xxvi.
10. Pervo, "Direct Speech," 299–303.
11. E.g., "apologetic historiography": Sterling, *Historiography*, 16–19, 392–93.
12. Alexander, "Fact," 382–85.
13. Peter Head, "Acts and the Problem of Its Texts," in *The Book of Acts in Its Ancient Literary Setting*, eds. Bruce W. Winter and Andrew D. Clarke (Grand Rapids: Eerdmans, 1993), 420.
14. Mikeal C. Parsons and Richard I. Pervo, *Rethinking the Unity of Luke and Acts* (Minneapolis: Fortress, 1993), 115; Luke and Acts have separate reception histories; unity of authorship continues to be questioned by some, e.g., Patricia Walters, *The Assumed Authorial Unity of Luke and Acts: A Reassessment of the Evidence* (Cambridge: Cambridge University Press, 2009); *contra* Tannehill, *Narrative Unity*, 1:xiii; Borgman, *Way*, ix.
15. Soards, *Speeches*, 10–12.
16. Rudolf Bultmann, *The History of the Synoptic Tradition*, trans. John Marsh (Oxford: Blackwell, 1963), 334–37, 358–67.
17. Dibelius, *Studies*, 124; David E. Aune, *The New Testament in Its Literary Environment* (Philadelphia: Westminster, 1987), 129; Johnson, *Acts*, 4, 12, asserting a paucity of source material for chs. 1–12.
18. E.g., from 120 (1:15) to tens of thousands (21:20); from Palestine, across the known world.
19. In terms of time, place, characters, and themes (Marguerat, *How to Read*, 32), the transition to 10:1 has the least links; there are weak links at 9:31–32; 11:19; 18:24; 19:1, only.
20. Bultmann, *Synoptic Tradition*, 360, 363, 367.
21. Witherington, *Acts*, 252–53.
22. 17:3 and 23:22, the only other ambiguous transitions to direct speech, are less tricky.
23. Stanley E. Porter, "The 'We' Passages," in *The Book of Acts in its Graeco-Roman Setting*, ed. David W. J. Gill and Conrad Gempf (Grand Rapids: Eerdmans, 1994), 545–74.

24. Kurz, *Reading*, 112. The hearer might not consciously notice the narrator's arrivals and departures, but even subconsciously, the first person has the same effect.

25. Pervo, *Acts*, 15, treats "omniscient" narration as coming "from the biblical tradition." Actually, it is ubiquitous (except where a character narrates), but not all narrators provide a heavenly perspective (as Scripture and Homer do).

26. Zechariah, "filled with the Holy Spirit" (1:67, cf. Simeon, 2:26); Anna, a "prophetess" (1:36); Jesus grew in favor with God (2:52).

27. Jesus's temptation (Luke 4:1–13) could not be known unless recounted by Jesus, and therefore does not depend on the narrator's authority; "Satan entered Judas" (Luke 22:3) is evident from subsequent events; men in dazzling clothes (24:4) are claimed to be angels only by disciples (24:23). The only exception is the disputed text reporting an angel in Gethsemane (22:43–44). But it seems more likely that a pious scribe, having heard this tradition, would add this to the text than that it would be deleted, *contra* Joel Green, *The Death of Jesus: Tradition and Interpretation in the Passion Narrative* (Tübingen: Mohr-Siebeck, 1988), 56–57, who argues that three *hapax legomena* point to Lukan authorship—illogically, since insertion by a later scribe would better account for this change in vocabulary.

28. Except perhaps 1:20, which might be spoken by Peter or the narrator. The narrator quotes the passage read by the Ethiopian, but it is Philip who claims fulfillment (8:35). In the Third Gospel, Luke 3:4–6 is the only instance of the narrator claiming fulfillment.

29. Sterling, *Historiography*, 363, "*sacred narrative.*"

30. *Contra* Talbert, *Acts*, 83, who presumes narrator more authoritative than characters.

31. Haenchen, *Acts*, 9–14; Sterling, *Historiography*, 321.

32. Eckhard J. Schnabel, *Acts* (Grand Rapids: Zondervan, 2012), 21.

33. Satterthwaite, "Background."

34. Sterling, *Historiography*, 370–74.

35. Sterling, *Historiography*, 352–63.

36. Witherington, *Acts*, 52; Sterling, *Historiography*, 329.

37. Septuagintal links might suggest a Jewish author, Jacob Jervell, *Die Apostelgeschichte* (Göttingen: Vandenhoeck, 1998), 84–85.

38. Perhaps, Alexander, *Preface*, 132–3.

39. Witherington, *Acts*, 63; Alexander, *Preface*, 198, perhaps hosting a house-church.

40. Witherington, *Acts*, 65; uncertain, Alexander, *Preface*, 191.

41. Tyson, *Images*, 19–41.

42. Tyson, *Images*, 35–36.

43. Tyson, *Images*, 38–39.

44. Shiell, *Lector*; Tyson, *Images*, 22.

45. Tyson, *Images*, 36.

46. Similarly, "a Sabbath day's journey" (1:12) and "Symeon" (for Simon, 15:14) provide Jewish flavor but risk confusing a Gentile. Paul's comment that Jesus spoke from heaven in Hebrew (26:14) makes the account more distant for a Gentile hearer,

but more engaging for a Jew. Paul's comment that he has no charge against his nation (28:19) is of sharper concern for Jews than for Gentiles.

47. Tyson, *Images*, 36.

48. Harry Y. Gamble, *Books and Readers in the Early Church* (New Haven and London: Yale University Press, 1995), 4, 10; Keith, *Literacy*, 73–85.

49. Keener, *Acts*, 1:426, n. 25.

50. Keener, *Acts*, 1:325–34.

51. Reference to the supernatural was common, e.g., Herodotus, *Histories* 1:13, 34, 59 etc. Philostratus, *Life of Apollonius* 1:4–5, 19, 21; 8:26, etc. In contrast, Thucydides excludes it (*Peloponnesian War* 1:21); Polybius (*Histories* 1:4) limits it to a sense of fate, Walbank, *Polybius*, 59–65; Theophrastus, *Characters*, 16, denigrates the superstitious; Lucretius, *On the Nature of Things* 1:62–79; 2:600–660, is dismissive of religion.

52. E.g., Sterling, *Historiography*, 375.

53. Further, a hearer familiar with the MT might not be persuaded by James's quotation (15:17), based on the LXX of Amos 9:12. Jews well-educated in the MT are not the implied audience.

54. In the Third Gospel, the only point at which an uninformed hearer would need help is when Jesus says, "Remember Lot's wife" (Luke 17:32; a cautionary tale that is not hard to explain).

55. And some versions of 4 Macc 17:6 (although more often used of Moses or David).

56. Exod 21:1 indicates corporate context for chapters 20–31.

57. Ezek 18 provides a rare treatment by a prophet of the individual.

58. The Third Gospel may demonstrate a corporate focus in using a plural generalization (Luke 8:21, *contra* Mark 3:35; Matt 12:50), but, in contrast, picks out Peter as an individual "catcher of men" (Luke 5:10, *contra* Matt 4:19; Mark 1:17).

59. Even house-to-house ministry (2:46; 5:42; 20:20) probably involved domestic groups.

60. Strikingly, Peter shows no more respect to Centurion Cornelius than to his household, and the narrator treats the group as inviting Peter to stay (10:48).

61. Shiell, *Lector*, 30–33, 102–07.

62. The implication "obey" might be possible at 28:28, but hardly at Luke 11:28, where "obey" is added separately: οἱ ἀκούοντες ... καὶ φυλάσσοντες (those who hear ... and keep/obey).

63. 1:19; 4:36; 9:36.

64. Or, indeed, the closely related Jewish worldview.

65. Frederick F. Bruce, *The Acts of the Apostles: The Greek Text with Introduction and Commentary*, 2nd. ed. (London: Tyndale, 1952), 13–14.

66. Haenchen, *Acts*, 9; Bruce, *Acts* (1952), 1, 8–10, 14.

67. Bruce, *Acts* (1952), 11; whereas Pervo, *Acts*, 5, 12, suggests early second century; for overview, see Hemer, *Setting*, 365–70.

68. Pervo, *Acts*, 5–7.

69. Bauckham, "For Whom."

70. Bruce Winter, *After Paul Left Corinth: The Influence of Secular Ethics and Social Change* (Grand Rapids: Eerdmans, 2001), 22.

71. Peter Lampe, *From Paul to Valentinus: Christians at Rome in the First Two Centuries* (London: T. & T. Clark, 2003), 410.

72. Peter Oakes, *Reading Romans in Pompeii: Paul's Letter at Ground Level* (London: SPCK, 2009).

73. Immanuel, *Repent*, 45, 215–18.

Chapter Eight

Narrative Persuasion in Acts

In this approach to the Acts of the Apostles, the last chapter has provided the starting point—that is, the basic literary analysis of narrator, audience, context, and any purpose mentioned within the text. This chapter moves on to consider the persuasive aspects of the text, using the aspects of this method that are distinctively different from conventional literary analysis. Particular attention is given to the disagreement over John Mark, and to the expectations that, by the end of Acts, have been established about what may come next. A more detailed analysis of the Cornelius episode is provided in the case study in Chapter 9.

ACCREDITING AND DISCREDITING

Both the Third Gospel and Acts have a remarkably high density of narrative devices for establishing characters as trustworthy or untrustworthy (Appendices C and D give details). There is also a remarkably wide variety of these accrediting and discrediting devices.

The most common device involves *positive characterization*, usually by the narrator (e.g., Stephen was "full of faith," 6:5), but sometimes by a trusted character (e.g., the Lord, the most trusted of characters, tells Paul, "I am with you," 18:10a) or onlookers (responding with joy, or praise to God, 8:8) or even, very rarely, an untrustworthy character (an evil spirit acknowledges Jesus and Paul, but not Sceva's sons, 19:15). Accreditation can also be through *commissioning* or appointment by or association with a trusted character (e.g., "the apostles whom he [Jesus] had chosen," 1:2).

There are various claims that (OT) *prophecy has been fulfilled*, sometimes in general terms (e.g., "God fulfilled what he had foretold through the mouth of all the prophets," 3:18), sometimes involving a specific quotation (e.g., at 3:22, Peter quotes Deut 18:15, claiming that Jesus fulfills Moses's promise of another prophet); this primarily provides attestation to the one fulfilling the prophecy;[1] in Acts, such claims are made by the trusted characters. There are also fulfillments of recent prophecies, e.g., Sapphira's abrupt death (5:10) fulfills Peter's words (5:9); this primarily provides attestation to the one who made the prophecy.[2] *Signs and wonders* attest those who perform them, e.g., Peter is accredited by healing the disabled beggar (3:7; he then also gives credit to Jesus, 3:12–13). The *amazed response* of onlookers (e.g., 3:10–11, or fear, 16:29), affirms miracles and thus those who perform them. *Evidence* is also sometimes mentioned overtly (e.g., "many proofs," ἐν πολλοῖς τεκμηρίοις, 1:4), but it can also be presented more subtly, such as words that reveal self-sacrificial willingness to suffer (e.g., Paul: "I am ready . . . to die . . . for the name," 21:13).[3] *Answered prayer* attests those who prayed, e.g., that the believers spoke with boldness (4:31) promptly and directly fulfills their prayer (4:29, further affirmed by the place shaking and a further filling with the Holy Spirit, 4:31).[4] Lastly, *association with the Holy Spirit* provides the most distinctive and unambiguous accreditation in Acts,[5] whether in the mouth of the narrator, or of a trusted character (e.g., Paul affirming the Ephesian elders as appointed by the Holy Spirit, 20:28).

These accrediting/discrediting devices were identified throughout both Acts and the Third Gospel (which sets its context), showing which characters are trustworthy and which untrustworthy. Appendix C tabulates the results. Devices involving the "supernatural" (A7–27, D8–24) are far more frequent in Luke-Acts than in the other texts studied (Chapter 10 makes the comparisons). There is far more accrediting (324 in Acts) than discrediting (55 in Acts)—the tone of the text is positive, closer to encomium than invective.

Once a character has been established as trusted (accredited), then their words can accredit or discredit others. Care is therefore needed to keep track, as the narrative develops, of which characters are already established as trusted. In Luke-Acts, the only uncertainties arise when characters develop—Simon/Peter and Saul/Paul[6]—and with the enigmatic Gamaliel (5:34–39). Otherwise, throughout Luke-Acts, the trusted characters are Jesus and those associated with him (presented as God's people, in continuity with OT), and those to be distrusted are those who oppose them. Some, largely minor characters are neither accredited nor discredited (e.g., James, 12:17; 15:13; 21:18; the Ephesian city official, 19:35; tribune Claudius Lysias, 21:31–40; 23:18–25; Tertullus, 24:1–2; Festus, 24:27–26:32).[7]

It is the narrator and the trusted characters who dominate the establishing of trust/distrust, with other characters most relevant when they express awe or fear, or when their own words expose their character (e.g., the financial motivation accompanying Demetrius's pious words, 19:25–27). Indeed, negative characterization by a character who is not trusted has been listed (D3), for completeness, but may not play a significant part in persuasion. The only example in the Third Gospel is Simon the Pharisee's opinion of the sinful woman (Luke 7:39), promptly overturned by Jesus. (Otherwise, negative characterization is entirely in the mouth of the narrator or Jesus.) Similarly, in Acts, Tertullus's accusations against Paul (24:5) are negated by the surrounding narrative. In contrast, positive characterization by such "other characters" (A3) can be significant, for example in attesting the innocence of Jesus (by Pilate, Luke 23:4, 15, 22; a criminal, Luke 23:41; a centurion, Luke 23:47) and of Paul (by Lysias, Acts 23:29; Festus, 25:18–19, 25; Agrippa, 26:31, 32). It is especially because they are not associated with, and so not biased toward, Jesus or Paul that these comments carry weight, perceived as independent attestation.

The results (Appendix C, Tables C.1 and C.2) do not reveal any significant difference between the Third Gospel and Acts. In both, the narrator provides much positive characterization, but the trusted characters provide more. Claims that OT prophecy has been fulfilled come only once from the narrator (Luke 3:4–6)—they are otherwise left to the trusted characters: In the Third Gospel, twelve by Jesus,[8] and two by Zechariah (Luke 1:70, 72–73); in Acts, ten by Peter, eight by Paul,[9] three by James (15:16, 17, 18), two by believers (4:25–26, 28) and one by Philip (implied at 8:32–35).

The reporting of an amazed response (awe or fear) by onlookers has been included, as a device for demonstrating that something amazing did happen, thus accrediting the performer of that miracle (e.g., 2:7, amazed Diaspora Jews hearing various languages; 3:10–11, Peter healing a disabled beggar). Luke-Acts also makes use of reactions of joy and praise to God, by onlookers or by those healed. This device is hardly used in the First and Second Gospels,[10] but is remarkably frequent in Luke-Acts: χαίρω (to rejoice) is used in this way at Luke 13:17; 19:37; Acts 8:39; χαρά (joy) at Luke 24:41, 52; Acts 8:8; 12:14; ἀγαλλιάω (to rejoice) at Acts 16:34 (assuming attestation of the earthquake as well as of the gospel); δοξάζω (to praise) at Luke 18:43; 23:47; and αἰνέω (to praise) at Luke 19:37. These reactions do not involve direct speech, so they are treated as positive characterization by the narrator, who has chosen to mention them.

In the Third Gospel, there is a striking change in reactions to miracles. These all involve fear or awe until Luke 11:14 (fourteen instances),[11] but after that (starting at Luke 13:17), reactions are all of joy or praise (five instances),[12] until after the resurrection. This is not merely due to a change in source.[13] So, around the start of Jesus's journey to Jerusalem (Luke 9:51, cf. 13:22), there is a switch from awe to joy, which contrasts with increasing hostility from Jewish leaders. This may indicate the developing reaction desired from Luke's audience: If they identify with the narrative audiences, they move from expectation (e.g., Luke 1:66; 2:34–35) via awe to joy. There is further awe at the resurrection, consummated in the final verses (Luke 24:52–53) in praise (εὐλογέω) and joy (as anticipated, Luke 2:10, cf. 1:14). But such a pattern is not evident in Acts.

The Holy Spirit provides a distinctive and powerful form of accreditation in Luke-Acts[14]—everyone associated with the Spirit is to be trusted. At times, this seems to summarize their permanent state (e.g., Stephen, 6:5; Barnabas, 11:24); at others, it indicates inspiration at that moment (e.g., Peter, 2:4; 4:8; Stephen, 7:55; Agabus, 11:28; Paul, 13:9). The Spirit's arrival confirms the genuineness of conversion (8:17; 10:44–45, 47; 19:6–7; perhaps 13:52). In contrast, untrustworthy characters do not even mention, let alone claim authority through, the Spirit. Indeed, the narrative distances the Holy Spirit even from baptized believers if their heart is not right (8:18–24, cf. 5:1–11). It is intriguing that, although James is presented as an accepted leader (12:17; 15:13–21; 21:18) and Apollos as a powerful orator (18:24–28), the narrator never clearly associates the Holy Spirit with either of them. Acts may acknowledge their reputation but hardly contributes to it.[15] Although Barnabas and Saul/Paul are chosen by the Holy Spirit and commissioned (13:2–4), John (Mark) is mentioned only in a brief aside, as a helper (13:5). Thus the one who returned early (13:13), and is criticized for that by Paul (15:38), is never associated with the Holy Spirit, whereas those associated with the Holy Spirit are presented as faithfully undertaking their mission (to completion, 14:26).

Figures 8.1 and 8.2 show how accrediting devices are distributed through the chapters. (Appendix C gives more detail.) The expected pattern for accrediting and discrediting through a story involves using the devices early on, as characters are introduced. After that, they are only necessary as new characters appear, or if existing characters change. Indeed, the distribution of these devices through the Third Gospel shows an early burst of accrediting activity in the infancy narratives (chs. 1–2). Accreditation of Jesus reaches its peak in chapter 4, as he starts his ministry. It reduces after that, with gaps in chapters 15, 16, and 21, where discourse dominates. Narrative accreditation precedes the larger blocks of teaching, so that Jesus is by then already a trusted character, who will be listened to with respect. There is a final burst of accreditation during Jesus's trial, death, and resurrection (chs. 22–24). The shape of Figure 8.1 is in no way surprising.

But accreditation in Acts is, surprisingly, not concentrated at the beginning and end; rather, its peaks are near the middle. The low numbers at the beginning can be explained by characters continuing from the Third Gospel, rather than being introduced. There are then peaks in chapter 10, with a focus

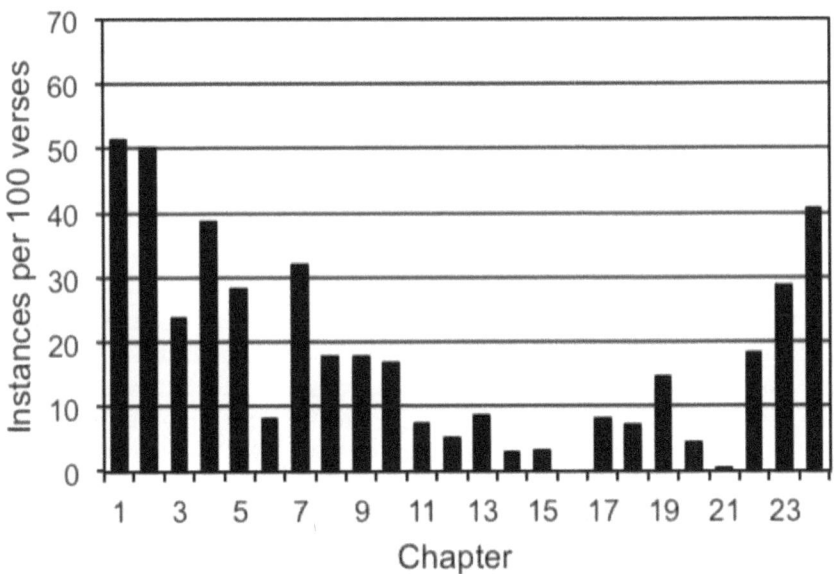

Figure 8.1. Distribution of Accrediting Through Luke

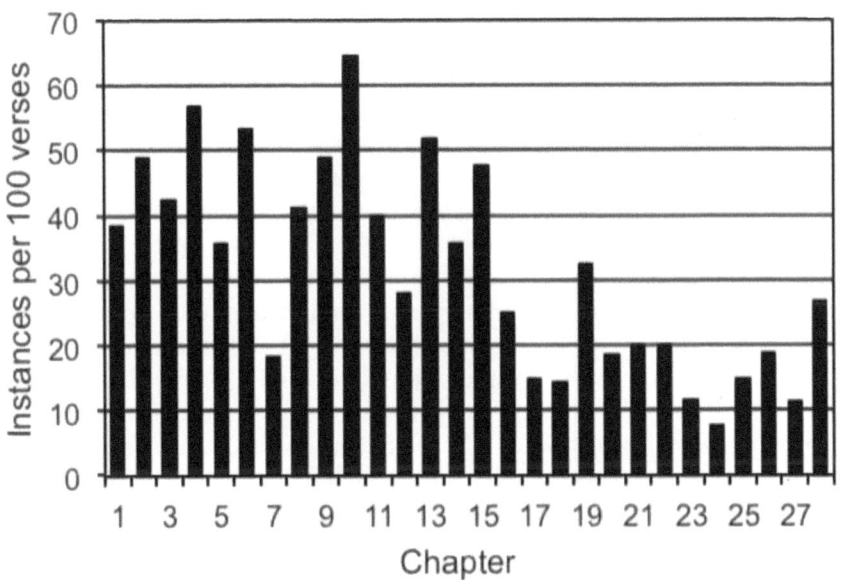

Figure 8.2. Distribution of Accrediting Through Acts

on Cornelius and his household, and chapter 13, as Barnabas and Saul/Paul start their missionary journey and speak about Jesus at Pisidian Antioch (with a minor peak in chapter 15, the Jerusalem Council). In chapter 13, Paul suddenly comes to the fore as a trusted character speaking—he provides half of these accreditations. In chapters 14–28, Paul becomes the main character accredited (sixty-six instances out of 111).

Accreditation in the Third Gospel is heavily focused on Jesus (about two-thirds, 154 out of 230 instances, Table C.3). After him come angels (twenty-two) and John the Baptist (eighteen)—and their narrative function, along with Simeon, is mainly to attest to Jesus. Thus Jesus, angels, and John the Baptist are the prominent trusted characters. The other trusted characters are those involved in the infancy narratives (Zechariah, Elizabeth, Mary, Simeon, and Anna), the disciples (the Twelve, Luke 9:1–2; 12:11–12; 22:28–30; 24:47–48; the seventy/seventy-two, Luke 10:1, 17, 19), Joseph of Arimathea (Luke 23:50–51), and, with Jesus providing reversals of their initial characterization, perhaps even Zacchaeus (Luke 19:9) and the "sinful" woman (Luke 7:47).

For the disciples, this positive characterization is not the whole story. Judas is, from the outset, singled out for negative portrayal (6:16; 22:3, 48), with the effect that his treachery does not reflect upon the others. Nevertheless, it is the disciples' failure to exorcize that prompts Jesus's sharp criticism of the entire generation (Luke 9:40); and Cleopas and his companion are described as "foolish and slow of heart to believe" (24:25). The other disciples are not strongly characterized as individuals, except for Peter, whose denial of Jesus is tempered by Jesus's earlier words, which amount to a personal commission (Luke 22:32). So the characterization of the disciples is mixed.

In Acts, there is much accreditation, but it is striking that Paul receives far more frequent accreditation (eighty-four instances) than Jesus (sixty-one), the Christian movement (fifty), or Peter (twenty-eight). This does not mean that Paul is accorded a status higher than Jesus, but that the text works harder to establish Paul as trustworthy.

Negative characterization is used sparingly (no comment is passed on Demetrius the silversmith, apart from his own words and actions, 19:24), but, at times, forcefully (e.g., Herod Agrippa I, 12:1–2, 20–23). It is applied mainly to opponents, but at times to believers: Ananias and Sapphira (5:1–11), Simon Magus (8:20–23), John Mark (15:38), and perhaps even Peter, through God's emphatic, threefold warning (10:15–16; 11:9–10) and his own admission that he was in danger of hindering God (11:17). Negative characterization is initially (until 6:13) only in the mouth of Peter: against Judas (1:18), Jerusalem Jews (2:23, 36, 40; 3:13–15, 26), their leaders (4:10; 5:30), and, later, Simon Magus (8:20–23). Negative portrayal of Jews and their leaders is continued by Stephen (7:9, 27, 35, 39, 51–52), Paul (13:27–28, 51; 18:6; 23:3 cf. 13:6), and the narrator (6:13; 8:1; 9:23, 28; 13:45; 17:5; 21:27–36; 23:12–15; 25:3), ameliorated by mention of many Jews responding positively (e.g., 2:47; 4:4, 21; 6:1, 7; 9:31, 35; 13:43; 21:20).

The most interesting aspect of negative characterization is the one that is fully reversed: Although the early Saul/Paul is portrayed negatively (8:1; 9:1, cf. 9:13; 26:11), after his encounter with Jesus (9:1–19), he is only and repeatedly portrayed positively (eighty-four positive accreditations of various kinds), except for the untrustworthy accusations of Tertullus (24:5) and the (presumably exaggerated) suspicions of circumcised believers (21:21). This dramatic change in Saul/Paul's characterization is exceptional;[16] in the texts studied, only Aseneth provides a comparable transformation.

In summary, the key trusted characters in Acts are Jesus, Peter, Stephen, Philip, and Paul (from 9:15 onward).[17] John and Barnabas provide (largely nonvocal) support. Concerning Gentiles, although the earlier positive characterization of the centurion in Capernaum (three accreditations, Luke 7:4–5, 9) is significant, that provided for Cornelius and his household is far more extensive (sixteen accreditations, combined with a further seventeen of Gentiles in general, as believers). Overall, the text provides noteworthy accreditation of Gentile believers, but far more accreditation of Paul than of anybody else.

EXCURSUS: DISAGREEMENT OVER JOHN MARK

An appreciation of this general thrust of accreditation in Acts sheds some light on the disagreement between Paul and Barnabas over John Mark (15:36–40; apparently Barnabas's cousin, Col 4:10). The narrative does not take John Mark's point of view, and is therefore not primarily a cautionary tale for hearers who empathize with him. The narrator does not provide enough information for the hearer to be sure which side to take in the disagreement—one does not discover whether Mark's return home (13:13) was due to lack of commitment or, perhaps, simply ill health (cf. Epaphroditus, Phil 2:25–30). But the episode does account for Paul's change in companions—of which hearers might already be aware from other sources (initial founders of churches were long remembered, 1 Cor 4:15; Gal 4:14; cf. 1 Thess 2:1, 10–11).

The account might conceivably be designed to answer a possible accusation against Barnabas—that "Paul refused to work any longer with Barnabas"—by indicating that it was only Mark to whom Paul objected. But the text elsewhere shows no hint of accusations against Barnabas (except, alongside Paul, those of unbelieving opponents, 13:50; 14:5, which the narrative discredits). Acts shows much more concern to defend Paul. This episode gives prominence to Paul: He takes the initiative (15:36) and provides the only direct speech (15:36). So the function of the episode is, much more likely, to defend Paul against the possible accusation that "Barnabas refused to work any longer with Paul." The text does not mention (nor quite deny) this accusation, but it does deflect it by giving the reader the counter-message that it was Paul who did the refusing, and that their parting did not reflect badly on either Paul or Barnabas, but only on Mark. In this way, not only is Paul accredited by his early association with Barnabas (9:27; 11:25–26; 13:2–15:35), but the text also avoids discrediting Paul over their separation.

NOTABLE EXAMPLES OF PERSUASIVE TECHNIQUES

- P1a) *Overt instruction by narrator*. The narrator does not take on the overt role of instructor. For instance, Acts contains many quotations of Scripture (outside Stephen's speech, 7:2–53, there are eighteen that are overt, introduced as quotations; within that speech are a further twelve quotations of varying degrees of overtness), yet these are all in the mouths of the characters; none is provided by the narrator. Rather, the narrator plays his part in establishing the trusted characters (e.g., as filled with the Holy Spirit: Peter, 4:8; Stephen, 6:5; 7:55; Barnabas, 11:24; Paul, 13:9). He also affirms that miracles have taken place—although this is subtle, because it is combined with reference either to specific witnesses (e.g., Jesus's resurrection appearances to the apostles, 1:3) or to the public nature of the events (e.g., 3:11; 5:11–12). The narrator does not presume that the audience will accept his personal word either for these miracles or for the gospel message. Instead, he provides narrative accreditation for the trusted characters and their message.
- P1b) *Overt instruction by trusted characters*.[18] It is mainly through trusted characters that teaching is provided in Acts—especially through Peter, Stephen, and Paul. The speeches are addressed to their various narrative audiences, but the teaching also aims beyond these immediate addressees:[19] Peter aspires to address all (πᾶς) Israel (2:36; 4:10) and "all who are far away" (2:39); Paul considers "people always" (διὰ παντός, 24:16), "both small and great" (26:22); and "all who are listening" (not only Agrippa, 26:29). So the hearers of Acts may reasonably interpret the teaching as aimed at them also, especially when expressed as generalizations, e.g., "whoever (πᾶς ὃς ἄν) calls on the name of the Lord will be saved" (2:21); "whoever does not (πᾶσα ψυχὴ ἥτις ἐὰν μή) hear/obey that prophet [Lev 23:39 applied to Jesus] will be destroyed" (3:23); "there is no other (οὐδε

... ἕτερον) name under heaven ... by which we must be saved" (4:12); "in every (πᾶς) nation the one who fears him [God] and does what is right is acceptable to him" (10:35); "all (πᾶς) those who believe in him [Jesus] receive forgiveness of sins" (10:43); "every one (πᾶς) who believes in this man [Jesus] is acquitted" (13:39); "God ... is not far from each one (ἕκαστος) of us" (17:27); "God ... now commands all people everywhere (πάντας πανταχοῦ) to repent" (17:30).[20]

In these generalizations, hearers can detect a message directly relevant to themselves and their own community. Through the overall narrative, the hearer is invited to imagine being one of the original hearers of the characters' speeches. It is not impossible for a believing hearer of Acts to identify with the trusted character who is doing the speaking, but the narrative does not generally encourage that (see P3 below). One more naturally imagines listening to them. Early in Acts, the speakers are explicitly accompanied (Peter by John, 3:1; Peter by six others, 10:23; 11:12; Paul by Barnabas and others, 13:13; Paul by Silas, 16:25).[21] Haenchen regards John's presence in the Temple as an addition to a story originally about Peter, because of the awkward way John seems to be inserted, e.g., at 3:4.[22] But whatever the sources or redaction, the effect of the extant text mentioning John is to make it easy for a believing hearer of Acts to imagine observing events and overhearing speeches from the point of view of such a companion. Thus a hearer may engage with the speeches either (if convinced) from the point of view of a believer accompanying the speaker or (whatever their conviction) from the point of view of a member of the crowd.

- P1c) *Overt instruction by untrustworthy characters.* The Jewish leaders are characterized negatively—for example, when Peter implies that their instructions are in direct opposition to God (4:19). Yet even they admit, reluctantly, that a notable sign (γνωστὸν σημεῖον, 4:16) was done through Peter. As a member of the Sanhedrin, Gamaliel may also be classified as an untrustworthy character, even though he is introduced as widely respected (5:34). He provides a wise voice of moderation, persuading the council not to kill the apostles. By the time Acts was written, the church had certainly spread and grown; thus, although the council probably expected the movement to fail, the hearer of Acts will note an ironic prophecy in Gamaliel's assertion that "if it is from God, you will not be able to stop them; rather, you may be found to be opponents of God" (5:38-39). Gamaliel was more right than he knew. If the hearers of Acts included Christians familiar with persecution, they might cheer at this point, or at least give some gesture of approval.

Saul/Paul is introduced as an untrustworthy character—indeed, a villain, persecuting believers (7:58; 8:1-3)—before becoming a hero. So, not surprisingly, he provides no teaching in his initial role as an untrustworthy character.

- P2a) *Worldview of the text.* The general worldview of Acts includes the assumption that miracles happen, including resurrection, healings, exorcisms, visions, and prophecies. Some supernatural events provide trusted characters with guidance (8:26, 29, 39–40; 9:3–6, 10–16; 10:3–6, 11–16, 19–20; 11:28; 13:2; 16:7, 9; 18:9–10; 20:23; 21:4, 11; 22:17–21; 23:11; 27:23–24). Others provide accreditation; for example, Peter, with John, heals a disabled beggar (3:6–7, cf. 5:15–16; 9:34–35; 9:36–42)—performing, in Jesus's name, a miracle such as Jesus had performed. Similarly, Saul/Paul is accredited, not only through his supernatural calling (9:3–19, cf. 22:6–16; 26:12–18), but also by his subsequent miracles (13:10–12; 14:8–10; 16:16–18; 19:11–12; 20:9–12). Supernatural release from prison is provided to the apostles (5:19–21), Peter (12:3–17), and Paul and Silas (16:25–34); other protection is also mentioned (27:24; 28:3–6). However, safety is not guaranteed, as demonstrated by the deaths of Stephen (7:60) and James (12:2), nor is release portrayed as primarily for the safety of the apostles, since they are promptly sent to be rearrested (albeit more gently, 5:26), nor of Paul and Silas, who do not flee but remain with their jailor (16:27–34). Rather, these events act as public signs that God's power exceeds that of the authorities and that his servants act, not secretly or fearfully, but publicly and boldly. Acts makes extensive use of the supernatural both in directing and in explaining events.

Such miracles were already part of the worldview of the Septuagint (e.g., the Shunammite's son raised, 4 Kgdms 4:18–37; Naaman's leprosy, 4 Kgdms 5:1–19; exorcism, Tob 8:1–14). Miracles of healing, vision, and prophecy were often reported also in the pagan world (e.g., Herodotus, Philostratus), so miracles in Acts are not unprecedented. But Acts is careful to distinguish Christian miracles from those of magicians—not only as superior (8:9–13; 13:11; 19:13–17), but also as divine (not demonic, 16:16–18) and motivated by grace, not money (8:20; 19:19; 20:33–35, cf. 19:25). Resurrection is evidently more countercultural, because although accepted by Pharisees, it is admitted to be contentious among both Sadducees (23:8) and Greeks (17:32).

Acts is also distinctive in its emphasis on the Holy Spirit.[23] Pagans understood that the divine might communicate through particular individuals, especially oracles at shrines such as Delphi, or priests, such as the *augures* and *haruspices* (diviners) who discerned the auspicious from the inauspicious.[24] But it was not common for devotees to expect divine power to be manifest in their whole group. Similarly, Judaism accepted the idea of divinely inspired prophets (although 1 Macc 4:46; 9:27 admits that prophecy had ceased), some of whom performed miracles; and there was some ongoing legacy, at least in Jewish attempts at exorcism (19:13, cf.

Luke 11:19). But the activity of the Holy Spirit in Acts does not indicate a mere resumption of that described in the Septuagint; rather, it far exceeds it, in terms of the numbers of believers involved, the numbers of miracles involved, and the frequency of divine intervention and guidance. This is portrayed as no mere resumption or continuation, but a dramatic fulfillment of ancient prophetic promise (2:16–21, quoting Joel 2:28–32).[25]

Through quotations of Scripture, Acts portrays itself as being related to the Septuagint, indeed (with the Third Gospel) as its fulfillment. Thus it gives the impression of having the same worldview as the Septuagint, with the extra step of identifying Jesus as the promised Messiah (e.g., 2:36; 3:20; 17:3; 18:5, 28, cf. 4:26–27; 13:33–35; 26:23) and prophet like Moses (3:23–24). The reality is more complicated, because Judaism, based on its Scriptures, maintained a strict separation from Gentiles, which, at times, became disdain or hostility (e.g., 1–4 Maccabees), yet Acts describes the overturning of that separation and distinction.

- P2b) *Worldview of trusted characters.* The worldview of the text is identical to the worldview of the trusted characters.[26] The content of the speeches, although tailored to the specific situation and audience within the narrative, represents a remarkably consistent worldview,[27] to the extent that Paul, the educated Pharisee from Tarsus, can sound strangely similar to Peter, the Galilean fisherman (e.g., Psalm 16:10 is cited by Peter, 2:31, and by Paul, 13:35, both emphasizing David's death, so that only Jesus fulfills this).[28] There is repetition in speeches of events already described by the narrator—concerning Paul's conversion/call (9:1–30; 22:1–21; 26:2–29) and the Cornelius episode (see chapter 9). These clearly provide emphasis,[29] but they do more than that; for example, repetition demonstrates that the speaker is truthful, so that their words can be trusted. These reiterations have a different "narrative point of view" (of the character, rather than the narrator), and include some variations in detail, but they do not betray any significant difference of fact or interpretation. Particular emphases are that Jewish believers should no longer treat Gentile believers as unclean[30] and that Paul had Jesus's commission for Gentile mission.[31]

- P3) *Characterization in the Third Gospel.* The Third Gospel establishes a precedent—which sets the scene for Acts—of the main speakers, John the Baptist and Jesus, being heard with respect rather than empathy. John the Baptist is presented as exceptional (μέγας, great; "filled with the Holy Spirit," Luke 1:15), making it unrealistic to identify with him. There is no *direct inside view* of his thinking. He is characterized with respect (receiving God's word, ῥῆμα, 3:2), not empathy. Thereafter, the main speaker is Jesus. The hearer naturally identifies with the crowd or the disciples and not with this respected speaker (introduced by Gabriel as God's son, an eternal king, 1:32–33).³² There are minor insights (direct inside views) into Jesus's thoughts and emotions (e.g., "how stressed I am [συνέχομαι, constrained, distressed] until it is completed," 12:50), but respect dominates over empathy. The hearer may overhear Jesus's emotions at some points, but the overall point of view is more that of those around him than that of Jesus himself (e.g., the account of Jesus's donkey follows the disciples who fetch it, 19:32–35).

After the start of Jesus's ministry (Luke 4:14), there are eleven insights into Jesus from the narrator,³³ plus four within Jesus's own words.³⁴ But there are many more insights into the thinking and emotions of his various narrative audiences: fifty-nine from the narrator,³⁵ plus five in direct speech³⁶—five times as many direct inside views into Jesus's audiences than into Jesus himself. The hearer of the Third Gospel more naturally imagines being a hearer of Jesus than being Jesus himself. This is especially true of the resurrection appearances (Luke 24), which give no direct inside view of Jesus, but there is much about the reactions of others. Whereas an average chapter of the Third Gospel contains less than five insights into characters, chapter 24 contains fourteen. In particular, empathy is built with Cleopas and his companion as they describe their hopes (24:21), amazement at reports of the empty tomb (v. 22), excitement at prophecies being fulfilled (hearts "burning," καίω, v. 32), and a hasty return trip.

There are some episodes that are naturally heard from the point of view of specific characters: Zechariah (1:8–23, 67–79); Mary (1:28–56; 2:19–51); and Peter (22:54–62). Descriptions of their emotions and thinking (1:12, 29; 2:19, 33, 48, 50–51; 22:61–62) evoke empathy, most dramatically in the case of Peter's weeping (22:62) as he recalls Jesus's prediction of his denial (22:61, fulfilling the anticipation set up by that prolepsis, 22:34).

Thus, in the Third Gospel, the main speakers (John the Baptist and Jesus) are portrayed with respect, so that one imagines hearing them rather than being them; a few, brief episodes encourage empathy (with Zechariah, Mary, and Peter); and sympathy, while not absent,³⁷ is not the main focus in any of the characterization.

- P3) *Characterization in Acts.* An overview will be helpful, before picking out examples of each type of characterization. In Acts, characterization follows a similar pattern to the Third Gospel, but with the complication that the prompted response to Peter switches³⁸ between respect (for someone *from* whom the hearer learns) and empathy (for someone *with* whom the hearer learns). The analysis of accrediting, above, has demonstrated how respect is generated; it is now necessary to consider empathy.

There are, in Acts, some *direct inside views* of the main speakers: one for the apostles (5:42), five for Peter (in Cornelius episode, 10:10, 17, 19; and in Peter's release, 12:9, 11), and seventeen for Paul[39] (nine in his own words, eight through the narrator). Of these, ten[40] out of twenty-three occur within the "we" passages[41] (and another occurs at 16:18, in an episode that starts within a "we" passage; all ten concern Paul's thinking). Since the "we" passages represent less than one-eighth of the text, this is disproportionately high—out of the twenty-three, one would expect about three, not ten. This suggests that the "we" passages arise from a source (perhaps the author's memory) rich in insights into Paul's thinking.[42] There are also frequent indications in Acts, as in the Third Gospel, of the emotions and reactions of the various crowds and audiences—at least fifty (compared with twenty-three for the main speakers).

Empathy is most strongly evoked in the episode about Peter's release from prison (12:6–17), an episode told from Peter's point of view; he even explains his thoughts aloud (12:11, a soliloquy, with no narrative audience). Similarly, the Cornelius episode (apart from Cornelius's initial vision, 10:1–8) is told from Peter's point of view—especially the account of his own vision (10:9–23). The audience hears of Peter's hunger (10:10), his vision, his objection to unclean food, the stern words from heaven (to him personally, "you" singular, 10:15), and his puzzlement (10:17). In Jerusalem, Peter retells the story (11:5–17, cf. 15:7–9), reinforcing empathy with him, especially through revelation of his thoughts at Cornelius's house (11:16–17).

Although there is no direct inside view into Philip's thinking, the episode with the Ethiopian eunuch (8:26–40) is told largely from Philip's point of view, including reports of the promptings he receives from the Spirit. Philip is earlier characterized with respect (6:3; 8:13) but, in this episode, the hearer can easily identify with him.

Empathy is not strongly developed with Saul/Paul. He is introduced as an aggressive villain, opposed to the movement (7:58; 8:1, 3; 9:1–2), a negative portrayal that evokes antipathy. The account of his call (9:3–9), although briefly adopting Saul's point of view, jumps quickly to that of Ananias (9:10–17). The episode (9:1–22) includes some direct inside view into Ananias's thinking (his concerns about Saul, 9:13) but not into Saul's (beyond his initial aggression, 9:1). This account may develop the hearer's understanding of Saul/Paul, but shows little sign of attempting to build empathy with him. This may be natural, since a hearer will not easily or quickly switch between antipathy and empathy. The episode, rather, begins the process of establishing respect for Paul, as chosen by God (9:15), amazing his initial audiences (9:21), and debating powerfully (9:22).

Paul retells this episode twice (22:6–16; 26:12–18), providing ample opportunity to develop empathy, if the author wished. The first retelling inserts his question, "What shall I do, Lord?" (22:10), which gently indicates his shocked but compliant response. But the main additional detail comes in Ananias's instructions (22:14–16). The second retelling adds Jesus's words, "It is hard for you to kick against goads" (26:14), which provides his insight into Saul's situation; and the main additional detail comes in Jesus's instructions (26:16–18). These retellings do not take the opportunity to develop empathy; despite being retold by Paul himself, they provide no significant extra inside view. Rather, the additional details contribute toward respect, giving more information about his divine call.[43] Another opportunity to develop empathy would be the release of Paul and Silas from prison (16:25–40, since Peter's release, 12:6–17, develops empathy with him). Certainly, their praying and singing (16:25) indicates piety and hope, but the narrative gives no further indication of their thinking. Rather, the emotions expressed are the despair (16:27) and joy (16:34) of the jailer and the fear of the magistrates (16:38). This contributes more to respect for Paul than empathy.

Sympathy is not significantly evoked within Acts. Whereas bowels (σπλάγχνα, inward parts) are generally, in Scripture, used to indicate compassion (e.g., Luke 1:78), in Acts, they are used only literally (of Judas's bowels spilling out, 1:18). Compassion for a man with lifelong disability (3:2) might be evoked by starting with a full description of his plight, but a significant detail—that he was over forty—is saved for the end of the episode (4:22), where it is clearly included, not to evoke sympathy (for a man whose plight has now ended), but to emphasize the magnitude of the miracle.

So, in Acts as in the Third Gospel, respect (for trusted characters) is strongly encouraged, with the hearer most naturally identifying with the various narrative audiences. Sympathy is hardly evoked. It is respect, rather than empathy, that dominates the characterization of Paul. In contrast, although respect is established for Peter,[44] there follow two episodes that encourage empathy with him.

- P3a) *Positive characterization with empathy*. The two significant examples involve empathy with Peter, in the Cornelius episode (10:9–11:17, see chapter 9) and prison release (12:6–17). These have the effect of encouraging the audience to develop, with Peter, openness to the idea that God accepts all kinds of people without discriminating (διακρίνω, 11:12; 15:9, cf. 10:28) and confidence that God has power, greater than Herod's, to protect his servants.

- P3b) *Positive characterization with respect.* Accrediting devices are used to establish respect for Jesus; the movement; the main speakers (Peter, the apostles as a group, Stephen, Philip, and Paul); and Cornelius, his household, and Gentile believers as a group. This reinforces respect for Jesus (as already established in the Third Gospel) and his followers, and it encourages the hearer to take to heart the contents of speeches by these trusted speakers.
- P3c) *Positive characterization with sympathy.* This is not significantly used.
- P3d) *Aversion.* The negative characterization in Acts provokes "antipathy" (P4) rather than aversion. John Mark is a character with whom a hearer could identify, whose failure to persist in mission (13:5, 13; 15:37–39) could have been presented as a cautionary tale, but it is not. The episode may emphasize how committed one had to be to accompany Paul, but there is little opportunity for empathy with Mark and the verdict on him is left disputed.
- P4a) *Repulsive character (via traits).* Judas is introduced with an account of his betrayal of Jesus (1:16; condemned as wickedness, ἀδικία, 1:18) and of his gruesome death (1:18, a classic "negative outcome"), in keeping with the woe Jesus had pronounced (Luke 22:22). This encourages antipathy toward Judas—although it is not clear whether he had successors to whom such antipathy might also apply.

Herod emerges as one who harms believers, killing James (12:1–2) merely for popularity (12:3).[45] When acclaimed as a god, he fails to "give glory to God" by denying this, so an angel causes his gruesome death (12:23; cf. Antiochus Epiphanes, 2 Macc 9:9–12, 28). To some extent, this serves to warn the hearer against blasphemy (cf. 2 Macc 9:28) or offensive pride (ὕβρις). But the hearer identifies with Peter, not Herod, so the emphasis is more that the hearer should, as God does, take sides—Herod deserves antipathy—confident that God can protect believers and destroy opponents, even kings.

The Jewish leaders are negatively characterized through their words and actions (unjustly hostile to the believers), but not through comments by the narrator. There does not seem to be prejudice against them simply as Jews, because other Jews respond positively (e.g., many priests, 6:7) and Paul's decisive moves toward Gentiles (13:46–47; 18:6; 19:9; 28:28) do not exclude Jews (rather, Jews and Greeks are mentioned together, straight after Paul's departure from the Ephesus synagogue, 19:9–10). The Jewish leaders act as a foil, a contrast to believers;[46] for example, when the high priest shows unrestraint, ordering Paul to be struck (23:5), Paul ends up showing restraint and remarkable respect. Believers have repeatedly been in trouble, but Acts consistently lays the blame for this on the authorities.

The effect of this negative characterization is to encourage the hearer to dismiss allegations made against believers and, in the hearer's own context, to distrust any Jewish leaders who continue to oppose Christianity.

Similarly, those involved with idols, although often strongly condemned in Jewish texts (e.g., Isa 41:24; 44:9–11, 18; Jer 10:14–15), receive in Acts a mixed (although generally negative) portrayal—not nearly as negative as magicians (see P4b below). Demetrius is negatively portrayed only by his own words (revealing his financial concerns, 19:25) and the silversmiths by their rowdiness (19:28–29, 32–34; and the Ephesian official's rebuke, 19:36–40). Other pagans mistake Paul for a god (in Lystra, 14:11–13; and Malta, 28:6), but Paul's response in Lystra (14:15–17) falls short of a rebuke, and no response is reported in Malta. The characterization of Gentiles in Athens is neutral (17:21), involving interest (17:32) and a divided response (17:32–34). So the portrayal of pagans is generally negative, but does not amount to antipathy. The effect of this negative characterization is to encourage the hearer to see pagan beliefs as misguided, to dismiss the allegations made, within the text, against the believers, and, in their own context, to distrust any pagans who continue to oppose Christianity.

- P4b) *Antipathy: Repulsive character (via identity)*. There is strongly negative characterization of those involved in magic and related practices. The trusted characters contribute most forcefully to this: Simon the magician is rebuked by Peter with words that almost amount to a curse (8:20–23; although baptized, Simon seems still motivated by money and power); and Bar-Jesus/Elymas is rebuked and blinded through Paul (13:10–11). The narrator's contribution is much less forceful, but it includes exposing the anger of the owners of the exorcized fortune-teller as arising from their loss of income (16:19; in contrast to the joyful response to the most recent exorcisms, 8:7–8). Ironically, it is a demon who exposes the Jewish exorcists (whose attempt at a formulaic use of Jesus's name is magical in tone, 19:13)—they are dismissed as unknown, and overpowered (19:15–16). These characterizations tend to build antipathy toward anybody associated with magical practices. Converts who burned their expensive magical books (19:18-19) have the last word on this—encouraging a complete break with magic.[47]

- P5a) *Plot: Positive outcome*. The prison releases of Peter (12:3–19) and Paul (with Silas, 16:19–40) show God intervening miraculously on their behalf, discrediting those who imprisoned them and providing these missionaries with strong accreditation. The hearer is encouraged to trust them and their teaching, and to follow their example of trusting in God.

As in the Gospels, the miracle stories in Acts include positive outcomes for those healed or raised, e.g., Eutychus (20:9–12). But the episodes are most naturally heard from the point of view of an onlooker. The narrative function of these demonstrations of God's power is primarily to accredit the performers of the miracles and their message, not to encourage the hearer to identify with the beneficiaries. The Eutychus episode focuses on Paul; there is not enough detail about Eutychus to encourage identification with him. Indeed, although Paul claims that Eutychus is alive again (20:10), the narrative then follows the rest of Paul's meeting (20:11), postponing confirmation of the miracle to a final analepsis (20:12) that comments, not on Eutychus's response, but on the comforted (παρακαλέω, 20:12) believers. The episode is not structured to function as a cautionary tale about sleeping in sermons. It gives general reassurance that God looks after believers, but, mainly, it accredits Paul and his ministry.

Tabitha is characterized in more depth, as a shining example of good works (9:36, 39) who can certainly be seen as a positive example to emulate. Nevertheless, the focus of that episode is on Peter (whose actions and words, 9:40, are reminiscent of Jesus's, Luke 8:51–54).

- P5b) *Negative outcome*. The account of Ananias and Sapphira (5:1–11) relies on the negative outcome (their abrupt deaths) for its narrative impact. The preceding narrative has focused on the Jerusalem believers (4:23–37), whose positive characterization includes selling property and giving the proceeds to the apostles for distribution (4:34–35). At this point, the hearer naturally identifies with this excellent group. Ananias and Sapphira are mentioned next, with no overt characterization by the narrator, except that δέ (but, 5:1) gently indicates a contrast. Their retention of part of the proceeds is narrated negatively (νοσφίζω in the middle voice, implying embezzlement cf. Josh 7:1 of Achar/Aachan's sin and 2 Macc 4:32, of Menelaus's theft of temple vessels, the only two LXX occurrences, both heinous). It is Peter, amplifying this (5:3), whose words provide the most forceful denunciation (5:3–4, 9) as a satanic attempt to lie to God. Although the second account could easily have been abbreviated, Sapphira's death is described in no less detail than Ananias's. Their deaths have the last, and most forceful, word. This is surely a cautionary tale, where characters with whom the audience (both male and female) can identify make a clearly identified mistake and suffer a strongly emphasized negative outcome (reinforced by mention of the fearful response to this news, 5:11). The hearer is warned against making the same, or a similar, mistake—of attempting to deceive the Church and thus the Holy Spirit.[48]

Judas also comes to a sticky end (in an aside, 1:18–19, within Peter's speech, 1:16–22; an analepsis where it is unclear whether Peter or the narrator is speaking). This may be a cautionary tale, although the hearer has not at any stage in Luke-Acts had an opportunity to identify with Judas—

he is never mentioned without immediately being described as a traitor (Luke 6:16; 22:3–6, 47–48; Acts 1:16). This sticky end is certainly the culmination of negative characterization, developing antipathy through the trait of being a traitor (P4a). It also plays a part in the recharacterization of the apostles as a group who are, in Acts 1, cleansed from any possible association with betrayal or accusation of being incomplete. It helps with scene-setting, indicating the seriousness of being involved in killing Jesus, a theme then addressed by Peter (in 2:23—Jews in Jerusalem are treated as involved in Jesus's death).

Herod (Agrippa I) also comes to a sticky end (12:23; see P4a above). In contrast, the account of Simon Magus (8:9–24) seems inconclusive, in that his response (8:24) to Peter's call to repent (8:22) is ambiguous. Nevertheless, the outcome is undeniably negative, in that this reputed magician (8:9–11) ends up in disrepute. The plot contributes to negative characterization, developing antipathy, certainly through his traits (concern with money and power, 8:18–20), but more broadly through his identity as a magician (perhaps ex-magician). Irrespective of whether the hearer may have knowledge of Simon from other sources, this episode indicates unambiguously that the magician's power is dwarfed by God's power. The most forceful message is for the hearer to respect Christian leaders and neither to fear nor to use magicians.[49]

- P5c) *Polyphonic affirmation.* Paul's innocence is declared polyphonically, by himself (18:6, cf. 16:37), unbelieving Pharisees (23:9), Lysias (23:29), Festus (25:25), and Agrippa (26:31–32). The various speeches that present the gospel are also mutually reinforcing, although they are significantly adapted to each situation so that the variety of presentation may be more noticeable than the consistency of the basic proclamation.

- P5d) *Journey of discovery.* The hearer is encouraged to accompany Peter on his journey of discovery about God's acceptance of Gentiles (10:1–11:18, see chapter 9). The hearer is by now accustomed to responding with respect to Peter, as the Spirit speaks *through* him (2:14–36, 38–39; 3:12–26; 4:8–12; 5:3–4, 9, 29–32; 8:20–23, cf. words of power 9:34, 40). But in 10:9–20, there is a change, as the Spirit speaks *to* Peter (explicit in 10:19), in a way not much different from the address of an angel to Centurion Cornelius (10:1–8). With direct inside views, the hearer's response to Peter is changed from respect to empathy. The effect of the subsequent journey of discovery is to persuade the hearer, with Peter, that Jewish believers should accept Gentile believers without discriminating or requiring Torah observance (or, by implication, circumcision). By extension, if other grounds for discrimination had arisen in the hearer's own context (e.g., slave/free, fluency in Greek, availability to meet weekly, or living in a household that retained *Lares, Penates, Hestia*, or other household gods), this episode questions such discrimination.

It is remarkable that the Samaritan believers, unlike Gentiles, are not reported as causing any surprise among Jewish believers.[50] John, who had once suggested calling down fire to destroy Samaritans (Luke 9:54), later accompanies Peter in bestowing the heavenly fire of the Spirit upon them (8:14–17). But the text does nothing to highlight this irony. Acts could treat Samaria as a journey of discovery with Peter and John, but it does not. Neither is Paul's conversion/call (9:1–19) such a "journey of discovery" because the hearer develops little empathy for Paul—indeed, it is easier to identify with Ananias. In the retellings, the hearer discovers some new details, but Paul does not. For Paul, there may be a "shock of recognition," but this is not presented as a "journey of discovery."

- P5e) *Gentle steps*. The retellings of Paul's conversion/call are, rather, a gentle-steps approach, suitable for gradually winning over hearers initially suspicious of Paul's claim to divine appointment and ministry. In the third and final account, Paul hears directly from Jesus that he is appointed and sent to the Gentiles, with a promise of protection (26:16–18), yet this conversation technically happened in the Damascus road encounter first described at 9:5–6, where these words are omitted, and where Jesus is reported as communicating Paul's appointment only to Ananias. The middle of the three accounts omits Jesus's conversation with Ananias and adds Jesus mentioning this appointment directly to Paul (21:10). So, in these gentle steps, Jesus's appointment of Paul is described in more and more detail, and is presented as being communicated more and more directly by Jesus to Paul.

NARRATIVE PERSUASION

Acts puts considerable emphasis on accrediting Jesus's followers as trustworthy, with particular focus, in turn, upon Peter, Stephen, Philip, and Paul. Apart from Philip, these are the main speakers. The hearer of the Third Gospel is strongly encouraged to regard Jesus with respect, and therefore to heed his teaching; in the same way, Acts encourages respect for these trusted characters and for their teaching. It is not clear that the main purpose of the narrative is to encourage the hearer to follow their example, because much of their reported behavior could only be emulated by Spirit-filled miracle-workers. Admittedly, concerning exorcism, the Second Gospel provides details which might help exorcists (Mark 9:20–29, *contra* Matt 17:18–20; Luke 9:42), but Luke-Acts lacks such details. The descriptions of the corporate life of the Jerusalem believers (2:43–47; 4:23–37) seem ideal and unattainable rather than a realistic example to follow.

The narrative sets the scenes for the various speeches in Acts, not only by indicating the context, speaker, and narrative audience, but also by establishing trust in these speakers, so that the hearer is encouraged to take to heart their gospel proclamation (and encouragement to Christians, 20:18–35). Nevertheless, the persuasive message of Acts is not confined to the speeches. A compliant hearer of the narrative will be left with trust both in the Christian movement and in these particular leaders: especially Paul, but also Peter. A striking absence is that there is no clear accreditation (certainly, no direct association with the Holy Spirit) for any potential successor to these two. There are various ways in which Peter's ministry paves the way for Paul's, especially in accrediting ministry to Gentiles, but Paul's ministry does not (as presented in Acts) pave the way for any ongoing leader, except the local groups of elders he established (especially in Ephesus). Acts accredits no ongoing individual leader, only this general, corporate leadership. If there is any comment on future leadership it is, rather, Paul's warning that some will be savage wolves (20:29–30).

The most evident message of Acts is the gospel itself, building on the story of Jesus as recounted in the Third Gospel. The gospel is presented, not merely through speeches by evangelists (portrayed with respect), but also through narrative that indicates continuity between Jesus's ministry and that of the protagonists.[51] They carry out supernatural and teaching ministry with similarities to Jesus's ministry, and in Jesus's name. One contribution of the analysis here is to indicate that they are also accredited in similar ways to Jesus in the Third Gospel (e.g., amazed crowds).

Another key message of Acts is the appropriateness of mission to and incorporation of Gentiles. It is in the Cornelius episode (Acts 10) that there is the highest density of accrediting devices in Acts. In persuasion about this issue, the key role is played by the narrative rather than the speeches—the speeches serve to echo, clarify, and affirm what the narrative has already demonstrated. An array of narrative tools is used: prolepsis, as Saul/Paul's commission looks forward to his mission to Gentiles (9:15); positive characterization of Cornelius and his household (as devout, εὐσεβής, giving alms, ἐλεημοσύνη, 10:2); heavenly visions to Cornelius (10:3–6) and to Peter (10:10–16, including a puzzle to ponder); the opportunity, with Peter, to discover how the visions complement and clarify each other (10:20, 34); and the dramatic arrival of the Holy Spirit (10:44–46, A26), ensuring Peter's agreement that these Gentiles can be baptized (10:47–48) and encouraging the hearer to accept this. Peter's subsequent speeches (11:5–17; 15:7–9) do not pronounce a decision, but they guide his audiences through his experiences and thought processes. Having earlier listened with respect, learning *from* Peter (as the Spirit speaks *through* him), in this episode the hearer of Acts learns *with* Peter (as the Spirit speaks *to* him). The Cornelius narrative develops empathy with Peter so as to persuade the hearer by taking him/her on a journey of discovery.

On this issue, it would be reasonable to attempt to persuade Jews and God-fearers by a sermon or dialogue based on Scripture. Indeed, Paul comes close to this in Pisidian Antioch, when he cites Isaiah 49:6 (God's people are to be "a light" for the Gentiles, 13:47), as does James at the Jerusalem Council, citing Amos 9:11–12 ("that all peoples may seek the Lord," 15:16–17). Many such discussions must have happened; but they are likely to have included scriptural counterarguments, e.g., that Isaiah 49:23 goes on to suggest that approaching Gentiles must "lick the dust of your [Israel's] feet"; and that this Greek quotation of Amos 9:11–12 is significantly different from the Hebrew. It is not clear to what extent the author of Acts was aware of such discussions. It is clear that he chose a different approach—a narrative approach—to persuasion about this.

The character most often, and thus most forcefully, accredited in Acts is Paul; the text works hard to build respect for him. A compliant hearer is thus left reassured that Paul's mission to Gentiles was appropriate, despite the reservations of Jewish Christians, accusations of Jewish leaders and imprisonment by Romans. Paul is strongly accredited, which will tend also to accredit, in the hearer's own day, Paul's approach, the churches he founded and any leadership groups still associated with him.

Relatively minor episodes may also have persuasive impact; for example, the story of Ananias and Sapphira provides a cautionary tale. Peter's release from prison, in contrast to Herod's sudden death, encourages trust in the power of God. Similarly, relatively minor themes may also make a persuasive contribution; for example, negative characterization of those associated with magic, along with repeated demonstration of the Spirit's superior power, serves both to accredit the Jesus movement and to discredit magicians, even evoking antipathy toward them.

PERSUASION OF THE AUDIENCES OF ACTS

It is now possible to consider how persuasion within Acts can be expected to engage with various groups within the audience. Groups among the believers would be: converts from various Gentile backgrounds; Gentiles who had previously been proselytes or God-fearers; and Jews (and, in principle, possibly Samaritans). Among nonbelievers, similar groups would exist. It is not clear that the division in early audiences between "insiders" (believers) and "outsiders" would be sharp—unless current persecution made it impossible to remain "on the fence." Beyond the frequently mentioned God-fearers (who may be linked, at least in Syria, with Gentile "Judaizers" mentioned by Josephus, *J.W.* 2.463), Judaism had various other "fringes": Jews whose association with magic suggests that they were not entirely orthodox (Elymas, 13:6; sons of Sceva, 19:13–19); mixed marriages (Timothy's parents, 16:1–3); proselytes (mentioned among the Jews, 2:10; 13:43); apostate Jews (e.g., 1 Macc 1:11–15, 43; 2:16–18; 3 Macc 1:3; Alexander, Philo's nephew);[52] and household slaves.[53] After AD 70, many Jews were slaves (*J.W.* 6:418–19), and other Jews would have been tempted to apostasy by social pressure, by the Roman tax on Jews (*J.W.* 7:218), and possibly by revulsion at the reported Jewish atrocities. Proselytes and God-fearers would similarly have had their allegiance challenged at this time.

Torah observance ensured that Jews were among the groups with the strictest boundaries and therefore the smallest "fringe," so it is likely that Christian communities had a more extensive "fringe," given their loosening of Jewish boundary-markers (especially circumcision and food laws). The parable of the seed (Luke 8:5–15) mentions not only good soil (representing "insiders") and the path (unresponsive "outsiders"), but also rocky soil (where growth is short-lived) and thorny soil (where growth is eventually choked). These last two indicate the possibility, not merely of acceptance or rejection of the gospel, but also of some halfhearted responses. In time, that might effectively become a rejection, but there is an indication here that some hearers—perhaps even half of them—could initially be regarded as "fringe" rather than as either "insiders" or "outsiders." Specifically Christian examples would be that entire households are reported as being baptized (Cornelius, 10:44; 11:14; the Philippian jailer, 16:33; Crispus, 18:8), making it inevitable that, for each *pater familias* who believed, a whole group of others—relatives, children, slaves, and perhaps even friends (10:24)—suddenly found themselves within Christian community.[54] Acts might imply unanimity in these particular households, but it is not clear that this was verifiable—except, at times, by the initial, evident gift of tongues (10:44).[55] In general, in such household conversions, some would find themselves associated with the conversion, but not by their own choice. Some may not have been present at the time; and others, such as new slaves, would join the household subsequently. Although Philemon was a Christian (Phlm 5), Paul seems to treat Philemon's slave Onesimus as having become a believer only when he ran away and met Paul (becoming Paul's spiritual "son," Phlm 10, cf. 16). Before that, Onesimus would have been on the "fringe" of the Christian community. When women believed (5:14; 8:12; 17:12), or slaves, their lead would not necessarily be followed by husbands (1 Cor 7:13-16) or masters (implied at 1 Tim 6:1–2), so that a household not formally identified as Christian might have within it a mixture of Christians with others who knew them well and would not necessarily be hostile to their faith.[56] Mixed marriages, between believers and nonbelievers, are well attested.[57] The existence of God-fearers suggests the likelihood of there being a Christian equivalent—some who, having been exposed to the gospel, were positively disposed, and might even revere Jesus, but were unwilling to be baptized or formally identified as a Christian because of social pressure, unwillingness to abandon traditions, desire to revere Jesus alongside other deities, or reverence for Jesus combined with unresolved fear of (or even attachment to) magic.[58] Acts avoids suggesting these possibilities, but the invocation of Jesus's name by the sons of Sceva (19:13–15) is a step in this direction,[59] and modern experience in India suggests that such situations inevitably arise where the wider culture is accepting of multiple deities.[60]

Apostate Christians are also ignored by Acts.[61] Admittedly, under persecution, it would be hard for the embattled faithful to maintain any relationship with apostates, who would be seen as traitors. But one whose apostasy was less overt and arose from personal doubts, circumstances or relationships, might well maintain links with the Christian community.

For all these reasons, it makes sense to consider, not only "outsiders" (whether interested or hostile) and "insiders" (whether mature or new converts), but also a considerable "fringe." Indeed, 1 Cor 14:16–25 addresses a similar issue about the involvement of those on the "fringe." Paul urges that their entire approach to ordering the church meeting[62] should bear in mind, not only the presence of believers, but also the possible presence of unbelievers (ἄπιστος, presumably interested outsiders) and of the uninformed (ἰδιώτης). Paul assumes that these Corinthian believers will understand what he means when he mentions the "place" (τόπος) of the uninformed (1 Cor 14:16). Whether or not the uninitiated were normally present, Paul suggests that things be ordered on the basis that they may be present. If such Christian meetings were one of the occasions on which Acts was intended to be read, the author might well have a similar mindset—an awareness of the "place" of the uninitiated among his intended audience.

Most *Christians of Gentile origin* would naturally identify (at least aspirationally) with Cornelius and his household, but not with Judaizing Christians (15:1, 5, cf. 11:1–2).[63] They might not identify fully with Peter during Acts 10, while he is being persuaded to accept Gentiles, but can surely identify with him after that, when he becomes their advocate before Jewish believers. Gentile believers would be particularly interested in the theme of mission to Gentiles with minimal restrictions, which justifies their own incorporation into the Church by establishing continuity with the early Jesus movement, especially through Peter, and with historical Judaism, through claims that Jesus fulfills the Hebrew Scriptures. Acts does this without promoting antipathy toward Jews (although it does toward magicians). Gentile Christians would naturally accept and applaud the worldview presented in the text (although some might have a more hostile attitude toward persecutors such as the Jewish leaders). Churches with a significant proportion of Gentiles (as, apparently, at Antioch, 11:20, and in the churches Paul founded, e.g., 13:43; 14:27) would be the natural environment within which sources might have been available for the material in Acts. Gentile Christians may thus have contributed to the shaping of the material. They are also a key part of the implied audience.

Jewish believers would be engaged by Acts, most directly through empathy with Peter during the Cornelius episode. Especially in this episode, but also in the Jerusalem Council, the implied audience (once the persuasiveness of the text is allowed for) includes Jewish believers who need to be persuaded or reassured that it is right to accept Gentile believers and associate with them, with no more than minimal requirements (15:28–29; neither circumcision nor Torah observance).

The ongoing tension between believers and Jewish authorities is also significant. Acts indicates that believers do not behave badly even under provocation, including their behavior toward Jewish leaders. Paul is careful to avoid disrespect to the high priest (23:5) or unpatriotic complaints about his people (28:19)—details of more concern to a Jewish hearer than to a Gentile. Similarly, the narrative describes unethical behavior by Jewish leaders (e.g., "false witnesses" 6:13), but the narrator avoids directly criticizing them (despite coming close to it: "filled with jealousy, they contradicted . . . blaspheming" 13:45, cf. 17:5), and the negative comments are largely in the mouths of the trusted characters. Thus the narrator avoids sounding disloyal to Judaism, which would risk alienating Jewish hearers.

A Samaritan hearer of Acts, whether believing or not, would surely be frustrated that the text glosses over Samaritan concerns. Although Samaritans are presented as joyfully receiving the gospel, and receiving God's accreditation through the Holy Spirit, it is not stated that the Jewish Christians shared table fellowship with them—it is far from clear that they accepted them as brothers and sisters or as equals (although this issue is addressed for Gentiles, 10:34, 48; 11:12; 15:9). After centuries of hostility, that is a glaring omission from the point of view of a Samaritan. Samaritans are not among the implied audience.

It is not clear that *hostile nonbelievers* would listen to Acts. Hostile pagans would find no characters with whom they could easily identify, until the Lystrans (14:11–19), who are presented as misguided and fickle and are addressed by Paul in a hasty speech only three verses long (14:15–17). The pagan hearer's patience would finally be rewarded in Athens (17:16–34).[64] An interested pagan might engage with this narrative, but it is unclear that a hostile pagan would still be listening by this point.

If *hostile Jews* were the intended audience, it would be natural to encourage such hearers to identify with the early Saul/Paul and lead them on a journey of discovery about Jesus. Acts does not do that, suggesting that it was not written with hostile Jews in mind. Similarly, a hostile proselyte or God-fearer would naturally identify with the pious Cornelius. Peter's speech to Cornelius (10:34–43) could have focused on how, having already appreciated the God of the Jews, a God-fearer should take the extra step of accepting Jesus. That theme is not entirely absent (e.g., the prophets testify to Jesus, 10:43), but is far less prominent than the speech's opening theme, that God accepts Gentiles (10:34–35, 43)—but that was already the basis of a God-fearer's faith (albeit with limitations, e.g., limited access to the Temple or interaction with strict Jews). The account of this speech is not entirely unsuitable for persuading God-fearers to accept Jesus, but it is far more suitable for persuading Jewish believers to accept Gentile believers. The later "conversion" of the God-fearing Lydia is reported without any speech at all (16:14–15). So, the text is simply not structured to grasp these opportunities to engage with a hostile, God-fearing audience.

Once the persuasive aspects of the text are allowed for, the implied audience excludes Samaritans and those actively hostile to the Jesus movement, but could include believers of any (eastern Mediterranean) background. Nevertheless, if the text were intended only for believers, its contents would be incongruous because it neglects the life and concerns of ordinary believers. It recounts evangelistic addresses but almost nothing of ongoing teaching or catechism within the church (although such processes would be necessary and might be implied by κατηχέω, Luke 1:4). The episode describing controversy over support for widows (6:1–6) ends without explicitly stating whether the controversy was resolved; the focus is on neither widows nor church administration, but on introducing the Seven. The summaries of the life of the Jerusalem church (2:44–47; 4:32–37; 5:42) seem to be idealized (except for the episode with Ananias and Sapphira). After that, the focus is on outreach (including the basis for mission to Gentiles), with only the briefest of mentions of ongoing processes of discipleship (11:23, 26; 14:22–23; 15:41; 16:5; 18:11; 20:7, 11). The only speeches addressed to Christians are set within especially called leadership meetings (11:2–18; 15:6–29; 20:18–38), not normal church life. Issues concerning food are presented, unrealistically, as though resolved to the satisfaction of all (15:20–31, cf. Rom 14; 1 Cor 8; Gal 2:11–14). Although tensions over leadership were a significant issue as early as Paul's Corinthian correspondence (1 Cor 1:11–12), Acts glosses over such issues with its brief mention of the future possibility of ungodly leaders (20:29–30).[65] In summary, Acts focuses less on internal matters and more on the interface between the movement and the outside world—outreach, opposition, and persecution. It demonstrates little interest in internal issues such as leadership, administration, procedures, or even issues of lifestyle and ethics. Except perhaps in Paul's speech to the Ephesian elders (20:18–35), the agenda of Acts is thus very different from New Testament epistles or the *Didache*.

If presented to an audience of believers, who knew the reality of life within the church, Acts, which is often claimed to provide inspiring legitimation for the movement, would be in danger of ringing hollow by glossing over issues of immediate concern or frustration within the church. A conceivable and partial explanation might be that Acts was written a generation or more after Paul, so that even elderly believers could not contradict it. A more likely explanation is that Acts is intended for an audience extending beyond the community of believers, to interested outsiders, especially the "fringe" mentioned above. Acts can provide a "shop window" into the Jesus movement for interested outsiders at the same time as providing encouragement and shaping the worldview of believers. Luke 1:4 suggests that Luke-Acts aims, not merely to encourage those who are fully convinced, but to provide confidence (ἀσφάλεια) for those who are not yet sure that they have heard the truth. If believers in the audience understood from this that Acts is a "shop-window," they would be more likely to tolerate its focus on the external.

EXCURSUS: EXPECTATIONS AT THE END OF ACTS

The hearer's expectations are relevant to the questions of why Acts ends where it does, whether another sequel was planned, and whether publication was demonstrably after Paul's death or after the fall of Jerusalem[66] (two events of which every interested Greek-speaker would quickly become aware).

The Third Gospel provides some clear pointers to what will happen beyond the end of that text. Some are eschatological (e.g., Luke 1:33; 21:27); the siege and destruction of Jerusalem is explicit (Luke 21:6, 20, 24); and, from Jerusalem, the disciples are to witness internationally (Luke 24:47–48), with God's power (v. 49), strengthened by Peter (Luke 22:32), in the face of persecution (Luke 21:12). It is not explicit that there will be a sequel, but, if informed that there is one, the hearer already knows the starting point, main characters, and basic storyline.

Similarly, Acts sets some expectations. Eschatology is reiterated (e.g., Acts 1:11), but the destruction of Jerusalem is hardly hinted at (3:23 is very general; 6:14 is very indirect; Paul's judgmental words against Ananias, 23:3, are softened by more respectful words, 23:5). The Ephesian elders will not see Paul again (20:25) and are to expect "savage wolves" to arise among them (20:29-30). By reaching Rome, Paul fulfills his plan (19:21) and a heavenly prophecy (23:11), but must yet fulfill the prophecy that he will testify before Caesar (27:24). Mission "to the end of the earth: (1:8) is hardly complete (Rome being, for most, the center rather than the "end");[67] indeed Acts closes with a note of further expectation—Gentiles "will listen" (28:28).

Some suggest that Acts indicates that Paul will die in Rome—his farewell speech indicates his willingness to die (20:24); he does not expect to see these people again (20:25); and there is a *Gattung* of a final speech, which depends on the hero's subsequent death.[68] But, I suggest, weightier evidence actually indicates the opposite. Paul's assertion that he would not see the Ephesian elders again can be explained by his completion of ministry there and commitment to testify further west (Rome, 19:21, cf. Rom 15:23-29). God may have promised to reveal to Paul "how much he must suffer" (9:16), but such revelations never predict his death. Although Jesus prophesied his own death as inevitable (δεῖ, Luke 9:22, cf. 18:33), and he is in some ways a model for later martyrs (e.g., Stephen),[69] Acts does not present the death of any martyr as similarly inevitable. What Paul expresses is willingness to die (20:24; 21:13, cf. Thomas, John 11:16), not expectation of death. There are prophecies of his arrest (20:23; 21:11), but none of his death. Indeed, Paul's last comment about willingness to die is specific to Jerusalem (21:13), and by the end of Acts, this has already been shown *not* to have happened. In Acts, the bold witnesses have more often been saved (5:39; 12:3-11; 16:26-40) than killed (Stephen, 7:60; James, 12:2). Most telling, Paul has received from God the promise, not of death, but of rescue (ἐξαιρέω, middle voice, to set free, deliver) from both Jews and Gentiles (26:17). Although this promise is situated at the heart of Paul's call, it is not reported in the first two accounts (9:1-19; 22:6-16), only in the third. If it had been reported in chapter 9, the hearer might regard it as already fulfilled many times (e.g., rescued from Gentiles, 18:9-17). But, being reported only in chapter 26, it has been arranged to be fresh in the mind of the hearer at the end of Acts. Paul has recently been rescued from the Jews (21:35; 22:10, 12-35; and also from a storm, 27:24). The hearer naturally expects him now to be rescued from the Gentiles.

If a hearer of Acts was unaware of Paul's death, the text would give him/her no particular reason to doubt that God would rescue Paul and allow him to continue the unfinished mission. Although many suggest publication after Paul's death, the text itself suggests the opposite—that, after testifying before Caesar, Paul's release is anticipated.

There is also a question about whether the hearer is assumed to be aware of the destruction of Jerusalem. There is no hint of this in the text.[70] It is not clear that the hearer is assumed to be aware of it. However, if both author and hearer were aware of it, that would add significant color to the presentation of the leadership (including, by implication, the Twelve, 8:1) in Jerusalem. By the end of Acts, they remain in Jerusalem, apparently comfortably involved with the Temple (21:18–25). Thus, they would be presented (without any explicit comment) as sitting in cabins on the *Titanic*—caricatured as doomed.[71] But this leadership is not otherwise treated with reservations. In the case of James (Jesus's brother), Acts does not seem to further his reputation, but does acknowledge it (12:17; 15:19; 21:18) and, to some extent, employs it toward validation of the Gentile mission (15:13–29). It would therefore be surprising for Acts to include such implied criticism of this group. Even if they were to escape before the siege (as suggested by Luke 21:21), that would (unless the story were included in Acts, to provide some different emphasis) involve a loss of dignity compared with their position, represented as being ensconced in Jerusalem without having to do more than occasionally send emissaries to review the rest of the church (8:14; 11:1, 22; 15:22–30).

This suggests three possibilities. First, the author of Acts, despite generally showing respect for Christian leaders, was willing to show implied (but noticeable to all) disrespect to Jerusalem elders, by leaving them apparently doomed at the end of Acts. Secondly, he intended to write a further sequel, which would tell of how they fared when Jerusalem was destroyed. Or, thirdly, Acts was published before the fall of Jerusalem (or, just conceivably, might be ingeniously and deviously crafted to give that impression).

If a hearer of Acts were told that there is a sequel, their clearest expectation would be for it to tell of Paul's witness before Caesar. Other threads of the narrative have, by the closing chapters, been left aside. By the end of the Third Gospel, the main protagonists of the beginning of Acts, the apostles, have not only been introduced but have also been recently and overtly commissioned by Jesus. In contrast, by the end of Acts, it is not clear that there is any character other than Paul in a position to continue the story. None has been overtly commissioned through the Holy Spirit—unless the sequel were to revert to Silas (who, although largely silent,[72] was at least a prophet, 15:32), or Barnabas (commissioned at 13:2–4), in which case it would have to address the tricky question of John Mark's involvement (15:37–39). Apollos is never associated with the Holy Spirit (even his baptismal status is left uncertain, 18:25), and James is only associated with the Holy Spirit by his own claim (corporately, 15:28). No other character, apart from Paul, could continue the story in the way that Acts continues the story of the Third Gospel. Unless perhaps to continue Paul's story, it is not clear that any further sequel was planned at the time Acts was published.

CONCLUSIONS

A more detailed analysis of the Cornelius episode will be given in chapter 9, followed by a comparison between the five texts (Chapter 10) and further discussion of the purpose of Acts (Chapter 11). So the conclusions here will be brief.

This chapter has identified two features not encountered in the other texts studied: First, the Holy Spirit as the most powerful source of accreditation; secondly, a process of switching between respect and empathy for the same character, Peter, who plays different roles in the various stages of the author's persuasive narrative.

Almost all of the listed techniques of persuasion are built into Acts. There is a remarkable emphasis on authenticating trusted characters. A wide range of accrediting devices is used and they are frequent throughout the text. Paul is authenticated the most; but the highest density of accrediting devices is found in Acts 10, in the Cornelius episode. Paul is characterized with respect more than with empathy. In contrast, empathy with Peter is built in the Cornelius episode, so that the reader joins him on a "journey of discovery."

There is no shortage of material, for analyzing Acts as a persuasive narrative, and this kind of analysis gives some indications of the audiences and of the purpose of the text. Acts does not seem to be aimed at an audience hostile to the Jesus movement—whether Jewish, Gentile, or God-fearing. The narrative fails to take the steps that would be necessary to help them to identify with the characters and engage with the story. Acts mentions dialogue with Jews[73] (generally involving a hostile response), but it is not clear that Acts is itself designed to be a part of that dialogue; it describes the "conversion" of many Jews, many of whom must have initially been hostile, but it fails to invite the hearer to identify with anyone going through such a process.

The implied audience includes all sorts of (Greek-speaking) Christians, whether their background be Jewish, Gentile, or God-fearing (although not Samaritan). Believers are an inevitable audience for the work, and they seem to form a significant part of the target audience. For example, the cautionary tale of Ananias and Sapphira (5:1–11), while not inappropriate for an outsider, would be most pointed for a believing hearer. Nevertheless, the text does not seem designed purely for "internal" use among believers, because it shows far less interest in internal issues (e.g., relationships within local groups of believers, administration, ethics, hierarchy, routine, or discipline) than in external issues, such as outreach and persecution. Legitimating the Jesus movement to its own members is not convincing as the sole purpose of Acts, as it is not clear that it would be persuasive to those interested in internal matters and familiar with "warts-and-all" reality within the movement.

The text is suitable for an audience that includes not only believers, but also some who can best be described as "fringe"—who are interested, but not convinced about the movement. Such a fringe may not have been particularly numerous, may not have been ubiquitous and may not have been lasting (since a fringe would naturally evaporate under persecution). Nevertheless, there is evidence that believers had contact with a variety of such people, often through their households. The expectation that at least some interested outsiders would hear the work—that, alongside any other purposes, it must act as a "shop-window" for them—can explain both the focus on external issues and the tendency to gloss over internal issues.

On this basis, persuasion within the text includes both encouragement of interested "outsiders" wholeheartedly to join the movement and encouragement of "insiders" to have confidence in its legitimacy and power. The grounds for legitimacy include continuity with historical Judaism (claimed through fulfillment of Scripture), continuity with Jesus himself, and accreditation by the Holy Spirit. There is particular concern to authenticate Paul's ministry, with accounts of Peter's ministry providing a bridge between Jesus and Paul. Particular attention is given to legitimating the acceptance of Gentiles into the movement—a significant change from Judaism. This is achieved through narrative rather than argument, involving positive characterization of Cornelius, a journey of discovery with Peter, and multiple layers of accreditation. So the Cornelius episode will now be considered in more detail, as a case study.

NOTES

1. As God's agent (not always knowingly, e.g., Cyrus, Isa 45:1); Menken, "Fulfilment," 179–98.
2. Talbert, *Luke*, 233, 268; idem, *Acts*, 106, 225.
3. James A. Kelhoffer, *Persecution, Persuasion and Power: Readiness to Withstand Hardship as a Corroboration of Legitimacy in the New Testament* (Tübingen: Mohr Siebeck, 2010).
4. Holmås, *Prayer*, 262; positive outcomes (P5a) are also persuasive, encouraging prayer (265).
5. William H. Shepherd Jr. *The Narrative Function of the Holy Spirit as a Character in Luke-Acts* (Atlanta: Scholars, 1994), 246–47: "the Spirit is the narrative symbol of human reliability . . . to signal narrative reliability."
6. Perhaps Simon the Sorcerer, 8:9–24.
7. Although their actions (not included in Tables C.1 and C.2), may eventually show them in a positive or negative light: Introduced in neutral terms, Felix ends up negatively characterized, 24:26; Aquila and Priscilla finally receive some affirmation at 18:26.

8. Specific quotation: Luke 4:18–21; 7:27; 20:17–18, 41–44; 21:20–24; 22:37. General: 10:23–24; 18:31; 22:22, 37; 24:25–26, 27 (indirect speech), 44.

9. Specific quotation: Peter: 1:16–20 (perhaps narrator?); 2:16–21, 25–28, 31, 34–35; 3:22–23; 4:11. Paul: 13:23, 27–29, 33, 34, 35, 46–47 (with Barnabas); 28:26–27. General: Peter: 3:18, 24; 10:43. Paul: 26:22.

10. Magi's response to the star, Matt 2:10, and women's to an angel, Matt 28:8, are exceptional.

11. Luke 4:22, 32, 36; 5:9, 10, 26; 7:9, 16; 8:25, 37, 56; 9:34, 43; 11:14.

12. Luke 13:17; 17:15–16; 18:43; 19:37; 23:47 (cf. 19:48).

13. Luke 13:17 and 17:15–16 are in episodes peculiar to the Third Gospel. 18:43; 19:37; and 23:47 are in episodes shared with the First and Second Gospels, but where these "audience reactions" are peculiar to Luke.

14. Max Turner, *Power from on High: The Spirit in Israel's Restoration and Witness in Luke-Acts* (Eugene, OR: Wipf and Stock, 2000), 431–32; especially of new disciples, 433.

15. Although Jerusalem leaders as a group, including James, claim association with the Spirit (15:28) and Apollos's unspecified spirit (18:25) might be taken to imply the Holy Spirit.

16. Philip H. Kern, "Paul's Conversion and Luke's Portrayal of Character in Acts 8–10," *Tyndale Bulletin* 54, no. 2 (2003): 63–80, especially 63–64; Gerhard Schneider, *Die Apostelgeschichte: Kommentar*, 2 vols. (Freiburg: Herder, 1980–1982), 2:41–45, gives an overview.

17. The Holy Spirit might also be considered a character, Shepherd, *Narrative Function*.

18. Kurz, *Reading*, especially 73–110, 125–31.

19. Soards, *Speeches*, 203–04.

20. See also 15:11; 16:31; 20:35; 26:18, 29.

21. Later, Paul is alone for his Areopagus speech, 17:22–31, and perhaps for his defense speeches.

22. Haenchen, *Acts*, 199.

23. Shepherd, *Narrative Function*, 1–23.

24. Beard, *Religions*, 18–19.

25. Turner, *Power*, 349–51.

26. Or, if that develops, to the worldview finally adopted: Paul's attitude is transformed; and Peter's toward Gentiles (P5d below).

27. Soards, *Speeches*, 162, 183.

28. Witherington, *Rhetoric*, 47, 64.

29. Talbert, *Acts*, 57, 187.

30. Narrator indicates divine initiative, 10:15, 45, cf. Peter's words: 10:28; 11:12, 17–18; 15:9; the issue is presented as though fully agreed, 11:18; 15:13–29, especially 19–20.

31. Narrator indicates divine initiative, 9:15, cf. Paul's words: 22:15, 21; 26:17, 20.

32. For example, in Gethsemane, there is possible mention of Jesus's struggle (ἀγωνία, Luke 22:44), but omission of his emotions (ἤρξατο λυπεῖσθαι καὶ ἀδημονεῖν, Matt 26:37; ἤρξατο ἐκθαμβεῖσθαι καὶ ἀδημονεῖν, Mark 14:33). With little

direct inside view of Jesus, the scene is naturally envisaged from the point of view of the nearby disciples.

33. Luke 5:20, 22; 6:8; 7:9, 13; 9:47; 10:21; 11:17; 19:41; 20:23; 22:44.

34. Luke 9:41; 12:49–50; 13:34; 22:15.

35. Luke 4:28, 32, 36; 5:9, 26; 6:7, 11; 7:16, 29, 30, 39; 8:25, 35, 37, 47, 53, 56; 9:7, 33, 34, 43, 45; 10:29, 40; 11:14, 16, 38, 53–54; 13:14, 17; 14:1; 16:14; 18:23, 34, 43 (beggar), 43 (crowd); 19:6, 37, 47, 48; 20:19, 20, 26; 22:2, 6, 45, 61, 62; 23:8, 20, 27, 47, 48; 24:16, 31, 37, 41, 52, 53 (cf. 10:17, not a reaction to Jesus; 22:5; 24:4, 5, 8, 11, 12 in Jesus's absence).

36. Luke 5:8; 20:5–6; 24:21, 22, 32.

37. Having compassion (σπλαγχνίζομαι) is mentioned at 7:13 (Jesus, for the widow of Nain), 10:33 (the "Good Samaritan"), and 15:20 (the father, for his returning son), but these situations are promptly transformed for the better; any sympathy then evaporates.

38. Jack J. Gibson, *Peter between Jerusalem and Antioch* (Tubingen: Mohr Siebeck, 2013), 81, 140, notes only Peter's development from fallibility to authoritative "rock."

39. 14:9; 16:10, 13, 18; 17:16; 19:21; 20:7, 16, 22–23, 24, 25, 33; 21:13–14; 22:20; 26:9, 11; 28:15.

40. 16:10, 13 (including "we" with Paul); 20:7, 16, 22–23, 24, 25, 33; 21:13–14; 28:15.

41. Traditional definition: 16:10–17; 20:5–21:18; 27:1–28:16; Porter, "We," 545.

42. Porter's tighter definition (16:10–17; 20:5–15; 21:1–18; 27:1–19; 28:1–16) gives a similar conclusion: Five instances in "we" passages which are 1/14th of Acts; but less than two are expected.

43. Daniel Marguerat, "Saul's Conversion (Acts 9, 22, 26) and the Multiplication of Narrative in Acts," in *Luke's Literary Achievement*, ed. Christopher M. Tuckett (Sheffield: Sheffield Academic, 1995), 127–55, especially 154.

44. As Spirit-filled spokesman (2:14; 4:8); healer (3:7, cf. 5:16; 9:34) before amazed crowds (3:9–11, 16; 4:21) and amazed leaders (4:13, 14, 16); agent in bestowing the Spirit (8:15, 17); proclaimer of God's judgment on Ananias and Sapphira (5:5 10, 11) and Simon (8:20–23); and raiser of the dead (9:41–42).

45. O. Wesley Allen, *The Death of Herod: The Narrative and Theological Function of Retribution in Luke-Acts* (Atlanta, GA: Scholars, 1997), 77–78, characterized as a "ruthless tyrant."

46. Darr, *Character*, 92, Pharisees as "caricatures of a morality to be avoided," cf. 125.

47. Hans-Josef Klauck, *Magic and Paganism in Early Christianity: The World of the Acts of the Apostles* (Minneapolis: Fortress, 2000), 23; Steve Walton, "Evil in Ephesus: Acts 19:8–40," in *Evil in Second Temple Judaism and Early Christianity*, ed. Chris Keith and Loren T. Stuckenbruck (Tübingen: Mohr Siebeck, 2016), 233–34.

48. Although the apostles' authority is also emphasized, Johnson, *Acts*, 210.

49. Cf. the negative outcome for the sons of Sceva (19:13–17; P4b above).

50. V. J. Samkutty, *The Samaritan Mission in Acts* (London: T. & T. Clark, 2006), neglects this, despite noting that this is "a mission which is the first of its kind" (219).

51. Talbert, *Luke*, 93; idem, *Acts*, 77–78.

52. Daniel R. Schwartz, "Philo, His Family and His Times," in *The Cambridge Companion to Philo*, ed. Adam Kamesar (Cambridge: Cambridge University Press, 2009), 12–14.

53. Luke 12:42–49—slaves of Jews should have been Gentiles (Exod 21:2–11); there were also Jewish slaves in Gentile households (e.g., Neh 5:5–9).

54. Green, *Evangelism*, 321–22.

55. Further, the use of πᾶς (all, 10:44; 11:14) and πανοικεί (with whole household, 16:34) can bear a looser implication than "each and every" member—as indicated by "all the prophets" at 3:18: Christ's sufferings could hardly be claimed as foretold by "each and every" prophet. πᾶς can be hyperbolic, Witherington, *Acts*, 105–6.

56. Aristobulus and Narcissus seem to have been unbelievers, within whose households there were some believers (Rom 16:10–11); Lampe, *Valentinus*, 164–65.

57. With unbelieving husband: 1 Cor 7:13–16; 1 Pet 3:1–2, cf. Justin *2 Apol.* 2; Tertullian *To His Wife* 2:4–7; with unbelieving wife: *Apostolic Tradition* 41.

58. That the later *Apostolic Tradition* insists on catechumens ceasing from idolatry (16:8) or magic (16:13–14) shows that this was a concern, but does not guarantee that there was always a clean break.

59. Cf. Jesus's name in Paris Magical Papyrus IV, 3020; Winter, *Corinth*, 178, interpreting 1 Cor 12:3a in the light of archeological evidence, suggests that "the Christianisation of Hermes of the Underworld was in the minds of some converts who saw that now his tasks [including cursing] were performed by Jesus."

60. N. K. Das, "Religions Syncretism and Cultural Homogenisation in North-East India," in *Culture, Religion and Philosophy: Critical Studies in Syncretism and Inter-Faith Harmony*, ed. N. K. Das (Jaipur: Rawat, 2003), 295–324; cf., for a Roman example, *Augustan History, Life of Alexander Severus*, 29. For various types of ancient syncretism, see Irina Levinskaya, *The Book of Acts in Its Diaspora Setting* (Grand Rapids: Eerdmans, 1996), 197–205.

61. Pliny's letter reports converts who had abandoned Christianity, Nock, *Conversion*, 156–57; Eusebius, on Polycarp's martyrdom, also records Quintus's recantation, *Church History* 4:15. Green, *Evangelism*, 44 suggests that Jewish Christians were tempted to return to Judaism.

62. Edward Adams, *The Earliest Christian Meeting Places: Almost Exclusively Houses?* (London: T. & T. Clark, 2013), 24–30.

63. Unless they had earlier become full proselytes and been circumcised.

64. Esler, *Community*, 25, argues that, because persuasion in Acts overall is very different from this speech to Greeks, "outright pagans" can be excluded from the audience of Acts.

65. And disagreement over Mark (15:37–40).

66. Troy M. Troftgruben, *A Conclusion Unhindered: A Study of the Ending of Acts Within Its Literary Environment* (Tübingen: Mohr Siebeck, 2010), 7–36, 179–82; Loveday Alexander, *Acts in Its Ancient Literary Context* (London: T. & T. Clark, 2006), 227, who suggests that "the whole of Acts forms a narrative bridge between the story of Jesus and the world of the reader."

67. Keener, *Acts*, 1:429.

68. Talbert, *Acts*, 180, 231; Dibelius, *Studies*, 15. But the text arguably simply leaves uncertainty: Steve Walton, *Leadership and Lifestyle: The Portrait of Paul in the Miletus Speech and 1 Thessalonians* (Cambridge: Cambridge University Press, 2000), 78–79.

69. Talbert, *Luke*, 240; idem, *Acts*, 65.

70. Accusations about Jesus threatening the Temple (6:14) are presented as false. Luke 19:42–44; 21:6–24 (cf. Mark 13:1–19) might indicate awareness of AD 70, but it might simply echo 597–586 BC: Charles H. Dodd, *More New Testament Studies* (Manchester: Manchester University Press, 1968), 69–83.

71. Although James himself was killed even before AD 70, Josephus, *Ant.* 20:9.

72. Co-speaking briefly with Paul at 16:31.

73. Mentioned or implied at 6:9–10; 9:20–22, 29; 17:2–4; 18:4, 28; 19:8–9; 28:23–25.

Chapter Nine

Case Study
The Cornelius Episode, Acts 10:1–11:18

Chapter 8 gives an overview of narrative persuasion through the whole of Acts and shows how the method can be applied to the entire text. The next step is to consider a particular passage of Acts as a case study, to demonstrate that the method can also be used for more detailed analysis of a section of text. This will be done by working sequentially through the passage, in the style of a commentary; providing a distinctive explanation of how the retellings contribute; describing how the characterization of Peter contributes to persuasion here; and finally showing that the episode is constructed in a way that guides the hearer, with Peter, on a persuasive "journey of discovery."

SETTING THE SCENE FOR THE CORNELIUS EPISODE

The Cornelius episode (10:1–11:18) has been chosen for more detailed analysis because its high density of accrediting devices indicates that the author was working especially hard to be persuasive. The Peter-related events in the wider section 9:32–11:18 form a connected sequence, with only loose connections to the sections before and after.[1] The key function of the accounts of Aeneas and Dorcas (9:32–43) is to set the scene for the Cornelius episode, both in location (the house of Simon the tanner, 9:43; 10:6) and in setting the hearer's expectations of Peter. Although the inclusion of Dorcas's story has puzzled some,[2] its relevance to the Cornelius episode is that it sets a precedent of Peter responding positively when messengers ask him to come.[3]

NOTES ON FEATURES OF THE TEXT RELEVANT TO PERSUASION

Peter Is Persuaded

- *10:1.* The first phrases are very similar to the first phrases of the previous episode (9:36)—introducing a "certain" (τὶς) named person (a new character), in a named town (a new location), and describing them positively. This gives the feeling that this is a similar story over again, although this character is actually rather different from the Jewish Dorcas—a centurion and thus, although not necessarily Roman by race, certainly Gentile.
- *10:2.* Like Dorcas, Cornelius's positive characterization includes almsgiving. To this are added piety (εὐσεβής), fear of God,[4] and consistent prayer. Cornelius is no ordinary Gentile—he seems to be more religious even than the esteemed Dorcas! The terms used are universally positive, but they seem tailored to Jewish concerns.[5]
- *10:3.* Cornelius's vision is attested by the claim that he perceives it "clearly" (φανερῶς) and that the person in the vision is "an angel/messenger [ἄγγελος] of God." That Cornelius was praying at that time (cf. 3:1) is hinted at here and explicit at 10:30—further positive characterization.
- *10:4.* Cornelius stares (ἀτενίζω) at the angel, a focalizer that builds expectation of something important.[6] That he is terrified (ἔμφοβος) provides attestation for the angel—it takes a lot to terrify a centurion! To the narrator's positive characterization of Cornelius (10:2) is added heavenly attestation—his prayers and almsgiving have "gone up as a memorial [μνημόσυνον] before God," like the pleasing aroma of an acceptable sacrifice (Lev 2:2, cf. also atonement money, Exod 30:16, and prayers, Tob 12:12). This does not quite (yet, cf. 10:44) affirm that Cornelius is accepted by God,[7] but sets the expectation that his prayers, since heard, are about to be answered.
- *10:5–6.* That the angel mentions "a certain" (τὶς) Simon indicates that Simon/Peter is unknown to Cornelius. Specific information about Peter's name and whereabouts (with Simon the tanner, as the hearer knows, 9:43) accredits the angel as bringing unexplainable, therefore supernatural, knowledge. When the messengers confirm this by finding Peter (10:21), this will further accredit Cornelius, as having demonstrably received divine revelation. The added detail of the house being beside the sea (10:6, 32) is not confirmed by the narrator, but would be obvious to the messengers, and so is naturally assumed to be affirmed.
- *10:7.* The soldier who attends Cornelius is also pious (εὐσεβής); indeed, the three messengers must be part of his household (οἶκος) and, although presumably Gentiles, all fear God (10:2). One cannot fault Cornelius for the company and servants he keeps.

- *10:8.* That Cornelius makes his vision known straightaway adds to its credibility, through verifiability (at least, as perceived by the hearer) by these three. That he explains everything suggests trust and permits the messengers to speak for him (10:22). By sending messengers, Cornelius exactly and immediately obeys the angel's command (10:5). Empathy is not evoked—Cornelius must have felt strong emotions (10:24, 33 indicate enthusiastic expectation), but they are not mentioned here.
- *10:9–10.* The story shifts to Peter, praying on the roof at noon, implying heat. That he was hungry and having to wait for food gives the hearer further insight into his feelings. Peter is already a trusted and inspired character, unlike Cornelius, so the narrator can mention his trance/vision (ἔκστασις) without having to comment. The hearer naturally assumes it is from God, but, about this, is not "elevated" above Peter's knowledge, making it easy to imagine Peter's puzzlement (10:17).
- *10:11–14.* Peter sees heaven opened (ἀνοίγω, 10:11, which probably implies an authentically divine vision, cf. Luke 3:21; Acts 7:56),[8] and a collection of various creatures. Told to kill and eat, Peter refuses because he has never eaten anything "common" (κοινός) or "unclean" (ἀκάθαρτος). That Peter addresses the voice as "Lord" (κύριος) might simply represent respect, but suggests an assumption that the voice is divine.[9] There are presumably "clean" species, but Peter treats them as unfit to eat, presumably through contact with the "unclean."[10] Anybody familiar with Jews would recognize Peter's response as entirely natural—a similar response from Ezekiel even provoked a concession, not condemnation, from the Lord (Ezek 4:14–15). It has been suggested that Peter's hunger may have caused his trance,[11] made him receptive,[12] or at least inspired the theme of eating,[13] but its key relevance is surely this: Peter had no reason for refusing, except his Jewish scruples.
- *10:15–16.* The response is abrupt: "What God has made clean, do not treat as common" (κοινόω; the meaning "make unclean," as at 21:28, would not make sense here). The voice now asserts divine authority. This happens three times; God is being emphatic. Alert hearers will remember Peter's threefold denial of Jesus (Luke 22:34, 54–62)[14] and wonder whether Peter is again saying something wrong.
- *10:17–18.* The hearer gets a direct inside view—Peter is confused (διαπορέω), as is the first-time hearer.[15] The hearer has been anticipating the arrival of Cornelius's messengers, and their arrival at this moment indicates God's hand guiding events as well as the vision,[16] although the exact connection is not yet clear.
- *10:19–20.* Peter remains puzzled, thinking through (διενθυμέομαι, to consider) the vision. "The Spirit" (i.e., the Holy Spirit, 2:4b; 8:29, cf. 6:10)

gives him more direct guidance, accredited by being proved true moments later, when Peter will indeed meet the messengers. The claim "I have sent them" provides accreditation of the messengers to Peter (and, again, to the hearer). Peter is to go with them and not to "doubt/hesitate" (διακρίνω, middle) or perhaps "make a distinction" (a possible meaning, cf. Jas 2:4)—either meaning (or both) may apply.[17] Peter has not been told that these are Gentiles, and the last messengers (9:38) were Jews, so "without hesitating" would be a more natural interpretation for him to reach at this moment. This idea of going along with what you are told, at least for now, without arguing, even if you have doubts, is close to the way a reader or hearer naturally engages with narrative—suspending disbelief even if the story is an incredible fantasy. At this point, any hearer who shares Peter's doubts is encouraged nevertheless, like him, to go along with these events. For Peter, a way forward is authoritatively commanded; for hearers, overhearing this, the narrative guides them less overtly.

- *10:21.* Obediently going down, Peter meets the messengers and finds the Spirit's guidance confirmed. He would only now discover that these are Gentiles.
- *10:22.* The messengers provide a further positive characterization of Cornelius, as righteous (δίκαιος) and attested (μαρτυρέω) by the whole Jewish nation (hyperbolic—Peter is one example of a Jew who does not even know Cornelius). The hearer may recall the centurion of Capernaum, well-spoken-of by Jews (Luke 7:5; a man of faith, Luke 7:9, who could dispatch soldiers and messengers, Luke 7:8, 10). The messengers report that he has seen a "holy angel," adding the new information that Cornelius is to hear a message from Peter. Peter's vision begins to make sense—addressing willingness, not to eat, but to go to a Gentile's house and speak there.
- *10:23.* Peter offers hospitality to these Gentiles, overnight; in the light of the Spirit's guidance (10:19–20), the hearer accepts that. Most people would expect a tanner not to be a scrupulous Jew, thus the narrative can present the hospitality as Peter's without the hearer noticing that this was not entirely Peter's decision to make. The text avoids emphasizing that tricky negotiation would be needed before inviting Gentiles into a Jew's house; such negotiation is saved for Jerusalem (11:1–18). According to strict Jewish tradition (at least later), by living with a tanner, Peter would be unclean already.[18] But the hearer is not intended to assume that—otherwise Peter's earlier protests (10:14, 16) would be rather hypocritical; Peter was effectively rebuked three times, but not for hypocrisy.[19]
- The next day, Peter accompanies the messengers. A hearer familiar with Luke 7:2–11 would remember that Jesus was willing to accompany such messengers. Technically Jesus did not meet that centurion[20] or enter his

house, so Peter is about to take an unprecedented step. But the text does not emphasize this or provoke such critical reflection. Rather, Dorcas's contribution helps here. The hearer vaguely remembers that Jesus helped a virtuous centurion; but fresher in the hearer's mind is the precedent that, when messengers come to Peter making an urgent request on behalf of somebody virtuous, Peter goes without hesitating (ὀκνέω, 9:38, echoed by διακρίνω, 10:20). Desiring a satisfying story, the hearer wants him to go, to bring the threads of the story together and move toward resolution of a currently unsatisfactory situation (with Cornelius, Peter, and the first-time hearer still puzzled). Dorcas's story makes it feel natural and necessary that Peter should unhesitatingly accept this invitation—putting on one side, for now, any concerns about Cornelius being a Gentile. Peter is accompanied by local (Jewish, 10:45) Christians, who will not take any initiative, but will act as witnesses of the events to come.

- *10:24–26.* Cornelius gathers family and friends and, when Peter arrives, falls at his feet (προσκυνέω, possibly in worship, certainly showing great respect). Cornelius seems wholehearted, with high expectations. Gentiles who worship evangelists are always misguided; they are later characterized as fickle and foolish (14:11–19; 28:4–6), but there is no hint of that here. Hearers (especially Christians) will naturally imagine being Peter (or alongside Peter). A centurion was a powerful man, commanding respect and fear. The idea of a centurion prostrating himself publicly before Peter (a Galilean fisherman) would be incongruous—with hearers struggling to know how to react. It would be tempting to enjoy imagining a centurion groveling at one's feet; but Peter shows appropriate humility, defusing this tension, emphasizing that he is only human; such respect is due to God, not to God's servants, even apostles. King Ptolemy's exaggerated respect on the arrival of the law scrolls (*Let. Aris.* 177) is similar—a Gentile authority figure desires to pay great respect to the God of the Jews—a respect that indeed God, and only God, deserves.

- *10:27–29.* Peter goes in, meets the gathered crowd, and mentions that it is not permitted (ἀθέμιτος; against tradition—although not technically against the law)[21] for a Jew to visit a Gentile like this. Presumably some in the implied audience need to be informed or reminded of this. That it is introduced with, "You know," suggests that these Gentiles in Caesarea would know this (living among Jews) and, of the audience of Acts, that there are some who know this so well that they might be impatient with the explanation, were it not softened by this introduction. Peter goes on to apply his vision, not to food, but to people being declared clean by God. This provides an insight into his thinking, explaining why he came without objecting (ἀναντιρρήτως). He asks why they (surprisingly not addressing Cornelius personally, cf. 10:22) have sent for him.

- *10:30–33.* Cornelius explains his vision. The details are familiar (from 10:3–6), providing the hearer with a reminder and a further affirmation that Cornelius is a reliable witness, echoing the narrator. Cornelius reports seeing a man in shining (λαμπρός) attire,[22] an unembellished account of what he saw, with no added interpretation—appropriate for wooing any hearers suspicious of Gentiles like Cornelius. Whereas Jewish believers will later criticize Peter for coming (11:2), Cornelius shows appreciation. He assumes that God has commanded Peter to deliver them a message, presumably expecting some prophetic oracle. His piety is reflected by his solemn explanation that they have gathered "before God,"[23] which also raises the hearer's expectations. It has been suggested that "before God" (ἐνώπιον τοῦ θεοῦ) derives from the Septuagint.[24] But use there is almost entirely at the Tabernacle or Temple (e.g., Exod 23:15),[25] so the Septuagint hardly indicates the meaning here. Early Christian understanding, given their habit of meeting in houses (e.g., 2:46; 5:42), seems more relevant to the hearer of Acts. Among other places, Acts would surely have been heard in homes,[26] where Cornelius's comment would encourage those hearing Acts to consider themselves also as "before God."

- *10:34.* Mention of Peter opening his mouth prepares the hearer for a significant utterance.[27] Peter starts by revealing his thinking—he has realized (καταλαμβάνω, middle) that God is not "one who shows favoritism" (προσωπολήμπτης). The exact word is unique, and not a normal Greek way of expressing this (cf. 15:9 uses διακρίνω, I discriminate; 1 Tim 5:21 uses πρόκριμα, prejudice; and πρόσκλισις, favoritism). It seems to derive from θαυμάζω πρόσωπον in the Septuagint (e.g., Lev 19:15; Deut 10:17; perverting justice, e.g., through bribes).[28] Peter's meaning, that God now accepts Gentiles just like Jews (clarified at 11:15–17) is not a traditional Jewish understanding. This expression seems to have been standard among Christians (the abstract noun appears at Rom 2:11; Eph 6:9; Col 3:25; Jas 2:1), not Luke's creation, and might simply arise from them originally discussing this on the basis of the Septuagint. It has the effect of linking Peter's idea to similar-sounding ideas in the Septuagint—reassuring for hearers familiar with the Septuagint, while not unintelligible for others.

- *10:35.* Peter's generalization about who is acceptable to God echoes what the hearer has already heard about Cornelius—fearing God (10:2, 22) and righteous (10:22). The hearer, consciously or not, receives the suggestion that God accepts Cornelius and other Gentiles like him.

- *10:36–38.* Mentioning, "You know" (v. 37) provides attestation to the main, public facts of Jesus's ministry by suggesting that these details were widely known even among Gentiles in Caesarea.[29] It permits a compact speech, e.g., treating John the Baptist briefly, as a known person. Overheard by the audience of Acts, this suggests that these details are widely known, so that Peter's words are not contentious claims to be weighed up but reminders of reliable information already well-known. "Peace" (10:36) and Jesus "doing good" (εὐεργετέω, 10:38) are universally acceptable ideas particularly suitable when addressing Gentiles,[30] by which Peter accredits Jesus.

- *10:39–43.* Peter talks about the witnesses of Jesus's ministry and resurrection as "us," implying the apostles[31] (not his companions from Joppa, completely ignored since 10:23). Being commanded to preach by Jesus (v. 42) accredits Peter and the apostles, as commissioned. That "they" killed Jesus (v. 39, cf. 13:27–29) implies Jews in Jerusalem (echoing accusations addressed to Jerusalem Jews that "you" killed him; 2:23, 36; 3:15; 4:10; 7:52. cf. 5:28). Peter could here equally have accused "you" Romans, since the garrison in Jerusalem, which executed Jesus, was answerable to the headquarters here in Caesarea (23:23–33). It is possible that Luke follows sources in blaming Jerusalem Jews,[32] but the suggestion that he betrays "fundamental and systematic" hostility to Jews[33] goes too far, given positive mention of numerous Jewish believers (2:41; 4:4; 21:20). Certainly, Luke here avoids associating Cornelius and his household with any blame—there is no indication that Cornelius has anything to repent of, personally or by association.

    Peter mentions the general availability of forgiveness for those who believe in Jesus, fulfilling all the prophets; but he does not quote Scripture, perhaps because his audience are Gentiles.[34] He makes no direct appeal nor does he promise the Spirit; the next event is, rather, initiated by God.

- *10:44–46.* The Holy Spirit (identified by the narrator, leaving no doubt) interrupts by falling upon all Peter's hearers, who speak in tongues and praise God. Peter's Jewish ("from the circumcision") Christian companions are suddenly mentioned again, amazed at this (v. 45). Usually God's power is displayed through believers, and crowds of others are amazed (2:6, 43; 3:9; 4:13; 8:13; 9:21). This is the first time since the resurrection (Luke 24:12, 22) that believers are said to be amazed. (The other occurrence in Acts will be at 12:16.) This is a surprising reversal: God is amazing believers, not unbelievers. The Spirit's effects are described from the viewpoint of Peter's companions, who "heard" (v. 46) them and are presented as witnesses that this truly is the Spirit. The events echo Pentecost—the Spirit amazing onlookers by arriving upon a whole group (2:1–12; Peter makes the link explicit, 11:15; 15:8, cf. 10:47). It differs from Pentecost in being preceded rather than followed by an evangelistic speech[35] and, more surprisingly,

in lacking any indication of the recipients' point of view: 2:1–4 describes what the Jewish believers experienced ("saw," v. 3) when the Spirit came upon them. But, here, the point of view of the Gentiles who received the Spirit is not presented.
- *10:47–48.* Peter asks a rhetorical question, and this avoids presenting him as making a personal decision; rather, his hand has been forced by God: Baptism cannot reasonably be withheld,[36] since the Spirit has not been withheld. So, the Gentiles receive first the Spirit and then baptism, authorized by Peter. Peter (personally—with no mention of his companions) accepts "their" (not "Cornelius's," surprisingly) invitation to stay, eating with them (11:3). Such fellowship, which was not mentioned with Samaritans (8:5–25), is the final outcome with these Gentiles in Caesarea.

Peter Persuades

- *11:1–3.* News spreads. Peter goes up to Jerusalem, probably simply returning—there is no indication that he is summoned. There he faces criticism from Jews (οἱ ἐκ περιτομῆς, 11:2).[37] There is no indication of an organized group,[38] nor of any unusual attitude toward circumcision. Probably all the Jerusalem believers were concerned to some extent. Peter addresses some gathering of "the apostles and the brothers" (11:1), not necessarily formal. Jews "were criticizing him" (διεκρίνοντο, 11:2) for visiting and eating with Gentiles. If the aorist were used, that might imply an accusation made on one particular occasion; but the imperfect is used, suggesting an ongoing process of repeated accusations.
- *11:4.* Peter's speech is "orderly" (καθεξῆς, echoing the intention of the Third Gospel, Luke 1:3),[39] so the hearer anticipates a proper explanation.
- *11:5–10.* Peter retells his vision. The hearer finds the details familiar and accurate, so Peter is further accredited as a reliable witness. Peter already knows that the voice spoke for God (10:28), but he simply reports "a voice." He starts with the unembellished events he experienced, only then giving his final realization and conclusions.[40] Peter is not preaching, lecturing, or commanding, but inviting the Jerusalem believers (and the hearer of Acts)[41] to join him as he narrates his journey of discovery.
- *11:11.* Peter reconstructs the messengers' arrival (leaving Cornelius unnamed) in chronological order (not the sequence of his own experiences, 10:19–21).
- *11:12.* Peter's account echoes the narrator's, including identifying "the Spirit" (11:12; 10:19). He adds mention of "these six brothers" (οἱ ἓξ ἀδελφοὶ οὗτοι) accompanying him. "These" suggests either that some

of them accompanied Peter to Jerusalem or that he has (unreported here) identified them. Either way, they are presented as witnesses who could be questioned. In 10:45 they were described as οἱ ἐκ περιτομῆς—circumcised, like Peter's critics (11:2). In reality, there would be significant differences between Jewish believers from an outlying town like Joppa (who were willing to accompany Peter), and Jewish believers from the temple-city who objected to such a visit. Nevertheless, this phrase associates Peter's companions with his critics, which would both strengthen his companions' testimony and ease criticism of Peter, because of their participation alongside him.[42]

- *11:14.* Peter reports Cornelius's words, adding that Cornelius was to hear words "by which you will be saved, you and all your household." The flow of the narrative would have been disrupted had this been explicit at 10:6 (the narrator's account) or 10:33 (Cornelius's account), because this would forewarn Peter (and the hearer of Acts) that the Gentiles were about to be "saved," reducing the dramatic impact of the Spirit's arrival. This is not a "reader-elevated" episode; rather, the audience learns gradually, with the opportunity to empathize with Peter's journey of discovery.

- *11:15–16.* Peter reports how the Spirit's arrival on the Gentiles echoed Pentecost, and he adds a further direct inside view of his own thinking: This reminded him of words of Jesus, promising the Spirit (Acts 1:5, echoing Luke 3:16). Jesus's prophetic words have now been fulfilled (twice), accrediting Jesus. The promise was actually made to Jewish disciples, but Peter implies (without quite arguing) that the similarity between these two "Pentecosts" means that both are fulfillments. Jesus's promise accredits, first, Jewish believers and, now, these Gentile converts.

- *11:17.* Peter ends with a rhetorical question, echoing his words in 10:47, but strengthening them with the explicit claim that God gave this gift (the Spirit) to the Gentiles. This leads to a stronger question: not merely "Who can hinder/withhold (κωλύω) water" (10:47) but now, "Who was I to hinder (κωλύω) God?" (11:17). To refuse to accept these Gentiles would be to oppose God! Gamaliel had earlier, rightly, warned against becoming fighters-against-God (θεομάχος, 5:39). Peter's question implies that anybody who refuses to accept Gentile believers is opposing God. The narrative is not so direct as to lecture or threaten; the message is conveyed more gently—but it is undeniably conveyed.

- *11:18.* Criticism is silenced and replaced with praise, with the implication of unanimity in accepting that, "God gave even the Gentiles repentance unto life." The narrative audience has been persuaded; these Gentiles have been saved and God himself made it happen.

There are more levels to this communication than the hearer would naturally notice: The Jerusalem believers approve an account by Peter that includes an account by Cornelius of the words of an angel, which are attested by details provided by the narrator—a polyphonic web of mutual accreditation by different voices (P5c).

The episode closes with the impression that Gentiles are now, unexpectedly but clearly, fully accepted by both God and the Church.[43] Acts 15 shows that there was actually more to do: The question of what requirements should be imposed on Gentile believers remains. Indeed, the question of whether the gospel is open to all Gentiles, or only to the households of exemplary God-fearers, has not directly been addressed. Acts deals with such questions, not by articulating and discussing them rigorously, but through a narrative that addresses the issues little by little. By the end of Acts, there is still no clear answer as to whether Jewish believers are required (not merely permitted) to modify their eating habits and/or to share table fellowship with Gentile believers, whether Gentile believers should be permitted equal access to leadership positions, or (most sensitive of all) whether Jewish believers are permitted (or even expected) to intermarry with Gentile believers.

Despite the specific guidance drafted in chapter 15, Acts is far from being a manual of Christian policies and procedures. It establishes the idea that God has accepted Gentiles, so that Jewish Christians should not object to their conversion or to other Jewish Christians visiting them. It avoids further questions, such as whether Jewish Christians must not merely tolerate Gentile Christians elsewhere but also accept them within their local fellowship. Such omissions might be because outsiders form an expected part of the audience—to reveal more of the history of such tensions within the movement might not be a helpful introduction. Or they might be because the issue was not decisively resolved and Christians in the author's generation remained divided, so that any more specific conclusion would be rejected by one group or other.

THE RETELLINGS OF THE CORNELIUS EPISODE

There are multiple retellings built into this episode: Cornelius's vision is reported by the narrator (10:1–8) and retold by the messengers (10:22) and by Cornelius (10:30–33); and, in Jerusalem, Peter reports Cornelius's retelling (11:13–14). Peter's vision is reported by the narrator (10:9–21), interpreted by Peter to Cornelius (10:28–29), and reported by Peter in Jerusalem (11:5–12). The Holy Spirit's arrival, after Peter's speech, is reported by the narrator (10:34–48) and then twice by Peter (11:15–17; 15:7–9). The details could all have been included in a single chronological initial narrative, which would be more compact, allowing retellings to be omitted—Peter's entire speech in Jerusalem (11:5–17) could be omitted, leaving 11:4 simply to explain that he told the details "in order." What would be lost by doing this?

First, although Cornelius's and Peter's visions would still complement and confirm each other, Cornelius's retelling of his vision would be lost. The hearer would lose the accrediting effect of hearing him provide an accurate report of these (already narrated) events. Similarly, the accrediting effect of hearing Peter's accurate report in Jerusalem would be lost. Through retellings, Acts indicates the trustworthiness of Cornelius, his messengers, and Peter.

Secondly, hearers suspicious of the incorporation of Gentiles would be presented with a more abrupt challenge to their thinking. Before Acts 10, there has been no mention of fellowship with Gentiles and the one Gentile convert mentioned has disappeared to Ethiopia (8:39). Rearranged into chronological order, the angel tells Cornelius not only to send for Peter, but also (11:14, inserted at 10:32b) that Peter is to deliver words by which Cornelius will be saved, with all his household. The start of the episode would provide a clear statement of the outcome. A compliant hearer would have no problem with this. But a suspicious hearer (presumably a Jew, perhaps a proselyte or God-fearer), abruptly presented with this idea that a whole community of Gentiles is about to be saved (11:14), might respond negatively, questioning how authoritative this account is—losing their "suspended disbelief." Without retellings, the arrival of the Holy Spirit (10:44) would be less of a surprise (with less reason for "astonishment" 10:45), and the focus would be less on God's initiative, but would shift unhelpfully to the question: If Peter already knew this journey would involve Gentiles becoming Christians, was he even right to go? Rather, by using retellings, Acts leads the hearer through the events in gentle steps (P5e), wondering about the outcome,[44] with the Holy Spirit's arrival acting as a climax.

Thirdly, there would be some loss of multiple perspectives. In particular, although the narrator mentions an "angel/messenger [ἄγγελος] of God" (10:3), the messengers "a holy angel/messenger" (10:22), and Peter "an angel/messenger" (11:13), Cornelius only claims to have seen "a man in shining clothes" (10:30), indicating that he is a cautious, reliable witness. Without retelling, this accrediting detail would be lost. Although multiple perspectives provide accreditation most simply by agreeing with each other, differences like this can also contribute to persuasion.

Fourthly, Peter's memory of Jesus's promise of the Spirit (11:16–17) would be less convincing if reported chronologically (inserted at 10:46), at the moment of the Spirit's arrival. That promise was made near Jerusalem to Jewish disciples who were to stay there until it was fulfilled (1:4–5), so it is far from incongruous for Peter to mention it in Jerusalem to a group of Jewish believers. However, if reported by the narrator as his thought in Caesarea among a group of Gentiles, any hearer is more likely to question whether Jesus's promise is directly relevant. Peter's retelling is more persuasive, that the Gentiles have now received exactly what Jewish believers received at Pentecost (10:47; 11:15).

Fifthly, without retelling, the process by which Peter wins affirmation from the Jerusalem believers (11:18) would be less persuasive, leaving the hearer uncertain where the emphasis of Peter's case would lie. Peter's speech actually emphasizes the Spirit's arrival, in front of witnesses (11:15–17; 15:8). The chronological approach (without delaying details for retelling) would shift emphasis to the angel's initial announcement to Cornelius (proclaiming the outcome), but there were no other witnesses then, making that approach less convincing.

In summary, this episode emphasizes that God accepted Gentiles in the same way as Jews, without discriminating (10:34; 15:9), as affirmed by the Holy Spirit falling on them. A single, plain, chronological account would be adequate for hearers supportive of this idea but would be significantly less persuasive for unconvinced hearers. Others have noted that the process of retelling provides emphasis and indicates that these events are important. Changes in point of view, and extra details, provide variety and verisimilitude. Peter's own understanding and explanations develop.[45] But this study suggests that the process of retelling also (indeed, primarily) has a persuasive effect—that the development between retellings is due to changes not primarily in Peter's understanding, but in the developing attitude of the compliant hearer of Acts.

Retellings can give the impression of mutually validating accounts from different sources (P5c). If the reported retellings are historically accurate (which is not a question addressed here), then such multiple perspectives would truly accredit each other, and could have been checked[46] by those willing to travel and ask—both as the events unfolded (as mentioned at 22:5), and when Acts was first published. Thus there are logical grounds for finding retellings persuasive: If the account is based on details that could have been, and perhaps were, checked at the time, that makes it more credible. These different voices are not entirely independent—they all come from the pen of the same author. Nevertheless, this technique remains persuasive, although the process may be as much subconscious as logical, and it is not a technique that is likely to win over a critical and suspicious hearer. This narrative is best suited for hearers who, although unpersuaded, are open to persuasion.

CHARACTERIZATION OF PETER

In Acts 1–9, Peter is portrayed with respect rather than empathy—in particular, there is no significant direct inside view into Peter's thinking. After dropping briefly from the narrative (8:25–9:31), respect for Peter is then reinforced in the miracles with Aeneas and Dorcas (9:32–43). But in the Cornelius episode, the hearer suddenly gets many insights into Peter's thinking: his hunger (10:10), puzzlement (10:17, 19), interpretation of his vision (10:28–29, 34), and response to the Spirit's arrival (10:47; 11:16–17). These develop empathy, encouraging the hearer to engage with Peter's journey of discovery.

In this episode, Peter is more central than Cornelius—once Cornelius has introduced his household, the focus shifts to them rather than him personally (plurals at 10:29, 48). In contrast, when Peter and his companions are together, the focus is not on them but on Peter personally (singulars at 10:24, 26–28, 48), except for the moment when the companions are astonished at the Spirit's arrival (10:45–46a), which permits the narrator to gloss over the question of whether Peter was also surprised. His companions' role is limited to that moment of amazement—other mentions of them are the minimum necessary to explain their presence at that moment (10:23b) and to claim them as witnesses (11:12). Overall, Peter's is the dominant point of view in the episode (Cornelius is the focus for only twelve verses, 10:1–8, 30–33; Peter for forty-two verses, 10:9–23, 34–43, 47; 11:2–17).

PETER'S JOURNEY OF DISCOVERY

The episode seems primarily to act as a journey of discovery (P5d), upon which the hearer of Acts is invited to accompany Peter—indeed, Peter's own speech (11:5–17) invites the Jerusalem believers to do just that, and successfully persuades them. There is little evidence that hearers are expected to identify with Cornelius or his household. The only relevant insights that would encourage this are Cornelius's initial terror, which does more to accredit the vision than to characterize the centurion, and his high level of expectation as Peter prepares to speak (which the hearer naturally shares). However, although a gospel presentation is clearly required at this point, Peter's opening words shift the agenda back to God's message for Peter (10:34) more than God's message for Cornelius. It is Peter's perspective that is central to the persuasiveness of this episode.[47]

Comparison with Aseneth

Comparisons have been made between Paul's conversion and Aseneth's conversion,[48] since both involve heavenly visions and transformed lives. Cornelius's conversion also has some links to Aseneth's. But this research reaches the surprising conclusion that it is actually Peter who—at least in terms of persuasion—most closely resembles Aseneth. Aseneth is portrayed with empathy during her conversion, and then with respect afterward; in contrast, Paul is portrayed with antipathy before his conversion and, afterward, with respect but rather limited empathy. The persuasive effects of these two narratives are very different. Cornelius ends up, like Aseneth, accepted among God's people, having received messages from God and experienced divine presence. Both narratives make the case for the acceptability of such a character. But there is a significant difference: There is very limited inside view of Cornelius, who is portrayed with respect, not empathy. In the Cornelius episode, it is, rather, Peter with whom empathy is developed. At least in terms of persuasion, this is not presented as Cornelius's journey of discovery, but Peter's—persuading the hearer (by accompanying Peter) of the appropriateness of God welcoming these Gentiles.

CONCLUSIONS

Although this episode accredits the gospel and Peter, its persuasive thrust is accreditation of mission to Gentiles, presented as starting in Cornelius's house. So Acts 10–11 was not written for one authoritative Roman individual ("Theophilus"); the episode would have been an ideal opportunity to encourage such an individual to identify with Cornelius and be reassured of his acceptability through "repentance unto life" (11:18). But the account is not structured to do that. Gentiles could not fully identify with Cornelius, who is described in unattainably positive terms. The episode provides an important precedent, perhaps an ideal to aspire to, but not a realistic example to follow.

Although it is not inappropriate for interested Gentile outsiders, the account is most appropriate for hearers so conscious of Jewish boundaries that they are yet to be convinced about this development, mission to Gentiles. It would be suitable for presentation to Jewish Christians still struggling with this idea, and for Gentile Christians who knew Judaism and its Scriptures well, perhaps from being God-fearers before joining the movement. They would appreciate Peter's dilemma. They might be struggling to relate the beliefs and traditions of the Jews to the practices of the Christian movement and wondering whether Christianity could really claim to be rooted in Jewish Scripture. They might be under pressure to adopt Jewish practices and to be circumcised (15:1, cf. Gal

4:10; 6:12). This episode, along with Acts 15, goes out of its way to persuade the hearer that God accepts Gentiles and that this is through faith in Christ (accompanied by baptism) and not through Jewish practices.

NOTES

1. Most commentators separate 9:32–43 from 10:1–11:18, e.g., Rudolf Pesch, *Die Apostelgeschichte.* 2 vols. (Zürich: Benziger; Neukirchener, 1986), 1:330, regards 10:1–11:18 as the longest "Einzelerzälung" (single, complete episode) in Acts; so also Jürgen Roloff, *Die Apostelgeschichte* (Göttingen: Vandenhoeck & Ruprecht, 1988), 164.
2. Haenchen, *Acts*, 340.
3. Johnson, *Acts*, 178.
4. I.e., the God of Israel, James D. G. Dunn, *The Acts of the Apostles* (Valley Forge, PA: Trinity, 1996), 135.
5. Christoph W. Stenschke, *Luke's Portrait of Gentiles Prior to Their Coming to Faith* (Tübingen: Mohr Siebeck, 1999), 150; cf. Tob 12:8.
6. ἀτενίζω can simply mean looking carefully (Luke 22:56; Acts 11:6; and perhaps 1:10; 7:55); more frequently in Luke-Acts (Luke 4:20; Acts 3:4, 12; 6:15; 13:9; 14:9; 23:1), it builds tension for a significant speech or supernatural event.
7. Although Johnson, *Acts*, 194, goes that far.
8. Also Matt 3:16; John 1:51; Rev 19:11, cf. 11:19; 15:5; and LXX, Ezek 1:1; 3 Macc 6:18, cf. Isa 64:1.
9. Witherington, *Acts*, 350; although Haenchen, *Acts*, 348, suggests "mysteriously uncertain."
10. Witherington, *Acts*, 350, although uncleanness through contact was explicit only for dead, not living, animals, Lev 11:32–38.
11. Dunn, *Acts*, 137.
12. David G. Peterson, *The Acts of the Apostles* (Grand Rapids: Eerdmans, 2009), 329.
13. Haenchen, *Acts*, 347.
14. τρίς (three times) occurs in Luke-Acts only in these two incidents (Luke 22:34, 61; Acts 10:16; 11:10).
15. Johnson, *Acts*, 187, mentions sympathy, but empathy is more relevant here.
16. Dunn, *Acts*, 138.
17. Johnson, *Acts*, 185.
18. *m. Ketub.* 7:10; *b. Pesaḥ.* 65a; *Qidd.* 82b; Johnson, *Acts,* 179; Witherington, *Acts*, 333.
19. Dunn, *Acts*, 130; Johnson, *Acts,* 179.
20. Matt 8:5 presents them as meeting, but that is assumed to be unknown to the implied audience of Luke-Acts.

21. E.g., *Jub.* 22:16; although *m. Ber.* 7:1 assumes that Jews and Gentiles do eat together; Eckhard J. Schnabel, *Early Christian Mission*, 2 vols. (Downers Grove, IL: IVP, 2004), 1:710.

22. A common description of angels, e.g., Luke 24:4, glistening, ἀστράπτω; Acts 1:10, white, λευκός.

23. Although Codex Bezae et al. have "before you," i.e., Peter.

24. Haenchen, *Acts*, 351.

25. Job 42:7 is a rare exception.

26. Adams, *Meeting*, 200 (among other venues).

27. ἀνοίγω στόμα as at 8:35; Judg 11:35; Job 3:1; Ps 77:2 (78:2 MT); cf. 2:14. Formal speeches are more often introduced with mention of movement or gestures: 13:16; 15:7; 17:22; 21:40; 22:30–23:1; 26:1. Such introductions provoke the hearer to listen with expectation, also providing the lector with a cue for appropriate tone of voice—in this case, switching from Peter's conversation (10:27) to Peter's speech (10:34–43).

28. Johnson, *Acts*, 191. Also λαμβάνω πρόσωπον, e.g., Lev 19:15; 1 Esd 4:19.

29. Witherington, *Acts*, 356.

30. Lev 26:6. Peace herself (personified) is Tygaeus's quest in Aristophanes, *Peace*. εὐεργετέω is, in the LXX, used primarily of God's graciousness, e.g., Ps 12:6 (13:6, MT); Wis 3:5; (except when offered by a persecuting tyrant, 4 Macc 8:6). The benefactor (εὐεργέτης) played a respected and vital role in Greco-Roman society, e.g., Seneca, *On Benefits*.

31. Cf. qualifications of an apostle in 1:21–22.

32. Jon A. Weatherly, *Jewish Responsibility for the Death of Jesus in Luke-Acts* (Sheffield: Sheffield Academic, 1994), 272.

33. Jack T. Sanders, *The Jews in Luke-Acts* (London: SCM, 1987), xvi, approving of Gager.

34. Even if Cornelius himself were familiar with the Scriptures, it is unlikely that all his household and friends would be.

35. And in lacking the skeptical response of 2:13.

36. Cf. the Eunuch's question, 8:36, and immediate baptism, 8:38.

37. Rom 4:12; Col 4:11.

38. Here, simply "Jewish," as at Rom 3:1, 30; 4:9, 12; 15:8; Gal 2:7–8; Eph 2:11; Col 4:11; and throughout Luke-Acts, e.g., Acts 7:8; 10:45; 11:2; (even though there were groups of Jewish believers advocating circumcision for converts: Gal 2:4, 12–13; 5:12; 6:12–13, cf. Tit 1:10; Josephus *Ant.* 20.43–45).

39. "[I]n an orderly fashion," Alexander, *Preface*, 131–32.

40. Not necessarily "growth in [Peter's] own understanding" (Johnson, *Acts*, 201), but more is progressively revealed to the hearer of Acts.

41. Johnson, *Acts*, 195, 199.

42. Johnson, *Acts*, 198.

43. Peterson, *Acts*, 340.

44. Ronald D. Witherup, "Cornelius Over and Over and Over Again: 'Functional Redundancy' in the Acts of the Apostles," *Journal for the Study of the New Testament*

15, no. 49 (January 1993): 64, considers suspense as active questioning. But wondering may be more subconscious.

45. Witherup, "Cornelius," 64.

46. As Josephus points out for accounts of near-contemporary events, *J.W.* 1:14, 30.

47. Hence *"The Conversion of Peter and the Acceptance of Cornelius,"* Dunn, *Acts*, 131 [italics his].

48. Reviewed by John B. Polhill, *Acts* (Nashville: Broadman, 1992), 231 n. 3.

Chapter Ten

Comparison Between the Five Texts

The techniques of persuasion in five texts have been investigated, one by one. How does Acts compare with the other texts? Comparisons should make it possible to identify where a common technique is used in Acts, where an unusual technique is used in Acts, and any common techniques that are not used in Acts. So this chapter reviews persuasion in the texts as a group, summarizes what is distinctive about each text, and draws conclusions about Acts through comparison with each of the other texts.

OVERVIEW OF PERSUASION IN THE FIVE TEXTS—ACCREDITING AND DISCREDITING

One distinctive feature of Acts (and of Luke, even more) is how much of the accrediting and discrediting can be described as "supernatural." Appendix E, Table E.1, gives an overview of the devices, showing what percentages of them are positive (accrediting) or negative (discrediting), what percentages come from each kind of speaker (narrator, trusted character, or some other character), and what percentages are "supernatural" or "not supernatural." Accrediting or discrediting is taken as supernatural if it involves the action or attitude of God (or some other supernatural power), in particular: fulfillment of prophecy;[1] miracles;[2] or God's involvement through favor, rejection, answer to prayer, or commissioning.[3]

The narrator, rather than any character, provides the majority of accrediting and discrediting in all of these texts—with the exception of *Aristeas*, where the trusted characters (mainly King Ptolemy)[4] do more. Each narrator is to be trusted and speaks with authority—not merely as a literary "omniscient narrator," but also with the deeper authority to pronounce ethical and spiritual judgments, even claiming divine authority for these (although, in this, Josephus is more cautious than the others).

Accrediting and discrediting devices are mainly used to establish the trustworthiness of particular characters. At times, this accrediting might in itself achieve a persuasive aim (for example, Josephus showing himself in a good light), but it also consistently has the effect of allowing the words (and actions) of these respected characters to have persuasive force. Considering the proportions of negative, discrediting devices, *Aristeas* provides very few (less than 3 percent of instances), whereas Luke and Acts are very similar to each other (12 percent and 15 percent) and to *Aseneth* (11 percent). In contrast, both *Embassy* and *War* do much more discrediting (64 percent and 80 percent of instances) than accrediting—discrediting characters is in itself a persuasive thrust of these texts. Both are pro-Jewish texts, but *Embassy* affirms Judaism primarily by denigrating Gaius and his disrespect for Jewish beliefs and traditions, and *War* affirms Jewish aristocracy and traditions primarily by blaming the nation's destruction on upstart Jewish bandits.

Naturally, minor characters may be neither accredited nor discredited because they do not influence the hearer but simply move the plot forward (e.g., messengers, Acts 5:25; 16:35). Gamaliel (Acts 5:34–40) is unusual, as a member of a negatively characterized group (the Sanhedrin) who is personally characterized positively, leaving the hearer unsure whether to trust him. His moderate advice moves the plot forward, but does not quite provide a trustworthy comment on the Jesus movement. Similarly the character of Macro (Philo, *Embassy* 32–61) may be positive, but his association with Gaius is negative and proved his undoing; his role is not to instruct the hearer, but to move the plot forward by acting as a foil for and victim of Gaius's villainy.

The words of untrustworthy characters do not generally provide clear persuasion to the hearer. The exception is when such a character is used to demonstrate that even such a person agrees with a tenet of the narrator and/or trusted characters. This is evident in the pre-suicide speeches of Eleazar to his Sicarii (*J.W.* 7:323–388), admitting their fault. Similarly, Gaius, noting Agrippa's horrified reaction to his statue plan, correctly realizes that such a reaction can be expected from other Jews (*Embassy* 268). Also, in Luke-Acts, characters of high status but uncertain trustworthiness admit the innocence of Jesus (Luke 23:4, 14–15, 22; 47) and Paul (Acts 23:29; 25:25; 26:31–32); but Judas does not comment on his betrayal, nor do persecutors comment on their persecution (except for Paul, once he is trusted and no longer a villain).

The trustworthiness of most characters never changes. The exceptions are Aseneth, who starts as a flawed character, and Paul, who starts as a villain. They both end up changing decisively and then being strongly accredited.

Comparing the proportions of devices in the mouth of trusted characters, Luke and Acts are again similar to each other (35 percent and 44 percent) and most similar to *Aseneth* (35 percent). *Embassy* and *War* are far more dependent on their prominent narrators (with only 17 percent and 9 percent from trusted characters), whereas *Aristeas* uses trusted characters far more (60 percent—with most of these instances during the Symposium).[5]

In the proportion of supernatural accrediting and discrediting devices used, Luke (65 percent) and Acts (54 percent) are again most similar to *Aseneth* (46 percent), with the other texts using few such devices (13 percent or less). In accrediting, Luke-Acts is remarkable in its emphasis on the supernatural or divine, e.g., angels, visions, miracles, and claims of God's favor. Similar analysis of Mark's Gospel (showing 53 percent supernatural accrediting/discrediting devices, not reported in detail here) suggests that this focus is not peculiar to the author(s) of Luke-Acts, but may be characteristic of the way early Christians told the stories about Jesus and his followers.

In the style of accrediting and discrediting, Luke and Acts are most similar to *Aseneth*. This may arise from these three texts being in styles that seem deliberately to echo Scripture.

SIGNIFICANT ASPECTS OF PERSUASION IN *EMBASSY*

Philo's treatises show that he was a respected author who liked to teach. In *Embassy*, he makes autobiographical narrative persuasive in ways which are relatively easy to detect—including, not surprisingly, didactic asides (P1a).[6] In the narrative, his consistent discrediting of Gaius is reinforced by rhetorical sections that also denounce him. So narrative and rhetoric are used together for the same persuasive purpose, with the overt persuasion in the rhetoric confirming the force of the techniques of less-overt persuasion in the rest of the narrative.

The most striking technique of narrative persuasion is antipathy (to Gaius, and some others around him) through negative character traits (P4a) and exposing his distorted worldview (P2c, a technique not evident in the other texts). The device of sarcasm is employed, with biting force, within both rhetorical sections (91, 101) and narrative (60, 163, 203 by messengers, 206, 265 by Gaius, 352). There is also xenophobic negative characterization of Egyptians (P4b, through national identity, although also through association with idolatry; 120, 139, 162–163, 166). Polyphonic affirmation (P5c) is evident, as the narrator and various characters each indicate that Jews are horrified at the prospect of a statue in their Temple, preferring death to witnessing such a thing.[7] The way the text describes the pitiable condition and horrors experienced by Jews evokes sympathy for them (P3c), antipathy toward those responsible (P4a, Gaius; Alexandrians), and antipathy toward their ideas (especially erecting statues in Jewish places).

Although the text is undeniably pro-Jewish, its persuasive force is strongly negative—against Gaius and, through him, against the idea of interfering with Jewish traditions and sentiments.

RELEVANCE OF *EMBASSY* TO PERSUASION IN ACTS

The author of Acts does not assert personal authority as Philo does; rather, he emphasizes the authority of his trusted characters. This style arises in part from emulating scriptural narrators. *Embassy* addresses Jewish belief and tradition with reference to Greco-Roman mythology but not to Scripture.[8] In contrast, Acts works hard to accredit Jesus and his movement as fulfilling OT prophecy. The way Acts makes extensive reference to Scripture is a not simply a default set by Jewish predecessors.

Despite including many negative characterizations, *Embassy* provides only positive portrayals of Jews, with complete unity between them. In contrast, Acts provides not only positive portrayals of believers and their unity, but also exceptions: Ananias and Sapphira (5:1–10); Simon the Sorcerer (8:9–24); and Paul and Barnabas's disagreement over John Mark (15:37–40). Acts is a more nuanced account.

Embassy demonstrates how biting and sarcastic an author can be in his invective. Although Acts reports opposition and persecution by Jews, there are relatively few comments on this;[9] such Jews are portrayed negatively, but Acts does not amount to invective against them. Magicians are portrayed much more negatively—although more as overpowered than doomed. Acts does not so much instill hatred of magicians as dispel fear of them by pointing to the superior power available to believers.

Embassy illustrates how horror and pathos can be employed persuasively.[10] In contrast, Luke's account of the crucifixion largely avoids graphic details, as does the Acts account of Stephen's stoning, focusing more on his speech and vision. Although Philo at times evokes sympathy for suffering Jews, Acts evokes respect rather than sympathy for suffering believers.

The polyphonic persuasion in *Embassy* demonstrates that this technique (P5c) was already in use before Acts was written. In Acts, Paul's preaching includes echoes of Peter's. Despite significant differences between the various speeches, these echoes contribute some sense of continuity, making links back from Paul to Peter and to Jesus, thus accrediting Paul and his ministry. But comparison with *Embassy* further suggests that such echoes play a part in reinforcing the message preached—hearing the same ideas from a Galilean fisherman and from an educated Pharisee can deepen the persuasive impact. Multiple declarations of Paul's innocence function similarly.[11]

SIGNIFICANT ASPECTS OF PERSUASION IN *WAR*

In *War,* a Jewish author writes a history for a predominantly non-Jewish audience (1:3), with imperial patronage (*Life* 423–429), having himself surrendered and witnessed his nation's defeat. Josephus was expected to show Romans in a good light; he also displays concern for his own reputation (*J.W.* 7:448), mentioning his own prophecy of Vespasian's imperial destiny (3:401, cf. 6:313)—perhaps Josephus's claim to fame at the time of publication. So this text exposes personal issues, concerning the author's reputation, and sensitive issues of politics within the Roman Empire.

Blame for Jerusalem's destruction is directed, not against Romans, Jewish traditions, or established Jewish leadership, but against bands of Jewish brigands. The text portrays traditional, aristocratic local leaders positively[12] and sedition against them negatively—comfortable ideas, for educated hearers. Given the Gentile audience, it is not surprising that the supernatural is mentioned to only a limited extent and primarily in Greco-Roman terms of oracles and omens; nevertheless, the narrator comments on this destruction as being the judgment of (the Jewish) God upon these sacrilegious Jews.[13] Thus, while admitting Jewish fault, Josephus nevertheless defends Jewish traditions and the Jewish God. He deflects scorn and hostility away from Jews in general and onto brigands, portrayed as villains (P4a). Some Gentiles would surely have assumed that the Jewish God had suffered defeat, but the narrator's asides suggest the opposite—that the Jewish God was actually the one in control.

RELEVANCE OF *WAR* TO PERSUASION IN ACTS

Josephus is evidently concerned about the reputations of his people and himself. Similarly, Acts takes care over the way it portrays the Jesus movement, with mainly positive portrayals and any negative portrayals ameliorated: Judas, Ananias, and Sapphira are dead; Simon the Magician is discredited; and other false leaders are presented as a mere future possibility (20:29–30). But, although concerned with the reputation of his message,[14] the author shows no evidence of concern for personal reputation—remaining anonymous, claiming status as a participant only indirectly (using "we"), and letting characters speak with authority more than himself. In this, his style is much closer to Scripture than to Josephus. However authoritative the author's own status within his community, he treats material passed down by the original witnesses (Luke 1:2; 24:48; Acts 1:8, 2:32, along with the especially commissioned Paul), as more authoritative.

Aware that, for many, Romans are heroes and Jews villains (*J.W.* 1:2), Josephus attempts to shift the allocation of praise and blame. Similarly Acts admits, as would be common knowledge, that the Jesus movement faced opposition—allegations (e.g., as troublemakers, 16:20–21; 17:6; 24:5), riots, beatings, executions, and imprisonments, "spoken against everywhere" (28:22), but Acts suggests that it was always others who caused trouble[15] and, when investigated, such charges against the movement proved unfounded.[16] Acts assigns praise to Christians and blame to various instigators of aggressive opposition (Jews[17] and others, e.g., the Ephesian silversmiths, 19:24–29). This encourages Christians to follow these examples of blamelessness, and interested outsiders to abandon any prejudice against the movement.

Josephus provides mixed portrayals of Romans—criticizing the dead Nero (*J.W.* 2:250) but not subsequent emperors; mentioning Roman achievements (e.g., 2:271), but also abuses (2:272–279). He accepts Roman authority (discouraging rebellion, 3:108), but treats it as granted by the Jewish God (5:367). This provides some indication of imperial issues faced by the author of Acts. The portrayal of Romans in Acts is also mixed—concerned about proper legal processes (25:16, 27), yet hoping for bribes (24:26). In the light of *War*, the absence from Acts of direct criticism of Rome makes sense—it would have alienated any who supported the status quo and would have been dangerous for the text's author and distributors. Silence would not necessarily be taken as approval of Roman rule; most hearers would be listening for subversive undertones. Luke-Acts emphasizes declarations of innocence by those in authority, but its portrayal of bold outspokenness (5:29; 23:3; 24:25) does not suggest that the believers would automatically show the respect and obedience demanded by Roman authorities. Christians are portrayed as innocent of subversion, but not as unquestioningly loyal to the authorities.[18] So, although Romans and their supporters would not be offended by Luke-Acts, neither would those who resented Roman abuses be suspicious of or offended by this carefully-balanced portrayal.

SIGNIFICANT ASPECTS OF PERSUASION IN *ASENETH*

This text provides an expansion of Genesis and is written in the general style of Scripture, with visions and supernatural events reported by a reticent narrator, and religious poetry[19] providing commentary on the narrated situation. The elements of romance (chs. 1–22) and subterfuge (chs. 23–29) are entertaining, and Aseneth's vision includes mysterious symbolism[20] that would encourage the hearer to ask questions.

Characterization contributes forcefully to persuasion. Pharaoh's firstborn is a villain (P4a). The heavenly man is supernatural, from God. Joseph is portrayed with extreme respect (P3b, e.g., *Jos. Asen.* 5:1–7, more than in Genesis). The most interesting character is Aseneth—attractive (1:4–6) but flawed (2:1; 4:12); then, after a conversion experience that develops empathy (P3a), she ends up characterized with respect similar to Joseph's. The plot takes the hearer along with Aseneth on her journey of discovery (P5d). This presents Judaism positively and idolatry negatively (8:5; 12:9; 13:11). The strict boundary between Jews and Gentiles is emphasized (ethical behavior, 28:5; 29:3; sexual relations, 8:5–7; 21:1), but Aseneth is presented as wholeheartedly converting, as wholeheartedly accepted by heaven and by Jews, and as a "City of Refuge" for many Gentiles who will come to God in the future (15:7; 17:6; 19:5, 8, cf. 16:16). Thus the text promotes proselytism, but sets a high expectation of the wholeheartedness of converts.

RELEVANCE OF *ASENETH* TO PERSUASION IN ACTS

Aseneth makes deliberate reference to the style and content of Scripture. The result shows remarkable similarities to Acts in terms of style—with an omniscient, reticent narrator, describing supernatural occurrences without expressing uncertainty. Religious poems related to the narrative (Aseneth's soliloquies) are also a scriptural feature—absent from Acts but included in the Third Gospel (Luke 1:46–55, 68–79; 2:29–32).[21]

Scriptural style also indicates a desire to sound authoritative, perhaps even to speak for God. Both *Aseneth* and Acts include characters who claim to speak for God, so it is quite possible that the authors intended their texts to be seen as having divine authority and eternal significance. Aseneth's role as "City of Refuge" for future proselytes makes links to the hearer's own world. Similarly, generalizations in the gospel proclamation in Acts provide a message presented as relevant to all, including hearers of Acts. Quotations from Scripture accredit Jesus and his movement, but by associating Luke-Acts with the Septuagint, they also build the status of Luke-Acts itself as at least linked to Scripture, and perhaps as a continuation of it.

The mysterious symbolism of *Aseneth* is absent from Acts, which sets a tone, rather, of openness and clarity. An interested hearer of *Aseneth* would need to ask more questions. But Acts does not indicate the need for an ongoing process of explanation or catechism (Luke 1:1–4 suggests that the text itself is adequate); it gives the impression that one need only repent and be baptized (e.g., 2:38; 8:36–38; 16:30–34).

The character of Joseph is extreme—central, authoritative, yet without direct inside views. He illustrates the way a character portrayed with respect (not empathy) can be used persuasively, like Peter in Acts 1–6. On the other hand, Aseneth, an attractive but flawed character, is portrayed with empathy (not, until later, with respect), allowing the hearer to accompany her on a journey of discovery. In Acts, Cornelius is different: portrayed positively (10:1–2, 22) without mention of flaws or repentance—he is more incorporated than converted. Paul is also different: Ultimately respected, he is initially a persecuting villain (8:1, 3; 9:1–2, 13–14, 21), with little opportunity for the hearer to develop empathy (his initial conversion/call, Acts 9, giving little direct inside view). Rather, it is with Peter that the "journey of discovery" technique is used (concerning Cornelius, 10:1–11:18) and the hearer naturally joins him in that journey toward seeing Gentiles as acceptable.

SIGNIFICANT ASPECTS OF PERSUASION IN *ARISTEAS*

In *Aristeas*, an almost-certainly Jewish author writes under the guise of an educated Gentile narrator in order that his positive portrayal of Judaism, the Jewish Law, and its Greek translation may seem to come from a respectful outsider. This positive portrayal is polyphonic, with almost all the characters contributing to it. The diversity of styles suggests that the author hopes to impress the hearer with his literary ability. That Jews are wise by Greek standards is emphasized by the lengthy Symposium (*Let. Aris.*, 184–300), where the seventy-two Jewish elders provide wise sayings on kingship.

The connecting theme is the translation of the Law into Greek, so strongly accredited that accreditation of some version of the Septuagint is surely one significant purpose of the work. The text portrays relations of mutual respect between Jews and Alexandrian Greeks in terms that are extremely positive, with almost no negative characterization. Aristeas respects Judaism from the outset (12; 15–16), so his journey to Jerusalem does not change his point of view—it is as much a journey of affirmation as a "journey of discovery." It provides an opportunity to showcase Judaism, including the Temple (84–104) and the Law (130–169). The text accredits Judaism, with a special interest in the Jewish community in Alexandria. Mention of an annual Jewish festival in Alexandria (180) raises the possibility that the text was published for use at such an event, to act as a foundation myth for some combination of the Jewish community there, their Greek Scriptures, and their festival.

RELEVANCE OF *ARISTEAS* TO PERSUASION IN ACTS

Aristeas indicates extreme cordiality and mutual respect between King Ptolemy and the high priest, Eleazar (gifts, *Let. Aris.*, 51–82; 172; 319–320; letters, 35–46), which builds respect for Alexandrian Jews and their Greek Scriptures. Whether or not realistic, this certainly demonstrates the importance of respect and honor. In Acts, the embattled, scarred, imprisoned, shipwrecked Paul (14:19; 16:19–24; 21:30–33; 22:22–25; 27:41–44) would not fit the cultural expectation of a respected religious leader appointed by a venerated deity—any more than a crucified peasant would. The gospel and its proclaimers were countercultural and would face prejudice as a result. There was work to do to persuade believers, let alone interested outsiders, that a movement with no status—no temple full of treasure and tradition—could truly be from God. Whereas respect for education, wealth, and status are evident in *Aristeas*, it is striking that Acts focuses rather on miracles and the Holy Spirit—along with willingness to suffer in the process of serving.

The main Greek characters in *Aristeas* are portrayed positively and, without evidently any change in religious or communal identity, as surprisingly respectful toward Jews and Judaism. While admitting the earlier enslavement of many Jews in Egypt, the text presents this as fully resolved. The account may well have been published a generation or more after the events described, when a rose-tinted portrayal of these past events would be less implausible. Acts, in contrast, ends with Jews in Rome largely rejecting the gospel, no mention of whether Gentiles in Rome were actually responsive, and Paul remaining in custody—Acts does not gloss over these tensions. Comparison with *Aristeas* reinforces the strangeness of the ending of Acts. If Paul preached unhindered in Rome for two years, there would surely be some converts who could be mentioned, to alleviate this inconclusiveness. If the preexisting believers in Rome were hostile to Paul—a possible reason why they are hardly mentioned—even they could not reasonably be offended by such a mention. But such converts are not mentioned. Rather, the abrupt ending leaves the impression that the "jury was still out" both on Paul and on the responsiveness of Gentiles in Rome. This would make sense if the text were published at the end of those two years, so that Paul's fate really was still open ended.[22]

SIGNIFICANT ASPECTS OF PERSUASION IN ACTS

Much has been covered in the comparisons above, showing that the persuasiveness of Acts depends on techniques that were not created by its author, but were in general use. But are there aspects of persuasion in Acts that do not arise in these comparisons?

Supernatural accreditation is a key feature of persuasion in Acts, which, although prominent also in *Aseneth*, is not a major feature of the other texts. The claim that Scripture has been fulfilled is distinctive by its frequency of use in Acts: It provides twenty-two instances of accrediting (A8, A10) and two of discrediting (D10: 1:16–20; 28:26–27). In contrast, the only instance in the four nonbiblical texts is in *War* (4:385–388), where Josephus suggests that the destruction of Jerusalem fulfilled a specific prophecy—although the details he gives do not match texts available today. So this device is distinctive of the New Testament writers. Acts (twenty-four instances, A7–10, D8–10) uses it rather more than the Third Gospel (sixteen, cf. Mark has eight).

Fulfillment of recent prophecies (A11–12, D11) is also distinctive of Acts. This device is found occasionally in the other texts (*Embassy*, two instances; *War*, one; *Aseneth* three). It is common in Acts (thirteen instances) and the Third Gospel (twenty-two; Mark has five).

In making assertions of God's favor (A23–25), Acts (seventeen instances) is in line with *Aseneth* (sixteen) and *Aristeas* (eighteen). But Acts adds the closely related accrediting device (A26–27) of being filled with or associated with the Holy Spirit (thirty-three instances; Luke has thirteen; Mark five). In contrast, Philo and Josephus make only occasional assertions of God's favor (two instances in *Embassy*) or rejection (two instances in *War*). In Acts, mention of the Holy Spirit is used to provide the most forceful accreditation, implying not merely God's favor but also God's guidance and empowering, indicating that some of the speeches should be respected as though God himself were speaking. Thus Acts is presenting itself as an inspired text: By commenting authoritatively on which characters and words were inspired by God, the narrator presents himself as authoritative. However, the narrator remains reticent; the hearer is less aware of deciding whether to trust the narrator than of working out how to respond to the characters and their message. By the end of the story, the hearer is encouraged, not to pronounce upon whether this text should be respected as Scripture, but to form or maintain an allegiance, which the text has progressively been urging, to Paul, his gospel, and his Gentile mission.

SUMMARY

This comparison with other texts primarily affirms that the techniques of persuasion used in the narrative of Acts are not novel but were in common use—although Acts is significantly more similar to the Third Gospel than it is to the other texts. Persuasive processes common to all these texts include the following. Confidence in the narrator is built—relatively overtly, except for the reticent narrator of *Aseneth*, who employs scriptural style and scriptural allusions to associate himself with the narrator of Genesis. Trusted characters are established through a range of accrediting devices—most frequently, positive epithets in the mouth of the narrator (A1). There may be untrustworthy characters, but not always (none speaks in *Aristeas*). The worldview of the text is communicated through some combination of expression of the opinions of the narrator (through asides), expression of the opinions of trusted characters, and plot, especially through positive or negative outcomes. The idea of God's favor or rejection (as accrediting or discrediting) is used to some extent in all of the texts.

Although not always central to persuasion, it is remarkable that antipathy is evident in all of the texts: antipathy via character traits (P4a), toward Gaius, John of Gischala, Pharaoh's son, informers, and Herod (Agrippa I) in the five texts respectively; and antipathy via group identity (P4b), toward Egyptians, Idumaeans, Egyptian women, Egyptians, and magicians. The four nonbiblical texts consistently abhor idols and idolaters, with evident antipathy;[23] Acts also presents them negatively, although more gently—representing idolaters more as misguided than as abhorrent (14:11; 28:6; cf. 17:22–31). Such prejudices may not represent the main persuasive purposes, but certainly represent one aspect of the worldviews presented.

Comparison between the texts also indicates which persuasive techniques existed but were unusual. For example, overt teaching in the mouth of untrustworthy characters (P1c) is relatively rare but evident from Eleazar before suicide (*J.W.* 7:327, 332), Joseph's plotting brothers in defeat (*Jos. Asen.* 28:1, 3), and perhaps one remark by Gaius (*Embassy* 268). Sarcasm is rare, although Philo uses it forcefully; subtler forms of irony are arguably ubiquitous. The persuasive "journey of discovery" (P5d) seems uncommon, but it is significant for Aseneth and for Peter during the Cornelius episode.

Luke-Acts is distinctive, among these texts, in quoting Scripture frequently, to accredit Jesus and his movement or, occasionally, to discredit Jewish opponents. Luke-Acts is also distinctive in its emphasis on the supernatural—ancient audiences were used to divine and supernatural elements, but their frequency and prominence in Luke-Acts is remarkable. This limited initial study suggests that a typical first-time hearer of Luke-Acts would be surprised by this intensity of supernatural events. Luke-Acts is also distinctive in the role played by the Holy Spirit, who has been considered here primarily from the point of view of accreditation. In Luke-Acts, association with the Holy Spirit is more than an expression of God's favor, but implies divine inspiration. The phrase "Holy Spirit" is not used in the other texts, but

Pentephres says of Joseph that "the spirit of God is upon him" (*Jos. Asen.*, 4:7); the narrator describes Levi as a prophet (*Jos. Asen.*, 22:13; 23:8; 26:6), which is affirmed by his supernatural awareness of distant events; Eleazar describes Moses as endowed by God with wisdom and knowledge (*Let. Aris.* 139), and the seventy-two elders describe the king as endowed by God with various gifts (e.g., sound reasoning, *Let. Aris.*, 267). Philo is more cautious concerning God's guidance of Petronius, with the generalization that "We find that to good men God whispers good decisions" (*Embassy* 245). Thus, in these Jewish texts, a few highly respected Jews might be seen as endowed with God's spirit, giving their words divine accreditation, and highly respected others, even Gentiles, might be described as endowed and guided by God, giving them respect but not necessarily giving their words divine accreditation. Nevertheless, it is only in Luke-Acts that the idea arises of God's Spirit coming frequently, coming obviously, and coming upon entire groups of believers (16:20–21; 17:6; 24:5).

Reactions of amazement, approval, or joy are used to provide accreditation (except in *War*). Disapproval or horror from onlookers (D17–18) is sometimes used as a discrediting device, especially in *Embassy*, which also provides some graphic descriptions that evoke horror or sympathy (P3c), but, along with *Aristeas,* Acts does not use these negative techniques.

Overall, in terms of persuasive techniques, Acts has much in common with the other texts. In the aspects that make it distinctive, Acts seems more like Scripture—although further analysis of Septuagint texts would be needed to confirm this in detail. It would be reasonable to expect different genres of narrative to exhibit rather different approaches to persuasion, although this method has avoided prejudging that question. The comparisons in this chapter do give some indications. The prominence of the narrators in the historiography of *Embassy* and *War* is strikingly indicated by the fact that these narrators provide about 80 percent of the instances of accrediting and discrediting, whereas narrators in the other texts provide about 50 percent. Whether or not it is regarded as appropriate for historians to provide ideological comments, they certainly do provide their own personal judgments on characters, whereas the other texts provide a higher proportion of comments in the mouths of trusted characters. Philo and Josephus also make much more use than the other authors of discrediting, mainly through negative characterization expressed by the narrator (including some biting sarcasm). This may not be true of histories in general, but these particular works are far more concerned with blame than with praise. Their accrediting and discrediting involves (compared with *Aseneth*, Luke and Acts) rather few connections with the supernatural, suggesting that their main interest is in the human causes of events. These narrators are prominent and provide the hearer with their own, personal comments and judgments, claiming authority as eyewitnesses. *Aristeas* may also present itself as an autobiographical historical document, but this is questionable, and given also its very different subject matter, it is not surprising that its style of persuasion is very different.

Among these texts, in approach to persuasion, *Aseneth* is by far the closest to Luke and Acts. The narrators of *Aseneth*, Luke and Acts are reticent. They include many judgments in the mouths of trusted characters, yet they are also willing to assert the (narratorial) authority to comment on the divine and the supernatural. Rather than reflecting personal authority, this may well arise from composing a narrative that was already known and that depended on sources of authority other than the identity of the author or editor. Their style of persuasion seems to be related less to historiography (or even romance) than to Scripture.

Despite the significant differences between these texts, and between the styles of persuasion within them, this method for identifying persuasion has proved relevant to them all.

NOTES

1. But not wise insights, where no supernatural claim is implied: *Embassy* 349, 359.
2. Including response to or evidence of a miracle.
3. E.g., commissioning by the Holy Spirit or by Jesus after the Ascension. Human attitudes or action toward God, such as piety or impiety, are not included, except where supernatural language is added: e.g., not only impiety but also God's anger, Josephus, *J.W.* 4:150, 382.
4. Out of 221, the king provides ninety-four—although seventy-two of these are formulaic, during the Symposium.
5. 105 instances (out of 221, 47.5 percent) are in the mouths of trusted characters at the Symposium.
6. Philo, *Embassy*, 1, 14, 110, 123, 220, 245, 336, 367.
7. *Embassy*, 81–92 (narrator); 190–196 (ambassadors); 198–205 (messengers); 229–242 (elders); 276–329 (Agrippa).
8. Scriptural allusions are rare—indeed, only explicit at 308 (restricted Temple access, alluding to Num 3:10; 17:13; 18:7), with more emphasis on Jewish traditions. Philo initially employs only Greco-Roman themes (1–114). It is without obvious scriptural allusions that Philo mentions: Jewish law and writings (115; 195; 208; 210; 240; 322), ancestral traditions and customs (115; 117; 156; 232; 240; 268; 290; 293; 313; 333; 335), institutions (159; 161; 208; 322; 369; 371), temple (188; 198; 278; 290; 346), attitudes (154; 202; 208–210; 236; 265; 308), and practices (Sabbath, 158; temple restrictions, 212; Day of Atonement, 306–307; synagogue assembly, 311; 315; first-fruits, 311; 316). Agrippa describes the ban on images, not as scriptural law (Exod 20:4; Deut 5:8), but as ancestral opinion (290); and Day of Atonement rituals

(Lev 16:1–34, cf. 23:26–32; Num 29:7–11) as ancestral practice (306). When Gaius mentions pork (361), this arises more from Jewish practice than Scripture.

9. 5:26; 6:13; 9:23, 28; 13:45; 13:50–51; 17:5; 21:27–36; 22:22–23; 23:10, 12–15; 25:3, 24, with only indirect criticism: mention of false witnesses (6:13), jealousy (13:45; 17:5), blaspheming (13:45), and intent to kill (e.g., 25:3). It is in the mouth (and symbolic actions 13:51; 18:6) of trusted characters that the Jews are more overtly criticized (2:23, 36, 40; 3:13–15, 26; 4:10; 5:30; 7:51; 13:27–28, 46; 23:3), e.g., "you stiff-necked people, uncircumcised in heart" (7:51), yet, ultimately, Paul brings no charges (28:19).

10. Philo, *Embassy*, 120–131: "horrors" (δεινός, 123) inflicted by Alexandrians, including "most pitiful" (οἰκτρότατος, 130) details (cf. 243; 266–267).

11. From himself (18:6, cf. 16:37), unbelieving Pharisees (23:9), Lysias (23:29), Festus (25:25), and Agrippa (26:31–32), cf. declarations of Jesus's innocence from Pilate (Luke 23:4, 14, 15, 22), Herod (23:15), a criminal (Luke 23:41), and a centurion (Luke 23:47).

12. E.g., 4:141, 318–325, 335, 358.

13. 4:150, 171, 201, 323; 5:19; 6:3–4, 110.

14. The persuasion throughout Acts reflects this, echoing such concern in Luke 1:1–4.

15. 8:1, 3; 9:21; 13:50; 14:5, 19; 16:19; 17:5–6, 13; 18:17; 19:24–29; 21:27–36; 22:22–23; 23:2, 9–10, 12–15; 25:3.

16. 16:35–39; 18:12–16; 19:40; 23:29; 25:25; 26:31–32. C. Kavin Rowe, *World Upside Down: Reading Acts in the Graeco-Roman Age* (Oxford: Oxford University Press, 2009), 147–48.

17. 5:40; 7:54; 8:3; 12:1–3; 13:50; 14:5, 19; 17:5–6, 13; 18:17; 21:27–36; 22:22–23; 23:2, 9–10, 12–15; 25:3.

18. Cf. Jesus's comments on tax, Luke 20:25; Rowe, *Upside Down*, 149–51.

19. Soliloquies at 6:2–8; 8:9; 11:3–14, 16–18; 12:1–13:15; 21:11–21.

20. Especially the honeycomb (16:1–16; 17:1–4) and bees (16:17–23).

21. Aseneth's poems do not quite fit the narrative context (mentioning her persecution, 11:3–6; 12:5, 7, 9–13, absent from the narrative); Mary's reference to God bringing down rulers (Luke 1:52) is similarly disjointed from its narrative. These discrepancies probably arise from uneven editing of earlier material—the author could edit narrative more freely than carefully structured (and perhaps well-known) poetry. This suggests that the compiler of the final form of *Aseneth* played down the subject of persecution of proselytes, and that Luke played down the subject of a Messiah through whom God would disrupt the political order.

22. Or, conceivably, a later text might have been presented as published at that time—which would provide the accreditation of seeming to be a contemporary account.

23. E.g., *J.W.* 1:650; 2:169–174; *Jos. Asen.* 8:5; 12:9; *Let. Aris.* 138, and, in more moderate terms, *Embassy*, 290.

Chapter Eleven

Revisiting the Purpose of Acts

Various proposed purposes of Acts were listed, in broad categories, in Chapter 1. What has this study been able to contribute, in terms of supporting or undermining these suggestions?

POSSIBLE PURPOSES

1. *Further Scripture.* This research makes it possible to check how scriptural the narrator of Acts is, particularly in his style of accrediting and persuasion. It is characteristic of OT narrators that, at times, they claim not only to be omniscient in terms of human events, but also to know heavenly events (Job 1:6–12; 2:1–7; Tob 3:16–17), or the heavenly perspective (e.g., Num 22:22; Jdg 3:1–2; 3 Kgdms 15:5).[1] The narrator claims such authority at Luke 1:6 and 26, but it is not clear that this happens in the rest of Luke-Acts.[2] OT narrators also describe (without expression of doubt) encounters between characters and God or angels, where the authority for the account may lie with either that character (e.g., Elisha for 4 Kgdms 2:9–12) or the narrator (e.g., Balaam is hardly a trustworthy source, Num 22:20). Acts certainly follows this pattern in its accounts of heavenly visions, appearances, and messages. Authoritative utterance is more in the mouth of trusted characters than of the narrator—which is true also of the OT accounts of Elijah and Elisha (3 Kgdms 17:1–4 Kgdms 13:20). This research has shown that accreditation in Acts has a remarkably strong supernatural emphasis, compared with the other texts. In this, along with the Third Gospel and *Aseneth*, Acts seems to be adopting (perhaps even amplifying) scriptural style. Overall, the narrative style of Acts is thus entirely compatible with scriptural style. For the narrator to assert higher

authority than his trusted characters would amount to a claim to divine authority, and such a claim can be detected in Luke 1, suggesting that the Third Gospel may be presenting itself as Scripture. Acts is similar but, as in *Aristeas*, authority is slightly more with the trusted characters. So the style of narration does suggest that the Third Gospel and Acts were written with a desire to be accepted by Christians as Scripture, alongside the Septuagint.

2. *Church history.* Other texts demonstrate a concern for future generations (e.g., *J.W.* 3:204; 6:200; *Let. Aris.*, 38, 296); the narrator of Acts does not. The speeches include forward-looking generalizations that indicate the gospel's relevance in all places ("for you, for your children [τεκνόν] and for all who are far away," 2:39, cf. 1:8; 10:35; 17:27, 30), presumably until Jesus's return (1:11). But it is unclear whether this should be understood as pointing primarily to children already born to the audience within the narrative at the time of the speech, to the first hearers of the work (perhaps one generation later), or to generations after that.[3] Acts ends with the prospect of further fruitful mission among Gentiles (28:28), but this seems limited to Rome, since Paul is held there. Greek-speaking citizens of the Roman Empire would have assumed that Rome was the center and not the "end" of the earth, so it is far from clear that this conclusion completes the commission of 1:8. A text aimed primarily at future generations could surely have ended on a more conclusive note, in terms of completed or ongoing geographical spread of the gospel. If 28:31 is indeed the intended end of the text, this suggests a concern more immediate than providing a history for future generations.

3. *Christian teaching* (διδαχή). *Embassy* has a narrator who is quite willing to adopt a didactic tone. In contrast, most of Acts deals with the Jesus movement's engagement with outsiders and is evangelistic and apologetic in its themes, rather than overtly didactic. There are some consistent themes running through the speeches, but the wording and presentation are highly variable, according to the narrative context. In this, Acts is surely not promoting a particular fixed or formulaic approach to the message or to the required response.

There are a few episodes that indicate a more internal and more didactic concern. The episode of Ananias and Sapphira (5:1–11) is entirely suitable as a cautionary tale—a warning aimed at members of the movement against any act of apparent piety, attempting to deceive the community and thus the Holy Spirit himself (5:3, 9). The account might well have been preserved through becoming proverbial among believers ("Remember Ananias and Sapphira," cf. "Remember Lot's wife," Luke 17:32), but it is not obvious that this is an incident an outsider needs to know about, and later generations might be hesitant to recount it to outsiders for fear of showing believers in a bad light. So the inclusion of this episode in Acts may suggest some didactic intent. Also, Paul's speech to the Ephesian elders (20:18–35) provides six verses of direct instruction for elders (vv. 28–32, 35), emphasizing Paul's example (ὑποδείκνυμι, v. 35). This might indicate didactic intent, but the speech contains twice as many verses accrediting Paul's ministry (vv. 18–27, 33–34). The focus is much more on Paul and his ministry than on people following his example. Similarly, although Peter (3:1–8; 9:33–42), Stephen (7:59–60), and Paul (14:8–10) echo Jesus at times, to various extents, this is not presented as planned imitation of Jesus, but rather as spontaneous, through the inspiration of the Holy Spirit (7:55), with the direct link to Jesus provided by use of his name (3:6, 13; 9:34). Further, Paul cannot be seen as a deliberate follower of Peter's example, because contact between them is minimal (limited to 15:4–29, and possibly 9:28). The emphasis in Acts is not on learning from example.

There is emphasis on ongoing empowerment by the Spirit. Throughout, although the trusted characters provide worthy examples, the narrator promotes respect for them more strongly than empathy, and presents them (especially Paul,[4] with his unique calling, 9:15; 22:14–15; 26:16) as exceptional, not as models realistic for every believer (or even the community)[5] to follow.

Thus, although Acts surely has some didactic intent, it does not provide believers with much by way of specific instruction. It gives some summaries of the gospel and examples to be followed or avoided, but it does more to promote loyalty—to these early leaders, to Jesus whom they proclaim, and to the ongoing movement. Acts certainly seeks to win over those who are suspicious of Gentile mission or of Paul. But whereas the writers of the epistles and the *Didache* are willing to assert their authority directly, Acts takes a much gentler approach, through narrative persuasion, which can hardly be described as didactic.

4. *General publication.* This research affirms the (relatively uncontroversial) view that Acts is not suitable for presentation to an audience actively hostile to the Jesus movement. Along with the Third Gospel, its strong monotheistic worldview and septuagintal style would surely be rejected outright by hostile pagans, and its negative portrayal of Jewish authorities (except Gamaliel, 5:34–39) would risk hardening the opposition of hostile Jews. Hostility seems to have been widespread—Acts itself admits that the movement had the reputation of facing opposition everywhere (28:22). It is unlikely that the author hoped to appeal to a completely general audience.

5. *Self-promotion.* Might some part of the Jesus movement, especially those associated with Paul, have acted as patrons for the preparation and

publication of Acts, for the purpose of raising the status of the movement as a whole, or at least of their group within it? Yes. This research indicates that Acts is a text with suitable persuasion built into it—not for a hostile audience, but for any audience willing to give both the Third Gospel (which seems to be prerequisite) and Acts a hearing. For example, if the text is complete, then it seems to present itself as being published two years into Paul's detention in Rome, and if it had indeed been published in Rome at that time, it might well have been used by Paul's supporters, not only to win support for him from among the believers (whom he had not previously visited), but also to take advantage of any publicity about his case to reach out to a wider audience. Such a purpose would explain, not only the rather abrupt ending and its reference to two years (28:30), but also the level of detail about Paul's journey to Rome (27:1–28:15), which is surprising if aimed at later generations, but entirely reasonable if aimed at an immediate, local audience. Along with explaining Jesus and his widely maligned movement (28:22), Luke-Acts does very fully answer the question, "Who is this Paul, and how does he come to be here in Rome?"

6. *Paul's legal defense.* This research does nothing to contradict the broad consensus that Acts is not suitable as a legal defense—despite including some relevant material, most of the text is not really relevant.

7. *Defense of Paul's memory.* Some aspects of Acts would be suitable for this. It contains indications of Paul's innocence of all charges, whether of blasphemy or sedition, which would help to defend him (and his ongoing followers) against accusations from outsiders. It also contains consistent justification for his ministry, which would help to defend him against accusations from believers, especially those attached to Judaism. But this narrative analysis actually suggests a date of publication before Paul's death. The inclusion of God's assurance of protection from both Jews and Gentiles toward the end, at 26:17 (and not in the earlier accounts of Paul's conversion/call) would make little sense if Paul were dead by the time of writing; his death would seem to contradict that promise—since the only evident threat from the Gentiles after this mention at 26:17 was a negative outcome of his trial in Rome. Mention of the promise instead at 9:5–6, chronologically, would fully avoid such an embarrassing implication. This narrative detail suggests, rather, that the narrator is prompting the audience to expect a positive outcome of Paul's trial. The text seems to have been written before Paul's death, rather than in his memory.

8. *Defense of the Jesus movement.* This idea has generally assumed an intended audience of influential Romans, open to being persuaded that the movement is legitimate or at least worthy of toleration. Certainly, Acts presents the movement positively, but not in a way suitable for these in-

fluential Romans. Their main concerns would surely be law and order (concern about sedition) and social stability (aversion to influences that might destabilize communities or families). There is evidence elsewhere that the movement's teaching did encourage all its members to be responsible and law-abiding (Rom 13:1–7; 1 Pet 2:13–20), so Acts surely could have mentioned this, but it does not. Rather, the text emphasizes the bold outspokenness[6] of the movement's leaders, a trait that might be popular among "underdogs" who would not themselves dare to speak thus, but it would hardly be reassuring or endearing to those in authority; the text does not seem suitable for such hearers. There are insights into the thinking of various officials (16:38; 22:29–30; 23:10; 24:25–26; 25:9, 18–20; 26:24, 31–32), but these reflect on Paul's particular situations, and not directly on the movement as a whole. There are opportunities for encouraging an authoritative Roman hearer to identify with Sergius Paulus (13:6–12), but his point of view is reported only briefly (13:12), or with Cornelius (10:1–48), but the text ends up focusing on his entire household and not on him as an individual (10:44–48). Acts does not encourage the hearer to identify with these prominent Romans.

So, although Acts presents the Jesus movement, and its leaders, as innocent of all accusations, this presentation does not seem to be aimed at Roman officials responsible for making judgments about the movement; the text is more appropriate for providing reassurance about the movement's appropriateness to believers and interested outsiders.

9. *Defense of Roman authorities.* There is uniformly positive portrayal of those Romans portrayed as converts (Cornelius, 10:1–48; Sergius Paulus, 13:7–12), which demonstrates the sort of accreditation of which the author is capable. In contrast, Acts provides a mixed picture of Romans in their exercise of authority: There is some accrediting (e.g., Festus's concern for due process, 25:27), but also some discrediting (e.g., Felix hoping for a bribe, 24:26). Acts is admittedly restrained in its criticism compared, for example, with Josephus's account of Festus's successors, Albinus and Florus (*J.W.* 2:271–279). There is, nevertheless, a contrast between these Roman leaders and the Roman converts that strongly suggests that concerns related to the gospel are more significant in the persuasiveness of Acts than any concern with Roman authority. Acts is not designed to provide a defense for Roman authorities in general.

10. *Evangelistic proclamation.* The text, although not particularly suitable for a hostile hearer, is entirely suitable for interested outsiders. Although Acts uses septuagintal style and overt quotations, prior knowledge of the Septuagint is not necessarily assumed or required—to follow the narrative of Acts, the hearer need only be aware of its existence and of its

status among Jews. Even the internal meetings are of wider relevance: The Jerusalem deliberations (11:1–18; 15:4–29) are of great significance not only for existing Gentile believers, but also for ongoing mission among Gentiles; Paul's Miletus speech provides not only instruction for elders but also defense of Paul's own ministry. Admittedly, there may be warnings for insiders in the episodes of Ananias and Sapphira (5:1–11) and, perhaps, Simon Magus (8:9–24), and believers might naturally be reluctant to mention such material to outsiders. But, on the basis of Jesus's overt warnings to those wondering whether to follow him (Luke 9:57–62; 14:25–35), there is no reason to suppose that the author of the Third Gospel had such reservations; and it is reasonable to suppose that Acts follows the same approach.

So, along with the Third Gospel, Acts is entirely suitable for reading out to an invited audience of interested outsiders. The Third Gospel commends Jesus, despite his rejection and death, as fulfilling Scripture, as sent by God, and as accredited, especially by his resurrection. Acts commends the subsequent Jesus movement, especially among Gentiles and especially in the person of Paul, despite widespread opposition, as further fulfilling Scripture, appointed by Jesus and empowered by the Holy Spirit. Acts, where the speeches are largely addressed to outsiders, is suitable not only to reassure the believing hearer that they were right to "repent and turn to God" (3:19; 26:20), but at the same time to encourage the unbelieving hearer to do so. The analysis in this book does not aim to demonstrate to what extent, if any, the text was actually used in such a way; but it does suggest that interested outsiders cannot be excluded from the intended audience and that the persuasiveness of the text itself is suitable for them.

11. *Inspiration for evangelism.* Acts describes mission and evangelism in positive terms, suitable for encouraging not only assent to, but even active support for such activities. But it is not clear that the accounts are intended to inspire individuals toward evangelism. Peter may provide a helpful example but, in his evangelism and apologetics, is portrayed with respect more than empathy. As an appointed apostle, witness and the movement's leader in Acts 1–12, one is certainly encouraged to respect him and what he stands for, but it is not clear exactly how a typical Christian might be expected to emulate him a generation later. Similarly, Paul is presented as having a unique calling and, although settled elders should copy his hard work among a local congregation (20:18–35), he has no evident successor in his peripatetic ministry and is not presented, overall, as one whose ministry others could copy. Stephen is presented in unattainably glowing terms (6:5, 8, 10, 15). Even to follow the example

of the less prominent Philip, one would have to perform exorcisms and other signs (8:6–7), and receive specific instruction from the Holy Spirit (8:26—and cope if that instruction is unexpected and, initially, inexplicable). If Acts were a manual on evangelism, its main points would be that the gospel is for all (including Gentiles) and that mission depends on the Holy Spirit; but it is not clear that the text is intended to provide particular evangelistic techniques or strategies that hearers can realistically emulate. Rather, it provides general encouragement and examples of mission that need significant adaptation for other evangelists at later times and in different contexts. Acts is capable of inspiring and guiding evangelism, but since it does little to provide relevant inside views of the various trusted characters (which would help the hearer to learn from their situations), it is not clear that this is a significant purpose of the text. The point at which the text does most to develop empathy—with Peter during the Cornelius episode—is, ironically, the point at which Peter's example is least worthy of copying (indeed, the heavenly voice may even be rebuking him, 10:15). Acts is certainly capable of encouraging mission, but it does not seem to be intended as a mission manual.

12. *Promotion of one Christian faction.* Many have noted that Acts accredits Paul and his ministry, but this study has provided details of the persuasive mechanisms and demonstrated the sheer extent of this accreditation. This suggests that Acts has been shaped to allow for some in the implied audience—presumably a significant group—who need to be won over and persuaded to accept both Paul's ministry and the wider Gentile mission. Does the text provide evidence of factions? Acts evidently opposes Judaizers (15:1, 5; but it presents that issue as though resolved, 15:6–33), magicians (and any influence they might have within the movement, e.g., 8:9–24), and unspecified, future, wolf-like leaders (20:29–30). It is not clear that Acts opposes any particular, ongoing group among the believers. Nevertheless, the thrust of persuasion makes it entirely credible that Acts was intended to promote Paul and his teaching within the church, and it is plausible that this was necessary because of believers still attached to Judaism (whether born Jews or, perhaps, already attracted to Judaism before hearing the gospel) and therefore still suspicious of a Gentile movement that had largely abandoned Jewish practices. The "gentle steps" with which Gentile mission is introduced and justified in the Cornelius episode (10:1–11:18) are surely aimed at such an audience. Acts is suitable for an audience of believers who value the Jewish roots of the movement and are not (yet) convinced of the validity of Paul's approach. The persuasiveness of Acts would encourage acceptance of

Paul's approach to Gentile mission, and therefore also acceptance of the churches that arose from it.

Analysis of persuasion provides a mechanism for testing other specific suggestions. For example, Tyson sees Acts as intentionally anti-Marcionite, containing themes that contradict Marcionite ideas.[7] Since Marcionites accepted Paul as an apostle but not the Twelve, and accepted Jesus but rejected Jewish Scripture and practice, an anti-Marcionite text would need to accredit Scripture and the Twelve. But Acts does not do that. It does not put effort into accrediting Scripture, but simply presupposes its authority,[8] and Acts shifts its focus so strongly to Paul (called personally by Jesus, completely independently of the Twelve) and away from the Twelve (initially accredited, but then absent after 15:23) that it risks playing into the hands of Marcionites. Further, if Acts were intended to reverse the spread of Marcionite ideas among believers, it would make sense, not simply to "preach to the converted," but to present its message in a way that would be persuasive in winning over a wavering hearer with Marcionite tendencies. Analysis of persuasion demonstrates that it does not. To be persuasive for a Marcionite sympathizer, Acts could take for granted respect for Jesus and Paul and could then attempt to use them to provide accreditation for those this hearer is inclined to dismiss—for Scripture and the Twelve. But Acts presupposes the authority, not of Paul, but of Scripture. An anti-Marcionite text would surely attempt to use the respected Paul to accredit the Twelve, by acknowledging their authority.[9] But, in Acts, Paul does not accredit the Twelve; rather, the Twelve accredit Paul (as "beloved," 15:25). Although Judas and Silas are officially sent to accompany him (15:22, 27), the text avoids suggesting that the Twelve sent or commissioned Paul, thus avoiding the question of whether they had direct authority over him. Paul and his companions duly deliver the letter from the Jerusalem meeting (15:30, cf. 16:4), but it is striking that, in all Paul's speeches, he never mentions the Twelve. Paul does not deny the authoritative status ascribed to the Twelve by the movement (e.g., when he is sent to them, 15:2), but he is not presented as in any way adding to their status. Minor changes to the wording of Acts would allow it to be much more persuasive for winning back Marcionite-sympathizers—it could accredit the Twelve by indicating more forcefully (and without distorting the facts) that Paul did at least acknowledge the authority ascribed to them by the movement. But Acts is far from direct on that point. Rather, the text presupposes the authority of Scripture, but not of Paul, whose authority it works hard to establish, and it hardly uses Paul to accredit the Twelve. Thus, an analysis of persuasion strongly undermines this anti-Marcionite hypothesis.

13. *Legitimation of the Jesus movement.* This research affirms the widely accepted idea that Acts aims to reassure its audience of the legitimacy of the Jesus movement. The extensive process of accrediting within the text has two relevant effects. First, it establishes trust in some key characters. That, in itself, contributes toward legitimating the ongoing movement, at the time of the publication of Acts, by providing a positive portrayal of some of its key early leaders. Secondly, the hearer is encouraged to listen with respect to those trusted characters, so that the ideas and worldview expressed in their speeches and actions are also presented persuasively. This contributes toward legitimating the ideas and worldview of the on-going movement (to the extent that they are still identified with those expressed in the text). Esler is right to note that, although legitimation of a movement might be aimed at second-generation members who were born into the movement, the believers who heard Acts must be assumed to include significant numbers of converts.[10] That is inevitable in a rapidly growing movement. Indeed, it would only be untrue for a movement that had already stagnated for a generation—which does not accord with what is known about the early church. On the other hand, this study does not support Esler's assumption that, as the intended audience, those outside the movement may be disregarded. Rather, Acts offers evidence of the legitimacy of the movement in a form that is also suitable for interested outsiders.

For Esler, the basis of legitimation includes portraying the Jesus movement as linked to Judaism (e.g., through fulfillment of Scripture), as compatible with allegiance to Rome, and, in incorporating Gentiles, as a faithful development with continuity provided especially through the role of Peter. This might give the impression that the movement is portrayed as legitimate by reference primarily to the established values and laws of Judaism and of the Roman Empire. But the term "legitimation" is far from adequate in expressing the persuasive impact of Acts. For instance, Proconsul Gallio's legitimation of the movement through his dismissal of allegations against it (18:12–17) is hardly a climax within the narrative. Jesus and his movement are indeed presented as innocent rather than guilty, but the text does far more than encourage the hearer to assent to that. The Jesus movement is not presented simply as something legal, which should therefore be permitted and in which one can participate without a sense of guilt. Rather, the gospel message is presented primarily as accredited, not by Jewish or Roman laws or values, but by God himself, through a wide range of supernatural accrediting devices such as angels, visions, and miracles. The hearer is encouraged to regard the gospel message as not merely legitimate, but as a vital, imperative, and compelling message (e.g., 2:40; 3:21–23; 10:42; 17:30–31) from God himself. This persuasive presentation within Acts is entirely suitable for both believers and interested outsiders.

CONCLUSION

This research suggests that the purpose of Acts can be summarized as the promotion of the Jesus movement, as initiated by Jesus (in the Third Gospel), as extended by the incorporation of Gentiles (in Acts), and, in particular, as embodied in Paul. The narrator speaks with authority about the supernatural, but does not himself provide authoritative instruction, so that Acts is more persuasive than didactic. The text seems suitable, not only for existing members of the movement, but also for any Greek-speakers interested enough to listen (to the Third Gospel, as well as to Acts)—although not for those actively hostile to the movement. The text seems designed, not merely to answer accusations or defend the movement (although it does that), but actively to promote it.

In particular, in promoting Gentile Christianity without Torah observance, legitimation of Gentile mission (and its resulting churches) is a significant purpose of the text. The "gentle steps" approach to persuasion suggests that the text does not "preach to the converted" on this issue, but aims to win over hearers suspicious of the idea—presumably Jews, proselytes, or God-fearers with an attachment to Jewish practices.

Through its focus on Paul, detailed account of his arrival in Rome and abrupt ending two years later, the text presents itself as having been published at that time, presumably in Rome itself, where publicity and rumors about Paul's case would naturally have aroused interest among Jews and Christians, and perhaps among others also.[11] Although most scholars suggest a later date, this analysis of persuasiveness suggests that the text is less suitable for publication after Paul's death, but entirely appropriate for publication at the end of those two years.

NOTES

1. Some pseudepigraphal, noncanonical Jewish texts also adopt this style. They were written with knowledge of some or all of the OT, so it is reasonable to assume that such texts were claiming authority alongside Scripture, whether or not others would concur.

2. Except perhaps in the disputed Luke 22:43–44.

3. Keener, *Acts* 1:440, sees 2:39 as applying to "all subsequent generations." But there is no explicit future reference. This would have been resolved had there also been mention of "children's children" as at: (also using τεκνόν), Exod 34:7; Prov 17:6; and (using υἱός) Gen 45:10; 4 Kgdms 17:41; Ps 102:17 (Ps 103:17, MT); 127:6 (128:6, MT); Jer 2:9; (cf. Ezek 37:25, Alexandrian text). These LXX references (except perhaps Jer 2:9) are to future generations (certainly at 4 Kgdms 17:41, onward "to this day"; Ps 127:6, a wish for future blessing; Ezek 37:25, for ever).

4. Portrayed as without successors: Barrett, "First," 100.

5. Keener, *Acts* 1:440, suggests that these characters are not models for the individual believer, but "for the Christian movement as a whole." But if Acts teaches, it is more about following God's initiative than particular human approaches or methods.

6. παρρησία, 2:29; 4:13, 29, 31; 28:31; παρρησιάζομαι, 9:27, 28; 13:46; 14:3; 18:26; 19:8; 26:26.

7. Tyson, *Marcion*, 76–78.

8. E.g., Peter presumes the authority of Scripture at 2:16–21, since the mystery of apparent drunkards can hardly accredit the prophet Joel, but the prophecy can explain the disciples' mysterious speech, cf. Luke 4:4, 8, 12, Jesus quotes Scripture as already authoritative, not as needing his accreditation.

9. Tyson, *Marcion*, 76.

10. Esler, *Community*, 16.

11. An interest suggested by Phil 1:13, whether or not this refers to the same imprisonment.

Chapter Twelve

Conclusions

REVIEW

The main aim of this book has been to address the question: *What can be learned, from the way Acts has been constructed, about the persuasive influence the text would have exerted on its original audiences?* Whatever genre one may suggest for Acts, it is certainly a narrative, so narrative criticism has been taken as the appropriate approach for addressing this question. But this discipline has not traditionally focused on issues of persuasion. Rhetorical criticism has begun to address persuasive influence, but it uses tools developed from speeches, which require considerable adaptation for application to narrative texts. So, this book has also aimed to provide *a systematic method for identifying techniques of persuasion within ancient narratives*. This method has been described and then used with five texts. For Acts, this has made it possible, first, to identify specific techniques of persuasion; secondly, to identify of what the hearer is being persuaded; and, thirdly, where possible, to assess for what particular group of hearers this persuasion is suitable. Comparison between the texts gives some indication of what is common and what is distinctive about the persuasion in Acts. The final aim of the research has been, in this way, to provide *evidence for or against various suggestions about the author's purpose*.

The method outlined in Chapter 2 builds on conventional narrative criticism, especially analysis of narrator and implied audience. It makes significant adaptations, necessary for addressing persuasion, and these take the form of a taxonomy of techniques of persuasion relevant to narrative. The vital issue of trust is addressed by considering, in detail, the devices used for accrediting or discrediting each character (and even the narrator).

Analysis of four nonbiblical texts has demonstrated that the persuasive techniques presented in the taxonomy can be identified in a range of texts comparable to Acts and roughly contemporary with it. This has also demonstrated how the method can draw conclusions about persuasive influence. For each text, this method provides new evidence about persuasiveness. This has not suggested entirely new ideas about purpose, but largely agrees with scholarly trends and consensus (to whatever extent there is consensus), which provides some grounds for confidence in the method.

Philo's *Embassy to Gaius* demonstrates how a narrative text may include sections of conventional rhetoric (in the mouth of the narrator), providing strong evidence that this text has persuasive intent. Indeed, *Embassy* provides a helpful comparison between persuasive speeches and persuasive narrative that, as parts of the same text, surely share the same purposes. Invective is prominent, against Gaius and emperor-worship, including the use of biting sarcasm. As an interpreter of political events, Philo emphasizes the unreasonableness of those who caused trouble for the Jews. For this, he uses Greek standards more than Jewish, while also emphasizing the commitment and unity of the Jews. This text is certainly suitable for encouraging his fellow Jews to stand firm despite troubles, but this study suggests that it is also suitable for eliciting tolerance or even support from influential Alexandrian Greeks (but not native Egyptians). *Embassy* supports Judaism by denigrating those who had persecuted the Jews. In contrast, Acts supports the Jesus movement, which was persecuted by Jewish leaders, with some aversion to these opponents, but although Philo uses biting techniques to generate hostility (antipathy), Acts does not resort to this.

Josephus's *Jewish War* demonstrates how an author may have to give careful consideration simultaneously to a range of different audiences, whether intended or inevitable. He seems primarily to address those interested in the recent Jewish war—educated, Greek-speaking subjects of the Roman Empire, including posterity. But his work would inevitably be checked for "political correctness" by cronies of the Emperor and by Josephus's personal enemies, seeking any evidence against him. It would also inevitably be checked by his fellow-Jews for "correctness" by Jewish standards. *War* indicates how a text may have multiple audiences and multiple, simultaneous purposes, for the text betrays concern with attitudes toward Jews (countering Roman hostility), toward emperors (an inevitable, rather than voluntary, concern), toward Josephus himself and, on careful reading, toward non-Roman aristocrats (like himself) within the Empire. Acts shows similar concern for attitudes toward the Jesus movement and, similarly, handles issues of Roman authority with some care, but in contrast, Acts shows little concern for the reputation of the author.

Joseph and Aseneth demonstrates how a text may build on acknowledged Scripture (which gives the text a respected starting point) and may depend strongly on the supernatural (especially the appearance of a man from heaven) to justify a particular idea—that a penitent pagan who turns to the God of the Jews can be fully accepted into the community. Its use of obscure imagery suggests that symbolic meaning may also be built into the text, encouraging the interested hearer to ask further questions of the lector (reader), or of the community that laid claim to these mysteries. Whereas Joseph is portrayed with respect and speaks with authority, this text shows how a reader may also be persuaded through developing empathy—with Aseneth, accompanying her on a journey of discovery. The implied audience seems to be in a situation where involvement with Gentiles, even proselytes, was unacceptable to at least some Jews. The text is suitable for persuading Jews that wholehearted proselytes can and should be accepted, without compromising Jewish values. It is also suitable for encouraging potential converts to follow Aseneth's example. Acts makes similar claims to be founded on both Scripture and further divine revelation but, unlike *Aseneth*, Acts recounts events of the recent past and emphasizes witnesses and evidence to which the (earliest) audiences may have access in other ways, beyond the text.

The *Letter of Aristeas* demonstrates the need to distinguish clearly between narrator and author and between the stated audience and the implied audience, since it seems to have been written by a Jew, yet has both a fictitious, Greek narrator and a fictitious, Greek recipient. The text seems designed to encourage respect for Judaism, its traditions and Scriptures, especially some particular Greek translation (presumably a version of the Septuagint). It attempts to encourage this respect according to Greek standards, portraying a situation of mutual respect between Jews and Alexandrian Greeks, using a striking variety of literary styles. Although scholars have tended to conclude that the text was written by a Jew for Jews (probably in Alexandria), the persuasion within the text would also be suitable for presentation to well-disposed Alexandrian Greeks, perhaps at a local Jewish festival. *Aristeas* is not particularly suitable for a suspicious hearer, to whom it would give an impression of hyperbole, as it provides an unremittingly positive portrayal of Jews, along with an almost universally positive portrayal of Greeks. In contrast, Acts does not present believers as respectable and respected; it provides a more balanced and nuanced mixture of positives and negatives, along with various conflicts.

For each text, members of the author's own community form an inevitable part of the audience, but are not automatically the intended, "target" audience. This study has taken care not to presuppose that these texts are "preaching to the converted," i.e., that the implied audience already agrees with the narrator—indeed, the extent of persuasiveness detected within the texts suggests the opposite.

The issue here is not whether outsiders were numerous or could easily be persuaded to listen,[1] but simply whether these texts show evidence of being suitable for them, which gives some indication of whether the authors had them in mind when writing. A modern example illustrates the need for this approach: One might argue that the key audience for evangelistic tracts is Christians, as the ones most familiar with the worldview presented and with most interest in buying, reading, and distributing them. But if one presupposes that the Christian themes and language of the text exclude outsiders from the audience, one will completely miss the "point." Caution is needed—and has been exercised here—before narrowing down the implied audience.

There has been a tendency in modern scholarship to propose, for the texts studied here, audiences who already agree with the worldviews of the narrators—i.e., suggesting that *Embassy*, *Aseneth*, and the *Aristeas* were written by Jews to influence or encourage fellow Jews and, similarly, that Acts was written by a Christian for Christians. (*War* is an exception, because it clearly presents itself as written by a Jew primarily for Gentiles.) Admittedly, these narratives do not have hostile outsiders as their implied audiences and have rightly been distinguished from such confrontational apologies as Josephus's *Against Apion* or Justin Martyr's *Apology*, which directly address issues raised by and relevant to hostile outsiders.[2] But it is not clear that the "fringes" around either Jewish or Christian communities can be ignored. This research has failed to find, within these texts, evidence that would discount the presence of interested outsiders in the implied audiences. Rather, the techniques of persuasion are generally appropriate not only for insiders but also for interested outsiders.

The analysis of persuasion in Acts has shown that there is a remarkable concern with accrediting the trusted characters (more than accrediting the narrator, who is relatively reticent) and that the means of accreditation are dominated by the supernatural—through divine approval or activity, including visions and miracles. Indeed, association with the Holy Spirit is used as the highest form of accreditation, implying not only God's favor but also divine empowering and inspiration, suggesting that words spoken immediately after such accreditation are not only to be trusted but to be treated with the greatest respect. Thus, the hearers of Acts are encouraged to listen with respect to the worldview and general teaching in the speeches of the trusted characters, and to note with respect the example set by their behavior.

Peter is initially characterized with such respect—the hearer learns *from* Peter. But, in the Cornelius episode (10:1–11:18), several insights are given into Peter's thoughts, developing empathy rather than respect. This encourages the hearer to identify with Peter and to accompany him on his journey of discovery about God's inclusion of Gentiles. Here, the hearer learns *with* Peter. God's announcement to Cornelius that he and his whole household will be saved through Peter's message is only revealed to the hearer on the third and final telling of this vision (11:14), as part of the conclusion to the episode, yet this technically happened at the beginning of the episode (but was unreported at that stage, 10:6). Analysis of persuasion suggests that this episode includes repetition not merely for emphasis (with some variations for interest), but rather as a persuasive, gentle-steps approach to winning over hearers initially suspicious of the idea that God might accept Gentiles in this way. The fact that Acts 10 has the highest density of accrediting devices of any chapter in Acts also suggests that this episode represents a climax of persuasion. The accounts of Paul's conversion/call also amount to a gentle-steps approach, introducing a suspicious hearer to the idea of Paul's call slightly more forcefully with each retelling.

Despite Witherington's suggestion that Acts is written for Theophilus—that is, for one, high-status individual[3]—this study has shown that the way Peter and Paul behave in the presence of centurions would risk alienating rather than engaging such an individual; rather, the implied audience of Acts is actually plural. They are already familiar with the Third Gospel, which gives a persuasive presentation of Jesus—despite his rejection and death, as actually sent by God (which is attested by the resurrection), in fulfillment of Scripture, to bring salvation to all kinds of people, with the apostles, although flawed, appointed by him and promised the Holy Spirit. Acts goes on to give a persuasive presentation of the Jesus movement—despite opposition, as faithfully and boldly proclaiming this good news, empowered by the Spirit. If the author of Acts were accused of writing pro-Christian propaganda, it is not clear that he would disagree; his emphasis on witnesses and evidence suggests that he would deny misrepresentation, but the text strongly suggests pro-Christian persuasive intent. The text is not suitable for hostile outsiders, as the necessary initial step of suspended disbelief, to enable them to engage with the narrative, would be too much. But the text is entirely suitable for interested outsiders. They would need to know that the Jews had well-respected Scriptures, but they would not need to be aware of much more about Judaism than that—indeed detailed knowledge of the Scriptures might be a disadvantage, raising questions that the text does not attempt to answer.[4]

The implied audience, once persuasion is allowed for, includes both Gentiles (who receive some explanations of Judaism) and Jews (the ones most in need of persuasion about God's incorporation of Gentiles), both believers (who particularly benefit from the cautionary tale of Ananias and Sapphira and from Paul's warnings about future leaders) and "fringe" members, including interested outsiders—the ones most in need of the challenge of overhearing the gospel and seeing the impressive, publicly displayed character of the believers.

The text is suitable, not so much for soliciting toleration for Christianity from outsiders, as for encouraging their wholehearted conversion to it.

Persuasion in Acts includes a clear focus on encouraging the hearer to accept and approve of the inclusion of Gentiles. It also has a clear focus on Paul, encouraging the hearer to respect him and approve of his ministry. Persuasion is evident on these two points, which indicates the presence, within the implied audience, of a significant number of hearers who are, at least initially, skeptical about Paul and about Gentile mission. If these are believers, they are believers who do not owe allegiance to Paul, although the narrator of Acts does display such allegiance. It may be of interest to reconstruct a "Lukan community" by considering the implied author and audience, but one must avoid the mistake of presupposing that the audience's point of view coincides with that of the narrator. The presence of these persuasive devices suggests that it does not. Admittedly, it is highly likely that initial audiences would include some, perhaps a majority, who agreed with the narrator's point of view. But one cannot assume that they are the target audience, nor that the audience is monolithic. Rather, the implied audience of Acts is certainly wider than that group that already agrees with the narrator.

In summary, the text of Acts is entirely appropriate for encouraging believers to continue in their faith, by legitimating the movement to which they belong. On the other hand, the persuasion in Acts is also entirely appropriate for presentation to interested outsiders, to encourage them to join the movement. There is evidence of gentle but persistent effort to persuade hearers of the appropriateness of Gentiles being included and of Paul and his ministry—and the suspicious hearers in need of such persuasion would most likely be those well accustomed to the exclusion of Gentiles: Jewish Christians, along with believers who had previously been proselytes or God-fearers, rather than those from pagan background. Acts 15 is presented as providing, with the authority of the Jerusalem church, an approval of Paul (15:25), and an agreed conclusion to the issue of including Gentiles.[5] Despite this, the persuasion within the text of Acts indicates that, for its implied audience, years later, these were still significant issues.

Various proposed *purposes of Acts* have been discussed. This study provides relevant evidence, leading to the following conclusions. First, the primary thrust of persuasion within Acts is simply to commend the Jesus movement—an extension of the way Jesus himself is commended in the Third Gospel. Secondly, although it would not be wrong to see the behavior of the trusted characters as generally exemplary, this research points out that these exceptional leaders are characterized more with respect than with empathy, suggesting that the hearer is intended primarily to learn *from* them (i.e., accept their message with respect), rather than learn *with* them (i.e., imagine being them, and attempt to emulate their ministry). Indeed, it is not clear that

Acts presents any character as able to emulate or succeed Paul. So it is not clear that the narrative of Acts was intended as a manual for mission or ministry. Thirdly, Tyson's particular suggestion of an anti-Marcionite purpose is undermined by the absence of any clear accrediting of the Twelve (who were discounted by Marcion) via the authority of Paul (who was accepted by Marcion)—rather the opposite, Paul is presented as accredited by the Twelve. Fourthly, the persuasion is entirely appropriate for a text published at the end of Paul's two years in Rome (28:30), since this explains: the accreditation of and increasing focus on Paul, as a figure of public interest at that time, whom the text commends; the lack of accreditation of any clear successor, which would be unnecessary during Paul's lifetime; and the expectation left at the end of the text that Paul would stand before Caesar (27:24), and would be rescued (26:17), but with no further details—which would be appropriate if his actual trial were still imminent at the time of publication.[6] The structure of the retellings of Paul's conversion/call (especially the promise of 26:17) would provoke puzzlement and disappointment if published after Paul's death. Rather, this arrangement strongly suggests expectation of Paul's release and therefore that Acts was published before Paul's death.

Finally, various proposed purposes of Acts remain credible, in the light of this research. The aim here is not to select and promote any one of them, but to provide a more systematic method for gathering evidence about them. It remains likely that Acts has multiple, simultaneous purposes, especially since this analysis also indicates that the implied audience should be considered, not as monolithic, but as made up of various groups—Jewish believers, Gentile believers and interested outsiders, and the eventually inevitable hostile audience of opponents or Roman authorities checking the document for signs of sedition.

Thus this research has proposed a taxonomy-based method for discerning techniques of persuasion within narratives. Analysis of four nonbiblical texts has demonstrated the pervasiveness of persuasion and, through comparison with secondary literature, that the conclusions are reasonable. Analysis of Acts has identified a wide variety of techniques of persuasion and suggested their persuasive influence. This evidence has been used to reassess various proposed purposes of Acts.

WHAT IS THE SIGNIFICANCE OF THIS BOOK?

Until now, it is not clear that there has been a suitable, systematic method for identifying techniques of persuasion in ancient narratives, such as Acts. This book provides a method and gives some examples of how it can be used. Although narrative criticism has conventionally employed the concepts of empathy, sympathy, and antipathy toward characters, this method has added the important concept of respect, which is connected with trust and must be distinguished from empathy in terms of its persuasive effect. The idea of the hearer accompanying a character on a persuasive "journey of discovery" has, here, been applied to ancient narratives in a way that leads to new evidence about the persuasive thrust of the Cornelius episode, where the hearer learns *with* Peter (on the basis of empathy) rather than *from* him (on the basis of respect).

As applied to Acts, the study provides a new method for identifying persuasiveness and, by using it, develops new evidence for and against various possible purposes of the text. For example, the retellings of Paul's conversion/call provide evidence of an attempt to win over initially skeptical hearers by introducing them to his divine commission in gentle steps.

HOW CAN THIS BE USED?

Wider Application of This Method

This book has provided a brief study of the whole of Acts and then a more detailed case study on the Cornelius episode. I hope this will encourage readers to carry out their own, detailed studies on other parts of Acts. It should also be possible to apply this method to the Gospels, since they are primarily narrative. Redaction criticism has already contributed to scholars' understanding of the "tendencies" of the redactors of the Gospels, especially the Synoptics, and it would be helpful to compare conclusions reached by the two methods. This analysis of Acts would ideally be reviewed and extended in the light of a similar analysis of the Third Gospel. Indeed, an analysis of all the Gospels would allow Acts to be interpreted in the context, not only of nonbiblical texts (as here), but also of these biblical texts. For example, the accrediting and discrediting devices in Acts are much more similar to those in the Third Gospel than they are to those in the nonbiblical texts. It might be tempting to claim this as evidence of common authorship between the Third Gospel and Acts; but such a conclusion would only be valid if Acts could be shown to be closer (in this aspect of persuasive style) to the Third Gospel than to the other Gospels. Brief comparison with the Second Gospel suggests that, although Luke's style of accrediting is rather different from the nonbiblical authors, it is very similar to Mark's. Some features of style identified by this research may simply be distinctive of Gospel writers as a group. Nevertheless, more detailed work on the Gospels might allow this method to be used to identify what is distinctive about each of the individual Evangelists.

OT narrative was, at times, read by NT authors as expressing a persuasive message (e.g., warnings, Luke 17:32; 1 Cor 10:6–11; Heb 4:1, 11). This suggests that it is worthwhile to try to analyze persuasive techniques in Hebrew literature also—although this method will need checking and, perhaps, adapting.

Refinement and Development of the Method

This book provides a first attempt to define and use a method that draws on established ideas, but it is also a significant development of them. Over time, the method will hopefully be refined and improved through further and wider use and through more detailed comparison with conclusions reached by other methods. Although relevant material is limited, more could be done to investigate the extent to which ancient authors were conscious of using persuasive techniques in their narrative, and also the extent to which such persuasiveness succeeded or failed. Analysis of a wider range of nonbiblical Greek texts (and even Latin texts, such as Suetonius's biographies) would provide, not only a broader range of comparisons for the Gospels and Acts, but also, perhaps, adaptations and additions to the method. From the Apocrypha, 2–4 Maccabees would provide helpful comparison with Acts. Analysis of narrative texts from elsewhere in the Septuagint would provide a further dimension, through comparison with Greek translated from Hebrew or Aramaic—relevant here, since the author of Acts was familiar with and, presumably, influenced by much of the Septuagint. The prominence of supernatural elements in Acts, especially in accreditation, is exceptional among the texts studied, but would benefit from a more detailed comparison with the Septuagint. With OT narrative, much may be the same, but there is a danger that ideas from Greek narrative style (which have influenced this method) would distort the analysis, so the method should ideally be checked and adapted in the light of Hebrew thought and texts.

More careful consideration might be given to the significance for persuasion of plot, arrangement, and role. For example, beyond noting positive and negative outcomes (as in the taxonomy presented), nuanced understanding of the role of a particular character is also needed, if Judas (who plays a key role in the main plot, and therefore may not be included for any separate persuasive purpose) is to be distinguished from Ananias and Sapphira (whose omission from the text would not detract from the main storyline, suggesting that their episode may be included primarily as a cautionary tale). Although the method aims to be systematic, much flesh and, perhaps, further bones remain to be added to this skeletal starting point.

A Look Ahead

Persuasive influence is an important, but often neglected, aspect of the meaning and significance of a narrative such as Acts. This book has asked what persuasive influence Acts would have exerted on its original audiences; it has begun to answer this question and to suggest implications for understanding the audiences and purposes of Acts. This makes some contribution to understanding Acts as a whole, and the method can also make a contribution to understanding and interpreting particular episodes. It is in the speeches that one can most easily detect both persuasion and theology in Acts, but this analysis of "narrative persuasion" provides a method for engaging with the whole text and any episode within it.

Narrative criticism has already made significant contributions to scholars' understanding of biblical narrative, in a form that is useful not only for scholars, but also for preachers: Just as a preacher is concerned with how hearers engage with a sermon, narrative criticism takes an interest in how hearers engage with a story—a helpful perspective for those preparing to preach from narrative. In trying to discern the "point" of a story, narrative criticism has a valuable contribution to make, especially if persuasiveness is carefully allowed for in the analysis.

More can be done to refine the method and extend its use, and thus to refine and develop these conclusions. Indeed, the method has deliberately been presented in a form—a taxonomy, with examples—designed to be easy for other narrative critics to understand, use, and develop. I hope that this book has provoked your interest in "narrative persuasion" and, perhaps, persuaded you to get involved in using and improving these ideas.

NOTES

1. Nor even how effective the text would actually have been, Alexander, "Apologetic Text," 44.
2. Alexander, "Apologetic Text," 23–25.
3. Witherington, *Acts*, 63.
4. Whereas apologies engage directly with counterarguments, e.g., Josephus, *Ag. Ap.* 1:1–2.
5. Although Acts avoids the further question of whether Jewish believers must remain observant Jews, touched on at 21:21.
6. Whether the text was actually published then, or simply presents itself as such, lies beyond the scope of this study.

Appendix A
List of Techniques of Persuasion

The techniques of persuasion, explained in more detail in Chapter 2, are listed here for convenient reference.

P1) *Overt instruction*

- P1a) *By the narrator:* A familiar example would be, "The moral of the story is . . ."
- P1b) *By a trusted character:* when accrediting devices have established that trust.
- P1c) *By an "other" character:* e.g., villain ends up relenting.

P2) *Worldview*

- P2a) *Worldview of the text* is revealed by a narrative event or narrator's description.
- P2b) *Trusted character's worldview* is revealed.
- P2c) *Untrustworthy character's worldview* is revealed.

P3) *Characterization:* Involving some degree of identification

- P3a) *Positive characterization and empathy:* e.g., a realistic, good example to follow.
- P3b) *Positive characterization and respect:* e.g., a trusted adviser, or an ideal to admire.
- P3c) *Positive characterization and sympathy:* e.g., a "sob story."
- P3d) *Aversion:* e.g., a realistic, bad example to avoid.

P4) *Antipathy:* Generally with hostility and without identification

- P4a) *Repulsive character (through personal traits):* a typical villainous character.
- P4b) *Repulsive character (through group identity):* e.g., xenophobic caricature.

P5) *Plot and arrangement*

- P5a) *Positive change or outcome:* e.g. comedy.
- P5b) *Negative change or outcome:* e.g. a cautionary tale.
- P5c) *Polyphonic affirmation:* The same idea comes from multiple, mutually reinforcing voices.
- P5d) *Journey of discovery:* The audience develops empathy with a character and accompanies them in learning a lesson as the story unfolds, e.g., Aseneth; and Peter (Acts 10:1–11:18).
- P5e) *Gentle steps:* The hearer is led, ideally unaware, through a cumulative series of minor developments in their attitude or thinking.

Techniques that are conceivable, but that this study has not identified actually being used persuasively in relevant narratives, include reporting a dialogue within the narrative (which might permit the arsenal of techniques of philosophical argument to be deployed); a repulsive narrator (e.g., Lucian's treatise, *A Professor of Public Speaking*); a shock of recognition (e.g., Nathan's impact on David, 2 Kgdms 12:1–7); and subtle indications of whether an action is good or bad (e.g., through omens or associations).

Techniques that might have been persuasive for early audiences, but that modern scholars are not likely to be able to interpret reliably include covert devices such as omission, symbolism, allusion, allegory, figured speech, irony, humor, and hints at esoteric knowledge—in cases where these are not explained within the text.

Appendix B
List of Accrediting and Discrediting Devices

The devices for Accrediting or Discrediting (see Chapter 2) are listed here.

Table B.1. List of Accrediting Devices

	Accrediting Device	Speaker
A1	Characterization (positive)	Narrator
A2	Characterization (positive)	Trusted
A3	Characterization (positive)	Other
A4	Commissioning by trusted character	Narrator
A5	Commissioning by trusted character	Trusted
A6	Commissioning by trusted character	Other
A7	General claim of OT prophecy fulfilled	Narrator
A8	General claim of OT prophecy fulfilled	Trusted
A9	Specific OT prophecy fulfilled	Narrator
A10	Specific OT prophecy fulfilled	Trusted
A11	Recent prophecy fulfilled	Narrator
A12	Recent prophecy fulfilled	Trusted
A13	Signs and wonders	Narrator
A14	Signs and wonders	Trusted
A15	Reaction of amazement: awe or fear	Narrator
A16	Reaction of amazement: awe or fear	Character
A17	Reaction of approval or joy	Narrator
A18	Reaction of approval or joy	Character
A19	Reported evidence	Narrator
A20	Reported evidence	Trusted
A21	Answered prayer	Narrator
A22	Answered prayer	Trusted
A23	Claim of God's favor	Narrator
A24	Claim of God's favor	Trusted
A25	Claim of God's favor	Other
A26	Association with the Holy Spirit	Narrator
A27	Association with the Holy Spirit	Trusted

Table B.2. List of Discrediting Devices

	Discrediting Device	Speaker
D1	Characterization (negative)	Narrator
D2	Characterization (negative)	Trusted
D3	Characterization (negative)	Other
D8	General claim of OT prophecy fulfilled	Trusted
D9	Specific OT prophecy fulfilled	Narrator
D10	Specific OT prophecy fulfilled	Trusted
D11	Recent prophecy fulfilled	Narrator
D13	Signs and wonders	Narrator
D14	Signs and wonders	Trusted
D17	Reaction of disapproval or horror	Narrator
D18	Reaction of disapproval or horror	Character
D19	Reported evidence	Narrator
D23	Claim of God's rejection	Narrator
D24	Claim of God's rejection	Trusted

The speaker may be the narrator, a trusted character (already accredited), or some "other" character. With reactions of disapproval or horror (D18), it has not proved necessary to distinguish between types of character. The numbering is chosen so that each Discrediting device is the complement of the Accrediting device with the same number—i.e., a similar technique, used with the opposite effect. Other devices are possible (e.g., D4 Commissioning by an untrustworthy character, mentioned by the narrator), but their use has not been found in the texts studied.

Appendix C
Accrediting and Discrediting in Luke-Acts

The number of occurrences of each device in Luke and Acts is shown.

Table C.1. Accrediting in Luke and Acts

	Accrediting Device	Speaker	Luke	Acts
A1	Characterization	Narrator	30	54
A2	Characterization	Trusted	33	55
A3	Characterization	Other	14	14
A4	Commissioning	Narrator	2	6
A5	Commissioning	Trusted	8	17
A6	Commissioning	Other	1	0
A7	General OT prophecy	Narrator	1	0
A8	General OT prophecy	Trusted	7	5
A9	Specific OT prophecy	Narrator	1	0
A10	Specific OT prophecy	Trusted	6	17
A11	Recent prophecy	Narrator	21	9
A12	Recent prophecy	Trusted	1	3
A13	Signs and wonders	Narrator	30	34
A14	Signs and wonders	Trusted	1	5
A15	Amazement: awe/fear	Narrator	26	13
A16	Amazement: awe/fear	Character	6	3
A17	Approval/joy	Narrator	6	9
A18	Approval/joy	Character	1	0
A19	Reported evidence	Narrator	10	12
A20	Reported evidence	Trusted	0	13
A21	Answered prayer	Narrator	0	3
A22	Answered prayer	Trusted	1	2
A23	God's favor	Narrator	3	3
A24	God's favor	Trusted	7	12
A25	God's favor	Other	1	2
A26	Holy Spirit	Narrator	9	24
A27	Holy Spirit	Trusted	4	9
		Total	230	324

Note: The speaker may be the narrator, a trusted character, or some "other" character.

Table C.2. Discrediting in Luke and Acts

	Discrediting Device	Speaker	Luke	Acts
D1	Characterization	Narrator	11	19
D2	Characterization	Trusted	12	20
D3	Characterization	Other	1	6
D8	General OT prophecy	Trusted	1	0
D9	Specific OT prophecy	Narrator	0	0
D10	Specific OT prophecy	Trusted	0	2
D11	Recent prophecy	Narrator	0	1
D13	Signs and wonders	Narrator	0	2
D14	Signs and wonders	Trusted	0	0
D17	Disapproval/horror	Narrator	0	0
D18	Disapproval/horror	Character	0	0
D19	Reported evidence	Narrator	0	0
D23	God's rejection	Narrator	0	0
D24	God's rejection	Trusted	9	5
		Total	34	55

Note: The speaker may be the narrator, a trusted character, or some "other" character.

Table C.3. The Characters Accredited in Luke and Acts

Luke	
Character Accredited	Accrediting
Jesus	154
Angels	22
John the Baptist	18
Disciples (as a group)	7
Simeon	4
Zechariah	4
Capernaum centurion	3
Others	18
Total	230

Discrediting: other characters, 34 times

Acts	
Character Accredited	Accrediting
Paul	84
Jesus	61
The movement	50
Peter	28
Gentiles as believers	17
Cornelius and family	16
Apostles	15
Others	53
Total	324

Discrediting: other characters, 55 times

The characters most frequently accredited are listed in Table C.3. In this, the resurrection has been treated as accrediting Jesus (seven times in Luke, twelve times in Acts).

The exact references in Acts, for these Accrediting (A1–27) and Discrediting (D1–24) devices, are as follows:

- A1. Positive characterization by the narrator (fifty-four instances): Acts 2:41, 47; 4:4, 21, 33; 5:13, 14, 26, 34; 6:7, 8; 8:2, 26, 27–28; 9:22, 28, 31, 32, 35, 36, 39, 41–42; 10:2; 11:21, 24; 13:1, 7, 12, 48–49; 14:1, 3, 21, 27; 15:2, 32, 40; 16:1–2, 5, 10, 14, 29–30; 17:4, 11–12, 34; 18:8, 24–25; 19:17, 20; 21:8–9, 16; 24:25; 25:7; 27:31–32, 42–43.
- A2. Positive characterization by a trusted character (fifty-five): Acts 1:11; 2:24–25, 32; 3:15 (claiming God's involvement), 15 (claiming to be witnesses), 26; 4:10 (healing accredits Jesus), 10 (claiming God's involvement), 27; 5:20, 32; 7:20, 59; 9:15–16, 27; 10:4, 28, 30, 32, 33, 36, 38, 40, 41, 42; 11:12, 13; 12:11; 13:24–25, 30, 31 (accrediting resurrection), 31 (accrediting initial believers); 15:7, 8, 21, 25, 28; 17:31 (accrediting resurrection), 31 (accrediting Jesus); 18:10; 19:4; 20:33, 34–35; 21:20; 22:10, 12; 23:5, 11; 24:12 (cf. 18); 25:8; 26:10, 26; 27:23–24; 28:18, 28.
- A3. Positive characterization by some other character (fourteen): Acts 4:16; 10:22 (claiming God's approval), 22 (claiming Jewish approval); 18:14; 19:15, 17, 26, 37; 23:9, 29; 25:18–19, 25; 26:31, 32.
- A4. Commissioning by or association with a trusted character, as stated by the narrator (six): Acts 1:2, 14; 4:13; 6:6; 13:3; 14:23.
- A5. Commissioning by or association with a trusted character, as stated by a trusted character (seventeen): Acts 1:7–8, 21–22; 2:36; 3:26; 4:12; 7:34, 35, 60; 9:6; 10:42; 13:2, 46–47; 20:24; 22:14, 21; 23:11; 26:17.
- A6. Commissioning by or association with a trusted character, as stated by some other character: no instances.
- A7. General OT prophecy fulfilled (accrediting), as stated by narrator: no instances.
- A8. General OT prophecy fulfilled, as stated by a trusted character (five): Acts 3:18, 24; 4:28; 10:43; 26:22.
- A9. Specific OT prophecy fulfilled, as stated by narrator: no instances.
- A10. Specific OT prophecy fulfilled, as stated by a trusted character (seventeen): Acts 2:16–21, 25–28, 31, 34–35; 3:22–23; 4:11, 25–26; 8:32–35; 13:23, 27–29, 33, 34, 35, 46–47; 15:16, 17, 18.
- A11. Recent prophecy fulfilled, as stated by narrator (nine): Acts 2:4 (fulfilling 1:4), 4 (fulfilling Luke 3:16, cf. 11:16); 9:18 (fulfilling 9:17); 10:17 (fulfilling 10:5–6, cf. 9:43); 11:28 (fulfilling 11:28); 13:11 (fulfilling

13:11); 21:33 (fulfilling 20:23); 27:14–44 (fulfilling 27:10), 44 (fulfilling 27:22, 24, 26, 34).
- A12. Recent prophecy fulfilled, as stated by a trusted character (three): Acts 11:15–16; 13:23–25 (fulfilling 13:25, cf. Luke 3:16); 22:18 (fulfilling 22:14).
- A13. Signs and wonders, as stated by narrator (thirty-four): Acts 1:2, 9, 10; 2:2–3, 4, 43; 3:7; 4:31; 5:10, 12, 16, 19; 6:8, 15; 8:6–7, 13, 39; 9:3–4, 8, 11–12, 18, 34; 10:46; 12:7–10, 23; 13:11; 14:3, 8–10; 16:26; 19:11–12; 20:10–12; 28:3–6, 8, 9.
- A14. Signs and wonders, as stated by a trusted character (five): Acts 2:22; 7:36; 10:38; 15:12; 22:6.
- A15. Amazed response (awe/fear), as stated by narrator (thirteen): Acts 2:6–7, 43; 3:9–11; 4:13; 5:5, 11; 8:9–11, 13; 9:21; 10:45; 12:16; 13:12; 19:17.
- A16. Amazed response (awe/fear), as stated by a character (three): Acts 12:15; 14:11; 28:6.
- A17. Approval/joy, as reported by narrator (nine): Acts 8:8, 39; 11:23; 12:14; 15:3, 22, 31; 16:34; 21:20.
- A18. Approval/joy, as reported by a character: no instances.
- A19. Reported evidence, as stated by narrator (twelve): Acts 1:3; 2:6–12; 4:14, 22, 34; 5:41; 9:41–42; 13:44; 16:25; 19:18–19, 30; 28:31.
- A20. Reported evidence, as stated by a trusted character (thirteen): Acts 2:13–15, 22; 3:16; 5:32; 8:20; 10:26, 41; 14:14–18, 22; 15:26; 20:24; 21:13; 28:19. (Of these, 8:20; 10:26; 14:14–18 provide evidence of the speaker's good character.)
- A21. Answered prayer, as stated by narrator (three): Acts 4:31; 8:15; 12:12.
- A22. Answered prayer, as stated by a trusted character (two): 10:4, 31.
- A23. God's favor, as stated by narrator (three): Acts 4:33; 7:55; 11:23.
- A24. God's favor, as stated by a trusted character (twelve): Acts 2:22, 33; 3:13; 5:31; 7:9, 46, 56; 10:4, 31, 38; 13:22; 15:14.
- A25. God's favor, as stated by some other character (two): Acts 11:18; 16:17.
- A26. Holy Spirit, as stated by narrator (twenty-four): Acts 1:2; 2:4; 4:8, 31; 6:5, 10; 7:55; 8:17, 29, 39; 9:31; 10:19, 44–45; 11:24, 28; 13:2, 4, 9, 52; 16:6–7; 19:6–7, 21; 21:4, 10–11.
- A27. Holy Spirit, as stated by a trusted character (nine): Acts 6:3; 9:17; 10:20, 38; 11:15; 15:8, 28; 20:22–23, 28.
- D1. Negative characterization by the narrator (nineteen): Acts 6:13; 8:1; 9:1, 23, 28; 12:1–2, 22–23; 13:6, 45; 15:38; 16:19; 17:5; 19:28–29; 21:34–35; 22:22–23; 23:10, 12–13; 24:26; 25:3.

- D2. Negative characterization by a trusted character (twenty): Acts 1:18; 2:23, 36, 40; 3:13–15, 26; 4:10; 5:30; 7:9, 27 (cf. 35, 39), 51, 52; 8:20–23; 9:13; 13:10–11, 27–28, 46; 15:24; 16:37; 26:11.
- D3. Negative characterization by some other character (six): Acts 19:15, 25; 23:27; 24:5; 25:24; 28:22.
- D5. Commissioning by or association with an untrustworthy character: no instances.
- D8. General OT prophecy fulfilled (discrediting), as stated by a trusted character: no instances.
- D9. Specific OT prophecy fulfilled, as stated by narrator: no instances.
- D10. Specific OT prophecy fulfilled, as stated by a trusted character (two): Acts 1:16–20; 28:26–27.
- D11. Recent prophecy fulfilled, as stated by narrator (one): Acts 5:10 (fulfilling 5:9).
- D13. Signs and wonders, as stated by narrator (two): Acts 5:5, 10.
- D14. Signs and wonders, as stated by a trusted character: no instances.
- D17–18. Disapproval/horror: no instances
- D19. Reported evidence, as stated by narrator: no instances.
- D23. God's rejection: no instances.
- D24. God's rejection, as stated by a trusted character (five): Acts 7:42–43; 8:21; 23:3; and symbolic actions, 13:50–51; 18:6.

Appendix D
Distribution of Accrediting and Discrediting in Luke-Acts

Table D.1 shows how Accrediting and Discrediting devices are distributed through the chapters of the Third Gospel. The last column is plotted in Figure 8.1. Table D.2 provides similar data for Acts, as plotted in Figure 8.2.

Table D.1. Distribution of Devices Through Luke

Luke ch.	Accrediting	Discrediting	Accrediting per 100 vss.
1	41	0	51.3
2	26	0	50.0
3	9	2	23.7
4	17	0	38.6
5	11	0	28.2
6	4	2	8.2
7	16	3	32.0
8	10	0	17.9
9	11	1	17.7
10	7	1	16.7
11	4	4	7.4
12	3	2	5.1
13	3	2	8.6
14	1	0	2.9
15	1	0	3.1
16	0	2	0
17	3	0	8.1
18	3	1	7.0
19	7	2	14.6
20	2	2	4.3
21	0	2	0
22	13	5	18.3
23	16	2	28.6
24	22	1	40.7
Total	230	34	(average 20.0)

Note: The last column allows for variations in chapter length, permitting direct comparison, as plotted in Figure 8.1.

Table D.2. Distribution of Devices Through Acts

Acts ch.	Accrediting	Discrediting	Accrediting per 100 vss.
1	10	2	38.5
2	23	3	48.9
3	11	2	42.3
4	21	1	56.8
5	15	4	35.7
6	8	1	53.3
7	11	5	18.3
8	16	3	41.0
9	21	4	48.8
10	31	0	64.6
11	12	0	40.0
12	7	2	28.0
13	27	6	51.9
14	10	0	35.7
15	19	2	47.5
16	10	2	25.0
17	5	1	14.7
18	4	1	14.3
19	13	3	32.5
20	7	0	18.4
21	8	1	20.0
22	6	1	20.0
23	4	4	11.4
24	2	2	7.7
25	4	2	14.8
26	6	1	18.8
27	5	0	11.4
28	8	2	26.7
Total	324	55	(average 32.3)

Note: The last column allows for variations in chapter length, permitting direct comparison, as plotted in Figure 8.2.

Appendix E
Overview of Accrediting and Discrediting

Table E.1 allows comparison by showing what percentage of devices are Accrediting; are from each kind of speaker; and can be described as "supernatural." The raw data is shown below that.

Table E.1. Overview of Accrediting and Discrediting

Accrediting/Discrediting Devices	Embassy	J.W.[a]	Jos. Asen.	Let. Aris.	Luke	Acts
Percentage						
Accrediting %	35.8	19.8	89.0	97.3	87.1	85.5
Discrediting %	64.2	80.2	11.0	2.7	12.9	14.5
Narrator %	79.7	84.2	54.9	37.6	56.8	49.7
Trusted character %	16.9	8.9	35.4	60.2	34.1	43.7
Other character %	3.4	6.9	9.8	2.3	9.1	6.6
Supernatural %	4.1	10.9	45.7	13.1	65.2	54.1
Not supernatural %	95.9	89.1	54.3	86.9	34.8	45.9
Number of Occurrences						
Total	148	101	164	221	264	379
Total accrediting	53	20	146	215	230	324
Total discrediting	95	81	18	6	34	55
Narrator	118	85	90	83	150	189
Trusted character	25	9	58	133	90	165
Other character	5	7	16	5	24	25
Supernatural	6	11	75	29	172	205
Not supernatural	142	90	89	192	92	174

[a] J.W. 4:120-397 is analyzed (a passage of length comparable to the other texts).

Table E.2. Accrediting Devices in All the Texts

A	Speaker	Accrediting Device	Embassy	J.W.[a]	Jos. Asen.	Let. Aris.	Luke	Acts
1	N	Characterization	28	18	38	58	30	54
2	T	Characterization	15	0	33	110	33	55
3	O	Characterization	1	0	11	4	14	14
4	N	Commissioning	0	0	0	2	2	6
5	T	Commissioning	0	0	3	1	8	17
6	O	Commissioning	0	0	0	0	1	0
7	N	General prophecy	0	0	0	0	1	0
8	T	General prophecy	0	0	0	0	7	5
9	N	Specific prophecy	0	0	0	0	1	0
10	T	Specific prophecy	0	0	0	0	6	17
11	N	Recent prophecy	2	0	3	0	21	9
12	T	Recent prophecy	0	0	0	0	1	3
13	N	Signs & wonders	0	0	9	1	30	34
14	T	Signs & wonders	0	0	1	0	1	5
15	N	Amazement	2	0	14	4	26	13
16	C	Amazement	1	0	0	0	6	3
17	N	Approval/joy	2	0	17	16	6	9
18	C	Approval/joy	0	0	0	1	1	0
19	N	Reported evidence	0	2	0	0	10	12
20	T	Reported evidence	0	0	0	0	0	13
21	N	Answered prayer	0	0	1	0	0	3
22	T	Answered prayer	0	0	0	0	1	2
23	N	God's favor	2	0	1	1	3	3
24	T	God's favor	0	0	15	17	7	12
25	O	God's favor	0	0	0	0	1	2
26	N	Holy Spirit	0	0	0	0	9	24
27	T	Holy Spirit	0	0	0	0	4	9
		Total	53	20	146	215	230	324

Note: The speaker may be the narrator (N) or a character (C), whether trusted (T) or other (O).
[a] *J.W.* 4:120-397 is analyzed (to give comparable length).

Table E.3. Discrediting Devices in All the Texts

D	Speaker	Discrediting Device	Embassy	J.W.[a]	Jos. Asen.	Let. Aris.	Luke	Acts
1	N	Characterization	69	56	6	0	11	19
2	T	Characterization	10	9	6	4	12	20
3	O	Characterization	0	7	5	0	1	6
8	T	General prophecy	0	0	0	0	1	0
9	N	Specific prophecy	0	1	0	0	0	0
10	T	Specific prophecy	0	0	0	0	0	2
11	N	Recent prophecy	0	1	0	0	0	1
13	N	Signs & wonders	0	0	0	1	0	2
14	T	Signs & wonders	0	0	0	1	0	0
17	N	Disapproval/horror	13	4	1	0	0	0
18	C	Disapproval/horror	3	0	0	0	0	0
19	N	Reported evidence	0	1	0	0	0	0
23	N	God's rejection	0	2	0	0	0	0
24	T	God's rejection	0	0	0	0	9	5
		Total	95	81	18	6	34	55

Note: The speaker may be the narrator (N), or a character (C), whether trusted (T) or other (O).
[a] *J.W.* 4:120-397 is analyzed (to give comparable length).

Bibliography

Adams, Edward. *The Earliest Christian Meeting Places: Almost Exclusively Houses?* LNTS 450. London: T. & T. Clark, 2013.

Alexander, Loveday. *Acts in Its Ancient Literary Context.* JSNTSup 298. London: T. & T. Clark, 2006.

———. "The Acts of the Apostles as an Apologetic Text." In *Apologetics in the Roman Empire: Pagans, Jews and Christians*, edited by Mark Edwards, Martin Goodman, and Simon Price, 15–44. Oxford: Oxford University Press, 1999.

———. "Fact, Fiction and the Genre of Acts." *New Testament Studies* 44, no. 3 (July 1998): 380–99.

———. *The Preface to Luke's Gospel: Literary Convention and Social Context in Luke 1:1–4 and Acts 1:1.* SNTSMS 78. Cambridge: Cambridge University Press, 1993.

Alexandre, Manuel, Jr. *Rhetorical Argumentation in Philo of Alexandria.* BJS 322. Studia Philonica Monographs 2. Atlanta: Scholars, 1999.

Allen, O. Wesley. *The Death of Herod: The Narrative and Theological Function of Retribution in Luke-Acts.* SBLDS 158. Altanta, GA: Scholars, 1997.

Aristophanes. Translated by Jeffrey Henderson. *Aristophanes.* 4 vols. LCL 178–80, 488. Cambridge, MA: Harvard University Press, 1998–2002.

Aristotle. Translated by John H. Freese. *The "Art" of Rhetoric.* LCL 193. London: Heinemann, 1975.

———. *Poetics.* Translated by Stephen Halliwell. *Aristotle, Poetics; Longinus, On the Sublime; Demetrius, On Style.* Vol. 23. LCL 199. London: Heinemann, 1953.

Aune, David E. *The New Testament in Its Literary Environment.* Philadelphia: Westminster, 1987.

Barclay, John M. G. "The Empire Writes Back: Josephan Rhetoric in Flavian Rome." In *Flavius Josephus and Flavian Rome.* Edited by Jonathan Edmondson, Steve Mason and James Rives, 315–32. Oxford: Oxford University Press, 2005.

———. *Jews in the Mediterranean Diaspora from Alexander to Trajan (323 BCE– 117 CE)*, Edinburgh: T. & T. Clark, 1996.

Barrett, Charles K. "The First New Testament." *Novum Testamentum* 38, no. 2 (April 1996): 94–104.

Bartlett, John R. *Jews in the Hellenistic World: Josephus, Aristeas, The Sybilline Oracles, Eupolemus*. Cambridge Commentaries on Writings of the Jewish and Christian World, 200 BC to AD 200. Vol. 1. Part 1. Cambridge: Cambridge University Press, 1985.

Bauckham, Richard. "For Whom Were the Gospels Written?" In *The Gospel for All Christians: Rethinking the Gospel Audiences*, edited by Richard Bauckham, 9–48. Grand Rapids: Eerdmans, 1998.

———, ed. *The Gospel for All Christians: Rethinking the Gospel Audiences*. Grand Rapids: Eerdmans, 1998.

Beard, Mary, John North, and Simon Price, eds. *Religions of Rome: Volume 1: A History*. Cambridge: Cambridge University Press, 1998.

Beavis, M. A. L. "Anti-Egyptian Polemic in the Letter of Aristeas 130–165 (The High Priest's Discourse)." *Journal for the Study of Judaism* 18, no. 2 (1987): 145–51.

Bennema, Cornelis. *The Theory of Character in New Testament Narrative*, Minneapolis: Fortress, 2014.

Bohak, Gideon. *Joseph and Aseneth and the Jewish Temple in Heliopolis*. EJL 10. Atlanta: Scholars, 1996.

Bonner, Stanley F. *The Literary Treatises of Dionysius of Halicarnassus: A Study in the Development of Critical Method*. Cambridge: Cambridge University Press, 1939.

Booth, Wayne C. *The Rhetoric of Fiction*. Chicago: University of Chicago Press, 1961.

Borgen, Peder. "Philo of Alexandria." In *Jewish Writings of the Second Temple Period: Apocrypha, Pseudepigrapha, Qumran Sectarian Writings, Philo, Josephus*. CRINT Section 2 The Literature of the Jewish People in the Period of the Second Temple and the Talmud, vol. 2, edited by Michael E. Stone, 233–82. Assen: Van Gorcum, 1984.

Borgman, Paul C. *The Way According to Luke: Hearing the Whole Story of Luke-Acts*. Grand Rapids: Eerdmans, 2006.

Brock, Timothy C., and Melanie C. Green, eds. *Persuasion: Psychological Insights and Perspectives*. 2nd ed. Thousand Oaks, CA: Sage, 2005.

Bruce, Frederick F. *The Acts of the Apostles: The Greek Text with Introduction and Commentary*. 2nd ed. London: Tyndale, 1952.

———. *The Acts of the Apostles: The Greek Text with Introduction and Commentary*. NICNT. Rev. ed. Grand Rapids: Eerdmans, 1988.

Bultmann, Rudolf. *The History of the Synoptic Tradition*. Translated by John Marsh. Oxford: Blackwell, 1963.

Burchard, Christoph. *Gesammelte Studien zu Joseph und Aseneth*. Leiden: Brill, 1996.

———. "Joseph and Aseneth." In *The Old Testament Pseudepigrapha*. Vol. 2, edited by James H. Charlesworth, 177–247. New York: Doubleday, 1985.

Burridge, Richard A. *What Are the Gospels?: A Comparison with Graeco-Roman Biography*. 2nd ed. Grand Rapids: Eerdmans, 2004.

Carbonaro, Paul. *La Lettre d'Aristée et le Mythe des Âges du Monde*. CahRB 79. Pende: J. Gabalda, 2012.

Cassidy, Richard J. *Society and Politics in the Acts of the Apostles*. Maryknoll: Orbis, 1987.

Charlesworth, James H., ed. *The Old Testament Pseudepigrapha*. 2 vols. New York: Doubleday, 1983–1985. [OTP]

Chesnutt, Randall D. *From Death to Life: Conversion in Joseph and Aseneth*. JSPSup 16. Sheffield: Sheffield Academic, 1995.

Churchill, Timothy W. R. *Divine Initiative and the Christology of the Damascus Road Encounter*. Eugene, OR: Pickwick, 2010.

Cicero, Marcus Tullius. Translated by Edward W. Sutton. *De Oratore*, [*On the Orator*] vols. 1 and 2. Cicero. Vols. 3 and 4. LCL 348, 349. London: Heinemann, 1967.

———. *Orator*. Translated by Harry M. Hubbell. *Cicero*. Vol. 5. LCL 342. Cambridge, MA: Harvard University Press, 1962.

Cohen, Shaye J. D. *Josephus in Galilee and Rome: His Vita and Development as a Historian*. Columbia Studies in the Classical Tradition 8. Boston: Brill, 2002.

Connor, W. Robert. *Thucydides*. Princeton: Princeton University Press, 1984.

Curran, John. "Flavius Josephus in Rome." In *Flavius Josephus: Interpretation and History*. Supplements to the Journal for the Study of Judaism 146, edited by Jack Pastor, Pnina Stern and Menahem Mor, 65–86. Leiden: Brill, 2011.

Darr, John A. *On Character Building: the Reader and the Rhetoric of Characterization in Luke-Acts*. Literary Currents in Biblical Interpretation. Louisville: Westminster/John Knox, 1992.

Das, N. K. "Religions Syncretism and Cultural Homogenisation in North-East India." In *Culture, Religion and Philosophy: Critical Studies in Syncretism and Inter-Faith Harmony*, edited by N. K. Das, 295–324. Jaipur: Rawat, 2003.

Demetrius, On Style. Translated by Stephen Halliwell. *Aristotle, Poetics; Longinus, On the Sublime; Demetrius, On Style*. Vol. 23. LCL 199. London: Heinemann, 1953.

Devillers, Olivier. "The Concentration of Power and Writing History: Forms of Historical Persuasion in the *Histories* (1.1-49)." In *A Companion to Tacitus*, edited by Victoria E. Pagán, 162–86. Chichester: Wiley-Blackwell, 2012.

Dibelius, Martin. *Studies in the Acts of the Apostles*. Edited by Heinrich Greeven. Translated by Mary Ling. London: SCM, 1956 (originally 1951).

Dionysius of Halicarnassus. On Literary Composition. Translated by Stephen Usher. *Dionysius of Halicarnassus: The Critical Essays*. 2 vols. LCL 465, 466. 3–245 of vol. 1. Cambridge, MA: Harvard University Press, 1985.

Dodd, Charles H. *More New Testament Studies*. Manchester: Manchester University Press, 1968.

Downing, F. Gerald. "Common Ground with Paganism in Luke and Josephus," *New Testament Studies* 28, no. 4 (October 1982): 546–59.

Dunn, James D. G. *The Acts of the Apostles*. Valley Forge, PA: Trinity, 1996.

Eberhard Nestle, Barbara Aland, Kurt Aland, Johannes Karavidopoulos, Carlo N. Martini and Bruce M. Metzger, eds. *Novum Testamentum Graece*. 28th ed. Stuttgart: Deutsche Bibelgesellschaft, 2012.

Edmondson, Jonathan, Steve Mason, and James Rives, eds. *Flavius Josephus and Flavian Rome*. Oxford: Oxford University Press, 2005.

Edwards, Mark, Martin Goodman, and Simon Price, eds. *Apologetics in the Roman Empire: Pagans, Jews and Christians*. Oxford: Oxford University Press, 1999.

Ehrman, Bart D. *Lost Christianities: The Battles for Scripture and the Faiths We Never Knew*. Oxford: Oxford University Press, 2003.

Esler, Philip F. *Community and Gospel in Luke-Acts: The Social and Political Motivations of Lucan Theology*. Cambridge: Cambridge University Press, 1987.

Evans, Gillian R., ed. *The First Christian Theologians: An Introduction to Theology in the Early Church*. Great Theologians. Oxford: Blackwell, 2004.

Fink, Uta Barbara. *Joseph und Aseneth: Revision des griechischen Textes und Edition der zweiten lateinischen Übersetzung*. Fontes et subsidia ad Bibliam pertinentes 5. Berlin: De Gruyter, 2008.

Finnern, Sönke. *Narratologie und biblische Exegese: eine integrative Methode der Erzählanalyse und ihr Ertrag am Beispiel von Matthäus 28*. WUNT 2, 285. Tübingen: Mohr Siebeck, 2010.

Fiorenza, Elisabeth Schüssler, ed. *Searching the Scriptures: A Feminist Commentary*. 2 vols. London: SCM, 1995.

Gamble, Harry Y. *Books and Readers in the Early Church*. New Haven: Yale University Press, 1995.

Gaventa, Beverly R. *The Acts of the Apostles*. ANTC. Nashville: Abingdon, 2003.

Gibson, Jack J. *Peter between Jerusalem and Antioch*. WUNT 2/345. Tubingen: Mohr Siebeck, 2013.

Green, Joel B. *The Death of Jesus: Tradition and Interpretation in the Passion Narrative*. WUNT 2/33. Tübingen: Mohr-Siebeck, 1988.

Green, Melanie C., and Timothy C. Brock. "The Role of Transportation in the Persuasiveness of Public Narratives." *Journal of Personality and Social Psychology* 79, no. 5 (November 2000): 701–21.

———, Jeffrey J. Strange, and Timothy C. Brock, eds. *Narrative Impact: Social and Cognitive Foundations*. Mahwah, NJ: Lawrence Erlbaum Associates, 2002.

Green, Michael. *Evangelism in the Early Church*. Rev. ed. Eastbourne: Kingsway, 2003.

Gross, Nicolas P., *Amatory Persuasion in Antiquity: Studies in Theory and Practice*. Newark, NJ: University of Delaware Press, 1985.

Gruen, Erich S. *Heritage and Hellenism: The Reinvention of Jewish Tradition*. HCS 30. Berkeley: University of California Press, 1998.

Hacham, Noah. "The Letter of Aristeas: A New Exodus Story?" *Journal for the Study of Judaism* 36, no. 1 (2005): 1–20.

Haenchen, Ernst. *The Acts of the Apostles: A Commentary*. Translated by R. McL. Wilson. Philadelphia: Westminster, 1971.

Head, Peter. "Acts and the Problem of Its Texts." In *The Book of Acts in Its Ancient Literary Setting*. BAFCS 1, edited by Bruce W. Winter and Andrew D. Clarke, 415–44. Grand Rapids: Eerdmans, 1993.

Hemer, Colin J. *The Book of Acts in the Setting of Hellenistic History*. WUNT 1/49. Tübingen: Mohr Siebeck, 1989.

Herodotus. Translated by Alfred D. Godley. *Herodotus*. 4 vols. LCL 117–20. London: Heinemann, 1920–1925.

Holmås, Geir Otto. *Prayer and Vindication in Luke-Acts: The Theme of Prayer within the Context of the Legitimating and Edifying Objective of the Lukan Narrative.* LNTS 433. London: T. & T. Clark, 2011.
Honigman, Sylvie. *The Septuagint and Homeric Scholarship in Alexandria: A Study in the Narrative of the Letter of Aristeas.* London: Routledge, 2003.
Hornblower, Simon, ed. *Greek Historiography.* Oxford: Clarendon, 1994.
Humphrey, Edith M. *And I Turned to See the Voice: The Rhetoric of Vision in the New Testament.* STI. Grand Rapids: Baker Academic, 2007.
———. *Joseph and Aseneth.* Guides to Apocrypha and Pseudepigrapha. Sheffield: Sheffield Academic, 2000.
Immanuel, Babu. *Repent and Turn to God: Recounting Acts.* South Perth, Australia: HIM International Ministries, 2004.
Ingarden, Roman. *The Cognition of the Literary Work of Art.* Translated by Ruth A. Crowley and Kenneth R. Olsen. Evanston, IL: Northwestern University Press, 1973.
Jellicoe, Sidney. "The Occasion and Purpose of the Letter of Aristeas: A Re-examination." *New Testament Studies* 12, no. 2 (January 1966): 144–50.
Jervell, Jacob. *Die Apostelgeschichte,* KEK 17. Göttingen: Vandenhoeck, 1998.
Johnson, Luke T. *The Acts of the Apostles.* SP 5. Collegeville, MN: Liturgical, 1992.
Joseph and Aseneth ("longer text"). Christoph Burchard. "Ein Vorläufiger Griechischer Text von *Joseph und Aseneth.*" In *Gesammelte Studien zu Joseph und Aseneth,* 161–212. Leiden: Brill, 1996.
Joseph and Aseneth ("shorter text"). Marc Philonenko. *Joseph et Aséneth: Introduction, Texte Critique et Notes.* StPB 13. Leiden: Brill, 1968.
Josephus, The Jewish War. Translated by Henry St. J. Thackeray et al. Vols. 2–4 of *Josephus.* 10 vols. LCL 203, 487, 210. Cambridge, MA: Harvard University Press, 1926–1997.
Kahle, Paul E. *The Cairo Geniza.* Schweich Lectures 1941. 2nd ed, Oxford: Blackwell, 1959.
Kamesar, Adam, ed. *The Cambridge Companion to Philo.* Cambridge: Cambridge University Press, 2009.
Kee, Howard C. "The Socio-Cultural Setting of Joseph and Aseneth," *New Testament Studies* 29, no. 3 (July 1983): 394–413.
Keener, Craig S. *Acts: An Exegetical Commentary.* 4 vols. Grand Rapids: Baker Academic, 2012–2015.
Keith, Chris. *Jesus' Literacy: Scribal Culture and the Teacher from Galilee.* LNTS 413. Library of Historical Jesus Studies 8. London: T. & T. Clark, 2011.
———, and Loren T. Stuckenbruck, eds. *Evil in Second Temple Judaism and Early Christianity,* WUNT 2/417. Tübingen: Mohr Siebeck, 2016.
Kelhoffer, James A. *Persecution, Persuasion and Power: Readiness to Withstand Hardship as a Corroboration of Legitimacy in the New Testament.* WUNT 1/270. Tübingen: Mohr Siebeck, 2010.
Kennedy, George A. *New Testament Interpretation through Rhetorical Criticism.* SR. Chapel Hill: University of North Carolina Press, 1984.
———. *Progymnasmata: Greek Textbooks of Prose Composition and Rhetoric.* WGRW 10. Atlanta: SBL, 2003.

Kern, Philip H. "Paul's Conversion and Luke's Portrayal of Character in Acts 8-10." *Tyndale Bulletin* 54, no. 2 (2003): 63–80.

Klauck, Hans-Josef. *Magic and Paganism in Early Christianity: The World of the Acts of the Apostles.* Translated by Brian McNeil. Minneapolis: Fortress, 2000.

Klijn, A. F. J. "The Letter of Aristeas and the Greek Translation of the Pentateuch in Egypt," *New Testament Studies* 11, no. 2 (January 1965): 154–58.

Kraemer, Ross S. *When Aseneth Met Joseph: A Late Antique Tale of the Biblical Patriarch and His Egyptian Wife, Reconsidered.* New York: Oxford University Press, 1998.

Kurz, William S. *Reading Luke-Acts: Dynamics of Biblical Narrative.* Louisville, KY: Westminster/John Knox, 1993.

Laansma, Jon C., Grant R. Osborne, and Ray van Neste, eds. *New Testament Theology in Light of the Church's Mission: Essays in Honor of I. Howard Marshall.* Eugene, OR: Cascade, 2011.

Lampe, Peter. *From Paul to Valentinus: Christians at Rome in the First Two Centuries.* Edited by Marshall D. Johnson. Translated by Michael Steinhauser. London: T. & T. Clark, 2003.

Lausberg, Heinrich. *Handbook of Literary Rhetoric: a Foundation for Literary Study*, trans. Matthew T. Bliss, Annemiek Jansen, and David E. Orton. Leiden: Brill, 1998.

The Letter of Aristeas. Translated by Henry St. J. Thackeray. *The Letter of Aristeas: Translated into English with an Introduction and Notes.* London: Macmillan, 1904.

Letter of Aristeas. Moses Hadas. *Aristeas to Philocrates (Letter of Aristeas).* Translated by Henry St. J. Thackeray. New York: Harper, 1951.

Levinskaya, Irina. *The Book of Acts in Its Diaspora Setting.* BAFCS 5. Grand Rapids: Eerdmans, 1996.

Lewes, C. L. *Dr Southwood Smith: A Retrospect.* Edinburgh: Blackwood, 1898.

Libanius. Translated by Craig A. Gibson. *Libanius's* Progymnasmata*: Model Exercises in Greek Prose Composition and Rhetoric.* Atlanta: SBL, 2008.

Liddell, Henry G., and Robert Scott. *A Greek-English Lexicon.* 9th ed. Oxford: Clarendon, 1996. [LSJ]

Liggins, Stephen S. *Many Convincing Proofs: Persuasive Phenomena Associated with Gospel Proclamation in Acts.* BZNW 221. Berlin: De Gruyter, 2016.

Lucian. *On How to Write History.* Translated by K. Kilburn. *Lucian.* Vol. 6. LCL 430. Cambridge, MA: Harvard University Press, 1959.

———. *A Professor of Public Speaking.* Translated by Austin M. Harmon. *Lucian.* Vol. 4. LCL 162. Cambridge, MA: Harvard University Press, 1961.

Lucretius. Translated by W. H. D. Rouse. *On the Nature of Things.* LCL 181. London: Heinemann, 1924.

Lust, Johan, Erik Eynikel, and Katrin Hauspie. *A Greek-English Lexicon of the Septuagint.* Stuttgart: Deutsche Bibelgesellschaft, 2003.

Maddox, Robert. *The Purpose of Luke-Acts.* SNTW. Edinburgh: T. & T. Clark, 1982.

Mader, Gottfried. *Josephus and the Politics of Historiography: Apologetic and Impression Management in the* Bellum Judaicum. Mnemosyne Bibliotheca Classica Batava Supplementum 205. Leiden: Brill, 2000.

Marguerat, Daniel. *Les Actes des Apôtres*. Commentaire du Nouveau Testament 5. 2 vols. Geneva: Labor et Fides, 2007–2015.

———. "Saul's Conversion (Acts 9, 22, 26) and the Multiplication of Narrative in Acts." In *Luke's Literary Achievement*. JSNTSup 116, edited by Christopher M. Tuckett, 127–55. Sheffield: Sheffield Academic, 1995.

———, and Yvan Bourquin. *How to Read Bible Stories: An Introduction to Narrative Criticism*. London: SCM, 1999.

Mason, Rex. *Propaganda and Subversion in the Old Testament*. London: SPCK, 1997.

Mason, Steve. *A History of the Jewish War: AD 66–74*. Cambridge: Cambridge University Press, 2016.

———. *Josephus and the New Testament*. 2nd ed. Peabody: Hendrickson, 2003.

———. "'Should any wish to enquire further' (*Ant*. 1.25): The Aim and Audience of Josephus" *Judean Antiquities/Life*. In *Understanding Josephus: Seven Perspectives*, JSPSup 32, edited by Steve Mason, 64–103. Sheffield: Sheffield Academic, 1998.

———, and Honora Chapman. *Judean War 2: Translation and Commentary*. Flavius Josephus: Translation and Commentary. Vol. 1B. Leiden: Brill, 2008.

Matusova, Ekaterin. *The Meaning of the Letter of Aristeas: In Light of Biblical Interpretation and Grammatical Tradition, and with Reference to its Historical Context*. FRLANT 260. Göttingen: Vandenhoeck & Ruprecht, 2015.

Mauck, John W. *Paul on Trial: The Book of Acts as a Defense of Christianity*. Nashville: Thomas Nelson, 2001.

Maxwell, Kathy R. *Hearing Between the Lines: The Audience as Fellow-Worker in Luke-Acts and Its Literary Milieu*. LNTS 425. London: T. & T. Clark, 2010.

McDonald, James I. H. *Kerygma and Didache: The Articulation and Structure of the Earliest Christian Message*. SNTSMS 37. Cambridge: Cambridge University Press, 1980.

Meecham, Henry G. *The Oldest Version of the Bible: "Aristeas" on Its Traditional Origin*. London: Holborn, 1932.

Meek, James A. *The Gentile Mission in Old Testament Citations in Acts: Text, Hermeneutic and Purpose*. LNTS 385. London: T. & T. Clark, 2008.

Menken, Maarten J. J. "Fulfilment of Scripture as a Propaganda Tool in Early Christianity." In *Persuasion and Dissuasion in Early Christianity, Ancient Judaism and Hellenism*, edited by Pieter van der Horst, Maarten J. J. Menken, Joop F. M. Smit, and Geert Van Oyen, 179–98. CBET 33. Leuven: Peeters, 2003.

Murray, Oswyn. "Aristeas and Ptolemaic Kingship," *Journal of Theological Studies* n.s. 18, no. 2 (October 1967): 337–71.

Niehoff, Maren R. *Philo on Jewish Identity and Culture*. Tübingen: Mohr Siebeck, 2001.

Nir, Rivka. *Joseph and Aseneth: A Christian Book*. Hebrew Bible Monographs 42. Sheffield: Sheffield Phoenix, 2012.

Nock, Arthur D. *Conversion: The Old and the New in Religion from Alexander the Great to Augustine of Hippo*. London: Oxford University Press, 1965.

Oakes, Peter. *Reading Romans in Pompeii: Paul's Letter at Ground Level*. London: SPCK, 2009.

O'Neill, John C. *The Theology of Acts in Its Historical Setting*. London: SPCK, 1961.

On the Sublime (attributed to Longinus). Herbert L. Havell. *Longinus on the Sublime*. London: Macmillan, 1890.

Pagán, Victoria E., ed. *A Companion to Tacitus*. Chichester: Wiley-Blackwell, 2012.

Parsons, Mikael C., and Richard I. Pervo. *Rethinking the Unity of Luke and Acts*. Minneapolis: Fortress, 1993.

Pastor, Jack, Pnina Stern, and Menahem Mor, eds. *Flavius Josephus: Interpretation and History*. JSJSup 146. Leiden: Brill, 2011.

Patrick, Dale, and Allen Scult. "Rhetoric and Ideology: A Debate within Biblical Scholarship over the Import of Persuasion." In *The Rhetorical Interpretation of Scripture: Essays from the 1996 Malibu Conference*, JSNTSup 180, edited by Stanley E. Porter and Dennis L. Stamps, 63–83. Sheffield: JSOT, 1999.

Pearce, Sarah J. K. *The Land of the Body: Studies in Philo's Representation of Egypt*, Tübingen: Mohr Siebeck, 2007.

Pelletier, André. *Lettre d'Aristée à Philocrate*. SC 89. Paris: Editions du Cerf, 1962.

Penner, Todd, ed. *Contextualizing Acts: Lukan Narrative and Greco-Roman Discourse*. SymS 20. Atlanta: SBL, 2003.

———. *In Praise of Christian Origins: Stephen and the Hellenists in Lucan Apologetic Historiography*. Emory Studies in Early Christianity. London: T. & T. Clark, 2004.

Pervo, Richard I. *Acts: A Commentary*. Hermeneia. Minneapolis: Fortress, 2009.

———. "Direct Speech in Acts and the Question of Genre." *Journal for the Study of the New Testament* 28, no. 3 (March 2006): 285–307.

———. *Profit with Delight: The Literary Genre of the Acts of the Apostles*. Philadelphia: Fortress, 1987.

Pesch, Rudolf. *Die Apostelgeschichte.* 2 vols. EKKNT 5. Zürich: Benziger; Neukirchener, 1986.

Peterson, David G. *The Acts of the Apostles*. PNTC. Grand Rapids: Eerdmans, 2009.

Philonenko, Marc. *Joseph et Aséneth: Introduction, Texte Critique et Notes*. StPB 13. Leiden: Brill, 1968.

Philo of Alexandria. *Embassy to Gaius*. Translated by Francis H. Colson. *Philo*. Vol. 10. LCL 379, 1–187. Cambridge, MA: Harvard University Press, 1962.

Philo of Alexandria. *On Flaccus*. Translated by Francis H. Colson. *Philo*, 295–403 of vol. 9. LCL 363. Cambridge, MA: Harvard University Press, 1962.

Philostratus, Translated by Christopher P. Jones. *Life of Apollonius of Tyana.* 2 vols. LCL 16, 17. Cambridge, MA: Harvard University Press, 2005.

Plato. *Gorgias.* Translated by Walter R. M. Lamb. *Plato*. Vol. 3. LCL 166. London: Heinemann, 1925.

Plutarch. Translated by Bernadotte Perrin. *Plutarch's Lives*. 11 vols. LCL. Cambridge, MA: Harvard University Press, 1914–1971.

Polhill, John B. *Acts.* NAC 26. Nashville, Tennessee: Broadman, 1992.

Polybius. Translated by William R. Paton. *Polybius: The Histories*. 6 vols. LCL. London: Heinemann, 1922–1927.

Porter, Stanley E. "Excursus: The 'We' Passages." In *The Book of Acts in Its Graeco-Roman Setting*, BAFCS 2, edited by David W. J. Gill and Conrad Gempf, 545–74. Grand Rapids: Eerdmans, 1994.

―――, ed. *Handbook of Classical Rhetoric in the Hellenistic Period 330 B.C.–A.D. 400*. Boston: Brill, 1997.
―――, and Dennis L. Stamps, eds. *The Rhetorical Interpretation of Scripture: Essays from the 1996 Malibu Conference*. JSNTSup 180. Sheffield: JSOT, 1999.
Powell, Mark A. *What Is Narrative Criticism?* GBS New Testament Series. London: SPCK, 1993.
Quintilian. Translated by Harold E. Butler. *The* Institutio Oratoria *of Quintilian*. 4 vols. LCL 124–27. London: Heinemann, 1920–1922.
Rajak, Tessa. *The Jewish Dialogue with Greece and Rome: Studies in Cultural and Social Interaction*. Boston: Brill, 2002.
―――, Sarah Pearce, James Aitken, and Jennifer Dines, eds. *Jewish Perspectives on Hellenistic Rulers*. HCS 50. Berkeley: University of California Press, 2007.
Reinmuth, Eckart, ed. *Joseph und Aseneth*. Sapere: Scripta antiquitatis posterioris ad ethicam religionemque pertinentia 15. Tübingen: Mohr Siebeck, 2009.
Rhetoric to Alexander (attributed to Aristotle). Translated by David C. Mirhady. *Aristotle*. Vol. 16, 450–641. Cambridge, MA: Harvard University Press, 2011.
Rhetoric to Herennius (attributed to Cicero). Translated by Harry Caplan. *Rhetorica ad Herennium. Cicero*. Vol. 1. LCL 403. Cambridge, MA: Harvard University Press, 1964.
Rhoads, David M. *Israel in Revolution: 6-74 C.E.: A Political History Based on the Writings of Josephus*. Philadelphia: Fortress, 1976.
Roloff, Jürgen. *Die Apostelgeschichte*. NTD 5. Göttingen: Vandenhoeck & Ruprecht, 1988.
Rood, Tim. *Thucydides: Narrative and Explanation*. Oxford Classical Monographs. Oxford: Clarendon, 1998.
Rothschild, Clare K. *Luke-Acts and the Rhetoric of History: An Investigation of Early Christian Historiography*. WUNT 2/175. Tübingen: Mohr Siebeck, 2004.
Rowe, C. Kavin. *World Upside Down: Reading Acts in the Graeco-Roman Age*. Oxford: Oxford University Press, 2009.
Samkutty, V. J. *The Samaritan Mission in Acts*. LNTS 328. London: T. & T. Clark, 2006.
Sanders, Jack T. *The Jews in Luke-Acts*. London: SCM, 1987.
Satterthwaite, Philip E. "Acts against the Background of Classical Rhetoric." In *The Book of Acts in Its Ancient Literary Setting*, BAFCS 1, edited by Bruce W. Winter and Andrew D. Clarke, 337–80. Grand Rapids: Eerdmans, 1993.
Schnabel, Eckhard J. *Acts*. ZECNT. Grand Rapids: Zondervan, 2012.
―――. *Early Christian Mission*, 2 vols. Downers Grove, IL: IVP, 2004.
Schneider, Gerhard. *Die Apostelgeschichte: Kommentar*. 2 vols. HThKNT 5. Freiburg: Herder, 1980–1982.
Schwartz, Daniel R. "Philo, His Family and His Times." In *The Cambridge Companion to Philo*, edited by Adam Kamesar, 9–31. Cambridge: Cambridge University Press, 2009.
Septuagint. Edited by Alfred Rahlfs. *Septuaginta: Id Est Vetus Testamentum Graece Iuxta LXX Interpretes*. Stuttgart: Deutsche Bibelgesellschaft, 2006.

Sheeley, Steven M. *Narrative Asides in Luke-Acts*. JSNTSup 72. Sheffield: Sheffield Academic, 1992.

Shepherd, William H., Jr. *The Narrative Function of the Holy Spirit as a Character in Luke-Acts*. SBLDS 147. Atlanta: Scholars, 1994.

Shiell, William D. *Reading Acts: The Lector and the Early Christian Audience*. BibInt 70. Boston: Brill, 2004.

Shutt, R. J. H. "Letter of Aristeas: A New Translation and Introduction." In *The Old Testament Pseudepigrapha*, edited by James H. Charlesworth, 2:7–34. New York: Doubleday, 1985.

Smallwood, E. Mary. *Philonis Alexandrini Legatio ad Gaium. Edited with an Introduction, Translation, and Commentary.* 2nd ed. Leiden: Brill, 1961.

Soards, Marion L. *The Speeches in Acts: Their Content, Context and Concerns*. Louisville: Westminster/John Knox, 1994.

Stenschke, Christoph W. *Luke's Portrait of Gentiles Prior to Their Coming to Faith*. WUNT 2/108. Tübingen: Mohr Siebeck, 1999.

Sterling, Gregory E. *Historiography and Self-Definition: Josephos, Luke-Acts and Apologetic Historiography*. NovTSup 64. Leiden: Brill, 1992.

Sternberg, Meir. *The Poetics of Biblical Narrative: Ideological Literature and the Drama of Reading*. ISBL. Bloomington: Indiana University Press, 1985.

Strabo. Translated by Horace L. Jones. *The Geography of Strabo*. 8 vols. LCL. London: Heinemann, 1917–1932.

Strauss, Mark L. "The Purpose of Luke-Acts: Reaching a Consensus." In *New Testament Theology in Light of the Church's Mission: Essays in Honor of I. Howard Marshall*, edited by Jon C. Laansma, Grant R. Osborne, and Ray van Neste, 135–50. Eugene, OR: Cascade, 2011.

Stone, Michael E., ed. *Jewish Writings of the Second Temple Period: Apocrypha, Pseudepigrapha, Qumran Sectarian Writings, Philo, Josephus*. CRINT Section 2. The Literature of the Jewish People in the Period of the Second Temple and the Talmud, vol. 2. Assen: Van Gorcum, 1984.

Swete, Henry B., ed. *An Introduction to the Old Testament in Greek*. Cambridge: Cambridge University Press, 1902.

Talbert, Charles H. *Reading Acts: A Literary and Theological Commentary on the Acts of the Apostles*. Rev. ed. Macon: Smyth & Helwys, 2005. (New York: Crossroad, 1997).

———. *Reading Luke: A Literary and Theological Commentary on the Third Gospel*. Rev. ed. Macon: Smyth & Helwys, 2002. (New York: Crossroad, 1986).

Tannehill, Robert C. *The Narrative Unity of Luke-Acts: A Literary Interpretation*. 2 vols. Foundations and Facets. Philadelphia: Fortress, 1986–1990.

Tcherikover, Victor. "The Ideology of the Letter of Aristeas." *Harvard Theological Review* 51, no. 2 (April 1958): 59–85.

Tertullian. Edited by Alexander Roberts and James Donaldson. Translated by A. Cleveland Coxe. *Latin Christianity: Its Founder, Tertullian*. Ante-Nicene Fathers. Vol. 3. Peabody, MA: Hendrickson, 1994.

Thackeray, Henry St. J. "The Letter of Aristeas." In *An Introduction to the Old Testament in Greek*, edited by Henry B. Swete, 501–74. Cambridge: Cambridge University Press, 1902.

Theon, Aelius. *Progymnasmata*. Translated by George A. Kennedy. *Progymnasmata: Greek Textbooks of Prose Composition and Rhetoric*. WGRW 10. Atlanta: SBL, 2003, 1–71.

Theophrastus. Translated by Jeffrey Rusten and I. C. Cunningham. *Theophrastus: Characters. Herodas: Mimes. Sophron and Other Mime Fragments.* LCL 225. Cambridge, MA: Harvard University Press, 2003.

Thomas, Rosalind. *Herodotus in Context: Ethnography, Science and the Art of Persuasion*. Cambridge: Cambridge University Press, 2000.

Thucydides. Translated by Charles F. Smith. *History of the Peloponnesian War*. 4 vols. LCL 108–10, 169. London: Heinemann, 1919–1923.

Troftgruben, Troy M. *A Conclusion Unhindered: A Study of the Ending of Acts within Its Literary Environment*. WUNT 2/280. Tübingen: Mohr Siebeck, 2010.

Tuckett, Christopher M., ed. *Luke's Literary Achievement*. JSNTSup 116. Sheffield: Sheffield Academic, 1995.

Turner, Max. *Power from on High: The Spirit in Israel's Restoration and Witness in Luke-Acts*. JPTSup 9. Eugene, OR: Wipf and Stock, 2000. (Sheffield: Sheffield Academic, 1996).

Tyson, Joseph B. *Images of Judaism in Luke-Acts*. Columbia: University of South Carolina Press, 1992.

———. *Marcion and Luke-Acts: A Defining Struggle*. Columbia: University of South Carolina Press, 2006.

van der Horst, Pieter, Maarten J. J. Menken, Joop F. M. Smit, and Geert Van Oyen, eds. *Persuasion and Dissuasion in Early Christianity, Ancient Judaism and Hellenism*. CBET 33. Leuven: Peeters, 2003.

Walaskay, Paul W. *Acts*. Westminster Bible Companion. Louisville, KY: Westminster/John Knox, 1998.

———. *And So We Came to Rome: The Political Perspective of St Luke*, SNTSMS 49. Cambridge: Cambridge University Press, 1983.

Walbank, Frank W. *Polybius*, Berkeley: University of California Press, 1972.

Walters, Patricia. *The Assumed Authorial Unity of Luke and Acts: A Reassessment of the Evidence*. SNTSMS 145. Cambridge: Cambridge University Press, 2009.

Walton, Steve. "Evil in Ephesus: Acts 19:8–40." In *Evil in Second Temple Judaism and Early Christianity*, WUNT 2/417, edited by Chris Keith and Loren T. Stuckenbruck, 224–34. Tübingen: Mohr Siebeck, 2016.

———. *Leadership and Lifestyle: The Portrait of Paul in the Miletus Speech and 1 Thessalonians*. SNTSMS 108. Cambridge: Cambridge University Press, 2000.

———. "Rhetorical Criticism: An Introduction." *Themelios* 21, no. 2 (January 1996): 4–9.

Weatherly, Jon A. *Jewish Responsibility for the Death of Jesus in Luke-Acts.* JSNTSup 106. Sheffield: Sheffield Academic, 1994.

Williamson, Ronald. *Jews in the Hellenistic World: Philo.* vol. 1. pt. 2. Cambridge Commentaries on Writings of the Jewish and Christian World 1. Cambridge: Cambridge University Press, 1989.

Winter, Bruce W. *After Paul Left Corinth: The Influence of Secular Ethics and Social Change.* Grand Rapids: Eerdmans, 2001.

Witherington, Ben, III. *The Acts of the Apostles: A Socio-Rhetorical Commentary.* Grand Rapids: Eerdmans, 1998.

———. *New Testament Rhetoric: An Introductory Guide to the Art of Persuasion in and of the New Testament.* Eugene, OR: Cascade, 2009.

Witherup, Ronald D. "Cornelius Over and Over and Over Again: 'Functional Redundancy' in the Acts of the Apostles," *Journal for the Study of the New Testament* 15, no. 49 (January 1993): 45–66.

Wright, Benjamin G., III. *Praise Israel for Wisdom and Instruction: Essays on Ben Sira and Wisdom, the Letter of Aristeas and the Septuagint.* JSJSup 131. Leiden: Brill, 2008.

Index

accrediting and discrediting, 20, 26–28, 51, 143–49, 195–97, 204–6, 231–48
Aesop, 30
Agrippa. *See* Herod
Alexander:
    the Great, 111; Philo's nephew, 164
allegiance, 1, 164, 204, 217, 226
amazement, 154, 183, 189, 206, *233, 235,* 247. *See also* awe
Ananias:
    of Damascus, 155–56, 161; and Sapphira, 148, 159, 167, 198–99, 214, 229. *See also* cautionary tale, in Acts
Ananus, 66, 69, 72–77, 80
antagonism, 19, 68. *See also* antipathy
anti-Marcionite. *See* Marcion
antipathy, 31, 78; evoked, 31, 37, 222, 228, 232; evoked against a group, 160, 163, 166, 205; evoked through direct inside view, 31, 51, 197; evoked through discrediting, 20, 155, 157–58, 160, 190, 198, 205
Apollos, 146, 170
apologetics, 3, 50, 108, 111, 113, 119;
    Christian, 9, 10, 210, 214
Aristophanes, 2, 32
Aristotle, 6, 18–19, 24, 33, 37, 54, 111

aside:
    by character, 55; by narrator, 7, 23, 28, 205; by narrator, in Acts, 130, 132, 146, 159; by narrator, in other texts 52, 59, 67, 71–72, 90, 107, 113, 197, 199; by narrator, in Acts, 130, 132, 146, 159
assurance, 94, 127, 212
Athens, 158, 167
attestation, 78, 128, 131, 178, 180, 182, 186, 225. *See also* accreditation
audience, 4, 17, 22–23, 35, 38;
    compliant, 98, 162–63, 187–88; future generations, 18, 49–50, 68, 80, 110, 210. *See also* posterity; implied, definition of, 22–23, 35, 38; inevitable, 10, 23, 68, 99, 118, 171, 222–23, 227; real, 35, 35n92; stated, 35, 38, 67, 110, 133, 223; within the text, 27, 37
author:
    implied author, 35n92, 226; real author, 2, 35, 35n92, 118; stated author, 35
authority:
    of apostles, 131–132, 216, 226–27; of author, 23, 36, 71, 81, 133, 198, 207, 211; of character, 6, 26, 114,

138, 146, 198, 209–10, 223; divine, 146, 179, 196, 201, 210; of narrator, asserted, 22–23, 58, 130–132, 195–96, 207, 209–10, 218; of narrator, restrained, 27, 81, 90, 113, 130, 132–33; neglected, 136, 138; political, 79, 181, 200, 213, 222; of scripture, 52, 58–59, 132, 138, 207, 216
autobiography, 6, 22, 46–47, 65, 107, 197, 207
aversion, 213, 222; evoked through characterization, 20, 30, 32, 54, 75, 96, 157, 231
awe, as crowd's reaction, 144–46, *233*, *235*, 238. *See also* amazement

Bar-Jesus. *See* Elymas
Barnabas, 129–31, 146, 148–51, 170, 198
Bayesian analysis, 93n49
blame:
 absolution from, 70–72, 75–78, 81, 183, 199–200; allocation of, 48, 68–70, 72, 75–78, 81, 157, 199–200, 206
biography, 2, 34, 128, 229
boldness, 54, 130, 144, 152, 169, 200, 213, 225

cautionary tale, 1, 32, 77, 117, 232; in Acts, 149, 157, 159, 163, 171, 210, 225, 229; in Scripture, 2, 32
centurion, 133, 138, 181, 225; of Capernaum, 145, 149, 180–81, *236*; Cornelius, 130, 136, 138, 160, 178, 189, 225; Julius, 136, 138, 225
character development, 26, 74, 76, 144, 156, 188
Claudius Lysias. *See* Lysias
coherence, 19, 33, 129
comedy, 32, 34, 116, 232
commissioning, 146; by God, 195; by Jesus, 130, 143, 148, 162, 170, 183, 210; of Paul, 153, 162, 200, 216, 228; by trusted character(s), 143, 170, 216, *233–35*, 237, 239, *247*
Corinth, 138, 165, 167

David, 2, 24–25, 30, 33, 137, 153, 232
Demetrius:
 author of *On Style*, 19; Ephesian silversmith, 145, 148, 158; of Phalerum (Phaleron), 108, 112, 115, 117
Demosthenes. *See Philippic*
deterrence, 69–70, 81. *See also* dissuasion
dialogue, 28, 29, 34, 87, 127, 163, 171, 232; as a genre, 2, 21, 29, 31, 34, 36–37, 51
Didache:
 Christian teaching, 8, 210; the text, 168, 211
direct inside view. *See* view
discrediting. *See* accrediting
dissuasion, 37, 46, 78. *See also* deterrence
Domitian, 67–70, 74
Dorcas (Tabitha), 159, 177–78, 181, 189
drama, 19, 21, 34, 36, 47, 54–56

Egyptians, 87, 118, 197, 222; excluded from implied audience, 47–48, 91, 93, 110, 112; negatively portrayed, 46, 55–56, 90–91, 97, 116, 197, 205; as suggested audience, 92, 94
Eleazar:
 high priest in *Aristeas*, 108–11, 114–18, 203, 206; leader of Sicarii, 25, 73, 76, 196, 205
Elymas, Bar-Jesus, 158, 164
encomium, 74, 144
endorsement, 34
entertainment, 1–3, 18, 70–71, 81, 87–88, 101, 201
Ephesus, 134, 138, 144, 157–58; elders, 144, 162, 168–69, 211; silversmiths, 200

epic, 21, 30, 34, 36
epithet, 27, 55, 111, 114, 205
Ethiopians, 93; the eunuch, 133, 136–37, 155, 187
ethos, 23, 28
Eutychus, 158–59
evangelism, 3, 9–10, 38, 167, 183, 210, 213–15, 224
evangelist, 162, 181, 215, 228
example:
    bad, to avoid, 30–31, 75, 211, 231; good, in Acts, 158–59, 161–62, 190, 200, 211, 214–15, 224; good, to follow, 1, 30–31, 97, 99, 101, 119, 223, 231

fable, 21, 30
fear:
    as crowd's reaction, 144–45, 159, *233*, *235*, 238; as individual's reaction, 156
Felix, 133, 136, 213
Festus, 133, 144–45, 160, 213
fiction, 2, 3, 7, 19, 21–22, 34, 128
fidelity, 19
flattery, 20, 56, 69, 75–77, 81
foil, 54, 109, 157, 196
"fringe" of the believing community, 164–65, 168, 172, 224–25
fulfillment. *See* prophecy

Gaius, Roman Emperor, 6, 26, 28, 32, 45–59, 196–98, 205, 222
Gallio, 217
Gamaliel, 144, 151, 185, 196, 211
generalization:
    expecting assent, 116, 182, 206; indicating relevance to hearer, 28, 77, 95–96, 150–51, 201, 210
genre, 8, 21–22, 34, 36, 128, 206, 221
"gentle steps," 25–26, 32–33, 57, 76, 98, 117, 232; in Acts, 161, 187, 215, 218, 228

hearer. *See* audience
Herod:
    Agrippa I, in *Embassy*, 46, 48, 50, 52–53, 55, 57–58, 196; Agrippa I, in Acts, 131, 148, 156–57, 160, 163, 205; Agrippa II, 68–69, 72–74, 76–78, 136, 145, 150, 160; the Great, 65, 73, 79
Herodotus, 36, 152
historiography, 10, 22–23, 36, 87, 101–2, 128, 132–33, 206–7
history, as a genre, 7, 8, 10, 22, 34, 50, 107, 128, 210. *See also* reception history
hostility. *See* antipathy

identity, 93–94, 203; of audience, 8–10; of author, 132–33, 207; of character, evoking antipathy, 31, 56, 75, 97, 116, 197, 205, 232; of character, evoking antipathy, in Acts, 158, 160, 205
Idumaeans, 29, 31, 66, 73, 75, 205
instruction, 10, 133, 215; by character, 28, 52, 72–73, 95, 114, 150–51, 231; by narrative, 8, 10, 70, 80, 95, 150–51, 156; within narrative, 28, 156, 211, 214; by narrator, 28, 51, 71, 95, 113, 150, 218, 231
invective, 50, 52–53, 58, 144, 198, 222
irony, 25, 33, 161, 205, 232

James:
    apostle, 152, 157, 169; brother of Jesus, 133, 144–46, 163, 170
John:
    the Baptist, 135, 148, 153–54, 183, *236*; of Gischala, 26, 66, 71–72, 75, 81, 205; Mark, 143, 146, 148–50, 157, 170, 198
Joseph, 26, 87–91, 95–99, 101, 201–2, 205–6, 223
"journey of discovery," 32, 57, 76, 115–118, 167, 202, 232; Aseneth's,

97–99, 102, 115–118, 201–2, 205, 223; Peter's, 160–161, 163, 171–172, 184–185, 189–190, 202, 225, 228
joy, 206, *233*; as crowd's reaction, in Acts, 143, 158, 166, 206, *235*, 238, *247*; as crowd's reaction, in Luke, 145–46, *235*, *247*; as individual's reaction, 156
Judaizers, 164, 215
Judas, the betrayer, 148, 156–57, 159, 196, 199, 229
Justin Martyr, 224

lector, 17–19, 49, 130–31, 223
legitimacy, 12, 172, 212, 217
legitimation, 9–10, 118, 168, 171–72, 217–18, 226
Lysias, Claudius, 26, 144–45, 160

Macro, 26, 45, 54–56, 196
magic, 152, 158, 160, 163–66, 198, 205, 215. *See also* Simon Magus
Marcion, 9, 12, 216
Mark. *See* John Mark
Miletus speech, Paul's, 144, 168–69, 211, 214
miracle, 129–130, 137, 150, 156, 161, 203; as accrediting, 27, 144–45, 152–53, 158–59, 189, 195, 197, 217, 224
mission, 9, 146, 148, 153, 157, 169, 214–15, 227; to Gentiles, accredited, 153, 162–63, 165, 170, 190, 204, 214–16, 218; to Gentiles, suspicion of, 12, 190, 211, 215, 226
model, 9, 169, 211. *See also* example, good, to follow
moral:
  education, 2, 8, 50; of story or fable, 28, 231
Moses, 30, 111, 144, 153, 206
myth, 21, 34, 71, 114, 118, 198; "charter myth" or "foundation myth," 111, 113, 119, 202

narrative criticism, 37, 127, 230; methods, 17, 21; scope and limitations, 2, 4, 30, 34–35, 221, 227
narrator:
  omniscient, 22, 131, 195, 201, 209; reticent, 6, 90, 132–133, 138, 200–201, 204–5, 207, 224
Nero, 66, 70, 200

Onias, 92, 94, 113

parable, 2, 21, 25, 164
patron, 8, 115, 133, 199, 211
Paul, 8–9, 12, 26, 127, 129–132, 134–138, 143–153, 211–216; as author, 1, 7, 137, 164–65, 167; characterization of, 131, 144, 148–149, 151, 155–63, 171–72, 190, 196; conversion/call, 32, 152–53, 155–57, 161–62, 190, 225, 227–28; death, 12, 168–70, 203, 212, 218, 227
Pentephres (Petephres, Potiphera), 89, 91, 97–98, 206
Peter, 138, 225; characterization of, 7, 144, 154–59, 165–67, 214–15; his "journey of discovery," 155, 160–63, 171–72, 177–191, 202, 205, 224–25, 228; as link between Paul and Jesus, 152–53, 162, 198, 211, 217; in Luke, 25, 147, 154, 168; as trusted speaker, 33, 130–32, 135–36, 144–53, 161–63
Pharos, Jewish festival there, 119, 120, 202, 223
Philip, the evangelist, 129–30, 132, 136, 155, 215; as a trusted character, 145, 149, 157, 161
Philippic, 2, 50, 58
Philocrates, 35, 108–11, 118
Pilate, Pontius, 65, 135, 145
Plato, 2
plot, 19, 31, 33, 56, 116, 196, 205, 232; of Acts, 158, 160, 196, 229; of *Aseneth*, 91, 97, 201. *See also* "sticky end"

Plutarch, 2
polyphonic affirmation, 26, 32, 232; in
    Acts, 160, 186, 198; in other texts,
    57, 76, 97, 117, 197–98, 202
posterity, 68, 79–80, 222. *See also*
    audience, future generations
Potiphera. *See* Pentephres
prayer, 87–89, 95, 97, 109, 113–114,
    156, 179; answered (as accrediting),
    10, 114, 195, *233*, *235*; encouraged, 8,
    117; as positive characterization, 178
progymnasmata. *See* rhetoric,
    handbooks
propaganda, 3, 7, 80, 225
prophecy, 27, 134, 136–37, 152, 182,
    195; recent prophecy fulfilled, 26,
    67, 72, 79, 169, 199, *233–34*, *247*;
    recent prophecy fulfilled, in Acts,
    132, 151, 169, 185, 204, *235–36*,
    237–39, *247*; OT fulfilled, in Acts,
    143, 145, 153–54, 167, 183, 198,
    235–39, *247*; scriptural prophecy
    fulfilled, 72, 79, 204, *233–34*, *247*
proselytization, 7, 71, 99, 119
Ptolemy II, Philadelphus, 108–9, 112,
    181, 195, 203
purpose, author's in writing, 1–12,
    18, 20, 26, 33–35, 37–38, 209–18,
    226–30

reader, 3, 5–6, 13, 17, 19. *See also*
    audience
reader-response criticism, 4, 24, 37
reassurance, 53, 159, 213. *See also*
    assurance
reception history, 35, 93, 93nn48–49
redaction, 4, 35, 88, 90, 151; criticism,
    228
repetition, 7, 25, 32, 153, 225. *See also*
    retelling
reputation:
    of author, 20, 23, 26, 35, 66, 71, 199,
    222; of character, 20, 34, 115, 146,
    170; of group, 199, 211

respect, evoked by characterization, 2,
    6–7, 20–21, 28–31, 34, 36–37, 226,
    228
retelling:
    of material from elsewhere, 21, 70,
    113, 130; of the Cornelius episode,
    155, 177, 184, 186–88; of Saul's
    "conversion," 32, 156, 161, 225,
    227–28; within one narrative, 7, 11,
    24–26
revulsion, 19, 164
rhetoric, 2–3, 18–20, 22, 45–46, 70;
    abuse of, 7, 31, 46, 54–55; awareness
    of, 37, 46, 128; conventions and
    features, 24, 29, 37, 133; handbooks,
    17–19, 107; training in, 3, 49, 70,
    107; within narrative, 6, 45, 48–49,
    127–28, 197, 222
rhetorical criticism, 4, 7, 34–37, 221
rhetorical question, 51–52, 184–85
rhetorical situation, 18
romance, 22, 87–88, 94, 201, 207

Samaritans, 88, 130, 161, 163, 166–67,
    171, 184
Sapphira, 144. *See also* Ananias
sarcasm, 25, 31, 76, 205–6; in *Embassy*,
    46, 50–52, 57, 197–98, 205–6, 222
Saul. *See* Paul
self-promotion, 8, 211
Sergius Paulus, 213
shock, 33, 98, 156, 161, 232
"sob-story," 30, 231
Sicarii, 66, 73, 75–76, 78, 196
Simon:
    Magus (the magician/sorcerer), 148,
    158, 160, 198–99, 214; Peter. *See*
    Peter
socio-rhetorical criticism, 3, 37
Socrates, 30
soliloquy, 55, 87–89, 96, 155, 201
speech:
    as a genre, 2–4, 6, 18–19, 31, 34,
    36, 58, 221; direct or indirect, 53,

88, 127–28, 130, 145, 150, 154; "figured," 25, 33, 232; oration within a narrative, vii, 3, 7, 9, 22, 28–29, 33–34, 37

Stephen:
characterization, 129–32, 143, 146, 149–50, 157, 161, 214; death, 129–32, 152, 169, 198; speech of, 149–50, 211

"sticky end," 56, 76, 97, 157, 159–60
subversive undertones, 25, 76, 80, 200
suspended disbelief, 180, 187, 225
Symposium, 108, 197, 202

Tabitha. *See* Dorcas
temple speech, Peter's, 33
theater. *See* drama
Theophilus, 127, 130, 133, 138, 190, 225
Thucydides, 24, 30, 36
Titus, Roman Emperor, 25, 66–71, 74, 76–78
tragedy, 33–34, 54
trait, 30–31, 213; negative, 30–31, 54, 75, 97, 116, 197, 205, 232; negative, in Acts, 157, 160, 205; positive, 30
transportation, 20, 20n14, 24
treatise, as a genre, 2, 21, 22, 31, 34, 36, 45, 107–8

verifiability, 21–22, 128, 164, 179
Vespasian, 26, 66–70, 72–75, 77–79, 199
view:
direct inside, 20, 30–31, 51, 53, 55, 74, 96, 115; direct inside, in Acts, 153–155, 160, 179, 185, 189, 202, 215; point of, character's, 25, 28–29, 52, 136, 149, 153–55, 184, 189; point of, hearer's, 151, 159, 166, 226; point of, narrator's, 19, 28–29, 47, 51–52, 73, 109, 226
vividness, 24, 56, 108

warning, 32, 58–59, 70, 76, 95, 97, 117; in Acts, 1, 148, 162, 210, 214, 225; in Scripture, 1, 2, 10, 214, 228
"we" passages, 131, 155, 199
willingness to suffer, 144, 169, 203

xenophobia, 2, 31, 197, 232

Zealots, 66, 70, 72–75, 78

About the Author

Eric Clouston provides theological education by extension (TEE) in Asia, in a program where most of the students would never have the chance to go to a residential college. As a visiting lecturer, he occasionally teaches at local theological colleges. More regularly, he teaches physics to children who are, mostly, the first from their family to attend school. His first PhD, from Cambridge University, UK, was in antenna design (which some see as a mysterious art within the discipline of electronics). After some experience in management consultancy, he studied theology at Ridley Hall, Cambridge, and was ordained in the Diocese of Rochester, Church of England. His PhD in New Testament was awarded by the University of Surrey, after studying through St. Mary's University, Twickenham, London.

www.ingramcontent.com/pod-product-compliance
Lightning Source LLC
Chambersburg PA
CBHW050900300426
44111CB00010B/1319